THIRD SERIES
General Editors:
Richard Proudfoot, Ann Thompson
David Scott Kastan and H.R. Woudhuysen
Associate General Editor for this volume:
George Walton Williams

KING
HENRY VI
PART 3

THE ARDEN SHAKESPEARE

ALL'S WELL THAT ENDS WELL	edited by Suzanne Gossett and Helen Wilcox
ANTONY AND CLEOPATRA	edited by John Wilders
AS YOU LIKE IT	edited by Juliet Dusinberre
THE COMEDY OF ERRORS	edited by Kent Cartwright
CORIOLANUS	edited by Peter Holland
CYMBELINE	edited by Valerie Wayne
DOUBLE FALSEHOOD	edited by Brean Hammond
HAMLET, Revised	edited by Ann Thompson and Neil Taylor
HAMLET, The Texts of 1603 and 1623	edited by Ann Thompson and Neil Taylor
JULIUS CAESAR	edited by David Daniell
KING EDWARD III	edited by Richard Proudfoot and Nicola Bennett
KING HENRY IV PART 1	edited by David Scott Kastan
KING HENRY IV PART 2	edited by James C. Bulman
KING HENRY V	edited by T.W. Craik
KING HENRY VI PART 1	edited by Edward Burns
KING HENRY VI PART 2	edited by Ronald Knowles
KING HENRY VI PART 3	edited by John D. Cox and Eric Rasmussen
KING HENRY VIII	edited by Gordon McMullan
KING JOHN	edited by Jesse M. Lander and J.J.M. Tobin
KING LEAR	edited by R.A. Foakes
KING RICHARD II	edited by Charles Forker
KING RICHARD III	edited by James R. Siemon
LOVE'S LABOUR'S LOST	edited by H.R. Woudhuysen
MACBETH	edited by Sandra Clark and Pamela Mason
MEASURE FOR MEASURE	edited by A.R. Braunmuller and Robert N. Watson
THE MERCHANT OF VENICE	edited by John Drakakis
THE MERRY WIVES OF WINDSOR	edited by Giorgio Melchiori
A MIDSUMMER NIGHT'S DREAM	edited by Sukanta Chaudhuri
MUCH ADO ABOUT NOTHING, Revised	edited by Claire McEachern
OTHELLO, Revised	edited by E.A.J. Honigmann, with an Introduction by Ayanna Thompson
PERICLES	edited by Suzanne Gossett
ROMEO AND JULIET	edited by René Weis
SHAKESPEARE'S POEMS	edited by Katherine Duncan-Jones and H.R. Woudhuysen
SHAKESPEARE'S SONNETS, Revised	edited by Katherine Duncan-Jones
SIR THOMAS MORE	edited by John Jowett
THE TAMING OF THE SHREW	edited by Barbara Hodgdon
THE TEMPEST, Revised	edited by Virginia Mason Vaughan and Alden T. Vaughan
TIMON OF ATHENS	edited by Anthony B. Dawson and Gretchen E. Minton
TITUS ANDRONICUS, Revised	edited by Jonathan Bate
TROILUS AND CRESSIDA, Revised	edited by David Bevington
TWELFTH NIGHT	edited by Keir Elam
THE TWO GENTLEMEN OF VERONA	edited by William C. Carroll
THE TWO NOBLE KINSMEN, Revised	edited by Lois Potter
THE WINTER'S TALE	edited by John Pitcher

KING HENRY VI PART 3

Edited by
JOHN D. COX
and
ERIC RASMUSSEN

THE ARDEN SHAKESPEARE

LONDON • NEW YORK • OXFORD • NEW DELHI • SYDNEY

THE ARDEN SHAKESPEARE
Bloomsbury Publishing Plc
50 Bedford Square, London, WC1B 3DP, UK
1385 Broadway, New York, NY 10018, USA

BLOOMSBURY, THE ARDEN SHAKESPEARE and the Arden Shakespeare logo are
trademarks of Bloomsbury Publishing Plc

This edition of *King Henry VI, Part 3* by John D. Cox and Eric Rasmussen,
first published 2001 by the Arden Shakespeare
Reprinted by Bloomsbury Arden Shakespeare 2010, 2011, 2013 (twice), 2016,
2017 (twice), 2018, 2019, 2020 (twice)

Editorial matter © John D. Cox and Eric Rasmussen, 2001

The general editors of the Arden Shakespeare have been
W.J. Craig and R.H. Case (first series 1899-1944)
Una Ellis-Fermor, Harold F. Brooks, Harold Jenkins and
Brian Morris (second series 1946-82)
Present general editors (third series)
Richard Proudfoot, Ann Thompson, David Scott Kastan and H.R. Woudhuysen

A catalogue record for this book is available from the British Library.

A catalog record for this book is available from the Library of Congress.

ISBN: HB: 978-1-9034-3630-1
PB: 978-1-9034-3631-8

Series: The Arden Shakespeare Third Series

Printed and bound in Great Britain

To find out more about our authors and books visit www.bloomsbury.com
and sign up for our newsletters.

The Editors

John D. Cox is the DuMez Professor of English at Hope College, Michigan. He is author of *Shakespeare and the Dramaturgy of Power* (1989) and *The Devil and the Sacred in English Drama, 1350–1642* (2000) and co-editor with David Scott Kastan of *A New History of Early English Drama* (1997).

Eric Rasmussen is Associate Professor of English at the University of Nevada, Reno. He is joint editor with David Bevington of *Doctor Faustus* in the Revels Plays series (1993) and the World's Classics edition of Christopher Marlowe's plays (1995), author of *A Textual Companion to 'Doctor Faustus'* (1994), and co-editor of the forthcoming *Norton Anthology of English Renaissance Drama* (2002). He writes the annual review of 'Editions and Textual Studies' for *Shakespeare Survey*.

For our students

CONTENTS

LIST OF
ILLUSTRATIONS

GENERAL EDITORS' PREFACE

The Arden Shakespeare is now over one hundred years old. The earliest volume in the first series, Edward Dowden's *Hamlet*, was published in 1899. Since then the Arden Shakespeare has become internationally recognized and respected. It is now widely acknowledged as the pre-eminent Shakespeare series, valued by scholars, students, actors and 'the great variety of readers' alike for its readable and reliable texts, its full annotation and its richly informative introductions.

We have aimed in the third Arden edition to maintain the quality and general character of its predecessors, preserving the commitment to presenting the play as it has been shaped in history. While each individual volume will necessarily have its own emphasis in the light of the unique possibilities and problems posed by the play, the series as a whole, like the earlier Ardens, insists upon the highest standards of scholarship and upon attractive and accessible presentation.

Newly edited from the original quarto and folio editions, the texts are presented in fully modernized form, with a textual apparatus that records all substantial divergences from those early printings. The notes and introductions focus on the conditions and possibilities of meaning that editors, critics and performers (on stage and screen) have discovered in the play. While building upon the rich history of scholarly and theatrical activity that has long shaped our understanding of the texts of Shakespeare's plays, this third series of the Arden Shakespeare is made necessary and possible by a new generation's encounter with Shakespeare, engaging with the plays and their complex relation to the culture in which they were – and continue to be – produced.

THE TEXT

On each page of the play itself, readers will find a passage of text followed by commentary and, finally, textual notes. Act and scene divisions (seldom present in the early editions and often the product of eighteenth-century or later scholarship) have been retained for ease of reference, but have been given less prominence than in the previous series. Editorial indications of location of the action have been removed to the textual notes or commentary.

In the text itself, unfamiliar typographic conventions have been avoided in order to minimize obstacles to the reader. Elided forms in the early texts are spelt out in full in verse lines wherever they indicate a usual late twentieth-century pronunciation that requires no special indication and wherever they occur in prose (except when they indicate non-standard pronunciation). In verse speeches, marks of elision are retained where they are necessary guides to the scansion and pronunciation of the line. Final -ed in past tense and participial forms of verbs is always printed as -ed without accent, never as -'d, but wherever the required pronunciation diverges from modern usage a note in the commentary draws attention to the fact. Where the final -ed should be given syllabic value contrary to modern usage, e.g.

> Doth Silvia know that I am banished?
> (*TGV* 3.1.221)

the note will take the form

> 221 **banished** banishèd

Conventional lineation of divided verse lines shared by two or more speakers has been reconsidered and sometimes rearranged. Except for the familiar *Exit* and *Exeunt*, Latin forms in stage directions and speech prefixes have been translated into English and the original Latin forms recorded in the textual notes.

COMMENTARY AND TEXTUAL NOTES

Notes in the commentary, for which a major source will be the *Oxford English Dictionary*, offer glossarial and other explication of verbal difficulties; they may also include discussion of points of theatrical interpretation and, in relevant cases, substantial extracts from Shakespeare's source material. Editors will not usually offer glossarial notes for words adequately defined in the latest edition of *The Concise Oxford Dictionary* or *Merriam-Webster's Collegiate Dictionary*, but in cases of doubt they will include notes. Attention, however, will be drawn to places where more than one likely interpretation can be proposed and to significant verbal and syntactic complexity. Notes preceded by * discuss editorial amendations or variant readings from the early edition(s) on which the text is based.

Headnotes to acts or scenes discuss, where appropriate, questions of scene location, Shakespeare's handling of his source materials, and major difficulties of staging. The list of roles (so headed to emphasize the play's status as a text for performance) is also considered in commentary notes. These may include comment on plausible patterns of casting with the resources of an Elizabethan or Jacobean acting company, and also on any variation in the description of roles in their speech prefixes in the early editions.

The textual notes are designed to let readers know when the edited text diverges from the early edition(s) on which it is based. Wherever this happens the note will record the rejected reading of the early edition(s), in original spelling, and the source of the reading adopted in this edition. Other forms from the early edition(s) recorded in these notes will include some spellings of particular interest or significance and original forms of translated stage directions. Where two early editions are involved, for instance with *Othello*, the notes will also record all important differences between them. The textual notes take a form that has been in use since the nineteenth century. This comprises, first: line reference, reading adopted in the text and closing square bracket; then: abbreviated reference, in italic, to the earliest edition to adopt the accepted reading, italic semicolon and noteworthy alternative reading(s), each with abbreviated italic reference to its source.

Conventions used in these textual notes include the following. The solidus / is used, in notes quoting verse or discussing verse lining, to indicate line endings. Distinctive spellings of the basic text (Q or F) follow the square bracket without indication of source and are enclosed in italic brackets. Names enclosed in italic brackets indicate originators of conjectural emendations when these did not originate in an edition of the text, or when this edition records a conjecture not accepted into its text. Stage directions (SDs) are referred to by the number of the line within or immediately after which they are placed. Line numbers with a decimal point relate to entry SDs and to SDs more than one line long, with the number after the point indicating the line within the SD: e.g. 78.4 refers to the fourth line of the SD following line 78. Lines of SDs at the start of a scene are numbered 0.1, 0.2, etc. Where only a line number and SD precede the square bracket, e.g. 128 SD], the note relates to the whole of a SD within or immediately following the line. Speech prefixes (SPs) follow similar conventions, 203 SP] referring to the speaker's name for line 203. Where a SP reference takes the form e.g. 38 + SP, it relates to all subsequent speeches assigned to that speaker in the scene in question.

Where, as with *King Henry V*, one of the early editions is a so-called 'bad quarto' (that is, a text either heavily adapted, or reconstructed from memory, or both), the divergences from the present edition are too great to be recorded in full in the notes. In these cases the editions will include a reduced photographic facsimile of the 'bad quarto' in an appendix.

INTRODUCTION

Both the introduction and the commentary are designed to present the plays as texts for performance, and make appropriate reference to stage, film and television versions, as well as introducing the reader to the range of critical approaches to the plays. They discuss the history of the reception of the texts within the theatre and scholarship and beyond, investigating the interdependency of the literary text and the surrounding 'cultural text' both at the time of the original production of Shakespeare's works and during their long and rich afterlife.

PREFACE

The task of joint editing is happily not like the struggles between Lancaster and York, at least it has not been like that for Eric Rasmussen and me. I asked him to join the project when I realized that too many commitments on my part were going to make it impossible for me to meet the deadline for this edition without assistance. Eric had proved his ability as a textual editor of Marlowe, and he helpfully agreed to edit the text of *3 Henry VI* and to write the textual introduction and textual notes. The collaboration has produced a flood of e-mail messages, many phone calls, and pleasant working sessions in Reno and Stratford-upon-Avon. Little did I know when I first agreed to edit this play that it would result in my first chance, courtesy of Eric, to see Lake Tahoe from the ground.

Together, then, we echo Lady Grey in taking our leave of this edition with many thousand thanks. I am grateful to Richard Proudfoot for careful and inspired reading of the introduction, commentary notes and appendices. We have not always agreed, but the edition is far better for his conscientious scrutiny of it. George Walton Williams was the first to peruse the commentary notes, and his bracing and often very funny responses have improved them enormously, despite our starting with different assumptions, especially where stage directions are concerned. David Kastan read a draft of the critical introduction and offered valuable suggestions for improving it. Ann Thompson joined the other senior editors and the publisher Jessica Hodge as generous hosts at regular meetings of the Arden editorial team that coincided with annual gatherings of the Shakespeare Association of America and also convened each summer at King's College London. Jonathan Hope provided invaluable assistance with the fine points of Shakespearean grammar. Working with the Arden copy-editor for this edition, Hannah Hyam, has made me grateful for a strong safety net.

Hope College provided generous financial assistance that

made possible my research and collaboration with Eric. Barbara Mowat supported the project by inviting me to join a seminar at the Folger Shakespeare Library on 'Editing: Theory and Practice' in the spring of 1998. I owe much to her, to other members of the seminar, and to those who visited to help us think about recent developments in editing, as well as our own editing projects. The able staff at the Folger Library also assisted the research and writing of the critical introduction in the spring of 2000. I am grateful to Barbara Mowat and Gail Paster for publishing essays in *Shakespeare Quarterly* that Randall Martin and I had written, without each other's knowledge, on discoveries about Somerville in *3 Henry VI*. Louise George Clubb kindly sent me photographs of the amazing production of *3 Henry VI* that her mother had seen in Honduras in 1950. The photographs were made from Louise Wright George's fifty-year-old negatives. Elizabeth Juckett supplied a valuable reference from the *Bulletin of the West Virginia Association of College English Teachers*, which I could not have found any other way.

We have dedicated this edition to our students, who assisted each of us in various important ways. I am especially grateful to ten students who read and discussed all of Shakespeare's history plays with me in an invigorating seminar in the spring of 1999: T.J. Achatz, Meredith Arwady, Noah Dale, Mary Gehl, Erica Gray, Bill Kim, Tammi Konynenbelt, Beth Laskowski, Chris Vande Bunte and Mira Velasco. In King Edward's words, they are friends that deigned to follow me where few others would, and I learned a lot from them.

John D. Cox
Holland, Michigan

The text of this edition began to take shape in a graduate seminar on scholarly editing under my direction at the University of Nevada, Reno, in the spring of 1997. The dedication of this volume records my lasting gratitude to the participants in that seminar: Jennifer Forsyth, Dave Golz, Elizabeth Gruber, Robert

Lerner, Brad Lucas, Diana Smith and Marsha Urban. My close collaboration with John Cox has been a constant source of stimulation to my work on the text of the play. Although John had no previous experience in the field of textual editing, our edition's fidelity to the Folio is due in large part to John's knack for overturning centuries of editorial tradition by pointing to overlooked analogues that render emendation unnecessary and the Folio eminently defensible.

It has been a great pleasure to participate in the Arden 3 publishing project under the enthusiastic stewardship of Jessica Hodge. Richard Proudfoot, arguably the world's most conscientious general editor, reviewed multiple drafts of the text with extraordinary acumen and rigour, challenged every assumption and suggested inspired emendations. George Walton Williams, as associate general editor, offered comments that were invariably humorous, gracious and profound. The text was further perfected by Hannah Hyam, who takes the art of copy-editing to a new level of detailed and comprehensive inquiry.

The biannual meetings of Arden editors proved to be enormously useful in the evolution of the text of this edition, as did conversations about specific textual matters with David Bevington, Doug Bruster, Lars Engle, Peter Holland, Jonathan Hope, Trevor Howard-Hill, John Jowett, David Scott Kastan, Bernice W. Kliman, Katharine Eisaman Maus, Gordon Mc-Mullan, Ann Thompson and Steven Urkowitz. Jennifer Forsyth assisted with an early draft of the textual introduction. Paul Werstine provided me with a copy of his important but unpublished essay on actors' names in printed texts. Arthur Evenchik, as always, was unsparingly generous with his time and editorial talents. My eight-year-old son Tristan facilitated completion of this project by procuring a rare paperback edition of Shakespeare, while my three-year-old son Arden remains convinced that this book is named for him.

Eric Rasmussen
Orinda, California

INTRODUCTION

3 Henry VI is a remarkable play, revealing a confidence and sureness that very few earlier plays can rival. Written before the young Shakespeare had acquired the means to purchase expensive books, the play is based closely on two of the more expensive books then available, the chronicles of Hall and Holinshed. His commitment to his sources therefore indicates a commitment to finding a means of reading and studying them. The results speak for themselves. Faced with a dense and difficult narrative, Shakespeare clarifies it judiciously while attending carefully to its most important features and recalling many of its minor ones – characters such as John Mortimer and his half-brother Hugh, who appear briefly in only one scene. He was attentive to his sources in relationships between characters, in the major battles of the Wars of the Roses, and in the many shifts of political fortune. He did not merely read; he thoroughly studied and understood what he read.

But *3 Henry VI* offers more than versified chronicle history in dialogue form. Shakespeare freely shaped his material to make it theatrically effective, poetically innovative, and consistent in plot and theme with the two other *Henry VI* plays and *Richard III*. To include minor characters from the chronicles, he had to know how Elizabethan commercial acting companies assigned roles and recycled actors from one scene to the next. Assigning sixty-seven roles to at least twenty-one actors required either a chart something like the one in Appendix 2 or else an astonishing ability to remember who appeared in what scenes and who might play various parts. To the intellectual challenge of adopting the chronicles to a dramatic narrative was thus added the mechanical challenge of making the narrative work for a group of actors. The least of his headaches would appear to be the major one facing Tom

Stoppard's Shakespeare, in the film *Shakespeare in Love*, who worries about his ability to compose poetry. While the poetry of *3 Henry VI* is not the most original, the most powerful, or the most memorable that Shakespeare would write, it nonetheless shows confident mastery of rhetorical resources then available. Sometimes imitating his daring contemporary, Christopher Marlowe, Shakespeare never imitates slavishly; his striking variations on Marlowe show a complete understanding of what Marlowe was doing and an ability to exceed it at the same time.

Moreover, as part of the sweep of English history that includes three other plays, *3 Henry VI* reveals a level of political sophistication that Marlowe never achieved, even when he offered Shakespeare the most sincere form of flattery by imitating, in *Edward II*, Shakespeare's dramatic adaptation of English history. Shakespeare interpreted the struggle for power in the fifteenth century in late Elizabethan terms, so that *3 Henry VI* complements the other history plays in examining the tension between the three constituent elements of late Tudor government: the monarchy, parliament and the administration of justice. *3 Henry VI* is unique, furthermore, in its understated celebration of Shakespeare's own county, Warwickshire: this play is the source of the historical commonplace that Richard Neville, the Earl of Warwick, was the maker of kings. Shakespeare altered his sources by creating a scene (5.1) that places the Earl in Coventry, a city the playwright knew well, as he makes clear in a series of interpolated or invented local references. The character called Somerville, for example, who enters as one of Warwick's retainers, is not in the chronicles and was very likely inspired by events near Stratford-upon-Avon in the 1580s – events in which Shakespeare's family may have been caught up (Martin and Cox).

The history of response to this remarkable play begins in the theatre; in fact, an allusion to *3 Henry VI* in performance is one of the first allusions to any play by Shakespeare. After its initial burst of popularity, it was performed less frequently than other history plays, but it enjoyed unprecedented success in the second half of the twentieth century, not only in England but also around the world. Criticism of *3 Henry VI*, on the other hand, though surprisingly full, has been more patronizing than appreciative and more textual than interpretive. The first critical question that arose about *3 Henry VI* concerned Shakespeare's sole responsibility for it: believing its poetry to be uneven, some eighteenth-century critics thought Shakespeare could not have written either the first-published version of the play – the Octavo *True Tragedy of Richard Duke of York* (1595) – or weak passages in the Folio text of 1623. They therefore proposed alternative authors. Many solutions to the puzzle of authorship have been offered, but we argue below that it has not been solved because it is unsolvable. Moral criticism has illuminated much in this play, from Samuel Johnson's observations about particular passages to E.M.W. Tillyard's argument about providential punishment. The characters of *3 Henry VI* have attracted considerable critical attention, with major differences of opinion arising about King Henry VI and Richard Duke of Gloucester in particular. We argue below that due attention to the still-vital influence of the morality play in the 1590s helps to explain Shakespeare's treatment of characters as types in *3 Henry VI*: the saintly king, the demonic upstart, the shrewish queen. At the same time, Shakespeare places these characters in secular political situations that complicate both their dramatic heritage and audience response to them.

3 Henry VI came into its own with the so-called New Criticism, from the 1940s to the 1970s. Tillyard, the most influential critic of the history plays in the twentieth century, thought Shakespeare failed to control 'a great mass of chronicle matter' in *3 Henry VI*, so that a few 'splendid things in it' are like 'islands sticking out of a sea of mediocrity' (*History Plays*, 190). New Critics took this claim as a challenge to be overcome. Their assumption of imaginative coherence in works of art produced readings of *3 Henry VI* that revealed striking patterns in imagery, symbol and theme, as well as close ties to its companion plays. Though the more hermetic assumptions of New Criticism have long since been abandoned, the readings it produced remain fascinating revelations of the play. In the meantime, psychoanalytic critics have revealed unexpected depths in Richard Duke of Gloucester; performance critics have illuminated how the play works in the theatre; feminist critics have discovered new features of *3 Henry VI* by examining its patriarchal assumptions, from its belittling of women to its preoccupation with male honour.

In order to do justice both to the play and to responses to it, this introduction takes a narrative form, telling the story of written engagement with the play (at least in English) from the earliest comment to the latest. The narrative is organized topically and chronologically, beginning with a history of performance (at least as that can be assessed from chance comments, reviews and stage illustrations), because the first assumed manifestation of *3 Henry VI* is in the Rose Theatre in 1592. From performance history, the narrative moves to the first critical question that arose about *3 Henry VI* as noted above, i.e. the question whether Shakespeare was wholly responsible for writing it or whether others shared in the task. Other topics are narrated below in the order they in turn appeared in the historical record, and each is then brought up to the present. Feminist interpretation of *3 Henry VI* is thus the last topic treated, not because it is least important but because it is the latest distinctive question to arise about this particular play.

We have chosen this method of introducing the play because we think it is the fairest way to proceed in the present historical moment. To tell the story of *3 Henry VI* exclusively from a postmodern point of view would privilege ways of thinking about the play that were articulated for the first time only in the late twentieth century. On the other hand, to exclude those ideas in constructing a narrative about *3 Henry VI* would imply the unchallenged integrity of a paradigm for both interpreting and editing plays that postmodernism has in fact seriously questioned. In keeping with those questions, we do not claim to have achieved closure, positivistic certainty or a definitive account of *3 Henry VI*. We acknowledge the interpretive nature of our enterprise, and we endeavour to make clear where the present edition stands in a long tradition of editing *3 Henry VI* – a tradition often so various that from time to time one wonders whether any two editors or critics are discussing the same play. This narrative has its own point of view, as all narratives do, and our sense of the play emerges clearly in the story we tell, of *3 Henry VI* as a remarkable play, of its secular use of medieval dramatic tradition and of its creation (or perpetuation) of one of the strongest female roles that Shakespeare wrote.

A PLAY FOR THE STAGE

3 Henry VI was originally written for performance in an Elizabethan theatre, and its careful preparation as a text for read-ing and study (as in this edition) is a subsequent development that would have astonished those who originally performed it. The earliest reference we have to any play by Shakespeare (either in whole or in part) is in the form of three allusions in 1592 to two of the *Henry VI* plays in the theatre. On 3 March of that year, the theatrical entrepreneur Philip Henslowe recorded earnings of £3 16s. 8d. (a very good return) for a performance of 'harey the vi' by Lord Strange's Men at the Rose Theatre, noting it as 'ne' i.e. presumably 'new'.[1] Five months later, on 8 August, Thomas Nashe's *Piers Penniless His Supplication to the Devil* was entered for publication in the Stationers' Register (Arber, 2.292). Among other things, Nashe's little book defends stage plays, arguing that they are mostly 'borrowed out of our English chronicles' to reprove 'these degenerate effeminate dayes of ours'. For example, Nashe exclaims:

> How would it have joied brave *Talbot* (the terror of the French) to thinke that after he had lyne two hundred yeares in his Tombe, hee should triumphe againe on the

---

1 For Henslowe's reference, see Henslowe, 16; for the company in question, see Gurr, 22, 259.

> Stage, and have his bones newe embalmed with the teares
> of ten thousand spectators at least (at severall times),
> who, in the Tragedian that represents his person, imagine
> they behold him fresh bleeding.
>
> (Nashe, 1.212)[1]

The only Talbot we know of on the Elizabethan stage is in
Shakespeare's *1 Henry VI*, which seems to have made a major
impression, not only on Nashe but also on others. Nashe's 'sever-
all times' is confirmed by Henslowe's records, which show
fourteen more performances over the next twenty-two months.

Barely a month after the entry of Nashe's book, another chance
comment indicates that *3 Henry VI* was also known in the theatre
by 1592. On 22 September Robert Greene's *Groatsworth of Wit*
was entered in the Stationers' Register (Arber, 2.292ᵛ) with a different intent from that of Nashe's book. Warning the '*Gentlemen
. . . that spend their wits in making plaies*' not to trust players,
Greene singles out an 'upstart Crow' in particular, one:

> beautified with our feathers, that with his *Tygers hart
> wrapt in a Players hyde*, supposes he is as well able to
> bombast out a blanke verse as the best of you: and being
> an absolute *Johannes fac totum*, is in his owne conceit the
> only Shake-scene in a country.
>
> (Greene, 80, 84–5)

The exact meaning of Greene's comment has been debated since
it was first recognized as an allusion to *3 Henry VI* by Thomas
Tyrwhitt in the eighteenth century (Greene, 131–45). That it *is*
an allusion, however, has not been questioned. When Queen
Margaret is torturing York, he accuses her of having a 'tiger's
heart wrapped in a woman's hide' (1.4.137), a line Greene adapts
to describe the 'upstart Crow'. 'Shake-scene' is likewise a pun on
Shakespeare's name. The passage is no less remarkable a tribute to

---

1   For more extensive quotation from this passage and more extensive commentary on
it, see Ard³ *1H6*, 1–4.

the power of Shakespeare's early plays in the theatre than is Nashe's comment about Talbot. Since none of Shakespeare's plays was in print by 1592, Greene not only remembered the scene of York's death from seeing it in the theatre, but he also expected his readers to remember it and to recognize his adaptation of a line from it.

Just what version of this play Greene remembered we do not know. The version that was printed closest in time to the play's first productions is the Octavo *True Tragedy* of 1595 (O), which contains fuller stage directions than *3 Henry VI* in the Folio text of 1623 (F). Despite being shorter than F by about a third, O was not necessarily written with the makeshift conditions of a touring company in mind. In O Warwick enters 'on the walles' (sig. E, l. 5), where he converses with three others: 'posts' from Oxford and Montague, respectively, and Summerfield. This acting space above the main stage is required to hold four actors and is therefore the same that Ernest L. Rhodes identifies as the 'gallery' of the Rose: 'Typically in besieging episodes the defenders come onto the walls (the gallery) and talk to those seeking admission at the gates' (E.L. Rhodes, 80)[1] (Fig. 1).

The notes to the present edition contain specific information about the probable early staging of the play, but a general description is appropriate at this point, since the earliest productions would have been closest to the playbook Shakespeare wrote for the performers and would have been affected in various ways by his presence.[2] Nearly all the action of *3 Henry VI* would have taken place on the Rose's thrust stage that was newly remodelled in 1592, while the theatres were closed because of the plague, to a depth of 18 feet 4 inches (Eccles, 94). Its width was similar to that of the old stage: 36 feet 9 inches at the back, tapering to 26 feet 10 inches at the front (Eccles, 92). This large stage was surrounded

---

1 For discussion of the upper acting area in Elizabethan theatres, see Gaw, *Origin*, 39–63; Hosley; Hattaway, 'gallery' in index.
2 For 'playbook' as a technical term that describes the manuscript prepared by a playwright (or playwrights) for performance, see W. Long, 'Precious'.

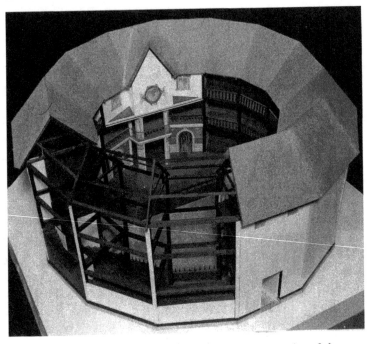

1   Jon Greenfield's model of the 1587 Rose, before construction of the stage
    roof in 1592

on three sides by an open space for those who were willing to stand
to watch plays, and this was enclosed in turn by three levels of
seating galleries, like those at the later (1599) Globe, reconstructed
in the 1990s on the south bank of the Thames. The primary purpose of Henslowe's remodelling in 1592 was apparently to add a
roof to the stage (Eccles, 126), thus introducing two downstage
upright roof supports for the first time. While enabling productions to continue in inclement weather, these posts must have
created new and unforeseen problems for the performers who had
to deal with them in the acting area. Behind the stage was the
'tiring house', where costumes and props were stored. The
tiring-house façade, which formed the background to action on
the stage, was probably decorated, but it was not designed to

accommodate scenic flats or any other means of surrounding the action with realistic effects (Hattaway, 24–7). Audiences were expected, as Shakespeare says, to 'piece out our imperfections with your thoughts' (*H5* Prologue 23). The imperfections he refers to included action on an undecorated stage, using a minimum of props.

Other impediments to credibility involved actors playing multiple parts. We calculate that twenty-one adult and four boy actors were required to play the sixty-seven parts in *3 Henry VI* (see Appendix 2). Moreover, all of these actors were male, with women's parts being taken by apprentices who were slighter, shorter and higher voiced.[1] Apprentices had to be capable performers, even if they were young. The role of Queen Margaret in *3 Henry VI* is the sixth longest and one of the most demanding in the play, certainly taken by an experienced senior apprentice, while less experienced counterparts played Lady Elizabeth Grey (afterwards Queen Elizabeth), the Lancastrian Prince Edward, Rutland, Richmond, and the Nurse to the Yorkist Prince Edward in 5.7.

Among the 'imperfections' Shakespeare acknowledges, the battle scenes in particular were singled out by Ben Jonson, Shakespeare's fellow actor and playwright, when he scoffed at actors in the *Henry VI* plays, who

> with three rustie swords,
> And helpe of some few foot-and-halfe-foote words,
> Fight ouer *Yorke*, and *Lancasters* long iarres:
> And in the tyring-house bring wounds, to scarres.
>
> (Jonson, 3.303)

But Jonson's critique needs to be understood in context. Nashe's comment about Talbot suggests that audiences were deeply

---

1   Hattaway points out that 'boy actors' does not mean 'piping choirboys' but 'mature youths whose voices may not have broken until they were fifteen or sixteen (assuming the onset of puberty to have been considerably later than it is now)' (Hattaway, 84).

moved by heroic soldiers, and the frequency of battle scenes in *3 Henry VI* (see Appendix 3) suggests that they were crowd pleasers, so Jonson's view was probably not representative. He was not, in any case, evaluating stage action by the criteria of later dramatic realism. He was more likely holding the public theatre up to the same standard that Sir Philip Sidney had used in his *Apology for Poetry* (published for the first time in 1595): the standard of Italian neo-classical drama. Decorum, as the Italians had learned from Horace, required that vigorous action be *reported*, not shown (Weinberg, 1.129, 167, 428), an expectation that Sidney assumes in condemning frequent scene changes: 'While in the meantime two Armies flye in, represented with foure swords and bucklers, and then what harde heart will not receiue it for a pitched fielde?' (G. Smith, 1.197). Jonson's antipathy to stage action echoes Sidney's, and it was not confined to the public stage: he later mocked the court stage designer, Inigo Jones, for believing (or so Jonson claimed) that the 'soul' of plays is not poetry but action and spectacle (Jonson, 3.402–6).

Despite his own remarkable poetic gifts, Shakespeare was as much on Jones's side in this quarrel as on Jonson's. His theatrical instincts were as sure as his poetic ones, and he exercised both with consummate ease and self-confidence, though the early plays are naturally less accomplished than the later ones. When he wrote *The Winter's Tale*, many years after *3 Henry VI*, Shakespeare obliquely addressed the issue of neo-classical expectation, or what he calls 'ancient'st order': 'Let me pass', his chorus, Time, commands the audience:

> The same I am, ere ancient'st order was
> Or what is now received. I witness to
> The times that brought them in; so shall I do
> To th' freshest things now reigning, and make stale
> The glistering of this present, as my tale
> Now seems to it.
>
> (*WT* 4.1.9–15)

10

Not surprisingly, Jonson also condemned *The Winter's Tale* as improbable, claiming of himself that he was 'loth to make Nature afraid in his *Playes*, like those that beget *Tales*, *Tempests*, and such like *Drolleries*' (Jonson, 6.16). But Shakespeare seems to have anticipated such criticism, and his prediction that his 'tale' would make contemporary plays stale by comparison has been amply vindicated.

THE POLITICS OF ADAPTATION ON THE ENGLISH STAGE

Does the closeness of early productions to Shakespeare's play-book and his likely involvement with them mean that those productions should be the standard for all subsequent ones? Even a director as historically conscientious as Harley Granville-Barker warned against taking historical practice as an undeviating criterion for theatrical performance: 'We shall not save our souls by being Elizabethan . . . . To be Elizabethan one must be strictly, logically or quite ineffectively so. And, even then, it is asking too much of an audience to come to the theatre so historically-sensed as that' (D. Kennedy, 130). Drama in all cultures includes performers and audience, but beyond those two common factors are infinitely more that distinguish one national tradition from another and one era of theatre in the same national tradition from another. Plays performed at Shakespeare's Globe Theatre as recently reconstructed in London are not necessarily closer to Shakespeare's playbook than plays performed elsewhere. For one thing, with the possible exception of part of *Sir Thomas More*, no playbook of Shakespeare's has survived, and early printed editions witness in varying ways to what happened in early productions.[1] Even if some miracle of serendipity and chance were to turn up a playbook of *3 Henry VI* in Shakespeare's hand,

---

1 The survival rate of Shakespeare's playbooks is not exceptional. Long states that 'only eighteen [playbooks] survive out of probably 3,000' written for the commercial London theatres between the 1570s and 1642 (W. Long, 'Precious', 414).

and even if a production were mounted from it at the new Globe Theatre, following everything we know about Elizabethan stage conditions, the result would not be an 'authentic' production that rendered others 'false'; it would simply be an interesting historical experiment that offered a provisional version of possibilities from 400 years ago, few of which could be represented by the playbook, and all, in any case, rendered and responded to by people who (and under circumstances which) would be unimaginably different from those in the 1590s (see Worthen, 1–43).

It should therefore be no surprise that the first known revival of *3 Henry VI* after the 1590s was an adaptation to a particular time and place that made it very different from the earliest productions. In 1680–1, John Crowne produced *The Misery of Civil War*, incorporating parts of *2* and *3 Henry VI* and setting a precedent for cutting, rearranging and conflation that continues to the present. The Elizabethan and Jacobean amphitheatres had been pulled down by the 1650s, and Crowne's Dukes Theatre was strongly influenced by early Stuart court drama. It was entirely indoors, it employed artificial lighting, and it used what contemporaries called a 'scene', or painted scenic backdrop for the action, that lay behind a curtain and could be altered in the course of the play (Odell, 1.102). Still, some points of continuity with early commercial theatres in London were apparent: action was performed principally on a semi-circular thrust stage in front of the curtained proscenium, and actors entered the stage through doors on either side of the proscenium arch. This configuration and the stylized means of entering and leaving the stage remained in use until well into the nineteenth century (Odell, 1.103) (Fig. 2).

Parts of Shakespeare's *3 Henry VI* were incorporated into Crowne's *The Misery of Civil War*. It heightened the romantic spectacle of Edward IV's courtship of Lady Grey with two added subplots. One involved a mistress of Edward, to whom he resorted from time to time and whom he finally (in a tribute to Francis Beaumont and John Fletcher's *Philaster*) killed unwittingly in battle when she was disguised as a boy. The other required Warwick

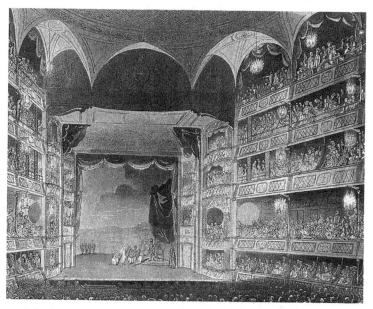

2   The Drury Lane Theatre in the early nineteenth century, when it still had two stage doors for all entries and exits and an apron stage before the proscenium arch (from R. Ackermann, *The Microcosm of London* (1808–10))

to meet Lady Grey immediately after the second battle of St Albans, where her husband had just been killed. Warwick's attempt to seduce Elizabeth (modelled on Richard's wooing of Lady Anne in *Richard III*) was futile, but it gave him a romantic motive for rejecting Edward when Edward fell in love with Elizabeth later and married her (Odell, 1.66–7). Crowne thus successfully adapted Shakespeare's history play to Restoration expectations for sentimental tragedy, with its strong appeal to the social outlook of the Court.

But Crowne had other motives too for adapting *2* and *3 Henry VI*. Twenty years after the Restoration, a play about civil war was unavoidably political, and Crowne's title leaves no doubt where the play stood – not surprisingly in view of the theatre's court patronage. His opening with Cade's rebellion and his addition of two painted scenes tend to the same effect. The first showed soldiers 'looting and raping' at a cottage; the second, 'Houses and Towns burning, Men and Women hang'd upon Trees, and Children on the Tops of Pikes' (H. Spencer, 304). In 1681, Crowne produced his *Henry the Sixth, the First Part*, incorporating elements of *1* and *2 Henry VI*, in which, despite his royalist outlook on the events of 1642–9, he adopted a more Whiggish stance. Aiming to whip up anti-Catholic sentiment in support of the Exclusion Bill of May 1680 – which barred the Catholic Duke of York from succeeding his brother, Charles II, to the throne – Crowne reshaped Winchester's plot to destroy Duke Humphrey in *2 Henry VI*, expanding the roles of the three murderers in 3.2 to make them more clearly the tools of the Machiavellian cardinal.[1] The Lord Chamberlain suppressed Crowne's play as a consequence, and 'the real wonder', as Odell says, 'is that the actors dared attempt it' in the first place (1.65).

Stage productions of Shakespeare's early history plays have repeatedly adapted them, as Crowne did, to prevailing political concerns, both conservative and oppositional. Crowne is unusual only in taking such different points of view in two successive plays. This kind of adaptation is an obvious way to make archaic material vital for a given audience, especially if that material deals with history in the first place, because the past inevitably functions in part as a mirror, in which seekers find themselves. When the past one is examining (or producing for the stage) has already been interpreted by Shakespeare, then his extraordinary cultural status becomes an additional motive for discovering and revealing what the writer cares most about. This was already a motive for Crowne, who describes Shakespeare as 'immortal' and acknowledges that his auditors' 'Mouthes are never out of taste with him' (H. Spencer, 309). Knowing his audience's appetite,

---

1 On the political context of Crowne's *Henry VI* and of other plays contemporary with it (including some supporting York), see Dobson, 62–98.

and presumably sharing it himself, Crowne boldly offered 'A little Vinegar against the *Pope*' when he served up his Shakespearean feast (Odell, 1.63).

Sometimes, to be sure, playwrights have been suspected of political motives when they appear to be innocent of them. In 1700, Charles Killigrew, Master of the Revels, refused Colley Cibber permission to perform the first act of his *Richard III*, which Cibber had borrowed from *3 Henry VI* 5.6 – the scene in which Richard of Gloucester murders Henry VI. Killigrew's concern was that 'the Distresses of King *Henry the Sixth* . . . would put weak People too much in mind of King *James* then living in France' (C. Spencer, 416). Cibber denied a political motive for the borrowing, but Crowne had set a precedent for political adaptation, and Crowne's particular way of dividing and conflating the early histories still influenced Theophilus Cibber in 1723, when he combined *2 Henry VI* with parts of *3 Henry VI*, following Ambrose Philips's example of adapting *2 Henry VI* the season before (Odell, 1.248, 250). In any case, Colley Cibber's conflation of *3 Henry VI* with *Richard III* was the most enduring version of the early histories on stage, continuing in its own right until well into the twentieth century (Sprague, 123–41) and setting a precedent for other conflations, such as Laurence Olivier's production of *Richard III* in 1944 (followed by a film in 1955), which began with Richard of Gloucester's soliloquy from *3 Henry VI* 3.2.

The second half of the eighteenth century saw, for the first time, a conscious contextualizing of Shakespeare's plays historically, prompted by growing antiquarian interest, a better understanding of how the texts had been established and a recognition (already asserted by Shakespeare in *The Winter's Tale*) that neo-classical standards of art were not timeless (De Grazia, 1–14). Shakespearean performance was affected by these changes. In 1817, when J.H. Merivale produced *Richard Duke of York; or the Contention of York and Lancaster*, he abandoned Crowne's pattern of adaptation, conflating all three parts of *Henry VI* into one play that concluded with York's death from *3 Henry VI* (Odell,

2.128–30). For Crowne's unifying conceptions, either social or political, Merivale substituted frequent allusions to plays by Shakespeare's contemporaries. A reviewer for the *European Magazine* thought that 'the piece is overloaded with this mass of incident which bears it down', though Edmund Kean, who played the Duke of York, was, 'in many scenes, unusually great' (Salgādo, 86). The historicizing impulse was evident in other ways when James Anderson revived *2 Henry VI* at the Surrey Theatre for the Shakespearean tercentenary in 1864. For the first time since the 1590s, an early history play by Shakespeare was performed with no additions and with attempts at doubling, as a contemporary noted, 'in the manner which [Anderson] imagines must have been resorted to by Shakespeare himself when the drama was first produced' (Salgādo, 88).

Anderson's experiment in historical revival was repeated at Stratford in 1906 by Frank Benson, who put on all three parts of *Henry VI* without conflating or adapting them. This was the first known performance of *3 Henry VI* since the 1590s, and it was inspired by the increasing recognition of historical context. An anonymous reviewer recognized Benson's attempt to recreate something like Elizabethan acting conditions: 'There was no changing of scenery, except of portable furniture, the action was continuous, and the auditors were expected to exercise not only their attention but their imagination'. Nonetheless, the realistic conventions of Edwardian staging still required so much attention to 'modern stage methods and machinery . . . that the work of Shakespeare is cut, and we do not see the whole' (*Herald*, 11 May 1906). The distance between another reviewer and Elizabethan taste is evident in his remark that in *3 Henry VI* 'there was an unnecessary amount of fighting, never very effective on the stage' (Dickins, 130).

Benson was frank about the political conception that lay behind his production. Ambivalence about empire, sentiment about Joan of Arc, idealism about the Whig view of history are all evident in his own description of what his production aimed to show:

> That the wanton aggression against France, was inevitably followed by civil disruption at home. That the Wars of the Roses, were practically a punishment, for a War of greed and spoliation, which reached its climax in the murder of Joan of Arc. . . . Finally how during the death and the ruin of so many nobles and gentry, the Commons of England were growing in power and importance, and laying the foundation of the English Empire; and how clearly Shakespeare rejects the machiavelian theory of politics which proved the ruin of Florence and Italian Liberties.
>
> (quoted in Sprague, 112)

Richard Dickins noted that to present *1 Henry VI* as Benson did, 'with La Pucelle appearing as a heroine and not as a minister of hell, is to deprive the play not only of its interest but of its meaning' (Dickins, 129). Dickins was also disappointed by Benson's portrayal of Richard in *3 Henry VI*. The part was so severely cut and underplayed that Dickins wondered if 'the heavy work entailed by the production of four practically new plays had left the manager no time for study' (129–30).

The ideal of authentic Elizabethan staging caught the fancy of many directors besides Benson; it was apparent in Robert Atkins's 1923 production of *Henry VI* at the Old Vic. This play was designed to celebrate the tercentenary of the First Folio by offering a version of all three plays for performance in a single evening, as Merivale had done in 1817. Atkins scrapped the venerable Victorian stage machinery, built a thrust stage in front of the proscenium, and largely replaced painted scenery with curtains (Rowell, 104–5). Atkins himself played Richard of Gloucester, and he seems to have worked harder at it than Benson, carefully distinguishing:

the younger from the older Richard, making him more care-free and less sardonic, though he had the right deep humour, the 'grumbling voice' that Margaret attributes to him, and a most intriguing laugh, loud and neighing, which would have been very inappropriate in the later play.

(Crosse, 58)

Where production is concerned, *3 Henry VI* came into its own after World War II. Since then, it has been produced more often than in the 350 previous years, and for the first time it has been recorded on videotape. In large part this remarkable record of performance is due to the success of John Barton and Peter Hall's adaptation of the *Henry VI* plays in 1963, called *The Wars of the Roses*, but all post-war productions have been characterized by the stage traditions we have seen thus far: conflation and adaptation, separate and largely uncut performance of the play by itself, historicizing, and politicizing. Recent directors have emphasized ensemble acting rather than star performers, but this emphasis also follows performance traditions for *3 Henry VI*, since we know of no star performers in productions from the 1590s, and few were drawn to the play in the eighteenth and nineteenth centuries. The point of emphasizing continuity between post-war performances and earlier tradition is not to dispraise recent productions but to view them in perspective, acknowledging both the limited range of possibilities and the contribution of earlier actors and directors to a more or less continuous tradition of performing the *Henry VI* plays in England.

Continuity was certainly a factor in Barry Jackson's production of *Henry VI* as three separate plays at the Birmingham Repertory Theatre in 1951–3, for Jackson had seen Benson's first production of the separate plays almost fifty years before, and they had left a strong impression on him (B. Jackson, 49). He was also aware of Merivale's *Richard, Duke of York* in 1817, though he mistakenly attributed the starring role in that play to Charles Kean rather than Edmund (50). Jackson referred to Merivale's production in defence of the Birmingham Rep's choice not to conflate three plays into one, as Merivale had done, and not to identify roles for star performers.

The company was young and relatively unknown, and Douglas Seale, who directed them, not only trained them to stand still when not speaking, thus achieving 'an undisturbed concentration upon the lines' (Kemp, 125) but also achieved effortless effects in doubling. 'Edgar Wreford changed from Humphrey of Gloucester to Richard so quickly and so radically that it took some time to realize that it was the same actor' (Leiter, 237). Seale solved inherent problems like the paper crown for York in 1.4. 'Paper crowns are not usually part of the impedimenta of battlefields. Where and how was it obtained?' (B. Jackson, 51). The solution was to create a ghost role, a boy jester wearing a paper crown, who entered and died with Rutland at Clifford's hand in 1.3. Leaving his body on stage for the next scene not only supplied the requisite prop in a seemingly impromptu manner but did so in a way that thematically reinforced Margaret's cruel taunting of York before she killed him. Of the three plays, Kenneth Tynan was most impressed with *3 Henry VI*: 'As staged by Mr. Seale, it stands up in its own right, shoulder-high at least to the twin peaks of *Henry IV*' (Tynan, 182) (Fig. 3).

The historicizing movement of nineteenth-century criticism and performance affected the design of Jackson's theatre, which was unusually small and intimate, with a seating capacity of just 464 (Cochrane, 6). But Jackson's idea was not to recapture 'history' on stage; it was to recapture historical stage conditions, including period costumes. Reducing the size of the theatre prevented the use of the elaborately realistic stage sets and huge casts that Herbert Beerbohm Tree had made famous and that Atkins also rejected at the Old Vic. Jackson believed that 'the impact of Shakespearean drama in an intimate house is intensified beyond belief' (B. Jackson, 51), apparently not realizing that the Globe held 3,000. His replacement of the Victorian orchestra pit with an

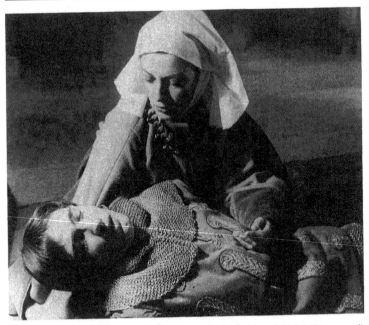

3   Queen Margaret (Rosalind Boxall) holds Prince Edward (John Greenwood) after the York brothers have killed him, in the Birmingham Rep production, directed by Sir Barry Jackson in 1953

apron stage which could be entered from either side was indeed a revival, but what it revived was more like Crowne's Duke's Theatre than the Rose or the Globe. Still, the shift of emphasis away from overpowering and cumbersome stage sets enabled less cutting and more fluid action. Jackson cut much of the fighting in *3 Henry VI*, 'so baffling to all producers', (51) and concluded the play with the opening lines of *Richard III*, which were 'finally submerged by the fanfares and bells marking [Edward IV's] supposedly permanent triumph' (52).

A decade after Jackson's production of *Henry VI*, John Barton and Peter Hall revived the Restoration custom of conflating the three plays in a production for the newly renamed Royal Shakespeare Company (Fig. 4). Their *Wars of the Roses* created

4 King Edward (Roy Dotrice) courts Lady Elizabeth Grey (Susan Engel) while Clarence (Charles Kay) and Gloucester (Ian Holm) look on, in the RSC's *Wars of the Roses* (1963)

two plays, *Henry VI* and *Edward IV*, out of the three, cutting in the process over half of the lines from the F text and adding 1,440 that Barton wrote himself (Leiter, 239). Their aim was to clarify the action so as to emphasize the roles of the two Gloucesters: Duke Humphrey's downfall and death, with the bungling connivance of the King, and the emergence of Richard as retribution for decades of baronial brawling and corruption. The adaptors' motives were various. In his introduction to the printed script, Hall said he had seen Jackson's separately produced plays in Birmingham and found them 'a mess of angry and undifferentiated barons, thrashing about in a diffuse narrative' (Barton and Hall, viii). For economic reasons, the RSC had determined not to stage more than two of the lesser known plays in a season, and both Barton and Hall wanted to produce the *Henry VI* plays along with *Richard III* (xvi).[1] Barton doubted that the *Henry VI* plays were by Shakespeare to begin with; rather, they represented 'the adaptation and partial revision of some earlier texts' (xxiii). Adapting adaptations was not as serious as adapting 'Shakespeare'. 'I wouldn't dream', Barton said later, 'of trying to write bits into *Lear*' (Addenbrooke, 206).

Hall, moreover, was explicit about a political motive. He was impressed by what he called the plays' 'sanctions' for political action that paralleled those he heard modern politicians using 'to mask the dictates of their party politics or their personal ambitions' (Barton and Hall, x). In the middle of a 'blood-soaked century' he thought that 'a presentation of one of the bloodiest and most hypocritical periods in history would teach many lessons about the present' (xi). He read Jan Kott's *Shakespeare Our Contemporary* while *Wars of the Roses* was in rehearsal, and he found it to be 'a great support to our production' (xi). Barbara Hodgdon pointed to the influence of Artaud's Theatre of Cruelty on 'a more truthful representation of war for a post World War II audience', and she noted the 'Brechtian (though not Marxist) appearance of the production – particularly in the focus on action for its own sake' and in the use of 'a *Mother Courage*-like "cart of war"' in the battle scenes (Hodgdon, '*Wars*', 174).

The appearance Hodgdon referred to was hard, metallic and lean. The armoury of Warwick Castle supplied the motif for John Bury's costumes and set. The latter was

> dominated by an enormous council table that provided visual continuity for the three plays: it remained, though those who sat at it changed with frightening regularity. A wall of rusty steel-plated *periaktoi*, turned to change

---

1   Despite generous state subsidy, the RSC was losing money heavily, and the new production had to turn the situation around. 'These productions were Peter's last chance; he sank or swam by them, and the fortunes of the company depended on them' (Beauman, 269).

locale and define playing area, backed the table. The set
provided an auditory, as well as visual comment on the
action.

(Leiter, 239)[1]

In staging *Henry VI* Barton and Hall thus rejected not only the
historicizing production values of Barry Jackson but also the
political conservatism of Frank Benson. Hall quoted Richard
Crossman approvingly on the 'Victorian or Edwardian blinkers' of
earlier interpretations (Barton and Hall, xi–xii). In its political
scepticism, *The Wars of the Roses* set a precedent for other post-
war productions, however reminiscent it was, in some respects, of
John Crowne's two Restoration adaptations of the *Henry VI*
plays, the second of which, after all, had daringly challenged the
prevailing power structure.

Despite the success of *Wars* (which indeed rescued the RSC
financially), each time the *Henry VI* plays have been produced in
Stratford since then, they have been done differently. In 1977,
Terry Hands returned to the separate play productions of Benson
and Jackson, almost certainly in reaction to the conflating tradition represented by Barton and Hall. In fact, *Wars* influenced the
new production, if only by default. In an interview with Homer
Swander, Hands insisted that his cast's principal challenge was to
find their way in uncharted waters: 'We had neither bad things to
avoid nor good things to be guided by. So we were very very much
out on our own'; but in the next breath he compared unfavourably
a scene in *Wars* with the rendering of the same scene in his production (Swander, 150).

Whereas Barton and Hall had achieved a lean plot by means of
heavy cutting, Hands cut almost nothing, determined to find out if
'warts' on the page could turn out to be 'beauty spots' in the theatre. Langdon Brown observed that Hands thus 'freed directors

---

1   G.K. Hunter noted that the council table may have been suggested by Kott's assertion that 'for Shakespeare, power . . . is a relentless struggle of living people who sit
together at one table' (Hunter, 'Royal', 104, n. 12).

from approaching the plays as flawed works requiring energy-sapping apologies and dramaturgic renovation, and allowed them to concentrate their energy on the substantial intrinsic merits' of the plays (Leiter, 236). Hands decided to use the remarkable O stage direction, for example: 'Enter Clifford wounded, with an arrow in his neck' (sig. C3ᵛ, 15–16) (Fig. 5). 'The first image was that it would be ridiculous, and in fact it isn't; it's amazing when you actually see it. It's so unexpected, it's so bizarre, that that moment has been following us all through the play' (Swander, 151). Whereas *Wars* had kept the same staging throughout *Henry VI* and *Edward IV*, Hands adopted different stage symbols for each of the three plays: four cannons for *1 Henry VI*, a green carpet for *2 Henry VI* ('we are in fertile England for the duration of this play'), and a black stage for *3 Henry VI*, 'empty now of furniture except for the throne, the crown, and swords' (Chillington, 568). Much was achieved by extraordinary lighting effects: 'many lights make

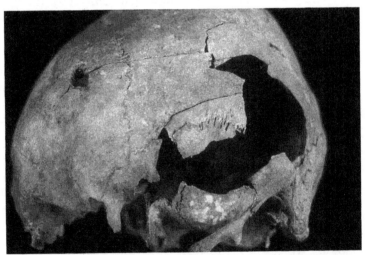

5   Arrow wound in the skull of a soldier whose skeleton was found in 1996 in a mass grave near the site of the battle of Towton, where some 24,000 died, among them Lord Clifford, who the chronicles report died from an arrow wound in his neck (see 2.6.0)

Hands' work', quipped David Daniell ('Opening', 267). Whereas *Wars* had emphasized rapid and continuous action, Hands encouraged his actors to explore the complexity of character, and Alan Howard was particularly memorable as Henry. Helen Mirren (Margaret) testified to the seriousness with which actors took their characterization. Discussing her response to Margaret's torturing of York in *3 Henry VI* 1.4 (Fig. 6), she remarked, 'After the death scene I am almost always ill. I actually vomit. Once I was ill just before it. I have been afraid that I will be ill right on stage, for the feeling of nausea is very strong' (Swander, 156). Her intensity was clearer to some viewers than to others. Roger Warren found the scene 'curiously *un*moving . . . they all seemed almost numbed by their excesses, but somehow missed the raw human emotions of an astounding scene' (R. Warren, 150). Daniell, on the other hand, found it 'as disturbing a thing as one can see' ('Opening', 274).

In still another contrast to *The Wars of the Roses*, Hands disavowed a political motive altogether:

> The *Wars of the Roses* was a study in power politics: its central image was the conference table, and Warwick, the scheming king-maker, was the central figure. But that's not Shakespeare. Shakespeare goes far beyond politics. Politics is a very shallow science.
>
> (Shaughnessy, 61)[1]

What Terry Hands could not know when he produced *Henry VI* is that the disavowal of political intent would itself shortly fall under the suspicion of having a political motive. In 1985, Alan Sinfield took the RSC to task for its conservatism, even when it tried hardest to be radical, let alone apolitical (Sinfield). His critique has been amplified more recently by Robert Shaughnessy, who argued that Hands's emphasis on character, choice and individual development in *Henry VI* 'also paralleled the ideological

---

1   This opinion of *Wars* and of political productions may well have been influenced by G.K. Hunter's judgement of Barton and Hall's work, though Hunter offered his opinion in an article that was hard on Hands's production as well (Hunter, 'Royal').

6   Margaret (Helen Mirren) taunting York (Emrys James) in Terry Hands's
     RSC production, 1977

manoeuverings on the political right which would eventually create the basis of its hegemony over the next decade, in its
reconstruction of the traditional nuclear family as the focus of
political and moral values' (Shaughnessy, 61–2). Pinning Margaret
Thatcher's policies on a revival of *Henry VI*, no matter how splendid or complete it was, sounds like political hyperbole, and
Shaughnessy's charge is reminiscent of Charles Killigrew's claim
about Colley Cibber's political intentions in *Richard III*, even
though Cibber denied them. Still, Sinfield's point about *inevitable*
politicizing is useful as a reminder that politics pervades every
culture, at least insofar as politics involves power relations, and that

most directors of *Henry VI* have not only been aware of their productions' politics but have also been ready to say what they are, because they are the convictions of the producers themselves.

When Michael Bogdanov produced a new *Wars of the Roses* with the English Shakespeare Company in 1987, he left no doubt about his political convictions. He conflated *3 Henry VI* with the second half of *2 Henry VI*, following the example of Barton and Hall and ultimately of John Crowne. But the resulting play was merely the sixth in a massive cycle of seven plays that were performed in regnal order, from *Richard II* to *Richard III*. Though Bogdanov was not the first to produce Shakespeare's histories this way, he was certainly the first to make such a huge production portable: after it opened at the Theatre Royal in Bath in December 1987, it played in Chicago early in 1988 and at the Spoleto Melbourne Arts Festival the following September, and it was also performed in France, Germany, Canada, Hong Kong and Japan (McElroy, 495).

Eschewing the historicizing production values of Benson and Jackson, Bogdanov created a 'double time scheme' (Potter, 173) by 'the calculated use of anachronism' (McElroy, 496), whose intent was to emphasize the contemporary political relevance of the medieval past as Shakespeare had interpreted it. While telling a continuous story of six successive reigns, the production moved visually between Victorian and punk costuming, becoming 'roughly speaking . . . more modern' as the cycle progressed (M. Jackson, *Wars*, 219), and thus implicitly telling another story: England's decline from imperial dominance to Thatcherism. More than one reviewer noticed that Margaret of Anjou, played by June Watson, bore resemblances to another Iron Lady with the same name. The pessimism of the cycle as a whole thus mirrored the pessimism of the English opposition in the late 1980s. As Lois Potter observed, 'When Bosworth Field is seen in the context of so many other bloody battles, it is hard to believe that the death of one ruler, or the advent of any other, can possibly make the slightest difference to the future of the country' (Potter, 173).

Anachronism was not an invention of the 1980s, of course; Shakespeare's staging of history was anachronistic to begin with: in *3 Henry VI* at least one reference was no less topically pointed (though a good deal less obtrusive) than John Crowne's anti-popery or Michael Bogdanov's anti-Thatcherism.[1] Shakespeare's staging of English history as a whole arguably had less to do with the medieval past than with the Elizabethan present. Bogdanov might thus claim to have revived the spirit of Shakespeare's histories more faithfully than Terry Hands, who produced them realistically and without conscious politicizing. Bogdanov's production values would seem to owe even more to Bertolt Brecht's 'alienation-effect' than did those of Barton and Hall in the 1960s, and Brecht significantly found inspiration for the idea in what he learned about Elizabethan and Jacobean staging, which he called 'a theatre full of A-effects' (Brecht, 58). What Brecht meant was that the anti-illusionistic conditions of Shakespeare's theatre prevented audience identification with the characters or action and thus assisted critical analysis of what they represented (Brecht, 51–7, 76–83). Brecht's assumption about the effects of open staging is not supported by what Nashe says about audience response to Talbot in *1 Henry VI*, but the alienating effects of Bogdanov's production are beyond question, and they would seem to function in roughly the way Brecht describes.[2] To be sure, Brecht's analysis depended on a recovered sense of the historical conditions of Shakespeare's theatre, and ironically Bodganov might therefore be said to be an historicizer of sorts in his own right.

1 See Martin and Cox for local references in the play and a possible allusion to one of Shakespeare's Stratford neighbours; for a suggestion of topicality involving Lancaster, see Dutton.
2 For Nashe, see above, pp. 5–6. Even more directly contradicting Brecht's assumption is Thomas Heywood's exclamation about the effect of history plays, since it involves specifically political and patriotic fervour: 'To turne to our domesticke hystories, what English blood seeing the person of any bold English man presented and doth not hugge his fame, and hunnye at his valor, pursuing him in his hart and all prosperous performance, as if the Personater were the man Personated, so bewitching a thing is liuely and well spirited action, that it hath power to new mold the harts of the spectators and fashion them to the shape of any noble and notable attempt' (Heywood, sig. B4). Heywood cites *E3* and *H5* in particular.

Almost exactly contemporary with Bogdanov's *Wars of the Roses* was the RSC's third staging of *3 Henry VI*, this time directed by Adrian Noble in a production called *The Plantagenets*. Noble reverted to the pattern of conflating the three *Henry VI* plays into two, which he called *Henry VI* and *The Rise of Edward IV*. They played in conjunction with a slightly adapted *Richard III*, in which Anton Lesser played Richard, as he had in Hands's *3 Henry VI*. Noble turned over the work of adaptation to Charles Wood, whom he called 'the greatest living writer on war and soldiers' (*Plantagenets*, xii). Wood had just completed *Tumbledown*, a television docu-drama about the Falklands War, and Noble compared Shakespeare's histories to the same genre, noting unapologetically that it had been accused of political bias:

> i.e. a marshalling of events to lead the viewer to a particular conclusion. I would argue that it is an absolutely proper ambition for the artist to attempt to lead his audience to a conclusion. The objection comes, of course, when one does not agree with the conclusion . . .
>
> (*Plantagenets*, ix)

In addition to Wood, Noble turned to Alan Sinfield, who wrote the programme notes for *The Plantagenets*. Having heard Sinfield's 1985 critique, the RSC would appear to have attempted to meet it by bringing the critic on board.

Despite Wood's initial work, the script was adjusted in rehearsal, as the actors and director negotiated cuts and restorations. Ralph Fiennes, who played Henry VI, found the process trying but the result satisfying: 'This was a strain because you always wanted more lines than you were allowed, but once you had swallowed the pill, as it were, good things started to happen and rehearsals became rather inspiring' (Jackson and Smallwood, 100). Only after the script had been settled did Bob Crowley offer a design that was much praised for its visual splendour. The battle of Tewkesbury, for example, was performed in a snowstorm, and the white cloth on which the defeated Lancastrians fell 'was then spectacularly hoisted to the vertical, horribly stained with the blood that has flowed from the multiple wounds of the slaughtered Prince Edward, stabbed in a vicious frenzy by the York brothers. Against that blood-stained cloth Henry VI is murdered' (Jackson and Smallwood, 89). The cloth stained with Rutland's blood, used by Margaret to taunt York, thus came back symbolically to haunt the Lancastrians in their defeat, and in the final scene King Edward stumbled over the body of the Lancastrian Prince, still on stage, when he reached toward his own son in his nurse's arms – another reminder that both sides had degraded themselves through wanton cruelty.

The visual sumptuousness of *The Plantagenets* contrasted with the fast pace and relative simplicity of Bogdanov's *Wars of the Roses*, and more than one commentator saw the lavish setting at Stratford and the Barbican as an inherent limitation to a 'radical' political production, since 'the political meaning of a production is inseparable from its theatrical effect', and 'the excessive decor . . . was itself a statement about the kind of audience that might feel at home there' (Potter, 180; cf. Shaughnessy, 16–20). By the same token, Noble's production was taken to task for its upbeat treatment of Richmond's success at the end of *Richard III*:

> Battered and overwhelmed by a relentless succession of images of devastation alternating with gorgeous pageantry, the spectator was in precisely this position of submission, to the autocracy of director and designer, and reactionary politics emerged on a large scale almost by default.
>
> (Shaughnessy, 86)

A reading of Noble's production as 'reactionary', despite the producer's attempt to be 'radical', is reminiscent of similar charges levelled at the RSC's two earlier productions of *Henry VI*. As Lois Potter noted, the contemporaneous staging of the early histories by both Bogdanov and Noble involved inevitable comparisons between them, 'and the game of "more subversive than thou" was widely played' (178). If the big house at Stratford is indeed partly to blame for the RSC's perceived political ambivalence, it may be significant that the company's fourth staging of *3 Henry VI* opened at The Other Place, Stratford's most experimental 'fringe' theatre, and then went on tour. This production was directed by Katie Mitchell in 1994 and marked the first time that a woman had directed *3 Henry VI* on stage in England. (Mitchell was anticipated in Canada by Pam Brighton in 1980.) Using an abbreviated *3 Henry VI* as her foundation, Mitchell adapted the other *Henry VI* plays to it, calling the result *Henry VI, The Battle for the Throne* (R. Jackson, 348). The production emphasized Christian symbols and ritual, thus throwing the political squabbling and increasing chaos into even stronger relief as hypocritical and self-deceived. Since 'religious symbolism appeared to be an integral part of the characters' moral world' (R. Jackson, 348–9), the treachery and infighting became virtually a defect in that world itself. No wonder that the production 'evoked images and situations related to current conflicts in Eastern Europe', i.e. to the civil war in Bosnia (R. Jackson, 349).

The RSC's most recent staging of the histories largely continued Mitchell's principle of avoiding the big house: over the course of two playing seasons, in 1999–2000 and 2000–1, all eight plays in the two tetralogies were performed in regnal order, but only *Henry V* was presented in the Royal Shakespeare Theatre. While the four parts of the second tetralogy were divided among three directors, the four earlier plays were all directed by Michael Boyd, and all were performed in the Swan Theatre. Boyd self-consciously eschewed politics, as Terry Hands had done, declaring that the production was 'not about politics; it's very much a spiritual journey' (Boyd). His production was certainly less visibly contemporary than Michael Bogdanov's, and its conception of 'spirituality' was less explicitly political than Katie Mitchell's.

'Magical realism' is a phrase Boyd used to describe the effect of this production. Dead bodies had to be dragged or carried off the stage only in *Richard III*; with one exception, they arose and walked off in the earlier plays, following a red-robed Edward Clayton with keys at his belt, who was identified in the programme as 'The Keeper' in all four plays. Clayton played all the 'keepers' (of the Tower, of forests, and so forth) and thus became, in effect, a keeper of 'hell', an upstage aperture which was lit with misty red when the dead followed The Keeper into it. Moreover, the dead had a disturbing habit of reappearing to interact unexpectedly with the living. Thus Talbot and his son re-entered with their trenched fatal gashes still on them to play the pirates who kill Suffolk in *2 Henry VI* and the Son who has killed his Father and the Father who has killed his Son at the battle of Towton in *3 Henry VI* 2.5. They accomplished the latter by simply changing places when the lament switched from Son to Father.

Henry VI was played with transcendent innocence and remarkable emotional transparency by David Oyelowo, usually costumed in white or gold and therefore a stark contrast with the black-garbed, hypocritical and emotionally tortured Richard of Gloucester, who kills Henry at the end of *3 Henry VI*. The contrast between these two did ample justice to the kind of magical thinking that constructed medieval religious drama and that arguably operates in the characterization by type, as well as the prophecies, curses, omens and prodigies of *3 Henry VI* (see pp. 57–64). Henry was the one exception to dead bodies walking off stage in Boyd's *Henry VI*. Perhaps to emphasize his Christ-like slaughter, he lay where Richard killed him, costumed in a long white gown and bleeding profusely, so that when Richard dragged him off, the body left a wide trail of blood. The actors who performed the final scene were thus compelled to walk about in Henry's blood while celebrating the Yorkist triumph and the birth of Edward's first son. Shakespeare's occasional pun on 'guilt' and 'gilt' has never been rendered more graphically.

Whether Michael Boyd's production marks a departure from a long history of interpreting *3 Henry VI* politically on the English stage, from John Crowne to Katie Mitchell, remains to be seen. Some critics might argue, after all, that a theatrical production emphasizing magical realism and spiritual pilgrimage has an affinity with the politics of Tony Blair. Boyd consistently treated violence with breathtaking acrobatic choreography: soldiers descended from the catwalk on ropes, sometimes upside down; they were suspended in mid-air on steel ladders, where they deliberated, fought and died in an explosion of cascading red feathers; they cartwheeled, tumbled and shouted in unison as much as they marched in formation or mimed real sword fights. In this respect, there was no distinction between 'real' warfare and the mob violence of Jack Cade. Yet not all violence was ballet-like, nor was all bloodshed quasi-symbolic, as in Henry's case. After Clifford died, the York brothers violated the corpse, cutting off its nose and flinging it audibly to the stage. Wounds were ghastly and bled profusely. This was the realistic side of magic realism, and it effectively suggested the horrors of war. The amplified sound of arrows striking in a rush was not all that different from machine-gun fire, and the jerking of soldiers who died as the 'arrows' struck them was as horrible as anything in the movies. Endless political squabbling at court, where the weapons were only words, too readily produced real and graphic violence from which others suffered and died. Only a slight adjustment would be required to create a similar disparity between a tense but quiet political chamber and the carnage of a modern battlefield.

3 HENRY VI ON THE SCREEN AND AROUND THE GLOBE

A portion of *3 Henry VI* in performance was captured permanently as early as 1906, when two scenes from the play were performed at Warwick Castle as part of a pageant that was recorded on silent film. Five years later, a brief silent film record was made of Frank Benson's *Richard III*, which opened with the battle of Tewkesbury and Richard of Gloucester's murder of Henry VI from *3 Henry VI* 5.5 and 5.6, thus setting a cinematic precedent for Richard Loncraine's feature film almost ninety years later. The first known spoken words from *3 Henry VI* to be recorded in a film – in fact, 'probably the first Shakespeare talking picture' (Rothwell and Melzer, 106) – are by John Barrymore in *Show of Shows* (1929). He is billed in the film as Richard III, but the soliloquy he recites, 'between turns by Ted Lewis and Rin Tin Tin', is from *3 Henry VI*, 'using the identical phrasing and intonation and spitting consonants that you can hear in his recording on disc' (Kitchin, 71). In 1944, Laurence Olivier opened his production of *Richard III* at the New Theatre with the same soliloquy and in another memorable voice, later recorded for posterity in his film version of the play (1955).

Though no feature film has yet been made of *3 Henry VI* in its own right, the play has been adapted for television four times since World War II. Two of these were televised versions of stage productions. John Barton and Peter Hall's *Wars of the Roses*, containing portions of *3 Henry VI*, was filmed in black and white at Stratford over an eight-week period in 1964, after the stage run had ended.

> The intention was to give a sense of the impact of the stage production televisually, rather than a plain record of the plays in performance. In this, and for its time, the result is very successful, the emphasis being laid on close-ups rather than scenery.
>
> (McKernan and Terris, 73)

Much the same could be said of the televised version of Michael Bogdanov's *Wars of the Roses*, filmed almost thirty years later in full colour. The same script and set were used as for Bogdanov's epic stage cycle, but film techniques were used, especially close-ups. These were done effectively, as Michael Manheim reported in his description of Richard of Gloucester, played by Andrew Jarvis:

> in the extreme close-ups in which we view Richard throughout, the camera often shoots him from below,

dwelling extensively . . . on the speaker's chin, mouth and even saliva to intensify the effect of his villainy. The actor then adds uniquely varied, sometimes clownish, facial expressions that lace a speech with vicious mockery that is relished by the speaker. By such means, the close-ups of Jarvis give the prospect of Richard's rule a perverse and frightening appeal.

(Manheim, 'English', 137–8)

In addition to these televised adaptations of stage plays, two films of *3 Henry VI* were purpose-made for television and broadcast about twenty years apart: first in 1960 as part of Peter Dews's *An Age of Kings* and second in 1983 as part of the BBC/Time-Life Shakespeare. *An Age of Kings* involved fifteen shows of between sixty and ninety minutes apiece, two for each of the history plays except *1 Henry VI*, which was cut to fit into a single programme. *3 Henry VI* appeared as parts 12 and 13, 'The Morning's War' and 'The Sun in Splendour', respectively. The series as a whole was reviewed by Milton Crane in 1961, and though he said nothing about *3 Henry VI* in particular, he praised various actors (the young Sean Connery in the role of Hotspur, for example), and remarked that 'the camera work was fairly primitive: middle-distance shots alternated with close-ups, and the camera angle was rarely changed. So the works came through as filmed plays' (Crane, 325). Crane probably revealed more about his own 'expectational text', to borrow Barbara Hodgdon's phrase,[1] than about *An Age of Kings* in his frequent complaint that Peter Dews's decision to present the plays in regnal order was anti-climactic, 'as must be expected when a lesser work follows a greater' (Crane, 326). More familiarity with the second tetralogy and reiterated admiration for its literary qualities make Crane's reaction understandable but not inevitable. Stage presentations of

---

1   Hodgdon describes the 'expectational text' as 'my private notions about the play and about performed Shakespeare, notions that I may not even recognize until I find them denied' (Hodgdon, 'Two *Lears*', 143).

the plays in regnal order (in Germany, the UK and US) have been widely admired and successful.

Most people who see *3 Henry VI* in the foreseeable future are likely to do so in the version directed by Jane Howell for the BBC/Time-Life Shakespeare. This is because its initial broadcast in 1983 was followed by successful marketing on videotape: individual plays were much cheaper if the whole series was purchased than if they were purchased separately.[1] The BBC/Time-Life version thus became by default the primary teaching production of the play, because so many academic libraries purchased the series. Economically the strategy succeeded: by 1982, four years into the project of taping all the plays and three years from its conclusion, 'the series had paid for itself and was even making a profit due to foreign sales' (S. Willis, 8). Aesthetically and politically the results were more mixed, but coming relatively late in the series, Howell's *Henry VI* benefited from earlier mistakes while not escaping criticism of televised Shakespeare *per se* or of the way the project as a whole was funded.[2]

One way of characterizing Jane Howell's production is to say that it combined aspects of recent productions on stage: it was indebted to the politics and production values of both Barton and Hall's *Wars of the Roses* and Giorgio Strehler's *Il gioco dei potenti* (see pp. 42–3), while it followed Terry Hands's 1977 production in its completeness. The BBC filmed *3 Henry VI* on an indoor set, as it filmed all other plays in the series after Cedric Messina's period as producer ended (S. Willis, 19). Howell thought 'that the behaviour of the lords of England was a lot like children – prep school children' (S. Willis, 167), and the set therefore resembled an adventure playground, 'a multi-level [jumble] of doors, ropes, platforms, catwalks, walls' (171), which became increasingly battered and even charred as the series progressed, in order to suggest

---

1   The marketing of the videocassettes was in fact crucial to the series' production in the first place. The BBC could not fund the project alone, and Time-Life agreed to help capitalize it because they expected 'a big videocassette market' (Pilkington, 22).
2   For critiques of Shakespeare on television, see Coursen, 'Bard'; Holderness, 'Boxing' and 'Radical'.

the degeneration of public order. As Howell remarked, 'with Gloucester's death, anarchy is loosed and you're left with a very different set of values – every man for himself. You're into a time of change in which there is no code except survival of the fittest – who happens to be Richard. What interests me is that I think we are in that sort of state today, a time of change' (S. Willis, 172). The stylization of this set and its relationship to the director's conception of politics as change and vicious child's play conveyed a grim effect, like the stylized council table and *periaktoi* of Barton and Hall's *Wars of the Roses*, which also originated in its directors' political values. For Howell, too, Shakespeare is our contemporary.

Howell's *3 Henry VI* is linked to Strehler's *Il gioco* not only by the playfulness of the set and costumes but also by the production's self-conscious theatricality: 'proclaiming the performance as performance, the actors proceed to confide to the camera and audience, to glance at the camera to emphasize a response, and to enjoy the potential of theatre and television in combination' (S. Willis, 176). This self-conscious style tends to disengage viewers from the production as 'real' and therefore has affinities with Brecht's alienation-effect – another influence on both Barton and Hall and Strehler. As we noticed in Bogdanov's case, however, Brecht formulated the 'A-effect' partly in response to what he learned about the historical circumstances of production on the Elizabethan and Jacobean stage, and those circumstances affected Howell's *3 Henry VI* as well. The single set, the rapid following of one scene upon another, the extensive use of doubling, all evoke what we have come to understand about staging at the time *3 Henry VI* was first produced. Howell intended the doubling of parts to be noticed, hoping that the appearance of familiar faces in widely differing roles would contribute to an increasing sense of nightmare in the series (S. Willis, 170). The choice to stage the dying Clifford 'with an arrow in his neck' is another Elizabethan detail, also used by Terry Hands in his 1977 *3 Henry VI*, but whereas Hands's aim was to produce the play 'warts and all', Howell included the arrow as an alienation effect – an 'old-fashioned theatre gag' (S. Willis, 176) that called attention to itself as a stage device.

Though most people who see *3 Henry VI* are likely to see Jane Howell's production on videotape, many opportunities to see it on non-English stages presented themselves in the second half of the twentieth century. These cannot be treated here in the detail they deserve, but a sampling of them is essential to suggest how extensively the play has been produced, despite the generally patronizing critical response to it, and how persistently the English tradition of politicizing the history plays has characterized their production elsewhere as well.

Outside England, *3 Henry VI* had little life on the stage before 1950, the most extravagant exception being Franz Dingelstedt's production in 1864 of eight plays, from *Richard II* to *Richard III*, in regnal order, a feat not attempted again until Frank Benson did it in 1906. Dingelstedt undertook the huge task as director of the Weimar Court Theatre and in celebration of the Shakespeare tercentenary that year, but he repeated the production as manager of the Hofburgtheater in 1875 and again in 1876 (Sarlos, 130). Though Dingelstedt conceived of the entire cycle as a single five-act play, he was the first to designate the eight plays as two 'tetralogies' (Sarlos, 121), and he and his audiences seem to have been undisturbed that the plays coming last in regnal order were first in composition and therefore putatively inferior. In keeping with his time, he cut and adapted the plays heavily in order to stage them illusionistically, responding to a contemporary demand 'for the apparent resurrection of the past in all its details' (S. Williams, 156), as Beerbohm Tree did on the English stage.

In the New World, the first staging of *3 Henry VI* probably took place about 1900 or earlier, and performances of the play were repeated every two years by the descendants of African slaves on the Caribbean island of Roatan off the coast of Honduras (Fig. 7). The performance in 1950, the first to have been recorded, attests to the fact that the production had been mounted 'as far back as can be remembered' (George, 359). (By

7   King Henry (Mac Johnson) and Queen Margaret (Alva Bennett), from the
production of *3 Henry VI* on the Honduran island of Roatan, 1950

contrast, no production of *3 Henry VI*, or any of the *Henry VI* plays for that matter, was offered in North America before 1953, and the first production of *3 Henry VI* in England after the 1590s was in 1906.[1]) The only report of the Honduran production supports the inference that the performers chose and adapted *3 Henry VI* and *Richard III* as an expression of communal hope for deliverance from social oppression. They cut both plays heavily and played them as one in order to emphasize Richard's villainy and eventual comeuppance, thus producing 'a very satisfactory finale, bringing forth much applause from the well-entertained audience' (George, 365). The performers were all labourers – longshoremen, cooks, fruit inspectors, painters – and their lives were so busy that they found time to mount their play only about every two years. The production was preceded by a procession of actors in costume through the town, reminiscent of medieval production customs, and a six-piece band accompanied the play with a rendition of 'The Washington and Lee Swing' (George, 364). Without knowing anything about Brecht or Kott, the Hondurans undoubtedly staged the most radical version of *3 Henry VI* before Bogdanov's *Wars of the Roses* in 1988.

The historicizing movement of the early twentieth century in England had a North American counterpart in the advent of 'Elizabethan' staging. The first instance of this exercise in historical nostalgia was constructed by Angus Bowmer in 1935 in Ashland, Oregon, ironically using funds supplied by Franklin Roosevelt's Works Progress Administration to revive the American economy (Sandoe, 6). At Antioch College, Yellow Springs, Ohio, in 1953, a purpose-built stage was constructed 'over the steps of the ivy-clad Main Building', and it included a discovery space and upper acting area in the supposed Elizabethan

---

1   Hennig Cohen's report of a '*Henry VI*' performed in Charleston, South Carolina, in 1773–4 is a typographical error for '*Henry IV*' (Cohen, 329). The correct information had been published thirty years earlier, together with the complete text of the newspaper reports in question (E.Willis, 72–3).

manner (Marder, 57). This stage saw the first performance of the *Henry VI* plays (the three compressed into one) in North America. It was produced along with the rest of Shakespeare's history plays, presented in regnal order from *King John* to *Henry VIII*. At almost exactly the same time, the town of Stratford, Ontario, persuaded Tyrone Guthrie to initiate a Shakespeare festival with a thrust and balcony stage designed by Tanya Moiseiwitsch (Somerset, *Stratford*, xiii). Covered by a tent during its first four seasons, the same stage design was rebuilt in a permanent theatre that opened in 1957.

A watershed in international productions of *3 Henry VI* came with the near coincidence of John Barton and Peter Hall's *Wars of the Roses* and the Shakespeare tercentenary of 1964. We have already seen the influence of their version on subsequent productions in England, but it was no less important elsewhere. Their text of *Henry VI* was used for a production directed by John Hirsch at Stratford, Ontario, in 1966 (Somerset, *Stratford*, 47). Though it ran for thirty-six performances, it did not do well financially, so the festival was forced to cancel plans to stage the Barton–Hall *Edward IV* the following season. Ontario's first attempt at a version of *3 Henry VI* thus came in 1980, when Pam Brighton adapted all three plays as a single play called *Henry VI* that saw only thirteen performances (Somerset, *Stratford*, 154–5). Brighton was not only the first woman to direct the play but also the first adapter since the Restoration to add a 'whore' for Edward IV, though the effect was very different from the Cavalier ethos of John Crowne's production.

Elsewhere in North America, the *Henry VI* plays fared better at the Ashland festival in Oregon. There the initial strategy was to stage one history play every year in a more or less continuous cycle, so the *Henry VI* plays were produced three times, with *3 Henry VI* coming in 1955, 1966 and 1977. From the beginning, it was well received. Horace Robinson reported that the 1955 production was 'the best offering of the season' (Robinson, 451), and Alan Dessen reviewed the 1977 production enthusiastically

(Dessen). Nonetheless, Ashland abandoned the pattern in the 1980s and did not return to *Henry VI* until 1991–2, when they staged the three plays in two parts, in the manner of the Barton–Hall *Wars of the Roses*. Still, Ashland boldly answered Russell Jackson's rhetorical question, 'Who wants to see Part Three of anything?', by staging *3 Henry VI* more often than anyone else except the RSC. On the east coast, a *Wars of the Roses* was again produced by a theatre facing financial disaster, as Peter Hall had produced it at the RSC in 1963. In this case, it was the New York Shakespeare Festival, whose funding had been slashed by the city at the last minute. Joseph Papp introduced the production with a speech comparing the treachery and infighting of the *Wars* to New York city politics, but in fact Stuart Vaughan's production was deliberately apolitical, staged conservatively in a traditional historicizing manner (Hirsch, 477).

Outside North America the influence of the RSC's *Wars of the Roses* was extensive. French productions in 1967 and 1981 conflated the *Henry VI* plays with *Richard III* and were pointedly political (Gouhier, Déprats). The first German production after the Barton–Hall *Wars* was as different from Dingelstedt's 'total theatre' as one can imagine. Peter Palitzsch's *Der Krieg der Rosen*, produced at Stuttgart in 1967, imitated not only the title of the RSC production but also its political realism. A frieze of skeletons, broken weapons and ruins decorated the stage (Fig. 8): 'The message that aristocratic power games produce nothing but carnage needed labouring no further' (Hortmann, 227). Palitzsch's production was extremely popular and set a German standard for years to come (Hortmann, 230). In Japan, *3 Henry VI* was first staged by Norio Deguchi, who led a young company's successful effort to produce all of Shakespeare's plays over the course of six years, from 1975 to 1981. The production eschewed historicizing: costumes were modern, sets were simple, and the music was rock (Sasayama, 20).

Giorgio Strehler's Italian adaptation of *Henry VI* was, however, the most striking and influential of those inspired by Barton

8   The stage frieze used in the Berlin production of Peter Palitzsch's *Der Krieg der Rosen*, 1967

and Hall. Produced at Milan in 1965, Strehler's *Il gioco dei potenti* ('The Game of the Powerful') influenced not only Palitzsch's German production but also Jane Howell's televised *Henry VI* for BBC/Time–Life (see pp. 36–8). Inspired by Brecht, Kott and Pirandello, Strehler emphasized the theatricality of power, beginning with a miniature model of the Globe Theatre on stage, then transforming the theatre itself into an imitation of the Globe, thus merging audience reality and theatrical illusion (Leiter, 241). Strehler was also influenced by Kott's idea of the 'Grand Mechanism', which became, in effect, an updated version of Fortune's Wheel (see 4.3.46–7). For Kott the Grand Mechanism describes Shakespeare's static view of history, which 'turns full circle, returning to the point of departure'. The one who overthrows a tyrant thus becomes a tyrant himself: 'He has ceased to be the executioner, he is now a victim, caught in the wheels' (quoted by Leiter, 241). This 'mechanism' is what Strehler turned into the game of the powerful. Children's games accompanied the funeral of Henry V at the beginning of the sequence, and the play motif continued throughout the production. 'Thus, Strehler's theatrical depiction of the Grand Mechanism joined with theatrical invention, dialectical analysis, and historical criticism to create a production filled with joy and bitter irony' (Leiter, 241).

THE FIRST CRITICAL QUESTION: SINGLE AUTHORSHIP OR COLLABORATION?

The staging of *3 Henry VI* long preceded critical commentary about it, and the rise of critical commentary parallels the rise of Shakespeare's reputation. Later seventeenth-century preference for refined courtly taste regarded Shakespeare as an untutored popular playwright, a child of nature, not of art. Thus Gerard Langbaine pointed out in 1691 that the *Henry VI* plays violate 'the strict rules of *Dramatick Poetry*' because they cover decades rather than days and thus fail to conform to the unity of time (Langbaine, 457). Similarly Charles Gildon complained in 1710 that Richard's long soliloquy in *3 Henry VI* 3.2 'is highly unnatural, for as the Duke of *Buckingham* justly observ'd they [i.e. soliloquies] ought to be few, and short . . . . Our young Poets shou'd never imitate our *Shakspear* in this' (Vickers, 2.248–9).

A change came with the historicizing movement of the later eighteenth century, which affected criticism, as well as performance, of *3 Henry VI*. 'In order to make a true Estimate of the Abilities and Merit of a Writer', wrote Samuel Johnson as early as 1745, 'it is always necessary to examine the Genius of his Age, and Opinions of his contemporaries' (Vickers, 3.165). Where the *Henry VI* plays are concerned, the first examination of this kind involved a question about whether responsibility for writing them should be credited to Shakespeare alone. The issue originated as an aesthetic judgement that was designed to preserve Shakespeare's rising reputation from association with bad writing. 'Tho there are several Master-Strokes in these three Plays which incontestably betray the Workmanship of *Shakespeare*', wrote Lewis Theobald in 1733, 'yet I am doubtful whether they were entirely of his Writing' (Theobald, 4.110). Johnson, however, thought better of the plays than Theobald did, and he sought to anchor his judgement by turning to 'the evidence given by the plays themselves' (S. Johnson, 8.612), as well as by Shakespeare's 'Age, and Opinions of his Contemporaries'. Accordingly he cited the ascription of the *Henry VI* plays to Shakespeare by Heminge and Condell in the Folio of 1623, Shakespeare's reference to the *Henry VI* plays in the epilogue of *Henry V*, and the close connection between the end of *3 Henry VI* and the beginning of *Richard III* (8.612). In keeping with this consideration of 'evidence' (to use Johnson's own word, in a sense borrowed from the emerging scientific paradigm), George Steevens's 1778 edition of Shakespeare included Thomas Tyrwhitt's discovery of Robert Greene's allusion to *3 Henry VI* in *Greene's Groatsworth of Wit* (Steevens[2], 6.565–6; quoted above, p. 6). Steevens took the passage as evidence of Shakespeare's authorship.

Theobald and Johnson set up two sides of a question that became the first critical issue connected to the *Henry VI* plays and has proved to be the most persistent one, argued with increasing sophistication (and repetition) but without resolution to the present day. What began as an aesthetic question quickly took quasi-scientific form, to be answered with hypotheses, evidence and deduction in a manner that became standard for scholarly editions of Shakespeare's plays. On one hand is the position that the *Henry VI* plays are only in part by Shakespeare; on the other, that he is sole author. When Edmond Malone considered the question, in his *Dissertation on the Three Parts of King Henry VI* (1778, reprinted in his edition of 1790), he had already entertained both sides of it, but he argued the first side in what was to become the most influential critical edition of Shakespeare's works. His response to Tyrwhitt was to interpret Greene's allusion as a charge of plagiarism, thus confirming Malone's argument that the *Henry VI* plays had been originally written by George Peele,

45

Greene and Marlowe, and *re-written* by Shakespeare (Malone, 6.397–9, sig. Ee–Ee2). In addition to 'external evidence' from Greene, Malone cited the evidence of Q *First Part of the Contention* and O *True Tragedy of Richard Duke of York*, both of whose title-pages say they were acted by Pembroke's Men, 'but not *one* of our author's plays is said in its title-page to have been acted by any but the Lord Chamberlain's, or the Queen's, or King's servants' (6.397). Malone's canny turn to theatre history as 'external evidence', to use his own phrase, set a long-standing precedent, but he could not know how much more would be discovered or how differently it would be interpreted.

So great was Malone's authority that he established the basic position on the authorship of the *Henry VI* plays for more than a century.[1] When opinion finally turned against him, his edition was described as 'the breach' through which 'has poured a flood of conjecture that threatens to obliterate every familiar landmark' (Alexander, *Shakespeare's*, 32). The phrasing is Peter Alexander's, in an argument made independently by him and Madeleine Doran. They reasoned that *2* and *3 Henry VI* are not Shakespeare's revisions of *The Contention* and *The True Tragedy*, but that the latter are reconstructions from memory by actors who had performed in the longer plays.[2] Alexander considered Malone's reading of Greene's allusion to the 'upstart Crow' and argued that Malone had misinterpreted it (Alexander, *Shakespeare's*, 39–50). Alfred Hart confirmed Alexander's argument by comparing the vocabularies of plays in F and the 'bad quartos', though Hart appeared not to know of Doran (Hart, *Stolne*).

---

1 This is not to say that he went unchallenged. See Knight, 5.ix–xcii; Kenny, 245–367; Tucker Brooke. For nineteenth-century supporters of Malone, see White; Fleay; J. Lee.

2 The idea of 'memorial reconstruction' had been broached in principle by Kenny (277–367), but the theory was formulated by Pollard, who called such reconstructions 'bad quartos' (Pollard, *Folios* and *Fight*), and by Greg, in his edition of *Merry Wives* (Greg, *MWW*). Alexander was also indebted to Smart, 198–201. Johnson's conjecture that O was 'taken by some auditor who wrote down, during the representation, what the time would permit' (S. Johnson, 8.612) has resurfaced from time to time but never gained as wide a following as memorial reconstruction.

While Alexander and Doran successfully answered Malone – at least for the time being – on the question of how F related to O, they did not settle the controversy originated by Theobald and Johnson on the extent of Shakespeare's responsibility for the *Henry VI* plays. John Dover Wilson gave Malone new life by suggesting a different source for Greene's allusion to a 'crow' (Horace, not Aesop) and rejecting Alexander's correction of Malone on that basis (J. Wilson). He thus provided a rationale for his identification of the various contributors to *3 Henry VI* when he wrote the notes for his edition of the play (Cam[1], 123–208). Wilson's sophisticated revival of Theobald's original position kept the debate alive. 'While this difference of opinion remains unresolved', wrote Andrew Cairncross in 1957, 'the question of authorship is also in dispute' (Ard[2] *2H6*, xxi).

The work of Alexander and Doran was widely accepted and refined, but recent developments suggest that the question of authorship has not been resolved because it is unresolvable.[1] Efforts have been made to write computer programs that would find a mechanical solution to authorship based on style, but wide variations in orthography and typography and poor proofreading of early printed texts inevitably render such efforts inconclusive at best and wildly inaccurate at worst.[2] Moreover, the scientific turn that the debate over authorship took in the late eighteenth century was questioned in principle by Roland Barthes's postmodern

---

1 For refinements of memorial reconstruction, see Jordan; McMillin; *TxC*, 197–200. Gary Taylor explains that he chose the title *The True Tragedy of Richard Duke of York* rather than *3 Henry VI*, because the former is the title of O and 'is probably closer to the title by which the play was contemporarily known than either Folio's "*The third Part*" or the 1602 transfer entry's "Second parte"' (*TxC*, 199).

2 As a basis for accurate computer analysis, texts need to be 'commonized', i.e. rendered identical in textual accidentals such as spelling, punctuation and word breaks, but this process requires editorial judgement, which is thus interposed between analysis and authorship – presuming, of course, that early printed texts transparently express authorship in the first place. The Shakespeare Authorship Clinic at Claremont McKenna College undertook such an analysis without adequate 'commonizing' and concluded that *Titus Andronicus* and *3 Henry VI* were not by Shakespeare (Elliott and Valenza). For discussion of their work, see Foster, 'Claremont' and 'Response'; and for another computerized analysis of authorship, see Merriam.

challenge to the idea of authorship itself. Barthes saw the concept of the author as a product of early modern individualism, and he asserted that the concept had died, since both the context that gave rise to the concept and the context in which historical authors (such as Shakespeare) wrote have disappeared. For him, 'a text is not a line of words releasing a single "theological" meaning (the "message" of the Author-God) but a multi-dimensional space in which a variety of writings, none of them original, blend and clash' (Barthes, 146). In other words, a text is a social product, not the product of an individual consciousness. This insight has been influential in the editing of Shakespeare, as well as in studies of authorship. Jeffrey Masten thus pointed out the collaborative nature of Elizabethan and Jacobean playwrighting – involving playhouse and printing-house practices and the Master of the Revels (Masten) – and Paul Werstine argued that the assumptions of editing in the twentieth century, even at its most rigorous, really involved something more like collaborative storytelling than science (Werstine, 'Editing', 49).

Equally damaging to theories of 'bad quartos' and memorial reconstruction have been several critical studies that begin with the same assumptions as the theories themselves. Beginning with *King Lear* in the 1970s, scholars have been increasingly inclined to view 'bad quartos' as alternatives to other printed texts, rather than corruptions or degradations, with varying explanations being possible for their differences.[1] Steven Urkowitz, for example, has revived the eighteenth-century argument that F *3 Henry VI* is a revision of O *True Tragedy* (Urkowitz, 'If'). Peter Blayney brought extensive information about the printing trade to bear against Arthur Pollard's notion of 'bad quartos', and Laurie Maguire devoted a book-length study to examining the hypothesis of memorial reconstruction, concluding that of the forty plays (or parts of plays) identified as memorially reconstructed, none is unquestionably so, and a strong case can be made for only four

---

1   On *KL*, see M. Warren; Urkowitz, *Revision*; Taylor and Warren.

(Maguire, 324–5). Her work did not dismantle the hypothesis, but she strongly qualified its application: 'Starting from a position of interrogative scepticism, my aim is to chart the topography of an area which is riddled with problems from ignorance at one end to false assurance at the other, with confusion occupying the middle ground' (9).

This is not to say that the debate about authorship of *3 Henry VI* has simply come back to where it started. A great deal has been learned in the meantime, and it would be impossible to advance an eighteenth-century idea without considerable refinement and qualification. Still, the question as posed by Theobald and Johnson remains unanswered, and their alternatives would appear to be the best alternatives, after all: either Shakespeare shared the composition of *3 Henry VI* with indeterminate others, or he wrote it himself. Of the two, the first is the more likely explanation, given the circumstances of composition, performance and printing in the Shakespearean theatre. As Michael Bristol points out, 'in such an account authorship would be understood dialogically', that is, the product neither of an autonomous creative intelligence nor of competing such intelligences but of a process of authorial revision, theatrical emendation, and printshop adjustment (Bristol, 38).[1]

MORAL CRITICISM

While the first critical question about *3 Henry VI* concerned the play's authorship, the first interpretive responses to the play outside the theatre were moral criticism and character analysis, and here again Samuel Johnson was a pioneer. It is not clear, in fact, that he would have seen these two kinds of interpretation as distinct, but they certainly became so over the course of time, and it

---

1   In the absence of evidence and method to support a definitive scholarly argument, the present edition's use of 'Shakespeare' as author is a reflection of the editors' best judgement and the desirability for a less clumsy reference than 'the author' or 'Shakespeare and others'.

is therefore useful to distinguish them from the outset. Johnson not only originated a quasi-scientific turn in criticism of Shakespeare but also offered perceptive judgements about the morality of actions and character. Behind both kinds of commentary lay the Enlightenment assumption of universal truth and its accessibility to human knowledge. Of York's determination to resort to force against Margaret, after having sworn to uphold Henry during his lifetime (1.2.34–46), Johnson remarks:

> I know not whether the authour intended any moral instruction, but he that reads this has a striking admonition against that precipitancy by which men often use unlawful means to do that which a little delay would put honestly in their power. Had York staid but a few moments he had saved his cause from the stain of perjury.
>
> (S. Johnson, 8.599)

Johnson's confidence in the universality of moral law is evident in his comment on Warwick's reference to envy in 3.3.127: 'Envy is always supposed to have some fascinating or blasting power, and to be out of the reach of envy is therefore a privilege belonging to great excellence' (8.605).

The character criticism of the nineteenth century (see pp. 65–8) can be understood as a development of moral criticism, if character is conceived in moral terms, but a different kind of moral criticism arose in the mid-twentieth century. E.M.W. Tillyard and L.B. Campbell seem to have independently invented an analysis of the history plays in what they took to be their Elizabethan context, identifying moral assumptions as particular and historical rather than universal.[1] Tillyard wrote his widely influential little book, *The Elizabethan World Picture*, as part of 'an attempt to write a

---

1 For immediate influences on Tillyard and Campbell, '*Histories*', see Ornstein, 14–15. Writing at the same time as Tillyard and Campbell but closer in spirit to Johnson, Alfred Harbage subscribed to 'universal moral principles' (Harbage 154) and asserted that Shakespeare's plays manifest them. What the histories manifest is justice: 'unhappiness is never the product of good, and happiness never the product of evil' (Harbage 162).

larger one on Shakespeare's Histories' (Tillyard, *Elizabethan*, vii). Emphasizing the cosmology ('world picture') of the Elizabethans, he called his third chapter 'Sin', describing in it the cosmic disjunction that occurred because of a moral failure in time: the fall of Adam and Eve. This theme also informs his book on Shakespeare's history plays, where Tillyard asserted that 'there is a general (and predominantly religious) doctrine behind the mass of particular events transacted in Shakespeare's Histories' and that 'the chronicles themselves point just the same way' (Tillyard, *History Plays*, 8). The doctrine in question concerns the discord in the cosmos and in human affairs that resulted from the primal sin of Adam and Eve. Tillyard saw this doctrine informing what he famously called 'The Tudor Myth', i.e. 'an organic piece of history' invented by the Tudors to explain their own success (29). In Hall's chronicle Tillyard found an interpretation of Henry IV's reign that was analogous to the sin of Adam and Eve: Henry's deposition of Richard II brought a curse on England that was realized in the reign of Henry VI and was lifted only with the advent of Henry VII (60–1). Tillyard understood Shakespeare to be working out the organic scheme in Hall in two groups of four history plays, or 'tetralogies'.[1] His analysis of *3 Henry VI*, the third play in the first tetralogy, was that in it 'Shakespeare shows us chaos itself, the full prevalence of civil war, the perpetration of one horrible deed after another' (188). God's curse on England because of Henry IV's deed is thus realized in the reign of his grandson.[2]

Tillyard offered the most influential interpretation of the history plays for the second half of the twentieth century, not only

1 In a suggestive paragraph published in 1941, Rossiter had outlined Hall's 'plot' for fifteenth-century English history and referred to Shakespeare's adaptation of it as 'two linked tetralogies' (Rossiter, 'Prognosis', 128). Tillyard cited other work by Rossiter but not this essay.

2 For a similar description of divine retribution, arrived at independently of Tillyard, see Campbell, *'Histories'*, 122–5. Sister Mary Bonaventure Mroz also analysed divine retribution in Shakespeare's history plays in 1941 (Mroz), though wartime disruptions of commerce and communication probably prevented Tillyard from seeing her book. In any case, his reading was certainly the grander and more imaginatively captivating of the two.

giving rise to further elaborations over thirty years but also affecting dramatic productions and provoking specific questions and challenges that continued to the end of the century. Though Irving Ribner did not think Tillyard's idea explained all English history plays, he agreed that it explained Shakespeare's (Ribner, 12), which depict 'God's punishment . . . upon England for Henry Bolingbroke's deposition and murder of King Richard II' (99). For M.M. Reese, Tillyard's 'Tudor myth' became 'The Tudor Image', which presented 'the three generations from Richard II to Richard III . . . as a dreadful example of what happened when God's kindly watchfulness was turned to wrath by the crimes, ambition and misgovernment of men' (Reese, 20). This image, Reese argued, is preserved in Shakespeare's sequence of eight history plays. Though puckishly confident that Tillyard would agree 'if I were to say that there is *no* Elizabethan world picture', M.C. Bradbrook was another who nevertheless accepted what she called 'the "New Look" in the reading of Shakespeare's histories' (Bradbrook, 123), by which she meant 'the moral view of history [that] was worked very hard in the interest of the Tudor dynasty' (125). Two highly respected and much-used resources endorsed Tillyard's idea in the 1960s. In his anthology of Shakespeare's sources, Geoffrey Bullough not only referred to Shakespeare's 'organic view of history as a moral process', citing Tillyard as his authority (Bullough, 3.36), but also selected his sources in part with that view in mind. Andrew Cairncross's Arden 2 editions of the *Henry VI* plays were deeply informed by Tillyard: their 'general plan', Cairncross wrote, involves 'a universal political and "moral pattern"', by which an 'original crime – the deposition and murder of Richard II by Henry IV' is expiated by the chaos of civil war in *3 Henry VI* and the domination of a tyrant in *Richard III* (Ard², 1).[1]

---

1 Having published a defence of Tillyard's view in Ard² (1964), Cairncross again defended this view of the early histories almost ten years later (Cairncross). For other late defences of Tillyard that include significant mention of the *Henry VI* plays, see Jump; Merrix; Siegel.

But Tillyard's view influenced a wider world than academic criticism, and one of its most remarkable effects was on John Barton and Peter Hall's *Wars of the Roses*, produced at Stratford in 1963 (see above, pp. 20–3). Barton and Hall met at Cambridge, where Tillyard taught, in 1950, so that by the time they worked together at the RSC they had learned 'about the Elizabethan world picture at school and again at university' (Barton and Hall, ix). Hall's view of the histories was that 'Bolingbroke *has* to depose Richard II in order to claim the garden of England (this is why his personal ambition is revealed so ambiguously), but he, and his family, suffer retribution for generations' (x). The idea certainly came through to the actors, at least judging from Peggy Ashcroft's view of her character, Margaret, whom she understood as 'the embodiment of the Curse which is one of the themes of the four plays' (Ashcroft, 7).

Yet in spite of its enormous influence, Tillyard's moral reading of the history plays eventually encountered doubts. The first qualifications concerned his idea of divine providence, for a particular notion of how God operates in history is implied by the assertion that divine retribution for human evil explains the sequence of events between the reigns of Richard II and Richard III. Some critics thought Tillyard had neglected a contemporary recognition that 'general providence' was compatible with secondary causation originating in human volition (Brownlow, Quinn). More trenchantly, A.L. French wrote a series of articles challenging the premise that providence is at work in the early history plays at all (for those dealing with *3 Henry VI*, see A. French, '*Henry VI*' and 'Mills'), and H.A. Kelly carefully examined the chronicle sources to see if they indeed promulgate the 'Tudor myth', as Tillyard claimed they did. Kelly found that various chronicles contain various accounts of divine providence in defence of various interests – York, Lancaster and Tudor – but none of them contains the myth Tillyard described, or at least not as Tillyard described it. The same is true of Shakespeare's early history plays: 'There is no indication in this play [*Richard III*] or in the whole of this tetralogy that Henry VI or his family was divinely punished because of the sins of his grandfather, Henry IV' (H. Kelly, 295). Moody Prior pointed out that the Bible was not the only influence on Tudor historians; they were also affected by classical history, with 'its concern for causes construed not in terms of cosmic history and divine justice but in terms of the characters of men and the nature of polity and war' (Prior, *Drama*, 16). Thus Henry's 'invocations to God's providence and justice' in 3.1.98–100 are not statements of a cosmic theme in the play so much as they are manifestations of Henry's character, 'his passive submissiveness and his pious acquiescence to the will of God' (41). John Wilders argued that the Tudor myth is not in Hall's chronicle to begin with (Wilders, 67–70); David Scott Kastan found it in Hall but noted that it is only one of Hall's many possible explanations for what happened (Kastan, *Shakespeare*, 15–16); while David Frey again took issue with the manifestation of the Tudor myth in the *Henry VI* plays, which he thought 'cast serious doubt on the Tudor view of history, by raising fundamental questions concerning the concepts of divine justice, personal providence, and divine intervention' (Frey, 2). Frey's vehement rejection of Tillyard offered a moral reading of the *Henry VI* plays with exactly the opposite import – denying cosmic justice rather than affirming it.

As it turned out, Frey's argument anticipated the movement in the 1980s that swept Tillyard and similar moral critics aside by proposing a rival and, for its time, a more appealing moral proposition as the basis for interpretation. This movement identified itself variously as new historicism or cultural materialism, and its proposition (usually unstated but always eminently inferable) was that concern for social justice required a reading of Shakespeare that promotes social justice, in place of readings that promote, connive at or even merely tolerate unjust social structures. For Jonathan Dollimore, Tillyard was the principal representative of the latter. Insofar as Tillyard's world picture existed for any Elizabethan, Dollimore argued, it 'was not shared by all; it was an ideological legitimation of an existing social order, one rendered the more necessary by the apparent instability, actual *and* imagined, of that order' (Dollimore, 'Introduction', 5). Whereas Tillyard described 'dominant' culture, Dollimore and other contributors to his critical anthology were 'concerned with the marginalised and subordinate of Elizabethan and Jacobean culture' (Dollimore, 'Introduction', 6), including women, the colonized, the urban poor and agrarian labourers – in short, the majority of the population, in contrast to Tillyard's preoccupation with an elite few and *their* 'world picture'.

The impact of this realignment in moral criticism is hard to overstate, but its effect on the history plays has been mixed. On one hand, Stephen Greenblatt's essay on power and social class in the *Henry IV* plays proved to be one of the most provocative and controversial discussions in the closing years of the twentieth century. Reading Shakespeare along with less well-known texts, Greenblatt described a structural principle of injustice in Elizabethan culture, whereby a powerful elite encouraged – even generated – political subversion in order to contain and suppress it:

> It is precisely because of the English form of absolutist theatricality that Shakespeare's drama, written for a theatre subject to State censorship, can be so relentlessly subversive: the form itself, as a primary expression of Renaissance power, contains the radical doubts it continually provokes.
>
> (Greenblatt, 'Invisible', 45)

For Greenblatt, Elizabethan providentialism functioned as a means of social and political control (in the vein of Frey's argument that providence in the history plays has nothing to do with cosmic justice), and Shakespeare's Henry V was his most potent example (41–4).

On the other hand, new historicists and cultural materialists have focused almost exclusively on the second tetralogy, thus largely ignoring other histories, including the *Henry VI* plays.

Graham Holderness has been the most prolific critic of the history plays from the new angle, contributing an essay to Dollimore and Sinfield's influential anthology, *Political Shakespeare*, and publishing some five books on the history plays. While he has written repeatedly about *Richard II*, the *Henry IV* plays and *Henry V*, however, his only comments on the *Henry VI* plays consist of a discussion of Jane Howell's televised productions (Holderness, *Shakespeare's*, 215–19) and a chapter on *1 Henry VI* (Holderness, *Shakespeare*, 109–35).

A possible reason for this imbalance in critical attention may have to do with the assumptions of materialist critique. A commitment to a radical rereading of power and its manifestations has had the unexpected effect of privileging the most admired plays, presumably because the view the critic hopes to displace can be most successfully challenged in plays that are best known and that therefore most influentially support the critical view being promoted. If *Henry V* can be shown to contain its own subversion or to reveal the political manipulation of providential belief, then it is easy to assume that the same must be true for lesser plays, which therefore merit no discussion. The implied aesthetic judgement (some plays are 'better' or 'more important' than others) has gone without notice, though materialist critique purports to displace aesthetic judgement.

Another reason for over-attention to the second tetralogy may be that postmodern criticism in general resists definitions and boundaries, whether generic, chronological or aesthetic, because boundaries exclude, and exclusion presumes privilege. What better way to problematize 'history' than by ignoring plays that *seem* to be history plays and by offering a critique that doesn't seem to be 'historical'. Holderness thus has a chapter on *Hamlet* in a book on the history plays, and he discusses *Richard III* before *1 Henry VI* (Holderness, *Shakespeare*, 57–78, 79–135). In this respect too, what has been called the critical 'turn to history' has had the ironic, though presumably unintended, effect of marginalizing most of the history plays.

Despite the determination of recent critics to bury Tillyard definitively, the choice in moral criticism does not necessarily have to be as stark as that effort at interment suggests; that is, we are not necessarily compelled to choose between him and those who would bury him. One way to avoid that dilemma is to restate the question that Tillyard asked. His question, in effect, was whether the early history plays – and *3 Henry VI* in particular – were designed to illustrate a moral principle, and he answered in the affirmative by arguing for a principle of divine retributive justice. His critics have asked the same question and answered it negatively, rejecting Tillyard's answer because they perceive too much in the plays that denies cosmic justice or affirms it at the expense of social injustice, or both.

Rather than ask whether *3 Henry VI* illustrates or embodies a moral principle, it is possible to ask what kind of moral thinking the play exhibits. This question draws on the insights of social anthropology (as many postmodern critics have done) by recognizing a category of 'magical' thinking.[1] Examples include belief in the ability of language to affect the material world directly, as in spells, incantations, curses and blessings. Magical thinking also includes prophecies, omens, 'prodigies', oaths and swearing, whose power goes beyond mere words, evoking a mysterious influence that operates in spite of human knowledge or intent. In the late sixteenth century, magical thinking was still deeply bound up with moral thinking.

It is evident that many of these examples of magical thinking are present in *3 Henry VI*, and they are inspired by a variety of sources, not merely the chronicle histories of Hall and Holinshed. The Bible is certainly one source, but so is the epic tradition – newly domesticated for English writers in Spenser's first instalment of *The Faerie Queene* in 1590, just before the first records of the *Henry VI* plays on stage – and so is Senecan tragedy, the most impressive model for serious drama in late Elizabethan England.

---

1   On magical thinking, see Clark; Geertz; K. Thomas, 'Anthropology' and *Religion*.

Indeed, so powerful are the cultural models for magical thinking in the *Henry VI* plays and *Richard III* that the burden of proof is on those who would deny its presence and influence.

Shakespeare reserves the magical power of curses for *Richard III*, but he treats oaths magically in *3 Henry VI*. Faye Kelly has analysed the way that 'the entire structure of *3 Henry VI*' is permeated by 'broken oaths, broken vows, and perjury' (F. Kelly, 366). An omen appears in *3 Henry VI*, when the York brothers see three suns in the sky, and O's SD clearly indicates that the play's auditors were meant to see this mysterious sign as well: 'Three sunnes appeare in the aire' (O, sig. B3ᵛ). Richard recognizes that 'In this, the heaven figures some event' (2.1.32), and Edward believes that it refers to the brothers' unity, determining to change his heraldic device accordingly: 'Whate'er it bodes, henceforward will I bear / Upon my target three fair-shining suns' (2.1.39–40). One remarkable example of a 'prodigy' is noticed by Margaret, in referring to York's son, Richard, when she is mocking York:

> And where's that valiant crookback prodigy,
> Dickie, your boy, that with his grumbling voice
> Was wont to cheer his dad in mutinies?
>
> (1.4.75–7)

She is referring not to Richard's precocious talent but to his deformity (hence 'crookback'), also noted by young Clifford when he calls Richard 'foul stigmatic' (*2H6* 5.1.215), and admitted by Richard later in soliloquy (*3H6* 3.2.153–71). As for prophecies, Henry utters one about the young Earl of Richmond, calling him 'England's hope' and 'our country's bliss' (4.6.68, 70), thus providing the reason for Richmond's sole appearance in the play, albeit in a non-speaking role.

The question, then, is not whether magical thinking exists in *3 Henry VI* but how it affects moral thinking. Oaths have been recognized and variously interpreted. Thus Kelly refers her analysis to 'an ordered society ordained by God, ideally upheld by king and supported by subject' (F. Kelly, 357) – in short, she refers it to Tillyard. French, on the other hand, refers his analysis of oaths to anti–Tillyardian scepticism (A. French, 'Mills', 318–21). The celestial omen seen by the York brothers is ironized by Richard himself, in the opening soliloquy of *Richard III* (1.1.1–27), and his sardonic reading effectively undercuts his brother's brave interpretation of the omen in *3 Henry VI*, though on close examination even Edward's affirmation seems half-hearted ('Whate'er it bodes . . .'). Henry's prophecy of Richmond's future success is a transparent affirmation of the Tudor regime – an indubitable trace of the Tudor myth in *3 Henry VI* – and Shakespeare takes it straight from Hall (see 4.6.68–76n.). This instance of magical thinking has not been addressed by most critics who are sceptical of providential readings, though by itself it is inadequate to resolve the many questions they have raised.[1]

The on-again, off-again quality of magical thinking in *3 Henry VI* reveals a deep ambivalence in the sixteenth and seventeenth centuries about the way the world worked. The 'oppositional thinking' identified by Stuart Clark was in an early state of terminal crisis but was still the only way of thinking about the natural world, human history, religion and politics, because it had not yet been superseded by scientific thinking – that would not happen until the eighteenth century (Clark, *passim*). Though challenged by scepticism, oppositional thinking remained essentially intact because it was buttressed by the lack of a credible alternative and indeed seemed to become stronger with rationalized responses to each doubt expressed about some aspect of it.

The most fundamental opposition was cosmic – the opposition of God and the devil – but it was closely related to the moral opposition of good and evil, and these complementary oppositions were

---

1 Frey notes that F's version of the prophecy substitutes 'secret powers' for O's 'Heavenly powers' as the origin of Henry's prophecy and comments that 'any evidence of Shakespeare's intention to remove the aura of Divine Providence from Richmond will prove to be important to our final conclusions concerning the Tetralogy' (Frey, 64).

the basis of other contrarieties which seemed to make sense of things. Here, then, is where magical and moral thinking merged indistinguishably. Magical thinking was not a violation of common sense or rationality; it was a confirmation of both, an instance of good and evil manifesting themselves mysteriously but comprehensibly in the world of human experience. These oppositions were pressed into the service of particular political interests, as H. Kelly has shown in the case of providential stories about York, Lancaster and Tudor, and indeed no regime could command respect without an account of itself that made sense according to fundamental cosmic and moral oppositions – the kind of oppositions that organize Jonson's masques for the first two Stuart kings. Ideas of monarchical divine right are thus explicable manifestations of oppositional and magical thinking.

In the late Elizabethan regime, when Shakespeare's history plays were staged, oppositional thinking was in the early stages of a crisis occasioned less by scepticism *per se* than by developments in the Protestant Reformation. Protestants offered a way of looking at the world that appropriated the familiar lineaments of binary thinking, but what they identified as evil and demonic was not paganism or disbelief but a rival system of Christian belief. The English Church under Elizabeth was Protestant, and it distinguished itself from the papacy by identifying features of traditional belief that it rejected, such as transubstantiation and exorcism, which were regarded as violations of the Protestant belief that 'miracles are ceased', as the Archbishop of Canterbury puts it in *Henry V* 1.1.67 – that is, that after the apostolic age God no longer permitted miracles to occur. How 'miracles' could have ceased when magical thinking was still in full flower is a question the English Church could not answer in the sixteenth century, because it could not get outside of itself, so to speak, to recognize that traditional oppositional thinking still lay at the heart of its identity. Scepticism about miracles and rejection of 'papist superstition' thus coincided ambiguously with open credulity about a magical world.

This ambiguity helps to explain the odd combination of magical thinking and scepticism in the history plays and in *3 Henry VI* in particular. Besides Henry's prophecy concerning Richmond, the most impressive manifestation of oppositional thinking in *3 Henry VI* is Richard of Gloucester. Margaret's remark that he is a 'prodigy' (1.4.75) is complemented by Henry's greeting when Richard arrives to kill him:

> Ay, my good lord. 'My lord' I should say, rather.
> 'Tis sin to flatter; 'good' was little better.
> 'Good Gloucester' and 'good devil' were alike,
> And both preposterous. Therefore, not 'good lord'.
>
> (5.6.2–5)

Henry refuses to associate 'good' with Gloucester, because he views his visitor oppositionally, as if Gloucester were the devil. That is why he says calling either of them 'good' would be 'preposterous', using the word in its literal Latin sense of 'back-to-front', in parallel with common iconography of the devil with a face in his rear end. Richard stabs Henry just as Henry seems about to describe a preposterous detail about Richard that Richard himself describes later: 'I came into the world with my legs forward' (5.6.71).[1] Preposterousness was characteristic of the demonic, as Nicholas Rémy points out in his description of witches' gestures:

> they love to do everything in a ridiculous and unseemly manner. For they turn their backs toward the Demons when they go to worship them, and approach them sideways like a crab; when they hold out their hands in supplication they turn them downwards; when they converse they bend their eyes toward the ground; and in

---

1 This and other preposterous details about Richard in *3H6* and *R3* derive ultimately from Thomas More's *History of King Richard the Third* (1513; see 5.6.49–56n.), and this continuity between More and Shakespeare helps to verify the continuity of magical thinking throughout the sixteenth century and across the Catholic/Protestant divide.

other such ways they behave in a manner opposite to that of other men.

(quoted in Clark, 14)

Richard of Gloucester is accurately described by saying that he behaves 'in a manner opposite to that of other men', and his implicit invocation is both preposterous and demonic: 'Then, since the heavens have shaped my body so, / Let hell make crook'd my mind to answer it' (5.6.78–9).

The emergence of a demonic, prodigious and preposterous character near the apex of Yorkist power is an effective way to orient *3 Henry VI* in the sequence of events from the death of Henry V to the accession of Henry VII. Tillyard called the play 'the culminating expression of the horrors and wickedness of civil war' (Tillyard, *History Plays*, 189), and he recognized Richard as 'a diabolic character' (195), but he did not see the apocalyptic suggestions of Richard's rise to power as a quasi-Antichrist who represents an oppositional threat to a godly ruler (see Clark, 382–4). Richard's demonism and Henry's prophecy of Richmond's 'hope' and 'bliss' for England are complementary examples of magical thinking in *3 Henry VI*, and they help to elucidate the plan of the play and of its place among the first four history plays.

At the same time, however, the moral and providential clarity suggested by magical and oppositional thinking is complicated by ambiguities. Henry himself is a poor excuse for a king, even though he is a good man; his gullibility, timidity, arbitrariness, poor judgement and inability to lead are specifically political failures that have no obvious relation to the oppositional scheme suggested by Richard's demonism (see below, pp. 75–81). Moreover, both sides are equally tainted by vengeance and wanton cruelty, which undermines the simple opposition of a saintly Lancastrian king and a demonic Yorkist aspirant. A providential moral pattern undoubtedly operates in *3 Henry VI*, but it operates only in broad outline amid the play's crowd of secondary causes, which bear no

9   Fifteenth-century portrait of King Edward IV, by an unknown artist

discernible relation to it – such causes as human weakness, miscalculation, marital incompatibility, aristocratic rivalry, treachery, anger and chance. As J.P. Brockbank pointed out:

> the plays of *Henry VI* are not, as it were, haunted by the ghost of Richard II, and the catastrophes of the civil wars are not laid to Bolingbroke's charge; the catastrophic virtue of Henry and the catastrophic evil of Richard are not an inescapable inheritance from the distant past but are generated by the happenings we are made to witness.
>
> (Brockbank, 'Frame', 98)

The principal moral concern in these events seems to involve the evil that human beings do to each other in civil wars, and the prophecy that Richmond will deliver the nation from such evil is not the essence of this story but a rare example of providential clarity in the chaos of the Wars of the Roses.[1]

CHARACTER CRITICISM

Moral criticism was an early interpretive method for understanding *3 Henry VI*, and it has remained a vital source of insight ever since, but closely related to it is the analysis of character, which became particularly influential in the nineteenth century. This is not to say that character analysis was a nineteenth-century innovation. Character was one of the elements of tragedy as analysed by Aristotle, and it was therefore important for neo-classical criticism. L.C. Knights documented the neo-classical admiration for Shakespeare's characters (Knights, 18–22), an admiration shared by Samuel Johnson, who was an astute critic of the most dogmatic neo-classical formulations. Speaking as an editor, he was struck by

---

1   To create this aspect of the Tudor myth, Shakespeare had to elide the accomplishments of Edward IV (see Fig. 9), who reigned prosperously for fourteen years (from 1471 to 1485) after the defeat of Lancaster and began to put into place some of the structures of effective centralized power that are now associated with Henry VII (Saccio, *Shakespeare's*, 159–65).

what he saw as an incongruous line by King Henry late in *3 Henry VI*: 'Let's levy men and beat him back again' (4.8.6). 'This line', Johnson wrote, 'expresses a spirit of war so unsuitable to the character of Henry, that I would give the first cold speech to the King, and the brisk answer to Warwick' (S. Johnson, 8.608).

Johnson was also the first to see complications in the oppositional reading of Richard as a devil – complications that arose from Johnson's imagining Richard as a real human being rather than a symbol of evil. Johnson thought Richard spoke 'the language of nature' in 3.2.151–71:

> Whoever is stigmatised with deformity has a constant source of envy in his mind, and would counterballance by some other superiority these advantages which he feels himself to want. Bacon remarks that the deformed are commonly daring, and it is almost proverbially observed that they are ill-natured. The truth is, that the deformed, like all other men, are displeased with inferiority, and endeavour to gain ground by good or bad means, as they are virtuous or corrupt.
>
> (S. Johnson, 8.605)

By 'the language of nature' Johnson means human nature, and his observations anticipate what would later be called an 'inferiority complex'.

The understanding of Shakespeare's characters as if they were real human beings, with complex histories and motives, fascinated critics in the nineteenth century, though they began with assumptions different from Johnson's. Whereas he regarded human nature as rational in essence and everywhere the same, nineteenth-century critics were informed by the romantic assumption that human beings are individualized by their emotional and imaginative make-up, as William Hazlitt indicates:

> All these several personages were as different in Shakespeare as they would have been in themselves: his

imagination borrowed from the life, and every circumstance, object, motive, passion, operated there as it would in reality, and produced a world of men and women as distinct, as true and as various as those that exist in nature. The peculiar property of Shakespeare's imagination was this truth, accompanied with the unconsciousness of nature: indeed, imagination to be perfect must be unconscious, at least in production; for nature is so.

(Hazlitt, 218–19)

Whereas Johnson took Richard for a real human being, Hazlitt's interest was in King Henry (see below, pp. 68–75), thus establishing a pattern of focusing on these two in character criticism of *3 Henry VI*.

Attention to character has produced some of the most extreme interpretations of Shakespeare's plays, because more than any other critical method it has drawn on the idea that Shakespeare was a genius who understood everything about human nature. If, as Hazlitt asserted, Shakespeare 'produced a world of men and women as distinct, as true and as various as those that exist in nature', then some have assumed that he must be a guide to every kind of human thought and endeavour. The Victorian physician John Charles Bucknill, for example, published a treatise on mental disease in 1859, using a number of Shakespearean characters as case studies (Bucknill). Nineteenth-century character criticism came to fruition in the early twentieth century in the magisterial work of A.C. Bradley on Hamlet, Othello, Lear and Macbeth, and Bradley's influence remained strong throughout the first half of the twentieth century, even when critics disagreed with it. Bradley had nothing to say about *3 Henry VI*, however, and in this he represents a tendency of character criticism to focus on 'great' characters and 'great' plays to the neglect of lesser ones.[1] Even

---

1 A notable exception is Thomas Whateley, who draws as much from *3H6* as from *R3* in his comparison of Richard and Macbeth (Whateley).

10 The birth of the future Henry VI at Windsor

when Charles Cowden Clarke addressed the subject of *Shakespeare-Characters; Chiefly Those Subordinate*, he left the *Henry VI* plays out of his account (C. Clarke). Lily Bess Campbell rejected Bradley's romantic assumptions in favour of a historicizing method that purported to explain Shakespeare's conception of character in Elizabethan terms, but she too focused exclusively on the four 'great' tragedies (Campbell, *Heroes*). Harold Goddard and Leeds Barroll discussed Richard of Gloucester, but only as he appears in *Richard III*, not in *3 Henry VI* (Goddard, 35–40; Barroll, 240–2). Arthur Kirsch combined trenchant character criticism with biblical and Freudian insights, but he left the history plays entirely out of account (Kirsch, *Shakespeare and Passions*). Harold Bloom kept the tradition of character criticism alive at the end of the twentieth century, identifying himself with Johnson, Hazlitt, Bradley and Goddard (Bloom, xviii) and affirming that 'no other writer, before or since Shakespeare, has accomplished so well the virtual miracle of creating utterly different yet self-consistent voices for his more than one hundred major characters and many hundreds of highly distinctive minor personages' (xvii). Yet Bloom paid the *Henry VI* plays little more than a backhanded compliment: '*Richard III*, whether in its strengths or its limitations, owes its energy and brilliance to the laboratory of the three parts of *Henry VI*. That is justification enough for Shakespeare's immersion in the Wars of the Roses' (Bloom, 50).[1]

Henry

Of the two characters who have been most discussed in *3 Henry VI*, Henry has been regarded least consistently. To some interpreters, he has appeared to be a good man in a bad situation, capable of doing no wrong himself but destroyed by the wrongs

---

1 Theoretical resistance to character criticism originated with Knights and remained vigorous throughout the twentieth century, but its critique neglected 'minor' characters in favour of 'great' ones, and it therefore contributed nothing, even indirectly, to character criticism of *3H6*.

of others. 'This gentle, bewildered soul makes the only human remarks in [*2 Henry VI*]', John Masefield observed. 'In Shakespeare's vision it is from such souls, planted, to their own misery, among spikes and thorns, that the flower of human goodness blossoms' (Masefield, 60). A fuller defence, though no less impressionistic, was mounted by Arthur Cadoux, who blamed Henry's problems on his early inheritance – 'authority is not easily recovered after a long minority among powerful and ambitious nobles' (Cadoux, 12) – and pointed out his public virtues: he 'never shows fear', and he 'loves England' (12, 13). The bias toward 'great souls' in character criticism is evident in Cadoux's commendation of Henry as an anticipation of Hamlet, the greatest of all great souls for character critics (14).

In similar vein, Harold Goddard thought Henry was 'a prophecy, in a sense a progenitor, of the most saintly character Shakespeare ever created – the divine Desdemona' (Goddard, 32). Deeply impressed by 'this childlike and saintly king', Goddard offered what is, in effect, a magical reading of the *Henry VI* plays: 'Had it not been for that Amazon, Margaret of Lancaster, and that fiend in human shape, the younger Richard of York', Henry would have achieved 'an understanding between the warlike factions of Lancaster and York' (Goddard, 31).[1] Among other things, this ignores the difficulties of Henry's minority kingship, his wilful and politically disastrous marriage, and his unwillingness to defend Humphrey, Duke of Gloucester, in *2 Henry VI*. A similar argument, though with a different emphasis, was made two decades after Goddard by Michael Manheim, who saw Henry as a virtuous but hapless victim of the Machiavellian schemers and politicians who surround him (Manheim, *Weak King*, 76–115). For Manheim, it was not Henry who lacked anything; the problem lay with his rivals, who lacked Henry's moral uprightness, and critics who find fault with Henry's political ability 'unwittingly

---

1   Cf. John Danby's remark that 'The axis of the [first] tetralogy is defined by Henry VI on the one hand and Richard III on the other. Henry VI is as nearly blameless as a king can be' (Danby, 59).

accept the barons' methods' (85). Manheim's identification of Henry's conversation with the keepers (3.1.72–95) as 'a paraphrase of Christ on the cross' (109) is hardly surprising, for Henry in this view is analogous to Socrates or Jesus – a good man destroyed by evil ones.

Most interpreters of Henry's character have recognized that he has problems in himself, as well as in his situation. Hazlitt contrasted Henry with Richard II, noting the 'effeminacy' of both but distinguishing them. Thus the effeminacy of Henry 'is that of an indolent, good-natured mind, naturally averse to the turmoils of ambition and the cares of greatness, and who wishes to pass his time in monkish indolence and contemplation' (Hazlitt, 219). Edward Dowden followed Hazlitt in seeing Henry as a 'saint of a feeble type'. In fact, Dowden was so confident in judgements of character that he invoked them as criteria in determining authorship. Thus Henry's characterization exhibited 'Shakesperian impartiality and irony' in *2 Henry VI* and *3 Henry VI* but not in *1 Henry VI*, which Dowden judged to belong 'to the pre-Shakesperian school' (Dowden, 173).

Not surprisingly, events leading up to World War II coloured contemporary views of Shakespeare's first English royal portrait. Dowden unwittingly anticipated this development in his comment about the compromise Henry makes in the first scene of *3 Henry VI*: 'Yet in Henry's conduct there has been no active selfishness; he has only accepted peace at the price required' (Dowden, 178). 'Appeasement' is the word that occurred first to Mattie Swayne, writing in 1941, who agonized with Henry's idealistic 'pacifism' in a world of self-seeking power-madness (Swayne, 146). Affirming the romantic belief that Shakespeare's genius 'seems to have left no part of our individual or collective humanity unexplored', Swayne read a sixteenth-century dramatic character as if the character were Swayne himself (Swayne, 143). Writing at the same time, Hereward Price refused to assert, as Swayne did, that Henry was a 'pacifist' (Price, 'Shakespeare', 395), but he nonetheless saw the mild King as Shakespeare's rejection of the Elizabethan 'delight in revenge' (394). Theodore Spencer may also have been influenced by recent events in Germany, Italy and Japan, when he identified the theme of *2* and *3 Henry VI* as 'the disaster that comes to a kingdom when order is violated through the weakness of its king' (T. Spencer, 70). The theme of violated order was identified again in *3 Henry VI* toward the end of World War II by Tillyard, but his analysis was providential, not explicitly political like Spencer's (see above, p. 50–1). Una Ellis-Fermor, on the other hand, argued that Shakespeare's portrait of Henry had less to do with providentialism than with contemporary Italian political science: she thought Shakespeare had 'marked and inwardly digested the admonitions of the 7th chapter of Machiavelli's *Prince*', including the lesson that 'a "dangerous lenity" has no place among the "king-becoming graces"' (Ellis-Fermor, 38).

In the 1960s two critics approached characterization in *3 Henry VI* for the first time as a product not of Shakespeare's universal insight but of his particular situation as a beginning playwright in the early 1590s. Both Robert Y. Turner and Norman Rabkin saw the characters of the *Henry VI* plays as static 'types' (Turner, 'Characterization', 242; Rabkin, 250), and Turner traced this attribute of the early histories to the influence of the morality play and its personified moral abstractions (Turner, 243). Both critics, moreover, saw *Richard III* as the turning point for Shakespeare from static moral characterization to the introspective characters of the later histories, who are capable of change because they are capable of self-examination. Given this analysis of Shakespeare's growth in ability to construct dramatic characters, both critics saw Henry as static, and both cited his soliloquy at the battle of Towton (2.5) to make their point (Turner, 'Characterization', 257; Rabkin, 250).

Larry Champion argued in contrast not only that Henry's character develops in *3 Henry VI* but also that it gives him 'near-tragic stature' (Champion, 45). In the first scene, Henry is naive and temporizing, in Champion's view, but he grows to become 'the realist who can appraise his own political weakness in act 4 and somewhat like Richard II, confront his death with dignity and courage in act 5' (47). Henry is thus proof, along with Richard, that in *3 Henry VI* Shakespeare 'clearly seems to realize that genuine dramatic involvement is founded on compelling characterization' (53).

The political realists would seem to have the edge in this debate over Henry's character, and Turner and Rabkin have shown why. Edward Berry decisively answered idealizations of the king as a Christian humanist surrounded by Machiavellian power-seekers by pointing to Erasmus's observation that 'It is quite possible to find a good man who would not make a good prince' (E. Berry, 50n.).[1] From the beginning of the tetralogy, though Henry is not vicious, he is consistently weak, in both his moral and political judgements. The weaknesses he reveals in each stage of his life are analogous to the developmental weaknesses revealed by the protagonist in the Tudor morality play *Mundus et Infans* (c. 1500–22), and Henry's youthfully callow response to the blandishments of Suffolk in *1 Henry VI* and *2 Henry VI* recalls the callow youthfulness exhibited in another morality play, *The Disobedient Child* (c. 1559–70), where the Rich Man's Son chooses an inappropriate mate, as Henry does, and deeply regrets it. These are distinctly youthful moral failings, and they emphasize Henry as a type, just as they emphasize the typical Vice-like temptation of Suffolk, to which he weakly succumbs.[2] Henry's abandonment of Humphrey, Duke of Gloucester, in *2 Henry VI* is a more serious weakness, since it permits the destruction of Henry's last public-spirited supporter, fatally endangering his minister, himself and his kingdom.

---

1   J.P. Brockbank pointed to a similar sentiment in Thomas Elyot's *The Governour*: 'The King, says Elyot, must be merciful, but too much *Clementia* is a sickness of mind; as soon as any offend him the King should "immediately strike him with his most terrible dart of vengeance"' (Brockbank, 'Frame', 97).
2   On Suffolk's echo of the Vice-like Aaron and Richard of Gloucester, see Spivack, 386–7.

In *3 Henry VI* Henry's weakness remains specifically political – the characteristic weakness of an adult king considered as a type. He manifests it in the disastrous first scene, where, as Raymond Utterback points out, Henry can offer no merit to set beside what he has inherited (Utterback, 49–50), so he falls back on his father's merit (1.1.107–9), which he has not maintained. He lamely fails to assert his right – 'I know not what to say. My title's weak' (1.1.134); blindly subscribes to Clifford's amoral declaration of allegiance (motivated by vengeance) whether Henry's title is good or not (1.1.159–60) – 'O Clifford, how thy words revive my heart!' (1.1.163); and finally agrees to a compromise that is politically and personally suicidal, as Margaret immediately points out, when she learns of it:

> Ah, timorous wretch,
> Thou hast undone thyself, thy son and me,
> And given unto the house of York such head
> As thou shalt reign but by their sufferance.
> To entail him and his heirs unto the crown,
> What is it, but to make thy sepulchre
> And creep into it far before thy time?
>
> (1.1.231–7)

Henry is undeniably pious and conscientious, but these very qualities, which make him morally admirable as an individual, are often the source of his political failures, and those failures assist the steady decline of England's fortunes that the *Henry VI* plays enact.[1] Seeing York's head on the battlements of York, for example, Henry laments the violation of the oath he took in the play's first scene: ''Tis not my fault, / Nor wittingly have I infringed my vow' (2.2.7–8). The tenderness of his conscience regarding oath-breaking is morally admirable, in the play's own oppositional terms, but Henry fails to reckon that the oath was politically inept to begin with, and his only response to his having broken it,

---

1   For a thorough analysis of Henry's political weakness, see Richmond, 56–74.

however unwittingly, is lament. Indeed, lament is his characteristic mode in *3 Henry VI*, and it emphasizes his inability to act in such a way that he would not be compelled to lament in the first place. As M.M. Reese remarks about Henry's pastoral lament after the battle of Towton: if Henry 'had had his wish to be a shepherd, he would certainly have lost his sheep' (Reese, 200). Johnson's comment on Henry's line, 'Let's levy men and beat him back again' (4.8.6), presumed that it implied only boldness and determination (see p. 65), but it could as easily be understood (and performed) as an instance of Henry's ineptitude when he attempts to lead, as in the first scene. Nothing seems to qualify Clifford's dying assessment of Henry's kingship:

> And Henry, hadst thou swayed as kings should do,
> Or as thy father and his father did,
> Giving no ground unto the house of York,
> They never then had sprung like summer flies;
> I and ten thousand in this luckless realm
> Had left no mourning widows for our death,
> And thou this day hadst kept thy chair in peace.
>
> (2.6.14–20)

Henry's weakness does not excuse Clifford's vengeful savagery, but Henry's failure to keep York in check amounts to a failure to keep Clifford in check as well, and as Edna Zwick Boris points out, 'The lesson that a king must rule is not necessarily discredited through its being spoken by a doubtful moralist' (Boris, 82). Henry in fact fails to live up to the humanist maxim that Thomas More seems to have taken for himself as a minister to Henry VIII: 'What you cannot turn to good you must make as little bad as you can' (More, 101).

To be sure, Henry faces death bravely in the end, as Richard II does, but Henry's recognition of his approaching murderer as demonic is an example of the play's characterization by type. The character of mature Good Man is revealed in his belated ability to recognize Vicious Man, whereas he had failed to recognize him earlier in the person of Suffolk, and Henry's recognition is characteristically moral and external to himself rather than political and introspective. Richard II realizes what a political muddle he has made of his reign and comes to a moment of intense self-realization in light of his political failure:

> But whate'er I be,
> Nor I, nor any man that but man is,
> With nothing shall be pleased, till he be eased
> With being nothing.
>
> (*R2* 5.5.38–41)

This is very close to the insight Lear gains in his destitution, even to the wordplay on 'nothing' throughout *King Lear*, but Henry VI never comes to such a realization, and his ending, while certainly pitiable, is far from fearful, because Henry is so consistently weak.

Richard

Critical responses to Richard as a character have also been divided from the beginning. While no one has questioned his wickedness, different views have been taken as to what causes it. We have seen Johnson's incisive attention to Richard's soliloquy in 3.2 (see p. 65), with its suggestion that Richard behaves anti-socially because society rejects him for his physical deformities. Another eighteenth-century critic, Thomas Whateley, asserted, on the other hand, that Richard's physical shape should be understood as a manifestation of his inherently evil nature:

> The deformity of his body was supposed to indicate a similar depravity of mind; and Shakespeare makes great use both of that, and of the current stories of the times concerning the circumstances of his birth, to intimate that his actions proceeded not from the occasion, but from a savageness of nature.
>
> (Whateley, 35–6)[1]

---

1   The Renaissance tradition that Whateley seems to refer to has been explored in detail by Torrey, 126–39.

11 King Richard III (Richard, Duke of Gloucester in *3 Henry VI*), by an unknown artist

To support his argument, Whateley pointed to 'an extraordinary gaiety of heart' in Richard when he is most treacherous and destructive (38), as well as to a 'total insensibility to every tender feeling' (44), including family loyalty, remorse, shame, and shock at the suffering of others (46–67). Far from seeing Richard as a social victim, as Johnson did, Whateley saw him as a personification of depravity.

Johnson and Whateley thus established two lines of interpretation for Richard that prevailed for the next two centuries. Samuel Taylor Coleridge thought that 'pride of intellect, without moral feeling' is Richard's 'ruling impulse', and he followed Johnson in explaining it by reference to the mechanics of Richard's psyche: 'The inferiority of his person made the hero seek consolation and compensation in the superiority of his intellect; he thus endeavoured to counterbalance his deficiency. This striking feature is portrayed most admirably by Shakespeare, who represents Richard bringing forward his very defects and deformities as matters of boast' (Coleridge, 2.181). Arthur Cadoux saw something else that explained Richard's behaviour. Noting Bacon on deformity, as Johnson had, Cadoux also pointed to Richard's admiration for his father, the Duke of York (2.1.9–20), and psychologized it:

His father's love and admiration had sheltered him from the scorn of his deformity, so that his grief added energy to the prowess which, while the war lasted, evinced his superiority as a fighter and allowed him even to be generous to the brave.

(Cadoux, 15)

The fullest exposition of this kind was offered by John Palmer, who elaborated on the same points Cadoux had made and added that Richard's soliloquy in 3.2 was the result of his transferring dependence and admiration from York to Edward, only to have Edward let him down (Palmer, 66–74). Robert Ornstein referred to 'This pre-Freudian intuition of the compensatory drive for power', again tracing Richard's behaviour to the death of York, which 'is Richard's spiritual turning-point because it leaves him without a single emotional attachment' (Ornstein, 58, 57). Janet Adelman was so impressed by Richard's soliloquy in 3.2 that she identified it as the first 'voice of a fully developed subjectivity' in Shakespeare (Adelman, 1).

Most critics, however, have followed Whateley in seeing Richard as a personification of evil rather than a character with a credible inner life. To be sure, Dowden noted Richard's attachment to York (Dowden, 188), but he made little of it, emphasizing instead the 'daemonic intensity' rather than 'mystery' in Richard's characterization (181). Cynicism, insolence, audacity, dissimulation and 'wantonness of *diablerie*' are the qualities Dowden emphasized (184–6). Theodore Spencer explained Richard's 'malformed body' as 'the outward sign of a malformed soul' (T. Spencer, 72), and Ernest Howse asserted flatly that 'Richard had no inward conflict. He has no struggle against his better impulses, for all his impulses are bad. He displays no change in character, no deterioration and no sign of redemption' (Howse, 80).[1]

Bernard Spivack was the first to suggest that the split in critical perceptions of Richard might have something to do with the particular circumstances of Shakespeare as a playwright in the early 1590s. Those who take Richard as a personification of evil are closest to Spivack's insight that the dominant influence on characterization in the early London theatres was the traditional morality play, and that the inspiration for Richard was the abstract personification of evil called 'the Vice'. Those who psychologize Richard, for example, have not addressed the question of why he alone has so many soliloquies and asides of the variety that invite the audience to watch his bravura performance as he deceives and exploits other characters, but this is a standard procedure for what Richard himself, in one such aside, calls 'the formal Vice, Iniquity' (*R3* 3.1.82). Whateley's 'extraordinary gaiety of heart' and

---

1   See also Manheim, *Weak King*, 86–7; Champion, 42–4; Bloom, 64–74.

Dowden's 'wantonness of *diablerie*' are both qualities of the Vice, but so are Richard's dissimulation, hypocrisy, cynicism, manipulativeness, connivance with other evildoers, treachery, and eventual comeuppance in the end. Spivack points to a precedent in *Appius and Virginia* (1559–67) for the agony of conscience Richard suffers on the eve of his defeat (*R3* 5.3; Spivack, 479, n. 6), suggesting that even this semblance of an inner life for Richard is in reality but one of the many qualities that 'project him homiletically as another exponent of the art and achievement of villainy' (Spivack, 387).

Two more points might be added to Spivack's. One is a morality play precedent for Richard's assertion 'I am myself alone', in his self-congratulatory soliloquy after murdering King Henry (5.6.83). The precedent comes from Ulpian Fulwell's *Like Will to Like* (1562–8), whose Vice, Nichol Newfangle, similarly addresses the audience while alone on stage, after dealing with other vicious characters:

> Ha ha ha ha ha ha ha ha!
> Now three knaves are gone, and *I am left alone*,
> Myself here to solace.
>
>   (Fulwell, 566–8; our emphasis)

To be sure, Nichol evinces none of Richard's deep social alienation, yet both survive when other knaves fall, partly done in by the treachery of the speaker in each case, and their boasts of 'alone-ness' in soliloquy are striking points of continuity. Moreover, Fulwell's play was not an archaic memory; it was still in the repertory of Pembroke's Men, playing at the Rose Theatre, in October 1600 (Henslowe, 164).[1]

The other point concerns the historical source of Shakespeare's characterization for Richard of Gloucester. Spivack observes that Shakespeare 'not only follows history, he *dramatizes* it for the theatre; and he does so by the techniques native to his

---

1   For identification of Henslowe's reference, see Greg, *Henslowe*, 2.228–9.

stage and unerring in their popular effect' (Spivack, 393). But 'history' for Shakespeare was primarily the English chronicles, and where Richard in particular was concerned, 'history' was Thomas More's *History of King Richard the Third*, as Edward Hall adapted it for his chronicle (see 5.6.49–56n. below). Spivack does not point out that in the early sixteenth century, More's model for a personification of evil (i.e. the model for his Richard) was almost certainly the personified vices in morality plays by More's contemporaries, Henry Medwall and John Skelton. To be sure, the Vice *per se* had not yet appeared in Tudor drama, but all the features associated with him were already present in the multiple personified vices that inhabit plays like Medwall's *Nature* (*c.* 1496) and Skelton's *Magnificence* (1515–26) (Cox, *Devil*, 53–9). More's interest in the drama of his day is well documented and was treated dramatically in Shakespeare's generation in the play called *Sir Thomas More*, in which Shakespeare may have had a hand. In this play, More is imagined to step impromptu into the part of a missing player in a morality play called *The Marriage of Wit and Wisdom*. In short, when Shakespeare turned to the Vice as the model for Richard of Gloucester, he was not combining 'history' and drama; he was perpetuating the mode on which 'history' had been based in the first place, or in other words, he was following More in offering a reading of history that was borrowed from the morality play.

The value of Spivack's insight is that it complements perceptions of characterization by 'type' in the *Henry VI* plays (Rabkin; Turner, 'Characterization'), and it helps to clarify the oppositional thinking that underlies the emergence of monstrous evil out of civil conflict in the course of the first tetralogy (see above, pp. 57–64). These are elements of traditional dramaturgy that remained vital in London commercial plays much longer than is often recognized, animating many of Middleton's city comedies, for example, as well as domestic tragedies such as *The Witch of Edmonton* (1621), and a saint's play such as *The Virgin Martyr* (1620) (Cox, *Devil*, 166–87). At the same time, however, the long-standing debate over characterization in *3 Henry VI* emphasizes the transitional quality of Shakespeare's way of imagining character. The *Henry VI* plays are primarily political plays, not morality plays: they elucidate how powerful men and women acquire and maintain power or fail in the attempt to acquire and maintain it. No morality-play precedent exists for this kind of elucidation, because the task does not lend itself easily to oppositional moral categories. Moreover, Richard's soliloquy in 3.2 does indeed manifest something remarkably like what we have come to think of as an inferiority complex, and no one has pointed to a morality-play precedent for it. Whether it supports the full-blown psychological portrait drawn by John Palmer, based on what Edward Berry calls 'shadowy outlines of psychological development' in *2 Henry VI* and *3 Henry VI* (E. Berry, 69), is a matter readers will decide for themselves. Arthur Kirsch has shown that readings based on depth psychology can complement traditional dramaturgy, even for a play as late as *The Changeling* (1622) (Kirsch, *Jacobean*, 80–5), so the acknowledgement of traditional dramaturgical influence need not foreclose the issue of characterization. Indeed, anything that opens up our sense of Shakespeare's characterization should be welcome.

HISTORICAL CRITICISM: DETERMINING SOURCES

A 'turn to history' marked criticism and critical theory since the 1980s, as a reaction against the 'linguistic turn' of deconstruction. But history has been frequently rediscovered as a source of information and inspiration in understanding Shakespeare, so the most recent turn was not *the* turn but only the latest of many, though it has been a turn of a different kind. The first critics of Shakespeare who turned to history did so in the late eighteenth century, when 'historical authenticity' was first discovered, as we noticed in the staging of *3 Henry VI* and again in the opening rounds of the debate about the play's authorship. Johnson used 'evidence' in the sense of the emerging scientific paradigm, and Malone similarly used the phrases 'external evidence' and 'internal evidence' to designate acceptable warrants for proof from outside or inside a text – proof that seemed to be consistent with the shaping historical circumstances of the text in question.

This quasi-scientific sense of a text as a historical artefact from a recoverable context in the past was rejected by Romantic critics in favour of an emphasis on character analysis and the assumption of Shakespeare's universal and trans-historical genius, as we have just seen, but the interest in history as a verifiable standard of truth was not thereby eradicated. It survived, most influentially, in the investigation into the sources of Shakespeare's plays, an investigation originally inspired by antiquarian curiosity of the sort Gerard Langbaine exhibited in 1691 when he listed several of the chronicle sources of the history plays (Langbaine, 457). Eighteenth-century editors knew the chronicles but seldom referred to them: even Malone referred to Hall or Holinshed only twice in the notes to his edition of *3 Henry VI* (2.1.25n. and 2.6.31n.). Yet he must have known the first separate investigation of Shakespeare's sources, by Charlotte Lennox in 1773–4, who had devoted seven pages to *3 Henry VI* (Lennox, 3.155–61). 'The Facts are all extracted from *Holingshed*', she reported, and she read the play as an attempt to display the cruelty of its characters, observing that to achieve this aim, the poet 'has not scrupled to violate sometimes the Truth of History' (3.155–6). In the early nineteenth century Henry Ellis undertook for the first time the massive task of transcribing and printing modern editions of several chronicles, impelled in part by recognition of Shakespeare's debt to them, and the first systematic study of Shakespeare's chronicle sources was published by Thomas Courtenay in 1840. Perhaps inspired by Lennox, Courtenay italicized the central questions of his study for emphasis: '*what were Shakespeare's authorities for his history, and how far has he departed from them? And whether the plays may be given to our youth, as "properly historical"*' (Courtenay, 2.xii). As these questions suggest, Courtenay proceeded by comparing the events of Shakespeare's plays to the chronicle sources, with the intent of showing that Shakespeare's departures from them made the plays 'unhistorical'. Conceding that the red and white roses work on stage to identify the opposing parties in *3 Henry VI*, for example, Courtenay nonetheless proclaimed that he could find no 'authority for the use of the roses themselves, as an especial and popular symbol' (2.42).

Courtenay's truculence seems naive in retrospect, but it high-lights a number of hard issues. He rightly noticed that Shakespeare's history plays were being taken as 'history' – even though Shakespeare often departs from his sources – as early as the reign of James VI and I (Courtenay, 1.4–5). While allowing for differences between plays and prose narratives about the past, he did not acknowledge that the chronicles Shakespeare consulted were themselves heavily invested in particular viewpoints, that they often disagreed with each other on large points as well as small, and that they reported only a small fraction of what had happened during the time they covered. It was not a question of whether Shakespeare dramatized 'history' 'accurately', then, but of what kind of 'history' he dramatized, with what purpose, and to what effect.

Investigation of Shakespeare's historical sources became increasingly sophisticated, and modern editions of his history plays (including this one) depend on work done over the last two centuries, some of it by inspired amateurs. In 1869 George Russell French, an architect, published carefully researched historical notes on the characters of Shakespeare's history plays. Acknowledging Courtenay and French, W.G. Boswell-Stone wrote a scene-by-scene analysis of all Shakespeare's plays that draw on Holinshed's chronicle, while pointing out the contribu-tion of other chronicles as well. W.H. Thomson, a retired schoolteacher, published a historical dictionary of the characters in the history plays and *Macbeth*, considerably extending the range of French's work, to which Thomson was heavily indebted, though often without acknowledgement. In a huge labour of many years and eight volumes, Geoffrey Bullough edited and published all the sources he could find for Shakespeare's plays, including sections from the chronicles of Hall and Holinshed and portions of *The Mirror for Magistrates* that he deemed to be relevant to *3 Henry VI* (Bullough, 3.157–217), though he concluded that 'The main historical source is Hall' (3.158).[1]

Bullough based his selections not only on his own reading but also on the research of others who had studied Shakespeare's debt to the chronicles. The medieval historian Charles Kingsford listed some 118 early printed histories of the fifteenth century and another 158 manuscripts in his survey of 'historical literature' of the period covered by Shakespeare's two tetralogies (Kingsford, *English*, vii–xvi). Unlike Courtenay, Kingsford was well aware of the 'prejudices' of the sixteenth-century historians Shakespeare read; that is why Kingsford endeavoured 'to mark clearly their sources and the use which they make of them'. Recognizing, as Courtenay had, that Shakespeare's histories were the principal influence on 'popular opinion' about 'history', Kingsford deemed that tracing Shakespeare's 'material to its ultimate original is therefore a proper conclusion to the study of English historical literature in the fifteenth century' (11). When he turned to that task in a later book, he identified Hall as the source of a 'dramatic unity that underlies the cycle of Shakespeare's "Histories"'. This unity was 'the downfall of Richard II, the troublous times of Henry IV, the glory of his son, the long struggle of Lancaster and York with its tragic conclusion . . . , to which the happy union of the rival houses . . . furnishes a fitting crown' (Kingsford, *Prejudice*, 3). Kingsford thus suggested the germ of an idea that was to be developed influentially by E.M.W. Tillyard some twenty years later.

---

1   Kenneth Muir's more impressionistic study added nothing substantial to source study of *3H6* (Muir, 31). Muir published his first volume on Shakespeare's sources (for the comedies and tragedies) in 1957, intending to follow it shortly with a volume on the histories. The latter never materialized, but he treated the histories along with other genres in *The Sources of Shakespeare's Plays*, published in 1977, after Bullough had completed his series.

As more scholars gave their attention to the sources of the history plays, they offered more detailed studies of how Shakespeare used the chronicles. Though Lucille King appeared not to know the work of Boswell-Stone, she nonetheless argued in three articles that Shakespeare relied on Hall as well as Holinshed, particularly for *3 Henry VI* (L. King, 'Hall'), that he used the 1587 edition of Holinshed (rather than the 1577 edition) for *2 Henry VI* and *3 Henry VI* (L. King, '*2* and *3*'), and that *2 Henry VI* and *3 Henry VI* make more extensive use of the chronicles than do *The Contention* and *The True Tragedy*, though in some nine instances the latter use chronicle sources that do not appear in the longer versions (L. King, 'Text'). Hall's influence was confirmed by Gordon Zeefeld, who had read the first of King's articles and found even heavier dependence on Hall than King had (Zeefeld). Writing with an awareness of King's articles but with no reference to Zeefeld, R.A. Law summarized the evidence for the chronicle sources of the *Henry VI* plays and speculated that different patterns of dependence among the three plays (particularly where invented action is concerned) 'imply some difference in authorship', i.e. that *1 Henry VI* is less likely to be wholly by Shakespeare than the other two *Henry VI* plays (Law, 'Chronicles', 32). While the differences are undeniable, they are not necessarily due to different authors; they could as easily be a consequence of one author working one way with sources in a particular play – preferring more invented action, say – and a different way in others.[1] The most thorough analysis of Shakespeare's sources for *3 Henry VI* was J.P. Brockbank's unpublished doctoral thesis (Brockbank, 'Shakespeare's', 133–205). Brockbank was less interested in which chronicles Shakespeare used than in how he used them, and his careful

---

1 Scholars from various points of view have repeatedly suggested that their particular method or angle of vision helps to solve the question of authorship, and sometimes they resort to mere assertion, as Kingsford does in his claim – supported only by an imperial and impersonal voice – that 'it is doubtful whether Shakespeare contributed more [to *1H6*] than the scene of the Two Roses in the second act' (Kingsford, *Prejudice*, 12).

analysis of both the play and its sources laid the groundwork for one of the most influential published essays on the *Henry VI* plays (Brockbank, 'Frame').

With the advent of postmodernism, source study has been challenged for many of the same reasons that authorship has, and source study in its traditional forms has been virtually abandoned. The notion of the author as an autonomous intellect and imagination interacting with a definable set of available texts also written by 'authors' has been recognized as the construct of a particular period, i.e. the late eighteenth century, when a particular notion of history also originated, as we have seen. If these ideas of authorship, source and influence were distinctively 'modern', then the recognition that they are historically relative and inherently problematic is 'postmodern'. As Stephen Lynch recently pointed out,

> The concept of the literary source has undergone in recent years an almost infinite expansion to include virtually all expressions of language in a culture: not merely literary or historical influences, but vast arrays of texts (written and unwritten, known and unknown to the author), along with endless networks of linguistic and discursive structures (patterns of thought and logic, commonplace analogies, habitual figures of speech). Shakespeare's plays are no longer seen as based on a few assorted borrowings, but are now seen as interventions in preexistent fields of textuality. The old notion of particular and distinct sources has given way to new notions of boundless and heterogeneous intertextuality.
>
> (Lynch, 1)

Yet Lynch begins with this acknowledgement in order to establish a context for his study of four Shakespearean plays in comparison with what looks like their traditional 'sources' (*3 Henry VI* is not one of the four). One reason he gives for doing so is 'to reconstitute the cultural embeddedness of Shakespeare's plays', thus helping to deny the timelessness and transcendence that often seem to be ascribed to Shakespeare (113). Lynch thus gives a post-modern rationale for a traditional ('modern') endeavour.

Something very like the intertextuality Lynch describes in fact characterizes the history of traditional source study for *3 Henry VI*, if one looks beyond the chronicles. Discussions of classical allusions and influences, for example, have included *3 Henry VI*, in part because the early plays are more stylistically decorated with classical references than later plays. Shakespeare was the beneficiary of a rigorous Latin education at the Stratford grammar school, as T.W. Baldwin exhaustively documented (Baldwin), and Ben Jonson's remark that Shakespeare had 'small *Latine* and lesse *Greeke*' (Jonson, 8.391) probably says more about Jonson's own formidable self-training in the classics than it does about Shakespeare's lack. The earliest editors of *3 Henry VI*, also benefiting from extensive classical training in school and university, identified many allusions to classical mythology in the play, often adding helpful notes. Lewis Theobald thus identified the source of Rutland's Latin line in 1.3.48, and remarked, 'It is a signal Instance, I think, that the Author knew perfectly well how to apply his *Latine*' (Theobald, 4.314). Still, Ben Jonson's comment about Shakespeare's meagre learning inspired Richard Farmer's sharp attack in his *Essay on the Learning of Shakespeare* (Farmer, 10–12). Farmer fenced satirically with Shakespeare's editors in an effort to prove that Shakespeare's classical allusions derived from other English authors. It took Malone's magisterial edition to set the record straight by means of specific classical parallels.

R.K. Root published the first general study in 1903, a useful dictionary of classical mythology in Shakespeare, specifying the plays in which each reference occurs and briefly identifying possible sources (Root). F.S. Boas discussed selected classical allusions in his British Academy Lecture of 1943, including one (to Proteus) in *3 Henry VI* 3.2.192 (Boas, 117–18). Without reference to Baldwin, J.A.K. Thomson summarized Shakespeare's grammar-school education (J. Thomson, 9–19) and briefly discussed the allusions in each of the plays without reference to Root.[1] D.T. Starnes and E.W. Talbert broadened the base of indebtedness to ancient mythology by studying Renaissance Latin dictionaries and emblem books as possible additional sources of Shakespeare's classical allusions. They suggested that Daedalus and Icarus in *3 Henry VI* 5.6.18–25, for example, might derive from Cooper (Starnes and Talbert, 117), and that Shakespeare might owe his interpretation of Phaëton (1.4.33–4, 2.6.11–20) to Alciati's *Emblems* (117–19).[2] Referring frequently to Thomson but only once to Root ('an interesting study'), Percy Simpson listed several Latin works and passages where Shakespeare alludes to them – all later challenged by Kenneth Muir: 'Percy Simpson's list of parallels does not contain a single one which is beyond dispute' (Muir, 2).[3]

Muir's disagreement with Simpson highlights the postmodern point about intertextuality, in that Simpson's preference for a broader range of references points forward to the postmodern sense of infinite textual allusiveness. Postmodern critics have wanted not only to expand the range of allusions in high literary culture but also to include the entire field of textuality across social classes and different kinds of writing. Stephen Greenblatt's reading of the *Henry IV* plays along with an obscure description of early settlement in the New World and a book on coney-catching is a case in point (Greenblatt, 'Invisible'). Greenblatt was not interested in traditional sources, never mentioning Hall or Holinshed and famously identifying source study as 'the elephants' graveyard of literary history' (Greenblatt, 'Exorcists', 163). His point was not to illuminate Shakespeare's imaginative

---

1 Thomson identified thirteen classical allusions in *3H6* (J. Thomson, 92–8), as opposed to Root's twenty-four.

2 Cooper's dictionary is frequently cited in the notes to *3H6* below, not to assert Shakespeare's indebtedness to it but to give a sense of what Elizabethans who had consulted this source might have brought to the play.

3 Simpson included six references to *3H6* (P. Simpson, 11, 34, 44, 50, 55), among them being the line quoted in Latin by Rutland from Ovid's *Heroides*. It is hard to see how this one could be disputed.

transformation of identifiable sources but to reveal an unsus-
pected social bias that in Greenblatt's estimation tells us
something about Elizabethan juridical power and its theatrical
manifestation. Greenblatt's way of construing intertextuality thus
complements the postmodern commitment to social justice as a
primary value and can be seen as a subcategory of moral criticism.
Unfortunately, it has had little effect on criticism of *3 Henry VI*.

The postmodern point about intertextuality seems particularly
relevant to attempts at identifying Shakespeare's sources when it
comes to the Bible and proverbial lore. In both cases, small publishing industries have sprung up, to which interested readers and
hard-pressed editors have gratefully turned for assistance. But
what is a biblical or proverbial reference, and how can it be verified? Nineteenth-century inquiries about biblical influence were
conducted with greater attention to piety and public morality than
to thorough research, careful comparison and critical judgement
(Brown, Rees, Wordsworth). The most useful of these,
T.R. Eaton's *Shakespeare and the Bible*, cites just three biblical
allusions in *3 Henry VI* (Eaton, 49–52). But not all such inquiries
have been so naive, and scholars in the twentieth century shifted
the priority to a consideration of translations used and the credibility of particular parallels (Daniell, 'Reading'; Marx; Noble;
Shaheen; Sims). Noble was the first to recognize that Shakespeare
sometimes alludes to the *Book of Common Prayer*, as well as the
Bible, but since large portions of the Bible were used in the *Book
of Common Prayer* (*BCP*, 423–7), it is not always possible to distinguish the influence of the Bible from that of the prayer book.

To take two instances from *3 Henry VI*, most readers will
probably recognize that when Richard of Gloucester kisses his
nephew and compares himself to Judas, he is alluding to the
betrayer of Jesus Christ (5.7.33–4), and only one gospel records
this incident (Matthew, 26.49), so the source would seem to be
evident. But is it? In the translation of the Bible that Shakespeare
used most frequently, the Geneva Bible, Judas does not say
'Hail', as Richard does, but all *other* sixteenth-century versions,

including the *Book of Common Prayer*, read 'Haile master' (Shaheen, 73). Shakespeare seems very unlikely to have consulted a source for a story so well known; more probably he remembered the story from the Bishops' Bible, or he remembered it from a non-biblical source, and if the latter is true, in what sense is it precisely a *biblical* reference? Shaheen asserts that the source for Richard's allusion was the *Agony and Betrayal* from the York mystery plays, because Shakespeare's version is closest to what the York Judas says, 'All hayll, maistir' (Shaheen, 73). If Shaheen is right, this is a dramatic echo, not a biblical one, but the York cycle ceased production in 1569, when Shakespeare was five years old, and the first published edition of the York plays was in 1885, so it seems highly unlikely that Shakespeare was influenced by it. The more plausible explanation is that he remembered 'hail' from the account of the betrayal in the *Book of Common Prayer*, which was read annually on the Sunday next before Easter (*BCP*, 121), and he gratuitously added 'All' because the phrase came naturally to him.[1] But if the *Book of Common Prayer* was the 'source', the question persists as to whether this is, strictly speaking, an allusion to the Bible or to the *Book of Common Prayer*. While there is no denying the parallel with the York pageant, such parallels would seem to illustrate the postmodern point about intertextuality, especially where the Bible is concerned, because Shakespeare's culture was saturated with the Bible, not only in various printed forms but in graphic and dramatic forms as well.[2]

The second instance concerns a long-standing textual crux that the present edition resolves in favour of the control text (F),

---

1 Shakespeare twice used 'All hail' without any apparent biblical import (*LLL* 5.2.158, 339; *TNK* 3.5.99).
2 In *MA*, Borachio refers to 'Pharaoh's soldiers in the reechy painting' and to 'god Bel's priests in the old church-window' (3.3.133–5). When Shakespeare was imagining Borachio, in other words, he thought first of biblical stories in graphic form, not in print. In that case, was he thinking first in graphic terms himself, was he imagining a *character* who would think first in graphic terms, was he even distinguishing graphic sources from print, and how can we possibly tell?

on the argument that it involves a biblical allusion as it stands, though editors have regularly emended it since the nineteenth century. The passage in question is Henry's speech in 3.1, when he crosses the English border from exile in Scotland. He begins with a difficult line: 'Let me embrace the sower Aduersaries, / For Wise men say, it is the wisest course' (TLN 1422–3). Puzzled by 'the sower Aduersaries', Samuel Weller Singer suggested in 1826 that the text was corrupt and should read 'Let me embrace thee, sour Adversity', and he defended his emendation by referring to *As You Like It* 2.1.12, 'Sweet are the uses of adversity'. Richmond Noble pointed to a biblical analogue to Singer's emendation in Ecclesiasticus, 2.4–5, and Naseeb Shaheen followed him. Morris Tilley and Robert Dent both found proverbial analogues. It is important to note, however, that all these are parallels to Singer's emendation, not to the original reading in F, and no one noticed that a biblical analogue exists to the original as well: 'Agre with thine aduersarie quickely' (Matthew, 5.25, Geneva Bible). Moreover, the text from Matthew also appears in the *Book of Common Prayer* (186), and the stage direction specifies that Henry enters reading a prayer book. Whether this is technically a *biblical* allusion is therefore, again, difficult to say, but in any case, the allusion means that F's reading requires no textual emendation, and it has the authority of that 'wise man', Jesus.

Where proverbs are concerned, the nineteenth century manifests the same combination of naive studies and scholarship as for biblical influence. One of the features for which neo-classical critics admired Shakespeare was his use of *sententiae*, because they were a feature of Latin style, both classical and Renaissance, and Alexander Pope appended an alphabetical list of memorable sayings in Shakespeare's plays to his edition to make the point (Pope, *Shakespear*, 8.323–5). In the nineteenth century, this tradition persisted but its rationale changed: it became a way to exhibit Shakespeare's putatively universal wisdom. Proverbs were thus extracted from editions and published separately. Mary

Cowden Clarke published such a list alphabetically without identifying the plays they came from (M. Clarke, *Proverbs*), but W.J. Rolfe added the source plays to his edition of her collection (a total of eleven came from *3 Henry VI*), along with a tribute to Shakespeare's transcendent mastery of human knowledge (Rolfe, 37–8). C.J. Walbran organized his list both alphabetically and by play of origin, including eight proverbs from *3 Henry VI* (Walbran, 159–60).

The study of Shakespeare's proverbs was transformed by the lifelong labour of one scholar, Morris Tilley, whose collection of 11,780 proverbs was published posthumously in 1950, all drawn from the sixteenth and seventeenth centuries, including almost 3,000 from Shakespeare and sixty-eight from *3 Henry VI* in particular (Tilley, 806). Tilley's motive was to exhibit neither Shakespeare's success by neo-classical standards nor his universal learning; it was to describe a systematic use of proverbs on historical principles, by analogy to the making of a historical dictionary (Tilley began his career as a lexicographer). With a powerful and well-researched tool like this, much more reliable conclusions could be drawn about proverbs in Shakespeare's plays than had been possible earlier.

Still, the conclusions to be drawn remained tentative and unavoidably interpretive, as Robert Dent made clear in the introduction to his massive revision of Tilley's work on Shakespeare, published in 1981 (Dent, xi–xxviii). Frankly acknowledging that even with the improvements he had introduced, his own dictionary 'remains a tool to be used with caution' (xii), Dent pointed to the impossibility of defining a proverb, to inadequacies in Tilley's bases for selection, to difficulties resulting from a single entry form for substantive variants in a given 'proverb', to the necessary incompleteness of any particular collection, and implicitly to the tentativeness of his own well-judged conclusions: 'this present index *nervously but dutifully* records . . .', 'the index *courageously* excludes' (14–15, 16; our emphasis). From Tilley's sixty-eight proverbs in *3 Henry VI* Dent thus excluded six while adding forty-four more of his own, for a total of 106. (Dent, 17–18).[1]

Two examples will serve to illustrate the highly interpretive process involved in identifying proverbs. The first is a quotation from *3 Henry VI* that Tilley includes as proverbial but that Dent excludes. Arguing her case at the French court, Queen Margaret asserts that 'heavens are just, and Time suppresseth wrongs' (3.3.77), a commonplace that Tilley refers to his proverb T325, 'TIME cures every disease'. Though Dent offers no explanation for excluding Margaret's line as an instance of this proverb, he presumably did not see the suppression of wrongs as a close enough parallel to the curing of disease. The second example is one of the forty-four that Dent adds to Tilley. When Henry objects to York's possession of the throne in the play's first scene, York asserts, 'It must and shall be so. Content thyself' (1.1.85). Dent compares this line to Tilley's proverb, 'I (etc.) MUST and will' (M1330.1), for which the parallel examples include four instances of 'I must' and one of 'You must', but none of '*It* must'. This is presumably why Dent makes this a 'cf.' reference, i.e. something less certain than a full proverbial reference. But the uncertainty raises important questions. If this is not a 'proverb', does it count as an addition to Tilley? (Dent so counts it, but should he?) Can the issue be decided without a firm definition of 'proverb'? Did the lack of a specific parallel disqualify this example for Tilley, or did Tilley simply overlook it? The second is always possible, of course, but if the first is true, then two experienced analysts of proverbs honestly disagreed about this particular reference, as they disagreed about the first example. In both cases, the issue comes down to a difference of judgement on the part of two knowledgeable and astute scholars. This is not to dismiss their work; they thought carefully about many more

1 In the spirit of Dent's remark that he would 'totally ignore' many of the proverbs in his dictionary 'were I an Arden or Variorum editor' (Dent, xxii), the present edition notes just thirty-seven of Dent's proverbs and fifty-one of Tilley's in the commentary notes below.

proverbs than most other people do, certainly most editors of Shakespeare, and their process of selection was clearly not arbitrary. On the other hand, it was far from scientific, despite the many numbers that Tilley and Dent compiled.

Listing proverbs alphabetically also decontextualizes them in such a way as to obscure information about proverbs and social class. We noticed that eighteenth-century editors sometimes included lists of Shakespeare's proverbs because they saw his sententiousness as an approvable trait in comparison to Latin literature. For their sense of taste, in other words, proverbs were a mark of the literate high style, which in turn was a social marker, both in the sixteenth and eighteenth centuries. To some extent, they were right. Shakespeare certainly knew that Seneca is full of *sententiae*, and Charles Smith showed that a significant number of Shakespeare's proverbs derive from two Renaissance collections of Latin proverbs (C. Smith). Moreover, Tilley noted a difference between proverbs of native origin, marked by rhyme and alliteration, and those that Shakespeare used in translation – the latter including Latin proverbs, of course (Tilley, vi). But the fact that the vast majority of Shakespeare's proverbs were native in origin points to a different social origin as well, one that was closer to oral culture than to literate, to the common people than to the educated elite. It is not at all clear, in short, that sententiousness was the social marker for Shakespeare that it was for his eighteenth-century editors. In *3 Henry VI*, at any rate, though the most sententious character happens to be Richard of Gloucester, proverbs are distributed across all social classes (being offered not only by the nobility but also by messengers, watchmen and the Son who has killed his Father). Richard's disproportionate number of them may have something to do with his origin in the Tudor Vice, who was known for his sententiousness and whose origin was in popular drama, not in classical or courtly tradition.

HISTORICAL CRITICISM: ESTABLISHING CONTEXT

Beyond the identification of literary sources, historical interpretation of *3 Henry VI* has sought to expand the sense of context in which the play was written. Eighteenth-century editors initiated this inquiry, as they initiated so many others. We noticed Malone's attempt to use theatre history in an argument about authorship, for example (above, pp. 45–6). Potentially this kind of inquiry moves toward closure, in that it aims to find all the evidence pertinent to a given play in elucidating that play's 'background'. In addition to classical allusions in general, critics have thus recognized that the Elizabethan infatuation with Seneca in particular left its mark on *3 Henry VI*. The play was first performed two years before *Titus Andronicus*, Shakespeare's early acknowledgement of contemporary interest in the first-century writer of Latin tragedy (Ard³ *Tit*, 69–70). 'As Plautus and Seneca are accounted the best for Comedy and Tragedy among the Latines', wrote Francis Meres in 1598, 'so Shakespeare among the English is the most excellent in both kinds for the stage' (quoted in G. Smith, 2.317–18). Since, of the tragedies, only *Titus* and *Romeo and Juliet* had been performed by 1598, though a number of the histories had been performed by that year, Meres seems to have used 'tragedy' loosely to refer to history plays, as well as to Shakespeare's first tragedy.

Senecan influence involved more than particular allusions, such as those to *Medea* in *2 Henry VI*, *3 Henry VI* and *Macbeth* (Ewbank; cf. E. Jones, 269–70); it also involved style and theme. In the first book-length study of Senecan influence in Elizabethan drama, J.W. Cunliffe pointed to the 'ruthless spirit of violence and bloodshed' and 'the crude horrors of physical repulsiveness' in *3 Henry VI* and *Richard III* as Senecan motifs (Cunliffe, 73).[1]

---

1 F.L. Lucas was not impressed with this claim. 'Most of the Shakespearian passages quoted by Cunliffe and Engel seem to me the merest coincidences', including those in *3H6* (Lucas, 123). For a more recent sceptical assessment of Seneca's influence, see Hunter, 'Seneca'. Jones is more receptive (E. Jones, 267–77), pointing out that the influence of Seneca's style on Elizabethan dramatists involved the imitation of his favourite words, as well as features of his rhetoric.

Revenge was a favourite Senecan theme, and Seneca's influence probably helps to account for the fact that *3 Henry VI* is second only to *Titus Andronicus* in the number of words with the root 'venge' (see 1.1.55n.). In this case, the classical heritage coincided with long-standing native traditions of familial and personal honour that had been recently encoded in sixteenth-century books describing (and often prescribing) appropriate courtly behaviour. Gareth Lloyd Evans saw Shakespeare borrowing from Seneca for the violent vengeance of Richard of Gloucester in *3 Henry VI* and *Richard III*, while going well beyond his classical source at the same time (Evans, 140–50). A similar historical coincidence concerned Seneca's use of prophecy, dreams, premonitions and fate, which seemed to some like a pagan version of Christian providence, for in this case an esteemed classical authority reinforced magical thinking (see above, pp. 57–64).

Senecan influence involved style, as well as content, and Hardin Craig identified eight declamations in *3 Henry VI* as Senecan, though he argued for a dramatic functionality in many of these speeches that is not characteristic of Seneca (Craig, 58–9).[1] Gladys Willcock analysed Margaret's speech in particular as an illustration of Elizabethan *elocutio*, a way of heightening language with rhetorical devices for which 'Seneca's responsibility was quite general' (Willcock, 109–10). Robert Y. Turner pointed out that Shakespeare departs from Seneca in distributing declamations among several characters for emotional effect throughout *3 Henry VI*, rather than concentrating 'in Senecan fashion upon the climax with retrospective reports' (Turner, *Shakespeare's*, 105). Acknowledging all three of these critics, Wolfgang Clemen elaborated on Shakespeare's stylistic 'integration' of declamations in *3 Henry VI*: 'The isolation of the set speech, a characteristic feature of Senecan tragedy, by which the speech becomes a self-contained declamation, is rarely to be found in Shakespeare' (Clemen, 'Style', 11). Clifford's speech to persuade Henry not to disinherit

---

1   For unspecified reasons, Craig omitted the declamations of the unnamed father and son (2.5.55–72, 79–93) and the shorter declamation of Queen Elizabeth (4.4.16–24).

Prince Edward (2.2.9–42) is one of the rare exceptions, and Clemen pointed out that Shakespeare acknowledges its set piece style in Henry's reply: 'Full well hath Clifford played the orator' (2.2.43) (13). In short, while Shakespeare was probably indebted to Senecan style in *3 Henry VI*, he was also exploring ways to distance his style from classical influence in the interest of speech that seems more natural. Senecan influence is less noticeable in the second tetralogy than in the first.

The postmodern position that 'influence' encompasses more than demonstrable literary indebtedness is helpful in assessing the Senecanism of *3 Henry VI*. *Titus* is arguably as much a tribute to neo-classical tragic expectation as *The Comedy of Errors* is to neo-classical comedy, but Shakespeare's fascination with both can be understood in broader terms than literary fashion and indebtedness. Why, after all, did this particular fashion take hold at this particular time? The prestige of classical standards arose in the sixteenth century with the rise of humanist-educated courtiers to social and political prominence (Cox, *Shakespeare*, 41–60), and fascination with Seneca as an exemplar of Latin 'high style' served the interest of newly made families and their ambitious sons, at the same time that Roman Stoicism – again exemplified by Seneca himself, as well as his tragic heroes – reinforced a particular self-conception based on the competition and uncertainty of life at court, which the Tudors had made the exclusive route to wealth, prestige and power. Translations and academic productions of Seneca's plays were undertaken from the 1540s onward (B. Smith, 199–215).

One way to understand *Titus* and the *Henry VI* plays, then, is to see them as opposite responses to Senecanism and its social implications. Whereas *Titus* models Stoic rectitude in the Senecan manner, both in 'his steely intrepidity and his explosion into vengeful insanity' (Cox, *Shakespeare*, 175), the early English history plays examine the same ideal critically and detail its destructive social and political consequences. The conflation of the Senecan hero with the native Vice is brilliantly suggested in

Richard of Gloucester's affirmation, 'I am myself alone' (5.6.83), which not only evokes the Stoic rectitude and self-completeness of a Senecan hero but also echoes the Vice Nichol Newfangle in Ulpian Fulwell's *Like Will to Like* (see above, p. 79). The breakdown of political stability in the first tetralogy is complemented, if not caused, by a movement from heroic warrior nobility (the likes of Henry V and Talbot) to courtly competitors such as Suffolk, York and Richard of Gloucester, who can be seen as examples of Tudor 'new men', manifesting the dramaturgy of the Vice as well as the emulation and self-possession of Senecan heroes. Shakespeare's perception of the Tudor 'new fashion' is thus akin to that of his dramatic predecessors, Henry Medwall and John Skelton, at the beginning of the Tudor era, though his analysis is more analytically political than theirs and less distinctively moral.

Medwall and Skelton belong to the native dramatic tradition, of course, and this too has been explored as a complement to classical influence in the effort to establish Shakespeare's literary context. Gerard Langbaine's *Account of the English Dramatic Poets* (1691) was the first description, though brief, of Shakespeare as one playwright among many, and Robert Dodsley's *Select Collection of Old English Plays* in twelve volumes in 1744 was inspired by curiosity about what preceded Shakespeare.[1] Thomas Warton's *History of English Poetry* (1775) offered the first detailed narrative account of early English drama, based largely on unprinted sources, some of which have since disappeared. Malone's *Historical Account of the Rise and Progress of the English Stage*, based closely on Warton, was explicitly inspired by curiosity about Shakespeare's context, for which Malone had little respect:

---

1   More explicitly inspired by the desire to discover Shakespeare's sources was John Nichols's two-volume collection of *Six Old Plays* in 1779. W.C. Hazlitt eventually expanded Dodsley's anthology to fifteen volumes in its fourth edition (1874), which still remains the most accessible source for several sixteenth-century plays, some of which have survived in only one or two copies.

the titles are scarcely known, except to antiquaries; nor is there one of them that will bear a second perusal. Yet these, contemptible and few as they are, we may suppose to have been the most popular productions of the time, and the best that had been exhibited before the appearance of Shakespeare.

(Malone, *Historical*, sig. B)

Malone's extraordinary authority perpetuated this dim view of early drama and encouraged the seemingly scientific explanation in E.K. Chambers's evolutionary account in *The Mediaeval Stage*, where Shakespeare is a quasi-biological product of gradual development towards fit, strong and dominant specimens (Chambers, *Mediaeval*).

With such a negative assessment of Shakespeare's predecessors and contemporaries, it is not surprising that the first serious attention to the *Henry VI* plays in their immediate dramatic context did not appear until the twentieth century. F.E. Schelling used the term 'chronicle play' to describe a

master influence in the development of the English drama. . . . This is the English national spirit, the spirit which, from the days of the early sacred drama to the present time, has animated those scenes which seek the simple dramatic representation of everyday life or strive to make real the deeds of great historical personages of the past.

(Schelling, vi)

With so broad a definition, Schelling included plays from John Bale's *King Johan* (1538) to *Edmund Ironside* (which Schelling dated 1647), claiming thirteen of Shakespeare's plays for his category: the ten English history plays in addition to *King Lear*, *Macbeth* and *Cymbeline*, which derive from chronicle sources (Schelling, vii).

Others have, from time to time, pursued Schelling's attempt to describe a new genre that would include Shakespeare's history plays. Irving Ribner took up the task in 1957, rejecting Schelling's category ('chronicle play') as too broad and suggesting instead the term 'history play':

> if a play appears to fulfill what we know the Elizabethans considered to be the legitimate purposes of history, and if it is drawn from a chronicle source which we know that at least a large part of the contemporary audience accepted as factual, we may call it a history play.
>
> (Ribner, 27)

Even with this definition, Ribner's list of plays extended from 1519 (Skelton's *Magnificence*) to 1653 (the academic Latin play, *Sanctus Edoardus Confessor*). Though he did not refer to Ribner, F.P. Wilson nonetheless pointed out difficulties with the effort 'to define a history play by its subject-matter' (F. Wilson, *Shakespearian*, 2). As fairly constant features in Shakespeare's histories, he suggested 'the clash of arms', 'looseness of structure' and an interest in politics 'or, with Shakespeare, in character revealing itself in politics' (3–4).[1]

The most thoughtful attempt to define history plays generically (or at least Shakespeare's history plays) is David Scott Kastan's suggestion that they are formally distinct (Kastan, 'Shape'). Acknowledging Ribner and Wilson, Kastan noted problems with definitions of the history play by title, authorial intent and content, and he proposed that Shakespeare's history plays 'have a unique and determinate shape that emerges organically from the playwright's sense of the shape of history itself' (263). Secular history is thus time-defined and open-ended, and so are Shakespeare's secular history plays, in contrast to his comedies

---

1 Despite reference in the title of his article to the 'origins of a genre', Paul Dean does not describe the *Henry VI* plays generically; rather, he identifies some motifs that they have in common with Elizabethan romance histories (Dean). The title of John Velz's collection of essays is also at odds with its content (Velz). Even G.K.Hunter's 'Notes on the Genre of the History Play' moves in another direction: Hunter writes without reference to earlier attempts at defining genre and devotes most of his attention to *Oth* (Hunter, 'Afterword'), while Naomi Conn Liebler's essay on *3H6* is a study of theme (game and play), not of genre (Liebler).

and tragedies. Characters' preoccupation with time is exemplified, Kastan pointed out, in the garden scene of *Richard II*, where the gardeners discuss their need to work constantly in order to control weeds and pests: 'The iterative imagistic links between garden and state clearly imply that the kingdom is no less a post-lapsarian entity', i.e. it is governed by the relentless pressure of time, in contrast to the timelessness of Eden (273). The open-endedness of time is suggested by the play's open-ended start and its insistent questions about who murdered Woodstock: 'Shakespeare keeps the fact *of* the murder of Woodstock continually before the audience, but, in spite of the repeated charges of responsibility, the facts *about* the murder are deliberately obscured' (270). Similarly, the play does not end with Richard's death: 'The historical process continues, and, indeed, it is Richard's murder itself that opens up the play's ending' (271).[1]

Kastan's sense of genre is helpful in thinking about *3 Henry VI*. Shakespeare's first king who loses his crown is less explicitly oppressed by time than Richard II, but both kings fail politically because of their ineptitude, and in both cases ineptitude consists of untimely decisions and actions.[2] Henry fantasizes longingly about a timeless world of imagined bucolic perfection:

> O God! Methinks it were a happy life
> To be no better than a homely swain,
> To sit upon a hill, as I do now,
> To carve out dials quaintly, point by point,
> Thereby to see the minutes how they run:

---

1 Kastan derived his conception in part from Tom Driver, also referred to by Wolfgang Clemen, in his essay on past and future in Shakespeare (Clemen, 'Past', 234). Clemen anticipated Kastan's idea in his remark that 'The study of past and future in Shakespeare's plays, if carried out on a larger scale, could indeed teach us something about the connexion between dramatic technique and the expression of inner meaning' (232), and Clemen saw the history plays as especially important in this regard (233–40). Still, he stopped well short of defining the history play generically, as Kastan did, by its treatment of time. For A.R. Humphreys's elaboration on Clemen's idea, see Humphreys, 281–6 (on the *Henry VI* plays, 284–5).

2 Ricardo Quinones argued for a similar sense of time and royal ineptitude in the *Henry VI* plays, though he did not relate it to genre (Quinones, 'Lineal', 25–30, and 'Views', 334–5).

> How many makes the hour full complete,
> How many hours brings about the day,
> How many days will finish up the year,
> How many years a mortal man may live.
>   (2.5.21–9)

The speech has long been admired as a rhetorical set piece, but its context is the raging battle of Towton, from which the King has withdrawn, though the battle intrudes on his meditation in the form of an emblematic son who has killed his father and a father who has killed his son. Their suffering has been caused in part by the King's weakness and indecision, which he manifests again when Exeter impatiently urges him: 'Nay, stay not to expostulate, make speed; / Or else come after. I'll away before' (2.5.135–6). Henry's inability to move in a timely and decisive fashion is a substantial aspect of his characterization in *3 Henry VI*, and it contributes in its own way to the carnage of civil war. Henry's nemesis, Richard of Gloucester, on the other hand, has more of the play's references to time than any other character (seven out of twenty), and they often suggest his awareness of the need to seize opportunity, as his father York had before him: 'But wherefore stay we? 'Tis no time to talk' (4.5.24). Richard always seems to act in awareness of 'the golden time I look for' (3.2.127).[1]

3 Henry VI is defined by time as a history play not only in theme and characterization but also in its open-endedness. The play begins in the midst of an ongoing conflict which is not explained by reminiscence or arriving messenger, so the past is not enclosed retrospectively in the present: soldiers enter boasting and bearing battle trophies; one occupies a throne; they are confronted by an angry party who claim the first group is illegitimate – all without explanation or resolution. To understand fully what is happening requires information from the preceding plays or from the chronicles (supplied in the notes to this edition), and the need for that kind of information is what makes the first scene a 'start'

---

1 For Richard's other references to time, see 2.1.158, 2.6.67, 4.5.18, 5.1.48, and 5.3.16.

rather than a true beginning, in the Aristotelian sense of 'that which does not necessarily follow on something else, but after it something else naturally is or happens' (Aristotle, 30). By the end of the play, one king has defeated another and proclaims a happy future, but the victorious king's younger brother threatens 'all harm' in an ominous aside (5.7.34). This is clearly not the end of the story, in the Aristotelian sense of 'that which naturally follows on something else, either necessarily or for the most part, but nothing else after it' (Aristotle, 30). To be sure, we may well ask how many of the play's original auditors would have been ignorant of what followed *3 Henry VI*, given Tudor propaganda about Richard III, but that information is just what makes the play open-ended: the closing scene insists that something necessarily follows, whether we know what it is or not, just as the first scene insists that something preceded it. This open-endedness, more-over, is not an ineradicable residue from the chronicles but a deliberate feature of the history plays: when Shakespeare used the same chronicle source for *King Lear*, *Macbeth* and *Cymbeline*, he had no difficulty establishing a comparatively strong sense of closure as he wrote the beginnings and endings of those plays.[1]

Robert Jones acknowledged Kastan's point about time and the history play (R. Jones, xvi) in a book-length argument that Shakespeare's history plays are historical by virtue of their characters' memory of the past. The *Henry VI* plays thus move from a strong sense of history in memories of the heroic Henry V to vindictive memories of nothing but injuries suffered by one's clan or one's self in *3 Henry VI*, with a consequent loss of the national heritage (R. Jones, 1–30). This devolution in historical memory is epitomized, Jones argued, by Richard of Gloucester, whose image of hewing his way out of a thorny wood (3.2.174–81) is a symbolic rejection of a meaningful past: 'In his stance toward history and

---

1 Indeed, the tragic sense of closure at the end of *KL* is so strong that Kent and Edgar refer to the end of time itself (5.3.261–2). Contrast Young Clifford's apocalyptic allusions in *2H6* 5.2.40–5, which are not placed in the play's closing lines and refer only to Clifford's personal loss, not to the imaginative sense that everything that matters has collapsed.

its authority, as in so many other respects, Richard is the nadir toward which this self-destructive English polity has been plummeting' (R. Jones, 30).

While some scholars have thought about history plays generically, others have attended to the influence of specific playwrights on Shakespeare's early histories, and vice versa. Initially this conversation was conducted almost exclusively in terms of authorship, and several contemporaries were identified as Shakespeare's possible collaborators or as the originators of plays that Shakespeare revised. Thus F.E. Schelling discussed the *Henry VI* plays in a chapter entitled 'The Marlowe–Shakespeare Plays', because he believed that these are 'dramas in which Shakespeare, whether in revision or in independent authorship, was working either with Marlowe or directly under his influence' (Schelling, 75).

Aside from the question of shared authorship, the interaction of Marlowe and Shakespeare is a striking aspect of their developing theatrical careers, and considerable attention has been paid to it. They were born in the same year, came from similar socio-economic backgrounds, and gained a public reputation by the same means, though the Cambridge-educated Marlowe certainly made his mark first: the attention of London was captured in the late 1580s by the stunning success of *Tamburlaine*, which left a strong impression on Shakespeare's early history plays. Marlowe in turn seems to have learned from Shakespeare's histories when he wrote *Edward II* (Rossiter, *Woodstock*, 53–65). F.P. Wilson's judicious survey of the fragmentary surviving evidence inclined him to the 'surprising conclusion' that Shakespeare's early histories were the first of their kind: 'there is no certain evidence that any popular dramatist before Shakespeare wrote a play based on English history' (F. Wilson, *Marlowe*, 106).[1] Similarities between *Edward II* and *Richard II* are as intriguing as similarities between

---

1 Wilson was certainly aware of Bale's *King Johan* (1538), but he ruled it out with his phrase 'popular dramatist', which refers to playwrights for the London commercial theatres.

The Jew of Malta and *The Merchant of Venice*, and it is hard to know what might have become of this extraordinary symbiosis if Marlowe had not been stabbed to death in the spring of 1593.

Specific indebtedness and similarities have been noted by several critics.[1] The most sustained comparison of Marlowe and the *Henry VI* plays, however, was offered by David Riggs. To be sure, Riggs was concerned with a group of about fifteen 'heroical-historical' plays of the late 1580s and early 1590s, but he began by 'using *Tamburlaine* as a rough paradigm for their "heroical" themes' (Riggs, 18), and where *3 Henry VI* in particular is concerned, he saw the 'rhetorical frame' of *Tamburlaine* still intact (137), while the values were no longer those of the Tamburlainian hero but of Barabas: 'For a dramatist writing in 1590, the Machiavel and revenger of the popular stage would already have intersected in *The Jew of Malta*' (135).[2]

While Shakespeare's dramatic context in the London commercial theatres has been the subject of serious inquiry since the eighteenth century, the same was not true for earlier English drama, because the prejudice against it was so strong. Yet the native dramatic context before the 1570s would seem to be the most influential, having been established more than 300 years before Shakespeare came to London, whereas permanent commercial theatres began operating for the first time fewer than twenty years before he arrived. Shakespeare's first encounter with drama of any sort was probably in Coventry, where a popular mystery cycle was performed every spring until 1580, and in Stratford itself, which was a regular stopping-place for touring players from 1568 until 1602 when 'the borough council ruled against any more players using the guildhall' (Somerset, *REED*). Though the records indicate no content for the visitors' performances, they are likely to have drawn heavily on the staple fare of travelling actors: the Tudor morality play. Prejudice against these early, but remarkably durable, forms of drama is evident not only

---

1 Brooke; Cox, '*3 Henry VI*', 48–58; Leech; Talbert, 214–16.
2 For application of Rigg's idea to *3H6*, see Billings, 43–5.

in Malone, as we have seen, but also in E.K. Chambers's evolutionary conception of English dramatic development from primitive to complex.

In 1958, Bernard Spivack brilliantly addressed prejudice against the morality play, thereby establishing it as a relevant context for *3 Henry VI*. He showed that Richard of Gloucester is based on the morality play figure called the Vice, and his argument that Shakespeare's early characterization is a combination of personification allegory and actual persons has been influential in other analyses of character in *3 Henry VI* (see above, pp. 64–81). In a complementary argument, David Bevington showed that the structure of Marlowe's plays is directly indebted to Tudor morality plays (Bevington, *Mankind*, 199–262). Spivack's and Bevington's arguments help to put the influence of other plays from the commercial theatres in perspective: since Shakespeare and his contemporaries had a common dramatic heritage, they might well achieve some of the same effects independently. Barabas in *The Jew of Malta* is also based on the Vice, for example (Spivack, 346–53; Bevington, *Mankind*, 218–33), so similarities between Richard of Gloucester and Barabas may have as much to do with a common debt to the Vice as with Marlowe's influence on Shakespeare, or vice versa.

Among other kinds of play from the mainstream of English drama before the advent of London commercial theatres, the saints' plays seem to have had the least influence on the Shakespearean history play, but they were common and popular at one time, and the paucity of surviving examples in England necessarily requires an open verdict in this case.[1] To what extent might early audiences have caught complex glimpses of a saint's play behind the long-suffering, pious and murdered King Henry? Though the process of his canonization was cut off by the Reformation, he was popularly venerated as if he were a saint until well into the reign of Henry VIII (Knox and Leslie, 1–7)

---

1   For an annotated list of well over one hundred lost examples, see Davidson.

12 King Henry VI holding a book and sceptre in a stained-glass portrait from a window in the chapel of King's College, Cambridge, which Henry founded

(see Fig. 12), and memory of his holy status may be recalled in his own lines:

> My meed hath got me fame.
> I have not stopped mine ears to their demands,
> Nor posted off their suits with slow delays.
> My pity hath been balm to heal their wounds.
> My mildness hath allayed their swelling griefs.
> My mercy dried their water-flowing tears.
>
> (4.8.38–43)

To the pious Henry alone come 'divining thoughts', sent by 'secret powers' that 'Suggest but truth', as he prophesies Richmond's future kingship (4.6.68–9). Yet even this moment of prophetic foreknowledge is tinged with political irony, as Henry himself acknowledges: 'for this is he / Must help you more than you are hurt by me' (4.6.75–6).

The mystery plays were certainly important, though they have been little recognized. Discussing Richard II's comparison of himself to Christ before Pilate, A.P. Rossiter reminded his readers 'how familiar to the Elizabethans was the staged spectacle of a sacrificial king of sorrows before his judges' because of the mystery plays (Rossiter, 'Prognosis', 136). Francis Berry noticed an analogy between the torture of York in *3 Henry VI* 1.4 and the buffeting and scourging of Christ in the York cycle, but he drew no specific parallels (F. Berry, 58–9). With some justification, then, Emrys Jones commented in 1977 that 'a major obstacle to a close historical understanding of Shakespearean drama, and particularly the histories and tragedies, has been the failure to bring into relation with it the great body of dramatic writing known as the mystery plays' (E. Jones, 31). Jones interpreted the sham trial and political assassination of Duke Humphrey in *2 Henry VI* against the background of medieval passion plays (35–54), and in *3 Henry VI* he pointed again to the death of York (54–6).

What went unnoticed in observations about York's death and the mystery plays is that Margaret's mockery of York repeats a game motif that runs through the buffeting and scourging of Christ in several of the mystery cycles. 'I prithee grieve to make me merry, York' urges Margaret (1.4.86), restating the principle of cruel play in the Towneley cycle: 'Bot more sorow thou hase / oure myrth is incresyng' (*Towneley, Scourging*, 85–6). But York's death is not the only parallel with the mystery plays in *3 Henry VI*. The play begins with a scene that repeats specific motifs and stage groupings from the fall of Lucifer, the first pageant in the York cycle (Cox, *Shakespeare*, 93–5), and the deaths of Rutland and Prince Edward similarly repeat motifs from the slaughter of the innocents (Cox, *Shakespeare*, 96–7).

To recognize these parallels is not necessarily to turn secular history into sacred history or even to suggest an analogy between them, as O.B. Hardison did:

> In the cycle of plays from *Richard II* to *Richard III* it is evident that we have a secular equivalent to the sacred cycle of the Middle Ages. The protagonist of the cycle is respublica rather than Holy Church, and its rationale is the religio-political synthesis of the Tudor apologists rather than Catholic theology.
>
> (Hardison, 290)

For one thing, it is not clear that Shakespeare's plays were intended as a cycle. If they were, why did Shakespeare begin in the middle (with the death of Henry V) and proceed to the end, then go back to the beginning (the overthrow of Richard II) and proceed to the middle? Moreover, each play in itself has the same open-ended shape, even *Richard II* and *Richard III*, which begin and end the sequence. The effect of the mystery plays in Shakespeare's secular histories would seem to have less to do with parallels or equivalence than with contrast. What these plays render is not sacred history, which is definitively begun, directed and ended by God, with little or no consideration for the secondary dependence of one event upon another in diurnal time. Rather, Shakespeare seems to draw on the force of emotionally and morally charged events from the drama of salvation history in order to emphasize the priority of human action in dramas of secular history, where the focus is on the attempts of powerful men and women to acquire and maintain political influence, and where emotional impact seldom coincides with moral significance, as it does in the passion plays.

Given the subject matter of history plays, the attempt to establish Shakespeare's historical context as fully as possible has involved an interest in more than dramatic tradition; it has also included an exploration of political relationships in his culture, and this exploration has also affected criticism of *3 Henry VI*. The notion that the play had a particular historical context was at odds with the romantic idea of Shakespeare's timeless transcendence, but the two assumptions co-existed and flourished throughout the nineteenth century. Along with studies of Shakespeare's characters as illustrations of the unchanging human heart thus appeared studies of Shakespeare's plays as interventions in contemporary political struggles. Richard Simpson first applied this kind of interpretation to *3 Henry VI* in 1874. Simpson thought that Shakespeare's depiction of a weak king led by overbearing courtiers alluded 'to the time when Leicester ruled the roast by playing on the weaknesses of the Queen' (R. Simpson, 421), and he related several passages in *3 Henry VI* to events in the 1580s and to the Catholic pamphlet, *Leicester's Commonwealth*, published, under another title, by Robert Parsons in 1584 (R. Simpson, 422–3). While Simpson's reading seems arbitrary and over-determined, it appears that 'Somerville' in *3 Henry VI* (5.1.7–15) is an allusion to Sir John Somerville, a Warwickshire nobleman who was executed in 1583 for attempting to assassinate Queen Elizabeth, and Somerville is known to have been inspired by Parsons (Martin and Cox, 339). One allusion is not enough to support Simpson's interpretation of *3 Henry VI*, but Shakespeare's oblique reference to a recently executed Catholic nobleman makes Simpson's reading less incredible than it otherwise seems to be.[1]

The most detailed study of *3 Henry VI* in its political context is Edna Zwick Boris's interpretation of Shakespeare's two historical tetralogies in light of the English constitution in the late sixteenth century. Boris noticed that all eight plays focus on the three constituent elements of Tudor government: 'the council [i.e. the monarch in council], parliaments, and the administration of justice', but that the first tetralogy differs from the second in its additional consideration of 'essentially feudal concerns . . . the making and breaking of fealty oaths and . . . references to status'. She suggested that the difference was due to 'Shakespeare's increased reflection of the contemporary constitution in English history plays the more he worked with historical materials' (Boris, 13). Boris's analysis helps to explain royal weakness in particular. 'The Crown was a composite body', Boris argued, coinciding 'with the king as head of the body politic, with the heir to a particular dynasty, and with those responsible for maintaining the inalienable rights of the Crown and the kingdom' (88). Seen in this light, both characters who wear the crown in *3 Henry VI* are failures. 'Henry's weaknesses as a man, as head of his family, and as head of state' are all matched by Edward, though in different ways (94). Boris's consideration of *3 Henry VI* according to Tudor constitutional expectations thus illuminated the play as an Elizabethan study of the Crown in crisis.

Studies of ideas and policies in the history plays are more credible, as David Bevington argued (Bevington, *Tudor*, 1–26), than studies of the history plays as allegories of contemporary political figures or squabbles, but more than overtly political ideas and

---

1 Research into the politics of Shakespeare's plays has not helped to illuminate *3H6* very much. Tillyard dismissed the play (*History Plays*, 189–90), and Campbell's discussion of Shakespeare's history plays as 'mirrors of Elizabethan policy' omitted the *Henry VI* plays because she found them 'quite impossible to discuss without reviewing and reconsidering the evidence concerning the sequence and dates of the three parts' (Campbell, *'Histories'*, vi). Bevington's survey of topical meaning in Tudor drama considered *3H6* only briefly as evidence of Shakespeare's putative attitude toward the populace (Bevington, *Tudor*, 240).

111

relationships have been considered as part of the context of *3 Henry VI*. In 1934 Alfred Hart noticed the relevance to the history plays of sermons officially written for regular delivery in services of the Church of England. Hart referred to these 'sermons or homilies', in the Elizabethan phrase, as a 'new source-book', but they would more accurately be described as part of the informing context than as specific sources. Hart pointed to no specific parallels with the homilies in *3 Henry VI*, in any case, but his argument that the homily on 'Disobedience and Wilful Rebellion' must have influenced Shakespeare was an important insight. This homily was first published in 1571, when Shakespeare was seven years old, and portions of it were read on nine Sundays of every year thereafter throughout Queen Elizabeth's reign (Hart, *Homilies*, 23). Tillyard was impressed with Hart's argument (Tillyard, *History Plays*, 18–20), and Dollimore agreed that 'the homilies were an important ideological underpinning' of what he saw as an increasingly authoritarian development under Elizabeth (Dollimore, *Radical*, 83). Indeed, Dollimore saw the homilies as a great deal more than 'context'; he saw them as helping to construct an ideological system that the plays as often as not subvert rather than merely reproduce or support.

Much the same could be said about another source of commonplaces for the history plays: *The Mirror for Magistrates*. When this collection of moralistic tales about the downfall of powerful people was first published, during the reign of Mary, it was suppressed because of its Calvinist interpretation of political authority, and the first extant edition is dated 1559 (*Mirror*, 5–7, 52–4). The relevance of the *Mirror* to Shakespeare's history plays was noticed as early as 1737 (*Mirror*, 3), but it found its first real scholar in Lily Bess Campbell, who published a critical edition of it in 1938 and depended on it heavily in her book on Shakespeare's history plays (Campbell, *'Histories'*, 106–16). Details occasionally appear in *3 Henry VI* that the *Mirror* records (as indicated in the notes below), and King Edward's lament when Warwick captures him after the battle of Edgcote is typical of laments in the *Mirror*:

'Though Fortune's malice overthrow my state, / My mind exceeds the compass of her wheel' (4.3.46–7). Though such a lament would appear to be more Stoic than Calvinist, the Marian suppression of *Mirror* says something about the political sensitivity of religious differences in the sixteenth century and indicates that what appears to be apolitical to us may have been different to Shakespeare and his contemporaries.

PSYCHOANALYTIC CRITICISM

Though Freudian psychoanalysis is a relative newcomer in the history of Shakespeare criticism, it has strong affinities with the inclination to see the human psyche as transcendent and homogeneous across cultures, including historical cultures, so that Shakespeare's characters can be called on as witnesses to modern observations about human motivation or neurosis. Freud was a great deal more insightful, intelligent, prolific and imaginative than the Victorian physician John Charles Bucknill, but it is possible to see a similarity between Freud's use of Shakespeare's characters to illustrate psychological problems and Bucknill's use of Shakespeare for the same purpose in *The Psychology of Shakespeare* (1859).

A pertinent example is Freud's reference to Richard III's soliloquy at the beginning of *Richard III*.[1] He cited Richard as an example of those who see themselves as an exception to social expectation, because of 'an event or painful experience from which they had suffered in their earliest childhood, one in respect of which they knew themselves to be guiltless, and which they could look upon as an unjust injury inflicted upon them' (Freud, 4.320). He thus summarized the soliloquy in his own words:

---

1 Richard's soliloquy in *3H6* 3.2 would have served Freud's purpose even better, but Freud did not cite it, and the point about his way of reading character in Shakespeare is the same regardless. We are grateful to James Siemon for assistance with the bibliography of this section.

Nature has done me a grievous wrong in denying me that
beauty of form which wins human love. Life owes me
reparation for this, and I will see that I get it. I have a right
to be an exception, to overstep those bounds by which
others let themselves be circumscribed. I may do wrong
myself, since wrong has been done to me.

(Freud, 4.322)

Looked at this way, Freud argued, the mystery of Richard's evil is
diminished: 'the appearance of wantonness vanishes, the bitter-
ness and minuteness with which Richard has depicted his
deformity make their full effect, and we clearly perceive the bond
of fellowship which constrains us to sympathy with the miscreant'
(4.322). In short, Freud saw the soliloquy as suggesting an understandable motive for Richard's behaviour, in contrast to the
'motiveless malignity' that Coleridge saw in Iago and in other
Shakespearean characters like him. Freud's reading of Richard
thus belongs to the Romantic tradition of character interpretation
represented by Bradley, who saw Iago's occasional mention of
motives as indicators of his humanity: 'if he really possessed no
moral sense, we should never have heard those soliloquies which
so clearly betray his uneasiness and his unconscious desire to
persuade himself that he has some excuse for the villainy he
contemplates' (A.C. Bradley, 234–5).

Perhaps because of Freud's influence, psychoanalytic interpretation of *3 Henry VI* has focused on Richard of Gloucester,
explaining his misogyny as a reaction to his mother and his nurse-
maids (Dayton), or arguing that he is a 'mimetic' character, not a
type, because of what Shakespeare shows about his psychological
depths (Paris, 'Richard III' and *Character*, 33–7). An exception
was Robert Ravich, who used the early plays to discern
Shakespeare's own state of mind, requiring yet another argument
regarding authorship, this one psychological (Ravich, 390).
Impressed by the 'powerful depiction of female vengeance' in
Margaret's torturing of York in 1.4, Ravich inferred that

'Shakespeare was deeply concerned with the possibility that a woman could drive a man insane' (395). He saw a similar situation in *Titus* and compared both to Venus's seduction of Adonis in *Venus and Adonis*, suggesting that the latter 'may have afforded Shakespeare an opportunity to express in poetic form his own feelings about being married at eighteen to a woman eight years older' (396).

A new turn in the argument was offered by Robert Watson, who followed Freud in analyzing the plays rather than their author but eschewed not only Freud's analysis of Richard but the whole method of character analysis itself: 'this book is not a psycho-analysis of individual ambitious characters, but rather a study of how Shakespeare uses the realistic psychological mechanisms of the characters in service of a larger, metapsychological commentary on the implications and consequences of self-transformation' (R. Watson, 4). Echoing Coleridge in mistrusting Richard's 'motive-hunting soliloquies', Watson cut the critical Gordian knot of Richard's physical disability (is it the cause or manifestation of his evil character?) by observing that 'Richard himself suggests his birth defects are both cause and symbol of his evil deeds' (15). To the Stoic and morality-play resonances of Richard's declaration, 'I am myself alone' (5.6.83), Watson added a Freudian insight: 'Such a declaration of autonomy verges on a claim to autogeny' (16). In Watson's view, Richard is the first of several Shakespearean characters who defy the patrilineal order and symbolically give birth to a new identity which is doomed to fail. In this canny reading, Richard's simile of hewing his way out of a thorny wood (3.2.174–81) becomes a metaphor of a Caesarean section performed by the foetus (R. Watson, 19–20).[1] Watson observed that 'Shakespeare saw metaphorically what Freud saw scientifically' (4), but it seems odd to invoke science to describe Freud's manifestly symbolic construction. It would be more

---

1 James Winny had offered a more traditional view: 'The thorny wood in which he [Richard] is lost is the nightmarish world of his own monstrously distorted and protesting humanity' (Winny, 29).

appropriate to say that both Shakespeare and Freud were perceptive poets of human nature, and that Freud's symbols often complement Shakespeare's, because Freud was an imaginative reader of Shakespeare and an incisive critic (a 'master of suspicion', to use Paul Ricoeur's phrase) of the Christian and patriarchal symbolic system that Shakespeare inherited.

Marjorie Garber's analysis of Richard returned to Freud's own analysis but not to make Freud's point. Noting that Freud explicated Shakespeare's Richard III because he could not address current case-histories 'for reasons which will be easily understood' (Freud, 4.321), Garber suggested that the case in question was Kaiser Wilhelm II, reigning in Germany at the time Freud wrote his essay, for the Kaiser had a withered left arm, and he compensated for his disability by aggression (Garber, 85). Her point was that Freud's use of Richard does just what Richard himself does in his soliloquies on his deformity: he 'provides a revealing narrative of the ways in which the line between the "psychological" and the "historical" is blurred' (85). She alluded to Watson's point about autogenesis (Garber, 85, 95), but her reason for doing so was again to psychologize the process of writing history, which in Richard's case foregrounds deformity, both in Richard's body and in narratives that distort (deform) the historical Richard: 'It is in the multiple narratives of birth that Richard comes most clearly to stand as an embodiment of the paradoxical temporality of history' (95). Garber thus offered the most sustained attempt to integrate Freudian insights with the generic history play in particular, though her emphasis on Richard's character resulted in a de-emphasis on *3 Henry VI* as a particular history play.

Richard's soliloquy in 3.2 was the focus of Janet Adelman's opening comments in her book-length psychoanalytic study of anti-feminism in Shakespeare's plays. She understood the passage as perhaps the first 'voice of a fully developed subjectivity' in Shakespeare (Adelman, 1), thus identifying, as we saw earlier, with the Romantic tradition of interpreting Richard's motives as if he were a real human being. Her reading of Richard's character omitted Freud's reading, as Watson's had done, and Adelman took issue with Watson's understanding of Richard's autogenesis, even as she acknowledged its force. 'Watson's account tends too easily to blur the distinction between matricide and patricide: in fantasies of rebirth, the hero may symbolically replace the father to recreate himself, but he often does so by means of an attack specifically on the maternal body' (Adelman, 239), and this attack is what interested Adelman in her introduction to a book on that subject. Referring to Richard's determined solipsism (5.6.83), Adelman remarked that Richard 'becomes himself alone by hewing and hacking his way through the maternal body and the matrix of relationships it engenders' (Adelman, 3).

NEW CRITICISM

Throughout the middle decades of the twentieth century, from the 1930s to the mid-1970s, *3 Henry VI* was affected by the dominant literary theory and critical practice called 'New Criticism', after John Crowe Ransom's book by that title, published in 1941. In reaction to literary history, New Criticism emphasized the aesthetic qualities of literary works in themselves, as words on a page, without reference to historical context, biography, literary sources, or theories other than New Criticism. W.K. Wimsatt thus called literary works 'verbal icons', emphasizing 'a verbal image which fully realizes its verbal capacities', both pictorially and as 'an interpretation of reality in its metaphoric and symbolic dimensions' (Wimsatt, x). Openly rejecting historical contextualization, Cleanth Brooks declared that it is 'heresy' 'to refer the structure of the poem . . . to something outside the poem' (Brooks, 184).

Though the movement gained its title from an American book, compatible ideas were expounded by F.R. Leavis at Cambridge and were published (on Shakespeare in particular) by G. Wilson Knight, a British scholar, critic and actor. Moreover, New Criticism of Shakespeare was given strong momentum by

Caroline Spurgeon, an American working in England, whose *Shakespeare's Imagery and What It Tells Us* was a model of, and inspiration for, the new method, and by Wolfgang Clemen, whose *Shakespeares Bilder*, published before World War II (1936), was reissued, much revised, in English in 1951.[1] Spurgeon was reluctant to define an image, 'because, however much one might discuss it, few people would entirely agree as to what constitutes an image, and still fewer as to what constitutes a poetic image' (Spurgeon, 8). Nonetheless she offered a broad description of 'image' as covering 'every kind of simile, as well as every kind of what is really compressed simile – metaphor' and 'as connoting any and every imaginative picture or other experience, drawn in every kind of way, which may have come to the poet, not only through any of his senses, but through his mind and emotions as well' (5). The breadth of this definition would prove to be problematic for New Critical claims, because it provided no interpretive limit and enabled readings which were incompatible with each other.[2]

Spurgeon noticed a pattern of 'iterative imagery' concerned with gardening in all the early history plays (*1 Henry VI* to *Richard II*) (Spurgeon, 216). She counted about a dozen instances in *3 Henry VI*, where 'the metaphor becomes more definite' (218). Other image patterns in *3 Henry VI* were 'the butcher and slaughter-house' (227), the symbolizing of Henry's enemies as 'lions, tigers, wolves and bears' (229), and 'an unusually large number of pictures of the sea and ships, more than in any other play' (230) (Fig. 13).

---

1 Clemen pointed out that the first study of Shakespeare's imagery was undertaken by Walter Whiter in *A Specimen of a Commentary on Shakespeare*, published in 1794 (Clemen, *Development*, 13). Whiter was influenced by Locke's notion of the association of ideas, and his 'discovery', as he called it, complements the 'scientific' model of late eighteenth-century editing, but his pioneering method languished until the twentieth century.

2 In a trenchant early critique of Spurgeon's book, Lillian Hornstein noted the variety of meanings attached to 'image' and argued that '*Image* must have a meaning and the same meaning to all who use the method' (Hornstein, 640).

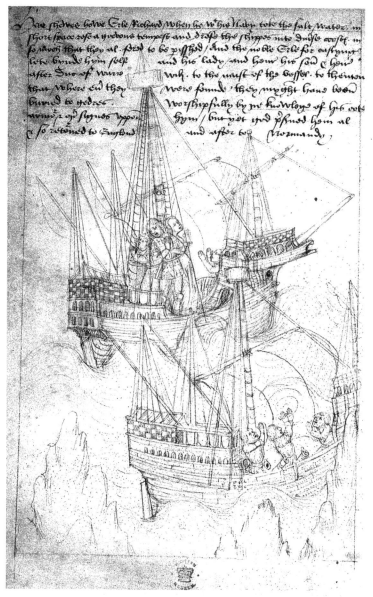

13 A storm at sea, often mentioned in *3 Henry VI*

Clemen was less interested in identifying and classifying the images Shakespeare used than in specifying where he used them, how they worked in that particular context, and how Shakespeare became increasingly artful in using them. In the *Henry VI* plays Clemen thus pointed out that images tend to cluster in monologues and when characters face death (Clemen, *Development*, 42–3). In the early histories Shakespeare also tends to elaborate the elements of his imagery, as when Henry VI uses the Icarus myth to describe the death of Prince Edward at Richard's hands:

> I, Daedalus, my poor boy, Icarus,
> Thy father, Minos, that denied our course;
> The sun that seared the wings of my sweet boy,
> Thy brother Edward; and thyself, the sea,
> Whose envious gulf did swallow up his life.
>
> (5.6.21–5; cited in Clemen, *Development*, 44)

As Shakespeare's imagery developed, Clemen argued, the playwright abandoned the obviousness of such elaboration in favour of understatement, subtlety and economy.

When later critics referred to images noticed by Spurgeon, they did not always acknowledge her precedent, but their omission was not necessarily deliberate, for the reading of images became so common that reinterpretations of the same imagery often seemed like first-time discoveries. Thus M.C. Bradbrook also discussed the garden imagery of *3 Henry VI*, but she defied New Critical orthodoxy by making historical comparisons to Edmund Dudley's *The Tree of Commonwealth* (1549) and the Jesse Tree of church windows (Bradbrook, 128–9). M.M. Reese alluded to garden imagery and predation imagery in the *Henry VI* plays (Reese, 173, 189), and he acknowledged Spurgeon when he mentioned 'the well-known image of storm and tempest' in *3 Henry VI* (190). His most original contribution to image study of *3 Henry VI* appeared in a footnote, where he described a pattern not noticed by Spurgeon:

In this play even the sun is the enemy of man. Instead of generating life, it parches and shrivels, dazzles the eye, breeds swarms of flies, attracts gnats, pierces at midday, sears, is clouded, brews a shower. Summer breeds no increase, but is associated with scalding heat, flames, fire, the parching of entrails.

(195, n. 1)[1]

Enumerating and interpreting imagery was not the only impact that New Criticism made on interpretation of *3 Henry VI*. The assumption behind image study was that the critic could discern implicit effects of the author's creative imagination, and the same assumption inclined critics to look for unifying patterns in a given play as a whole. What Spurgeon called 'iterative imagery' was an instance of this kind of pattern, but other kinds of patterns became the object of critical interest as well, and they inevitably yielded interpretations that assumed the unity or coherence of a given work. Though various deconstructive strategies have since rejected this assumption, it had the salutary effect of producing studies that took *3 Henry VI* seriously as a whole and separate play. In part, such studies reacted against analysis that extracted and interpreted characters apart from the play in which they appeared. 'Our duty as critics', L.C. Knights wrote, 'is to examine first the words of which the play is composed, then *the total effect* which this combination of words produces in our mind' (Knights, 7; our emphasis). This duty seemed self-evident to New Critics.

The effort to find unity and consistency in the *Henry VI* plays was given strong theoretical support by Hereward Price's seminal essay, 'Construction in Shakespeare'. Price traced the prejudice against Shakespeare's sense of formal coherence to the neo-classical judgement that Shakespeare 'artlessly' violated the dramatic 'unities'. A breakthrough came, Price argued, in Augustus Schlegel's observation of 'organical form', which 'is innate; it unfolds itself from within, and acquires its determination

---

1 For other enumerations of imagery in *3H6*, see Frey, 66; Kay; Brownlow, 50–7.

along with the complete development of the germ' (quoted in Price, 'Construction', 8), but Schlegel's point was missed by all but Coleridge. Price rejected contemporary historical contextualizing and the search for passages of lyrical beauty in the plays (10), because neither contributed to a sense of what Shakespeare was doing in a play as a whole. Price's debt to New Criticism (and his complementary contribution to it) is clear in his statement of what 'construction' in Shakespeare involved:

> Shakespeare's work is a strict intellectual construction developed from point to point until he brings us to the necessary and inevitable conclusion. He interrelates part to part, as well as every part to the whole. His inner idea is manifested in an action, with which it is intimately fused, so that the crises in the action which move us most deeply reveal at the same time most clearly the innermost core of Shakespeare's thought.
>
> (Price, 'Construction', 16–17)

Discovering an *implicit* design ('the innermost core of Shakespeare's thought') was also the goal of image hunters, and the notion that such a design characterized each play *as a whole* both derived from New Criticism of Shakespeare and was Price's most important contribution to it.

Where the *Henry VI* plays are concerned, Price offered an extended analysis of what he meant by 'construction' in *1 Henry VI* (Price, 'Construction', 24–36). Quoting W. Somerset Maugham that 'in a story as in a play, you must make up your mind what your point is and stick to it like grim death. That is just another way of saying that it must have form' (24), Price argued that the point Shakespeare sticks to in *1 Henry VI* is 'that discord follows the neglect of "specialty of rule"' (25). Without mentioning Tillyard, Price thus reiterated Tillyard's point about the Elizabethan regard for hierarchy (Tillyard, *History Plays*, 10–17), but he added to Tillyard the assumption of coherence in a given play, thus implicitly disagreeing with Tillyard's judgement that in

3 Henry VI 'Shakespeare had a great mass of chronicle matter to deal with and he failed to control it; or rather in paring it to manageable length he fails to make it significant' (Tillyard, *History Plays*, 190). Though Price himself offered no particular comments about organic form in *3 Henry VI*, he remarked in passing that 'Parts 2 and 3 are much better [than Part 1]' ('Construction', 37), thus inviting interpretation that would bear him out and refute Tillyard's negative appraisal of 'construction' in *3 Henry VI*.[1]

One of the most important contributions to the assumption of organic unity in the *Henry VI* plays was J.P. Brockbank's essay 'The Frame of Disorder: *Henry VI*'. Brockbank had written his doctoral thesis on the sources of the *Henry VI* plays, so he had no compunction about committing the New Critical 'heresy' of considering the chronicle context in his analysis of the three plays. Nonetheless, he asserted that Clifford's vengeful speech in *2 Henry VI*, 5.2.31–65, has an 'organic function in the plays' (Brockbank, 'Frame', 92), and he took his title from its opening lines:

> Shame and confusion! All is on the rout,
> Fear frames disorder, and disorder wounds
> Where it should guard.
> *(2 Henry VI, 5.2.31–3)*

'By not limiting the connotation of "disorder", "frame" and "confusion"', Brockbank argued, Shakespeare 'keeps the abstract force of the words and makes the image immense and the idea metaphysically reverberant' (91). In other words, Brockbank saw the three plays as united by their analysis of how political disorder affects a kingdom. While this judgement complemented Tillyard's notion of progressive chaos, with the outbreak in

---

1 Tillyard in turn reinforced the New Critical assumption of organic unity in his debate with Robert A. Law about the connections between one history play and another (Tillyard, *History Plays*, 264–5; Law, 'Links'; Tillyard, 'Cycle'; Law, 'Rejoinder'). The exchange helped to establish the authority of New Criticism of Shakespeare, even as it indicated the extent to which New Critical assumptions had taken hold.

3 Henry VI 'of civil war, the perpetration of one horrible deed after another' (Tillyard, *History Plays*, 188), Brockbank implicitly rejected Tillyard's providential thesis in favour of an emphasis on secondary causes:

> The plays of *Henry VI* are not, as it were, haunted by the ghost of Richard II, and the catastrophes of the civil wars are not laid to Bolingbroke's charge; the catastrophic virtue of Henry and the catastrophic evil of Richard are not an inescapable inheritance from the distant past but are generated by the happenings we are made to witness
>
> (Brockbank, 'Frame', 98)

Perhaps the most authoritative and influential New Critical interpretation of *3 Henry VI* appeared in Andrew Cairncross's edition of the play. Referring approvingly to Price's essay, Cairncross offered, in effect, a reading of 'construction' in *3 Henry VI* along the lines Price had offered for *1 Henry VI* (Ard[2], l–lxiv). Shakespeare solved his 'main dramatic problem – that of unity', Cairncross argued, both externally and internally (l–li). By external unity he meant the kind of coherence between all the *Henry VI* plays that Tillyard had argued for in his debate with Law. Shakespeare imposed internal unity on *3 Henry VI* itself by seizing 'the irreducible residue of disorder and chaos, the theme of disunity, and [using] it, with reinforcements of illustration and symbol, to create a unity of impression' (lii–liii). The theme of disunity appears in the state, the family and the individual, with most characters contributing to it through vicious self-interest, but Henry through political weakness (liii). Further 'unity of impression' (lv) is created by innumerable references to the past and by 'prophecies and curses that we know to predict events to come' (lvi). The latter create dramatic irony that 'is used consistently throughout as a typical reflection of the general theme' (lvii). Rejecting Romantic character analysis, as Knights had done, Cairncross argued that characterization subserves theme, so that characters are representative, rather than realistic:

they are almost Morality types . . . . They are so many
fragments in the chaos, ignorant and heedless of the general course of events as the wheel of Fortune turns and of
the consequences of their own actions, the victims of the
chain of revenge they have set in motion.

(Arden 2, *3 Henry VI*, lviii)

A 'pattern of alternation' also unifies the play, according to
Cairncross, whereby one party triumphs and then another, so that
'the very changes in the constantly changing situation are pressed
into the service of unity'. (Ard^2, lix)[1]

One of the hazards of thematic interpretation was repetition,
and this hazard increasingly inclined New Critics to reach for
innovation by seeking wider support than the text itself for
their analyses. Mark Rose's book *Shakespearean Design* seemed
to be inspired by Price's remark that 'We badly need a study of
Shakespeare's methods in the single scene' (Price,
'Construction', 21), and Rose acknowledged Price as a precedent to his own project (Rose, 4–6), but Rose integrated his
close reading of scenic construction with historical context,
arguing that the notion of structure held by 'the modern, "new
critical" approach to Shakespeare' was anachronistic (2), and
offering pre-Shakespearean parallels to the scenic design he
elaborated (3–4). In *3 Henry VI*, Rose cited the battle of
Towton to make his point. The 'scene' in question is actually
four scenes, he suggested, beginning with the Yorkists' rout
(2.3) and ending with that of the Lancastrians (2.6). 'The
sequence as a whole thus consists of two paired battle sequences
which frame the emblematic centerpiece' (Rose, 33). The
King's monologue and the scene with the bereaved Father and

---

1   In his doctoral thesis, Richard Henry Hawkins supplied a historical context for this
    alternation in *3H6* by relating it to the casting requirements of Elizabethan acting
    companies, as described in Bevington, *Mankind* (Hawkins). Once established, the
    New Critical method of looking for imagistic and thematic patterns quickly prolifer-
    ated, and numerous studies of this type appeared with *3H6* as their specific object,
    or at least as part of their object. See Berman; Bromley, 19–25; Gerould; Leggatt;
    Pierce, 76–82; Ricks, 83–97.

Son are 'emblematic' of the 'scene' as a whole and indeed 'of the entire play' (33), because they suggest that the meaningless existence of fluctuating fortune 'is not the end for which months and years were created. Nor were sons meant to kill fathers or fathers sons: this dual emblem defines the horror at the heart of civil war' (34). Despite Rose's disclaimer and his historical introduction, his mode and method of analysis were fundamentally New Critical.

The same is true of a book-length interpretive study of the *Henry VI* plays, Edward Berry's *Patterns of Decay*. Berry consistently integrated historical precedents and parallels into his study, but he identified it in New Critical terms as an 'extended argument for the dramatic integrity' of the first tetralogy, focusing on 'an underlying conception of historical process that provides each work with a thematic center and binds together the entire series' (E. Berry, ix). The theme of *3 Henry VI* is kinship, Berry argued: 'As a mode of action, a center of value, a measuring rod for the depredations of civil war, kinship, in virtually all its permutations and perversions, serves as the thematic center of the play' (57–8). Moreover, kinship takes its place in a pattern that characterizes the first tetralogy as a whole. Citing Cicero on 'the family unit as the bedrock of the state', Berry commented:

> In centering *3 Henry VI* on the concept of the family . . . , Shakespeare adapts a traditional conception of social structure to the theme of social devolution begun in Part I: chivalric community gives way to the narrower bonds of law, law to kinship, and kinship . . . to self-love.
>
> (E. Berry, 59)

Berry's book might well be described as the highwater mark of New Critical commentary on *3 Henry VI*. In elegant and precise language, Berry pointed to historical parallels, took other critics into account, such as Berman, Brockbank and Ricks, and offered an incisive reading of the play that sometimes made the same points others had made, but also took issue with them, and invariably did both in an eminently readable style.[1]

Though studies of imagery, theme and 'form' were the substance of New Criticism, this critical method also contributed to the debate about who wrote *3 Henry VI* by asserting Shakespeare's sole authorship. For if imagistic and thematic unity was a manifestation of organic imaginative processes, rather than an author's fully conscious intention, then such unity must be the product of a single creative mind, not of collaboration. As Karl Wentersdorf pointed out, 'It is precisely the predominantly subconscious nature of the processes leading to the evolution of a particular [image] cluster that makes this literary phenomenon valuable in questions of authorship' (Wentersdorf, 'Imagery', 257). A similar argument was made early on by Caroline Spurgeon, who devoted the first half of her book to 'The Revelation of the Man'. 'In the case of a poet', Spurgeon wrote, 'I suggest it is chiefly through his images that he, to some extent unconsciously, "gives himself away"' (Spurgeon, 4).

Hereward Price was equally certain that Shakespeare alone was capable of the kind of 'construction' Price identified. Those who assign different parts of the *Henry VI* plays to different dramatists on the basis of style 'never study Shakespeare's construction and yet they are continually denying that this or that part of a play is by Shakespeare' (Price, 'Construction', 37). To prove his point, Price offered a brief summary of 'construction' in *Titus Andronicus* (37–40), in order to refute John Dover Wilson's claim that the play was by several hands. 'By whatever test, then, you can apply', Price concluded, 'the exposition in *Titus* is Shakespeare's' (40). Cairncross did not address authorship in a separate section in his Arden 2 edition of *3 Henry VI*, but he repeated Price's argument in rejecting the position that the *Henry*

---

1 Despite the decline of interest in New Criticism in the course of the 1970s, some of its assumptions and methods persisted or reappeared in the close reading of poetry and attention to other formal qualities of a work (e.g., Kermode; McDonald). For essays of this sort dealing with *3H6*, see Candido; Hunt; Liebler.

VI plays are by multiple authors: 'even where Shakespeare was acknowledged as author [by other critics], though with reservations, the structural achievement and the dramatic purpose have seldom been adequately seen and appreciated' (Ard², xlix). Cairncross thus interpreted a perceived feature of the plays themselves (their thematic coherence) as evidence for an external fact about them, i.e. Shakespeare's authorship of them. Alvin Kernan compared the imagery in F *3 Henry VI* with that in O, and he noticed a remarkable falling off in the latter: not only does O have many fewer images, but they are also more conventional and less imaginative than in F. While Kernan made no explicit claim about authorship, he endorsed the theory of memorial construction for O, and he made comparative judgements, which strongly implied Shakespearean authorship for F: 'We may not appreciate obvious rhetoric today, but it is far less objectionable when handled by a master at the craft than when we find it in the debased form seen in the Q [i.e. O] passage' (Kernan, 439).

Despite widespread New Critical assumptions about authorship, they were no more effective in settling the question of who wrote *3 Henry VI* than any other analytical method. Lillian Hornstein strongly opposed Spurgeon's claim to be able to identify Shakespeare's personality behind his imagery: 'Miss Spurgeon's theory . . . is illogical and unsupported by the facts, in short, no more justified than the other biographical heresies which she herself dismisses' (Hornstein, 652). A debate between Karl Wentersdorf and Moody Prior concerning authorship and imagery was conducted over the course of almost twenty years and ended inconclusively.[1] Wentersdorf published the last word in this exchange in 1972, but no one replied. With the waning popularity of New Criticism and changing assumptions about the inspired genius of single authorship (see above, pp. 47–9), the question no longer appeared urgent or interesting enough to sustain debate in print.

1   Wentersdorf, 'Authenticity'; Prior, 'Imagery'; Wentersdorf, 'Imagery'.

The decline of New Criticism was hastened by Richard Levin's challenge to thematic criticism in particular.[1] Though he did not address *3 Henry VI*, Levin identified three kinds of logical error in thematic criticism of Renaissance drama in general that applies to criticism of *3 Henry VI* as well. First was circular reasoning in what he called 'the thematic assumption', when the critic assumes what is to be proved, i.e. that a given play has a unifying theme (Levin, *New*, 16–23). Second was 'the thematic leap', which 'is actually quite simple: it consists of seizing upon some particular components of the drama and making them the representatives or exemplars of a general class, which then becomes the subject of the play and of the critic's analysis' (23). One of the consequences of the thematic leap, Levin argued, was a competitive process of critical abstraction, whereby each successive critic of a given play proposed a theme of greater general abstraction than any previous theme and argued for this new candidate as the *real* meaning of the play (28–41). Finally, Levin pointed to another circular argument in thematic analysis: linking a given theme with 'structure'.

> The problem is not so much that the critic selects those facts of the play which support his thesis and passes over any which do not, but that the significance of the facts he does select has been defined in advance by the thesis they are intended to prove, for they present themselves to him, and so are presented to us, as representations of the central theme – as data already 'thematized'.
>
> (Levin, *New*, 41)

Levin's critique was not unassailable, but it came late in the vogue of New Criticism, thus manifesting a growing dissatisfaction with the method and responding to that dissatisfaction at the same time. Levin conceded that 'Some plays really are organized around a central theme and therefore require a thematic mode of

---

1 Levin's comments are cited here from his 1979 book, but his critique of thematic analysis had been published earlier, in a series of articles between 1972 and 1975.

analysis' (21), but he did not identify a way to distinguish such plays from those that are not thematic, in his view, and such a distinction is difficult to make for Renaissance drama, because it was still influenced by habits of personification allegory that had dominated English drama for two centuries before the advent of commercial theatres near London. In short, Levin emphasized logic at the expense of history, not only in dealing with plays themselves but in his dismissal of critics like Price, who incisively described the aesthetic assumptions of Renaissance drama as distinct from neo-classical assumptions. For Levin, Price was just another thematic critic:

> The author of a more general study entitled *Construction in Shakespeare* tells us that those who concentrate on the plot and emotional effects of the plays 'are far too narrow,' because 'they quite ignore design, the organization of parts with relation to an idea'.
>
> (Levin, *New*, 19)[1]

A particular kind of thematic interpretation, singled out for logical dismantling by Levin, made a considerable impact on *3 Henry VI*. Levin's description of it is characteristically wry, reductive and insightful:

> Critics pursuing this line are now revealing that play after play is actually about itself, since its real subject is the nature of poetry or drama or art in general; and thanks to their efforts, this growing field of reflexive thematics has recently been dignified with a name of its own: 'metadramatic criticism'.
>
> (Levin, *New*, 16)

---

1   Levin deleted the names and works of the critics he discussed, because he wanted to emphasize the similarities between them rather than the defects (as he saw them) of any particular essay. The result was reductive, however, because it failed to acknowledge differences between 1940 and 1970, and its homogenization of varied arguments understated the positive contributions of New Criticism and of thematic analysis in particular.

'Metatheatre' was a term coined by Lionel Abel and popularized by James Calderwood, who used 'metadrama' in the titles of three books he published on Shakespeare between 1971 and 1983. Abel offered more than thematic interpretation; he proposed a historical thesis about the change in consciousness associated with the Renaissance, and Levin again trumped history with logic by omitting this historical dimension. Still, Levin accurately identified the method of analysis, and much of his critique of thematic interpretation applied to metadramatic criticism.

The first contribution to what Levin called the 'field of reflexive thematics' was Anne Righter's *Shakespeare and the Idea of the Play*, a book that was even more historical than Abel's. Righter saw a distinction between Elizabethan drama, where 'the line dividing a world of shadows from reality came to separate the actors from their audience', and medieval drama, which 'drew its boundaries between a fragmentary, secular environment and the cosmos of the play' (Righter, 20), and she cited several fifteenth- and sixteenth-century plays to make her point. Tracing 'the play metaphor' through classical and medieval literature, she noted that 'this image of the world as a stage was associated almost entirely with non-dramatic literature' before the sixteenth century (65). The metaphor made the transition to the stage itself with the Vice, Righter argued (68), citing several morality plays in support (70–3). In a chapter on Shakespeare's early plays, she pointed to Warwick's response to the report of York's death in *3 Henry VI*:

> Why stand we like soft-hearted women here,
> Wailing our losses whiles the foe doth rage,
> And look upon, as if the tragedy
> Were played in jest by counterfeiting actors?
> (2.3.25–8)

Righter understood the allusion literally: 'all at once, the king-maker feels the unnaturalness of his own inaction. His momentary isolation from the battle which rages before him seems now to reflect an attitude more suited to the audience at a play' (92).

Increasingly, however, as Levin noted, critics read such passages thematically, i.e. they understood Shakespeare's plays to be about plays, and this is what Calderwood meant by 'metadrama':

> The more general argument of this book is that Shakespeare's plays are not only about the various moral, social, political, and other thematic issues with which critics have so long and quite properly been busy but also about Shakespeare's plays. Not just the 'idea of the play', as in Anne Righter's fine book of that title, but dramatic art itself – its media of language and theater, its generic forms and conventions, its relationship to truth and the social order – is a dominant Shakespearean theme, perhaps his most abiding subject.
>
> (Calderwood, 5)

Calderwood's own description of the method thus identified it as thematic and also distinguished it from Righter's study.[1]

The most rigorous metadramatic interpreter of *3 Henry VI* was John Blanpied, who focused attention on Henry's monologue during the battle of Towton. The monologue 'at first seems to contradict' the play's dominant view 'of a landscape abandoned by shaping consciousness', because the artful ornateness of Henry's speech seems so strongly opposed to the repetitive fluctuations and consequent shapelessness of the play as a whole (Blanpied, 66). Yet 'Henry's desire to escape the drama mires him in it; the radical incoherence of the war is a mirror image of his wish' (67). The first real relief we find from the 'exhausted drama of the war' in *3 Henry VI* is thus the emergence of Richard:

> My own view is that Shakespeare 'loses interest' volitionally – that is, willingly risks intelligibility in the interests of discovery. Thus from its own 'thorny woods' the play calls forth its own shaping consciousness. As the

---

1 For various applications of Calderwood's idea to *3H6* (whether influenced by him or not), see Bergeron; Neill; Van Laan, 130–7.

embodiment of disorder, Richard, in effect, is tempted into being.

(Blanpied, 70)

For Blanpied, Richard's hewing his way out of a thorny wood was an image neither of a foetal Caesarian section, as it was for Freudian critics, nor of 'getting loose', as it was for Joseph Candido, but of the artist discovering his own artistry:

> Though gruesomely distorted (he desperately toils, and hews with bloody axe), this is the dramatist we have been pursuing, who above all seeks through his woods to 'catch the English crown', meaning the symbolic appropriation of 'England' through her past.

(Blanpied, 72)

The effect of Richard's stunning force and style 'is that of self-creation, the first authentically new thing to occur in this dreamscape since York bespoke himself in the beginning of Part 2' (Blanpied, 70).

In effect, Blanpied thus interpreted *3 Henry VI* – and indeed all the history plays – as allegories of artistic creation. This is not to deny that they are 'about' history, but it is to assert that they are '*also* about' something besides history. Blanpied subscribed to Calderwood's term, 'duplexity', to describe this effect, which involves a combination of 'mimesis' and 'theatrics' (Blanpied, 254, n. 3). But history plays were not the only genre to feel the metadramatic interpreters' dissolving solution. As Richard Fly pointed out, 'Under the disenchanted gaze of the metadramatic critic, all of the plays may lose their distinctive generic features and become "metaphors for art"' (Fly, 134). This is the same observation that Richard Levin had made several years earlier about thematic interpretation in general: its tendency to seek for themes of ever greater abstract explanatory power ultimately seeks out the master theme that every play is 'really about', but if every play is 'really about' the same thing, then what value is the analytical method for the *distinctive* qualities of a given play?

14 Henry VI and Queen Margaret as a patroness of learning, being presented
with a book. Margaret founded Queens' College, Cambridge, in 1448. This
is the only contemporary portrait of her known to exist.

A late attempt to link metadramatic criticism with deconstruction is an example of keeping thematic thinking alive in a
changing critical world. Fly made the connection in the mid-
1980s, when deconstruction was dominant (131, 136). William
Hawley's later book-length study of the history plays interpreted
them in the light of 'critical hermeneutics', but his reading of *3
Henry VI* was metadramatic, despite his rejection of metadrama
as a 'monistic historiographical approach' (Hawley, 12). 'Theatre
is inherently well equipped to represent the complexities of
our historical being', he wrote in his introduction (13), and he

interpreted King Henry's 'primary fault' in *3 Henry VI* not as political but as 'artistic, stemming from his projection of exponential subjectivity in a theatrical world which even he fully comes to understand is anti-subjective' (52). Noting the 'theatrical mask' of the Dead Son in 2.5.97 ('The red rose and the white are on his face'), Hawley pointed out parallel facial imagery in *Venus and Adonis* and *The Rape of Lucrece*, where red denotes sexual passion, and white, chastity and virtue. But Hawley's point in the parallel was the theatrical effect: 'The bloody images of their faces, white walls with red marks, eclipse verbal signification in an unfolding world of theatricality' (48). Hawley's assertion that *3 Henry VI* 'openly inscribes its historiography in servitude to art' was metadramatic in all but name. His effort to fuse post-structuralist theory with metadramatic interpretation suggests that metadramatic criticism was really most at home with New Criticism, arising as it did in the 1960s and largely ceasing in the 1980s, when even Calderwood, its most enthusiastic practitioner and theoretician, moved on to other things.

PERFORMANCE CRITICISM

When thought of simply as commentary about plays in the theatre or on the screen, performance criticism is arguably the oldest form of Shakespearean criticism, since the first such commentary dates from 1592, as we noticed earlier (p. 6). As a form of modern critical interpretation with a distinctive label, however, performance criticism dates from the second half of the twentieth century, though at least one authority traces its origins to Harley Granville-Barker's *Prefaces to Shakespeare* (1927–74) and Muriel Bradbrook's *Elizabethan Stage Conventions* (1932) (Thompson, 16). Originally the point of such criticism was to illuminate a given playtext with reference to what we know about performing conditions at the time the play was first staged. Marvin and Ruth Thompson thus describe performance criticism as 'an approach that works toward defining a sense of the authentic' (15). This goal involves more than archaism: the reason for it is not only so 'we can judge any present-day performance for its appropriate authenticity' but also so 'we can better judge a performance for its "translation" into modern stage idiom' (15).

Some performance criticism conforms closely to the Thompsons' description. In discussing 'separated stage group-ings', for example, Charles Lower admonished editors to 'represent Shakespeare's drama as presentational art and, more specifically, as Elizabethan theatrical performance' (Lower, 55). Though Lower discussed an instance in *1 Henry VI*, a close par-allel occurs in *3 Henry VI*, even to the use of the same sexual *double entendre*: 'he shrives this woman to her smock' (*1H6* 1.2.119) and 'The ghostly father now hath done his shrift' (*3H6* 3.2.107). Lower's argument applies to both scenes: 'there is dra-matic necessity for some characters then on stage not hearing the dialogue involved' (Lower, 59), even though both parties' com-ments must be audible to the audience. His point was that editors need to edit with Elizabethan stage conditions in mind.

A model of the Thompsons' description was Bernard Beckerman's *Shakespeare at the Globe*. Taking a precisely defined set of plays (those performed at the Globe between its building in 1599 and the initiation of performances by the King's Men at the Blackfriars in 1608), Beckerman looked for common features in stage presentation in order to describe a distinctive dramaturgy at the time when the Globe was 'the only theater where [the Chamberlain-King's company] presented its plays in London' (Beckerman, ix). These limits necessarily ruled out *3 Henry VI*, which was performed at the Rose in 1592, but even if Beckerman had expanded his limits, it is not clear how substantially he would have added to criticism of *3 Henry VI*, since his method drew in part on other contemporary criticism whose contribution to *3 Henry VI* is well known. His 'premises for a study of Shakespearean dramatic form', for example, recalled Hereward Price's description of 'construction' in Shakespeare (Beckerman,

27–35). Beckerman did not refer to Price, but he contrasted 'Aristotelian causality' with 'organic structure' (31), as Price had done, and his description of non-linear structure (45–53), though more detailed than Price's, was based on similar assumptions.

Not all performance criticism fits the Thompsons' description, however. Peter Saccio used the production of *The Wars of the Roses* at the New Jersey Shakespeare Festival in 1983 to describe three reiterated features of *3 Henry VI* that are likely to appear in any production, because they arise from inherent demands of the action, quite apart from Elizabethan staging conditions. These features were 'the symmetrical arrangement of actors on stage, a pattern of repeated or parallel movement, and acts of killing' (Saccio, 'Images', 14). Among symmetrical groupings, Saccio mentioned the York brothers beholding '*Three suns . . . in the air*' (2.1.21 SD), the Towton interlude (2.5) and Edward's courtship of Lady Grey (3.2). Though Saccio confined his attention to the production he saw, his observation about symmetrical staging is supported by F's SD at TLN 2226–8 (4.1.7.1–3): '*Enter King Edward, Lady Grey, Penbrooke, Stafford, Hastings: foure stand on one side, and foure on the other*'. Instances of 'repeated parallel movement' in *3 Henry VI* include 3.2 and 3.3, where two ladies beg two kings for return of their husbands' lands, and numerous captures and escapes (the latter noticed at almost exactly the same time by Joseph Candido). As for acts of killing, Saccio discussed them in conjunction with battle scenes, noting that 'there is actually very little fighting in *3 Henry VI*', despite eleven scenes on the battlefield (18). 'My point is that atrocity has taken over from normal fighting to the extent that the latter is almost entirely excluded' (19). Saccio's careful attention to staging added critical insights to *3 Henry VI*, though his discussion, like Beckerman's, was influenced by other kinds of critical language, especially New Criticism (13, 19).

Performance criticism of *3 Henry VI* moved in a more deliberately postmodern – specifically New Historicist – direction in the analysis of Donald Watson. He discussed not only 'theatrical dimensions of the dramatic text' but also the theatricality of politics (D. Watson, 11–24), and the theatre as an institution (25–34): 'The connections among a play's theatricality, the culture's theatricality, and the theater's theatricality help to illuminate the problematic nature of the history plays' history' (12). In practice, Watson's analysis of *3 Henry VI* involved occasional references to modern performances (82, 83–4, 91–2) but otherwise offered a traditional reading of character (84–9) along with an argument that the play ritualizes atrocity: 'The transformation of murder and blasphemy into ritual increases [audience] anxiety, for the atrocities have been formalized and stylized into the ironic wit, elegant sarcasm, and sophisticated savagery of art and play' (93). In short, Watson offered performance criticism in focusing on audience response and referring to actual modern productions, but without attention to Beckerman's insistence that archaic scripts require attention to archaic staging. In discussing York's occupation of Henry's throne in 1.1, for example, Watson imagined the Yorkists 'scaling the balcony to occupy the visually superior position above the king who enters below, stage-directing their soldiers to take up their guard on the stage of politics' (82). But F's SD '*They goe vp*' (TLN 38) cannot refer to the balcony, as John Dover Wilson pointed out, because the dialogue allows no time for mounting the stairs, let alone for scaling the balcony (see 1.1.32n.). What the Yorkists 'go up' to must have been a throne (1.1.22, 26, 51) mounted on a movable platform – presumably the same platform that became the molehill on which York died, King Henry meditated during the battle of Towton and King Lewis sat to receive Margaret and Warwick. Repeated use of this platform in *3 Henry VI* would have ascribed a different semiotic value to it from the one Watson ascribed to the Yorkists on the balcony.

The most rigorously theorized discussion of *3 Henry VI*, from the point of view of performance criticism, was by Barbara Hodgdon, who used the term 'playtext' to describe the script, as distinct from 'performance text', or the theatrical performance of the script (Hodgdon, *End*, 18–19).[1] She used 'text' for both, because she was interested in the way history plays end, either in script or performance, and she argued that the end of a performance text is inherently different from the end of a playtext, because the theatrical context supplies meaning that the text cannot, especially at the conclusion of a history play. 'The king's a beggar, now the play is done' (*AW* Epilogue 1) is just the beginning of this kind of meaning in the theatre, as the common player who has been performing the role of nobleman steps forth to ask (or 'beg') for applause, but such meaning varies from one performance text to another, depending on the cultural context of the performance.

In keeping with her distinction between two kinds of 'text', Hodgdon divided her discussion of *3 Henry VI* into two, one concerning the playtext; the other, the performance text. The playtext ends, Hodgdon argued, with 'a number of signs associated with comic closure' (Hodgdon, *End*, 74) in the scene where Edward celebrates his family and his newly restored kingship. In the same scene, however, Richard's malevolent asides (5.7.21–5, 31–4) 'destabilize the comic signs that attempt to contain him' (76). Moreover, the end is anticipated in Richard's earlier sardonic soliloquy (3.2.124–95) (Hodgdon, *End*, 261, n.69), just as his killing of Henry is anticipated in his opening line of the play, when he displays Somerset's head and declares, 'Thus do I hope to shake King Henry's head' (1.1.20) (Hodgdon, *End*, 73). Most important, Richard belongs to a pattern in *3 Henry VI* that 'represents England's civil war as a conflict between patrilineal and matrilineal power' (69). Margaret is 'Joan's Amazonian apotheosis' (69), and Richard becomes Joan's 'antithetical double', relocating her witchcraft in his mother's womb (3.2.153–62), absorbing 'some of Margaret's (and Elizabeth's) more potentially threatening attributes' (71), and asserting his 'autogeny': 'I am myself alone'

---

1 For a useful discussion of Hodgdon's distinction, see Worthen (183–6), whose own distinction between text and performance suggests continuity with textual critics' distinction between 'text' and 'work' (Worthen, 1–43).

(5.6.83) (73–4). Hodgdon thus developed a feminist critique that took performance criticism of *3 Henry VI* in an entirely new direction.

The performance texts that Hodgdon considered were the RSC productions in 1963, 1977 and 1988, along with Michael Bogdanov's *Wars of the Roses* with the English Shakespeare Company. In each case she studied the performances themselves in order to see how their conclusion of the plays affected their meaning. In every case but Hands's, the three *Henry VI* plays were conflated into two plays, and this in itself profoundly affected the way they ended, especially when compared to the separate playtexts in F. John Barton's adaptation, for example, 'produced narrative and closural strategies more structurally and formally decisive than those of Shakespeare's originals' (Hodgdon, *End*, 77). Even Terry Hands's choice to stage the three plays separately and without *Richard III* involved 'representational choices for each close' that revealed 'the extent to which much more than "the text" is speaking' (82). Hodgdon's close attention to actual choices in modern performance texts of *3 Henry VI* involved more than theatre history; it was a substantially new way to understand 'the play'.[1]

FEMINIST CRITICISM

Until the last quarter of the twentieth century, feminism was a present absence in criticism of *3 Henry VI*, inferrable by the force it exerted, like the presence of planets around distant stars, while not perceivable in itself. Character critics, for example, who wrote at length about Henry and Richard (see pp. 68–81), had little or

---

1 Herbert Coursen's comments on Katie Mitchell's *3H6* at Stratford-upon-Avon in 1994 are really a review rather than performance criticism, since they offer a description of the production's opening moment, its particular strengths and at least one significant weakness (Coursen, *Shakespeare*, 156–60). Performance criticism makes its most distinctive claims when it describes how a production is both another 'text' and a substantial interpretation in itself.

nothing to say about Margaret of Anjou.[1] Yet Margaret is the only character who appears in all four plays of the tetralogy: she is courted by Suffolk as his mistress (and incidentally as Henry's Queen) at the end of *1 Henry VI*, becomes a major figure in English court politics in *2 Henry VI*, emerges as *de facto* head of the Lancastrian faction when war breaks out in *3 Henry VI*, and survives unhistorically to curse the successful Yorkists at the height of their power in *Richard III*.

The present absence of feminist critique is confirmed, where Margaret is concerned, by an early champion of her abilities, Thomas Heywood, Shakespeare's contemporary, who identified her as one of the nine female worthies of England, despite what he knew about her from Shakespeare's early history plays.[2] The mainstream opinion of Margaret, in contrast, started with Yorkist vilification of her in the fifteenth century and continued with the chroniclers, especially Polydore Vergil, who influenced Hall, Shakespeare's principal authority (P. Lee, 199–210). Shakespeare not only perpetuated the received view but reshaped and expanded it to emphasize Margaret's passionate affection (for Suffolk in *2 Henry VI*), dissimulation, strong will, determination, hot temper, cruelty and vengefulness.[3]

New Critics found a place for Margaret in the structure of the *Henry VI* plays (Matthews, 18–20; Ard² *1H6*, xlix). An exemplary and influential discussion of this kind was David Bevington's article on the 'the domineering female' in *1 Henry VI*. Noting that

1 Margaret does not appear in Mary Cowden Clarke's *Girlhood of Shakespeare's Heroines*, for example, though Clarke included characters whose roles are much slighter than Margaret's and whose girlhoods arguably offer less fruitful room for speculation.

2 Heywood's defence of Margaret was identified independently by Wright and by Williamson (43–4). Williamson noted that Heywood is unusual in being sympathetic to Joan la Pucelle as well (44), and that Peter LeMoyne's defence of both women was translated into English by the Marquess of Winchester in 1652 (57–8, n. 14). The seventeenth century thus saw a defence of Margaret that was overwhelmed thereafter by Shakespeare's point of view.

3 Gordon Zeefeld pointed out Shakespeare's debt to Hall in particular (Zeefeld, 337–8), and Thomas McNeal argued for the influence of Leir's wicked daughters from the old play *King Leir* (McNeal).

Talbot's confrontation with the Countess of Auvergne and Suffolk's courtship of Margaret are both Shakespeare's invention, Bevington argued that these episodes complement Joan la Pucelle's dallying with the Dauphin as statements of 'a unifying theme', creating 'structural integrity' in the play as a whole (Bevington, 'Domineering', 51). This theme is the usurpation of the man's place by the woman, appropriate to 'a play of disorder in which a main subtheme is the subjugation of reason by the flesh' (56).

Bevington's argument could be easily extended to *3 Henry VI*, where Margaret becomes most dominant in her relationship to Henry, exemplifying preposterous sexual inversion that signifies, as Richard does, the apocalyptic times of the later play (see above, pp. 75–81). Henry's uxoriousness in *1 Henry VI* reappears in *3 Henry VI*, when he declares that he follows Margaret into battle because he loves 'to go / Whither the Queen intends' (2.5.138–9). Little wonder that Richard later accuses Margaret of having 'stol'n the breech from Lancaster' (5.5.24). The symbolism of sexual inversion is typical of magical thinking; it reappeared, for example, in several of Jonson's anti-masques, where it served to magnify the patriarchal royal image by contrast. Margaret's cursing in *Richard III* is a relevant instance of magical language, closely related to the 'banning' of a witch like Goody Sawyer in *The Witch of Edmonton* some thirty years later. Richard calls Margaret a 'foul wrinkled witch' and 'hateful withered hag' (*R3* 1.3.164, 215). Alice Birney argued that Margaret's cursing makes her a proto-satirist, since it occurs 'at a point in literature at which magical curse and magical satire are still extremely difficult to differentiate' (Birney, 24).[1]

In short, Margaret is a type, and Bevington's 'domineering female' identified her type as well as any label has, but Richard and Henry are types as well, as we saw earlier, and that has not prevented critics as early as Johnson from interpreting them as

---

1   See also Aycock, 74–5; D.Willis, 190.

three-dimensional characters. Neglect of Margaret is all the more surprising in view of attention to Joan la Pucelle in *1 Henry VI*, who was the first character to attract feminist commentary, and who remains its principal object in the first tetralogy, though she appears briefly in only one play. Given this emphasis, the two principal women in *3 Henry VI*, Margaret and Lady Elizabeth Grey (Fig. 15), have been consistently seen as thematic adjuncts of Joan, even though many critics have believed that *1 Henry VI* is an afterthought to a 'two-part play' (i.e. *2* and *3 Henry VI* or whatever may lie behind them, as partially preserved in *The Contention* and *The True Tragedy*), and Joan would logically therefore be a thematic adjunct of Margaret, the dominant woman in *2* and *3 Henry VI*.[1]

Leslie Fiedler, who offered the first feminist critique of the *Henry VI* plays, identified Margaret as, 'in some real sense, Joan's successor', and he cannily noted that Joan blames Margaret's father for the pregnancy she claims in defence of her life: 'given a few more months, another act, Joan might have borne a half sister to Margaret, who succeeds her on stage as "the English scourge"' (Fiedler, 48). Fiedler thought Joan and Margaret were both manifestations of Shakespeare's own 'queasiness before the sexuality of women' (52), and Marilyn French similarly identified a 'disease' in Shakespeare 'with the sexuality supposedly incarnate in women', which 'grew, as he aged, into a terrified loathing' (M. French, 31). French adopted a binary scheme (hence her title, *Shakespeare's Division of Experience*), based on the opposed poles of feminine and masculine and their paradigmatic activities, 'giving birth and murder', which 'represent actions which cannot be changed although they can be concealed. They are in this sense absolutely true' (36).[2] 'Margaret takes over the role Joan plays', French argued, and

---

1 Liebler and Shea argue that Joan, Eleanor of Gloucester, and Queen Elizabeth are complementary foils to Margaret in each of the *Henry VI* plays, respectively, as Margaret moves successively through the stages of Jung's archetypal life cycle.

2 French's binary scheme had the paradoxical effect of preventing a conception of Margaret as a character, rather than (or in addition to) a type: 'Because the two gender principles occupy different conceptual realms – the human and ethical versus the type and the mythical – they cannot be synthesized' (M. French, 29).

15 Lady Elizabeth Grey (afterwards Queen Elizabeth), from the collection of Queens' College, Cambridge, which Elizabeth refounded in 1465

The implication – even young women who appear 'inlaw' are not to be trusted – is evident. And this scene [between Suffolk and Margaret] is in turn paralleled by *3 Henry VI*, III, ii, in which Elizabeth Grey appears, acting as virtuous and modest as Margaret had earlier, aware of her place in a way Edward is not.

(M. French, 49)

Coppélia Kahn, in contrast, thought that Shakespeare 'objects to the extreme polarization of the sex roles and the contradiction underlying it' (Kahn, 12), and she acknowledged Bevington's reading of the 'domineering female' while arguing that 'the traditional categories of male and female roles' are 'projections of male anxieties, consciously presented as such by Shakespeare' (55, n. 11). Similarly, she acknowledged Fiedler but disagreed that

> Shakespeare shares the misogyny of his characters; I see Shakespeare, rather, as criticizing a patriarchal world that bases the social order and the masculine identity on a destructively narrow and brittle foundation of identification with the father to the exclusion or repression of identification with the mother.

(Kahn, 55, n. 12)

Given her focus on masculine identity, Kahn had little to say about female characters, but she noted the association with supernatural power on the part of dominant women in *1 Henry VI*, adding that 'only Lady Elizabeth Grey in Part 3 has no associations with the demonic' (55).[1]

Despite comparative neglect of Margaret as a character, she is arguably as complex as Richard and Henry. One moment that exceeds the bounds of Margaret's type in *3 Henry VI* is her lament for her dead son, as she holds him in her arms:

---

1   That Margaret in *3H6* is an adjunct of Joan la Pucelle in *1H6*, rather than the other way around, has been argued by critics who otherwise began with different assumptions. See Hawley, 26; Hodgdon, *End*, 69; G. Jackson; Marcus, 66–89; Pitt, 150–7.

O Ned, sweet Ned, speak to thy mother, boy.
Canst thou not speak? O traitors, murderers!
They that stabbed Caesar shed no blood at all,
Did not offend, nor were not worthy blame,
If this foul deed were by to equal it.
He was a man; this, in respect, a child,
And men ne'er spend their fury on a child.
What's worse than murderer, that I may name it?
No, no, my heart will burst an if I speak –
And I will speak, that so my heart may burst.
Butchers and villains! Bloody cannibals!
How sweet a plant have you untimely cropped!
You have no children, butchers; if you had,
The thought of them would have stirred up remorse.
But if you ever chance to have a child,
Look in his youth to have him so cut off
As, deathsmen, you have rid this sweet young Prince!
                                        (5.5.51–67)

The stage configuration is a *pietà* (see Fig. 3, p. 20), anticipated not only by Mary's holding her dead son in her lap in the N–Town cycle but also by features of the medieval *planctus Mariae*, including the adjective 'sweet' and repetition of the beloved son's name (Woolf, 263–6). Such reminiscences of the mystery plays in *3 Henry VI* are neither blasphemous nor satirical. They parallel reminiscences of the crucifixion in the death of York in 1.4; (cf. Cox, *Shakespeare*, 95–6), and of the passion in the arrest, trial and execution of Gloucester in *2 Henry VI* (E. Jones, 35–54). In other words, Margaret's lament for her son is another example of Shakespeare's secularizing stage tradition by using an element from the dramatic history of salvation for its emotional effect while displacing it literally from its narrative and moral context. No one can think of Margaret merely as a domineering female while she laments for her young son, just as it is impossible to think of York as a Machiavellian power-seeker while Margaret is

146

torturing him.[1] Indeed, Margaret's cruelty generates so much sympathy for York that his diatribe against her gains credibility as a consequence, and critics have repeatedly cited it as evidence of Margaret's type: 'She-wolf of France', 'Amazonian trull', 'thy face is vizard-like, unchanging, / Made impudent with use of evil deeds', 'tiger's heart wrapped in a woman's hide' (1.4.111, 114, 116–17, 137). Margaret may indeed be all these things in 1.4, but she is very different in 5.5.

A description of Margaret's character might well connect her passionate lament for her son with her passionate affection for Suffolk in *2 Henry VI* 1.3. As Honor Matthews pointed out, Margaret anticipates Juliet in the first of these scenes, and it is 'the first passionate love-scene Shakespeare wrote', containing 'the rhythms of true grief and of true love' (Matthews, 18). 'Hot-tempered' is one way to describe Margaret, but 'passionate' has a different connotation, and her youth in *1 Henry VI* is not mentioned by critics who find her no more than a scheming seductress in the scene with Suffolk (she was sixteen when she married Henry in 1445). Her verbal facility is evident in all four plays, but to condemn her as a 'railer', as the York brothers do, is to perpetuate the misogynistic response to women who speak out in the presence of men. She also becomes increasingly determined, ambitious, politically crafty and warlike, but Margaret is blamed for these traits simply because she is a woman. They are not cited as detracting qualities of the many males who manifest them in the first tetralogy; indeed, Henry is sometimes blamed for lacking them. 'Women are soft, mild, pitiful and flexible; / Thou stern, obdurate, flinty, rough, remorseless', York complains to Margaret (*3H6* 1.4.141–2). This would seem to be less credible as a universal description of gender difference than as an expression of male fear and resentment of female boldness. Moreover, Margaret's strength may well be a compensation for her husband's weakness, rather than a cause or symbolic

---

1   Willis notes that York's and Margaret's speeches are linked by the accusation of cannibalism against their respective enemies (1.4.152 and 5.5.61) (D.Willis, 191).

symptom of political chaos.[1] There is still, it appears, much to be said on behalf of Margaret.[2]

THE TEXTS OF *THE TRUE TRAGEDY* AND *3 HENRY VI*

When we ask what sort of manuscript was handed to the Folio printer . . . we enter an altogether different field of criticism, a misty region of Weir, a land of shadowy shapes and melting outlines, where not even the most patient inquiry and the most penetrating analysis can hope to arrive at any but tentative and proximate conclusions.

Sir Walter Greg

With their seemingly contentious, chiastic titles, the Octavo text of 1595, *The true Tragedy of Richard Duke of York, and the death of good King Henry the Sixth*, and the Folio text of 1623, *The third Part of Henry the Sixth, with the death of the Duke of York*, call out for our divided attention. This edition includes both textual versions: a modernized, fully annotated text based on the Folio version, *3 Henry VI*,[3] and a reduced photographic facsimile of the Bodleian Library's unique copy of the Octavo, *The True Tragedy* (Appendix 1).[4] Although the plots are identical in the two

---

1   This is an open question historically as well: 'It is interesting to speculate about the pattern of Margaret's life and the fate of her reputation had she married a different kind of man' (P. Lee, 187).

2   Levine, 87–96, and Norvell have said a little already, in rare analyses of Margaret's character in *3H6*, but aside from Liebler and Shea's Jungian interpretation, no one has undertaken a study of Margaret as a continuous character (rather than a type) in all four plays of the first tetralogy, from a beautiful and youthful but impoverished princess to an aged, embittered and defeated queen.

3   In editing the Folio we have made judicious use of the Octavo. See especially 2.1.130, 2.6.8, and the SDs at 1.1.0.3, 1.4.60.1, 2.4.0.1–2, 2.4.11, 2.5.113, 2.5.122, 2.6.0.1–2, 3.1.12.1, 5.1.81, 5.1.82, 5.5.5, 5.5.6.

4   We use the short title *The True Tragedy* for the Octavo version and *3 Henry VI* for the Folio. The Oxford Shakespeare *Complete Works* adopted *Richard Duke of York* for both the Octavo and Folio versions of the play, an alternative that does have the advantage of distinguishing the Shakespearean text(s) from the anonymous play *The True Tragedy of Richard III* (1594).

versions, the Folio includes nearly a thousand lines that are not in the Octavo, and there are hundreds of minor variants between the two texts.[1]

Recent editors of the play have maintained that F was set directly from Shakespeare's original manuscript and that O represents a memorially reconstructed version of that original. We will present evidence that challenges both of these hypotheses – suggesting that O may not necessarily be a derivative text and that F may not have been set up from authorial 'foul papers' – but want to make it clear at the outset that we consider these conclusions tentative and proximate. Moreover, we realize that printing O in its entirety behind the modernized F version at once asserts and denies its status as a significant Shakespearean play. It is, we believe, a complete and internally consistent play, and deserves to be read as such. Nevertheless, its reduced size, its position behind the Folio text and its lack of independent commentary serve as reminders that it is considered at best a crookbacked prodigy, unable to stand on its own merits yet impossible to dismiss.

O (1595)

The Octavo (O)[2] was printed by Peter Short for the publisher Thomas Millington in 1595 with the following title-page:

> The true Tragedie of Richard | *Duke of Yorke, and the death of* | good King Henrie the Sixt, | *with the whole contention betweene* | the two Houses Lancaster | and Yorke, as it was sundrie times | acted by the Right Honoura- | ble the Earle of Pem- | brooke his seruants. | [ornament] | Printed at London by P. S. for Thomas Milling- | *ton, and are to be sold at his shoppe vnder* | *Saint Peters Church in* | *Cornwal.* 1595.

---

1   The Octavo runs to 2,313 total lines and the Folio to 3,217.
2   The Octavo is frequently denied its bibliographical identity by those who find 'quarto' a more convenient term. We trust that readers will not have difficulty with the designations O for the 1595 first edition, Q2 for the 1600 second edition, and Q3 for the 1619 third edition.

The speech prefixes are indented in the first part of the Octavo (quires A–B and the first five pages of the outer forme of sheet C) but are unindented throughout the remainder of the text (C5^v–E), suggesting that a compositor change took place midway through the setting of the outer forme of sheet C. The original price for a copy of the unbound Octavo was apparently eight pence (F. Johnson, 109). In the previous year, Millington had published *The First Part of the Contention betwixt the two famous Houses of Yorke and Lancaster, with the death of the good Duke Humphrey* (1594), a version of *2 Henry VI*. *The Contention* and *The True Tragedy* were part of a wave of twenty-seven play quartos printed between December 1593 and May 1595. A.W. Pollard argued that, given that the theatres had been closed because of the plague of 1592–3, the unemployed players were motivated by financial hardship to sell their manuscripts during this period (Pollard, *Folios*, 9). Peter W.M. Blayney has suggested that, since most of these quartos were, in fact, published *after* the theatres reopened, acting companies may have been prompted to flood the market with printed plays as a means of advertising the reopening and generating renewed interest in the stage after a two-year lull (Blayney, 'Publication', 386).

Millington secured his copy rights to *The Contention* by entering the play in the Stationers' Register on 12 March 1594: 'Entred for his copie . . . a booke intituled, the firste p*ar*te of the Contention of the twoo famous houses of york and Lancaster'. Some editors assume that this entry covered *The True Tragedy* as well, but others point out that the language refers specifically to the first part of *The Contention*. The absence of a separate entry for *The True Tragedy* has occasioned speculation that Millington acquired the text surreptitiously and was attempting to hide his piracy (even though he put his name on the title-pages of O and Q2). However, entrance in the Stationers' Register was an optional procedure that protected a publisher's rights. Blayney has observed that roughly a third of the books published in the period were not registered and that the absence of an entry in the

Stationers' Register 'is *never* sufficient reason for suspecting anything furtive, dishonest, or illegal' ('Publication', 404).

Q2 (1600)

A second edition – this time published in quarto format and so
designated Q2 – was printed for Millington by William White in
1600:

> THE | True Tragedie of | Richarde Duke of | Yorke, and
> the death of good | King Henrie the sixt: | VVith the
> whole contention betweene the two | Houses, Lancaster
> and Yorke; as it was | sundry times acted by the Right |
> Honourable the Earle | of Pembrooke his | seruantes. |
> [ornament] | Printed at Londou by *W.W.* for *Thomas
> Millington*, | and are to be sold at his shoppe vnder Saint
> | Peters Church in Cornewall. | 1600.

In this same year, Millington published Q2 of *The Contention* and
Q1 *Henry V*. The reference to the events of the *Henry VI* plays in
the epilogue to *Henry V* ('Which oft our stage hath shown') may
allude to a recent revival of the earlier plays on stage which might
have occasioned a revival of interest in the printed texts as well.

Previous editors have assumed that Q2 is an exact reprint of O,
but it is not. Dozens of irregularly divided verse lines in O are
relined in Q2; in some passages every line is changed to form a
perfect pentameter:[1]

> By Gods great mercies am *I* brought
> Againe, *Clarence* and *VVarwike* doe you
> Keepe the crowne, and gouerne and protect
> My realme in peace, and I will spend the
> Remnant of my daies, to sinnes rebuke
> And my Creators praise.
>
> (O sig. D8^r)

---

1   In one instance, Q2 adds words to fill out a metrically defective line in O: 'Ah
Warwike? should we report' (O sig. B4^{v}7) becomes 'Ah gentle *VVarwicke*, should we
but reporte' (Q2 sig. C1^{v}36).

151

By Gods great mercies am I brought againe:
Clarence and *Warwicke* do you keepe the Crowne,
And gouerne and protect my Realme in peace,
And I will spend the Remnant of my dayes,
To sinnes rebuke, and my creators prayse.

(Q2 sig. G1ᵛ)

Editors, of course, have emended the lineation of Shakespeare's
early printed texts since the beginning of the eighteenth century,
and mislineation remains today a much-debated area of editorial
theory (see Werstine, 'Line division'; Bowers). The fact that the
Q2 publisher/printer went to the trouble of recovering the submerged verse in O reveals that as early as 1600 mislineation was
thought to be a blemish on the O text that needed to be corrected.

Q3 (1619)

On 19 April 1602, Millington transferred his copy rights in '[t]he
first and Second *pa*rte of henry the vjᵗ ij bookes' to Thomas Pavier
who, in 1619, commissioned William Jaggard to reprint *The First
Part of the Contention* and *The True Tragedy* under the combined
title:

> THE | Whole Contention | betweene the two Famous |
> Houses, LANCASTER and | YORKE. | *With the Tragicall
> ends of the good Duke* | Humfrey, Richard Duke of Yorke,
> | *and King Henrie the* | *sixt.* | Diuided into two Parts:
> And newly corrected and | enlarged. Written by *William
> Shake-* | *speare,* Gent. | [ornament] | Printed at
> LONDON, for T.P.

This was the first printed text to attribute the plays to
Shakespeare. Greg's *Bibliography of English Printed Drama* classi-
fied Q3 as a reprint of O rather than Q2 (Greg, *BEPDR*, 1.223),
and no subsequent editor has questioned this identification.
However, we have found thirty-two places where Q3 follows the

lineation of Q2 rather than that of O.[1] Although one might argue that the controlling intelligence behind Q3 independently arrived at these identical relineations, the simpler explanation may be that Q3 was printed from an exemplar of Q2.

In 1619, Jaggard also reprinted for Pavier Q3 *Pericles*, Q2 *The Merry Wives of Windsor*, Q2 *The Merchant of Venice*, Q2 *A Midsummer Night's Dream*, Q2 *King Lear* and Q3 *Henry V* as well as two plays misattributed to Shakespeare, Q2 *A Yorkshire Tragedy* and Q2 *The First Part of Sir John Oldcastle* – now known as the 'Pavier Quartos'. The supposition that these individual quartos were intended to be bound together to form a collection of Shakespeare's plays is encouraged by the signatures, which are continuous from *The Whole Contention* through *Pericles*, and by the existence of several collections of the Pavier Quartos bound as single volumes.[2] Gerald Johnson has suggested that, given that Shakespeare's histories were the most popular of his plays in print in the early seventeenth century (*Richard II*, *Richard III* and *1 Henry IV* were each reprinted five times between the years 1597 and 1615), Pavier 'evidently viewed *The Whole Contention* as the sales leader for a more extensive collection' (G. Johnson, 37).

The King's Men apparently heard about Pavier's planned collection and invoked the protection of authority. On 3 May 1619, the Court of the Stationers' Company had before it a letter from the Lord Chamberlain, whereupon it was ordered that 'no playes that his Ma^tyes players do play shalbe printed w^thout consent of somme of them' (W.A. Jackson, 110). It seems that press work was already completed on three or four of Pavier's texts, which are correctly dated '1619', but the question was what to do with the plays yet to be printed. Greg suggested that since:

---

1   See Q3 lines I1^v3–4, I1^v21–2, I3^r20–1, K2^v32–3, K4^v14–15, N1^r18, N4^v22, O1^r25–6, O3^r20–2, O4^v6–8, P2^r2–6, Q2^r3–4, Q2^v19, Q3^r6–7, Q4^v2–3.

2   The Folger Shakespeare Library owns a set of the Pavier Quartos in which the ten plays are bound together in a single volume; another Folger bound set is missing *King Lear* but includes a note from the borrower apologizing for its absence; the Garrick copies in the British Library were also once bound together as were Capell's copies in the Trinity College Cambridge library. We are grateful to Richard Proudfoot for drawing these to our attention.

it was no longer safe to put the current date on the titles
. . . it was decided that the dates on the titles should be
those of the editions that were being reprinted, so that if
necessary the reprints could be passed off as copies of the
same, or at any rate as twin editions of the same date.

(Greg, *First Folio*, 16)

Thus, Pavier's quartos of *The Merchant of Venice*, *A Midsummer Night's Dream* and *Sir John Oldcastle* were dated '1600', and *King Lear* was dated '1608'; the title-page of *Henry V*, apparently printed immediately after that for *King Lear*, was mistakenly dated '1608' as well.

Although the dates on five of Pavier's ten reprints are indeed fraudulent, it is important to bear in mind that Pavier owned the legitimate copy rights to print both *The Contention* and *The True Tragedy*. There is no evidence to support Pollard's assertion that in printing Q3 Pavier committed 'fraud' (*Folios*, 114). But a cloud continues to hang over the Pavier Quartos, and textual scholars have tended to dismiss Q3 as merely 'the unauthorized 1619 Pavier reprint' (*TxC*, 111). Andrew Cairncross even accuses Q3 of false advertising, asserting that it is 'unjustifiably claimed on the title-page to be "newly corrected and enlarged"' (Ard[2], xiii). In fact, the title-page's claim is demonstrably justifiable: Q3 corrects Q1 of *The Contention* in specific details of the Duke of York's notoriously incorrect genealogy (see Ard[3] *2H6*, 123–4), adds eleven new lines to *The Contention* and one to *The True Tragedy*, and introduces nearly three hundred substantive variants. As Greg observed, 'what is interesting and possibly significant is the fact that even in this earliest and abortive collection of Shakespeare's plays some attempt was made to edit the text' (Greg, *Editorial Problem*, 34). McKerrow concluded that 'it is evident that these alterations are not merely proof-readers' corrections, but represent fresh authority' (McKerrow, '*Henry VI*', 157); more recent editors, however, have argued that 'the Q3 editor had reference to no authority other than his own imagination' (*TxC*, 198; see also Cam[2], 201).

Q3 of *The True Tragedy* includes two necessary stage directions that are missing from the earlier editions: '*Enter a Messenger*' (sig. K4ᵛ27) and '*Exit Mes.*' (sig. O1ᵛ7). An entrance for Richard of Gloucester, missing from a group entrance direction in O/Q2, is added in Q3 (sig. Q4ʳ5). The narrative stage direction 'the *Queene* is taken, & the prince, & *Oxf. & Sum.*' (O sig. E4ʳ30) is expanded and rewritten: '*the Queene, Prince, Oxford, and Somerset are taken*' (Q3 sig. Q1ᵛ21–2). In certain passages, the dialogue in Q3 differs markedly from that in O/Q2:

> For I will buz abroad such prophesies,
> As *Edward* shall be fearefull of his life,
> And then to purge his feare, Ile be thy death.
> *Henry* and his sonne are gone, thou *Clarence* next,
> And by one and one I will dispatch the rest
>
> (O sig. E7ʳ5–9)

> For I will buz abroad such Prophesies,
> Vnder pretence of outward seeming ill,
> As Edward shall be fearfull of his life,
> And then to purge his feare, Ile be thy death.
> King *Henry*, and the Prince his sonne are gone,
> And *Clarence* thou art next must follow them,
> So by one and one dispatching all the rest,
>
> (Q3 sig. Q3ᵛ31–7)

The editors of the Oxford *Complete Works* suggest that the Q3 compositor inaccurately cast off his copy, found himself two lines short at the end of Q3ᵛ, and so padded out his text with some wholly invented words to fill the space (*TxC*, 205). Given that the page following Q3ᵛ was still to be set, we wonder why the compositor would have employed these expedient measures at this juncture rather than waiting to see how much space-filling would be needed when he reached the end of the next page, Q4ʳ, the last of the inner forme (Q4ᵛ would presumably already have been set into type as part of the outer forme). The Oxford editors claim that the compositor did indeed encounter:

a similar problem at the bottom of the next page, the last in the forme, where he found it necessary to expand O's '*Clarence* and *Gloster*, loue my louelie | Queene' . . . to 'Brothers of Clarence and of Gloster, | Pray loue my louely Queene' [Q3 fol. Q4r].

(*TxC*, 205)

Although Q3 here includes a few words not found in O, the number of lines of text does not change; so, in this instance, the expansion can have had nothing to do with problems of casting off.

F1 (1623)

An understanding of the agent and authority behind the Q3 variant readings is of some importance because of certain links between the Q3 text and the version of the play that appeared four years later in the Shakespeare First Folio (1623) under the title

The third Part of Henry the Sixt, | vvith the death of the Duke of | YORKE

The play occupies pages 147–72 of the Histories section of the Folio, signatures o4^r–q4^v. The running titles on signatures o4^r–o6^v read *The third Part of Henry the Sixt* – the formula used in *Parts 1* and *2* – whereas those on signatures p1^r–q4^v read *The third Part of King Henry the Sixt*; Charlton Hinman demonstrated that after printing the first six pages of *3 Henry VI* (quire o), the Folio printers stopped work on the play in order to print the final nine pages of *Richard II* as well as the entire texts of *1 Henry IV* and *2 Henry IV* before returning to *3 Henry VI*. The play was set into type by two compositors (Hinman, 2.68–72, 108–17). Compositor A set quire o4–o6^r (Folio pages 147–52, corresponding to 1.1.1–2.1.75 in this edition), p4^r–p5^r (pp. 159–61, 3.2.2–3.3.151), p6^r–p6^r (pp. 163–4, 4.1.5–4.3.40), and q1^r–q3^r (pp. 166–70, 4.6.16–5.5.43). Compositor B was responsible for p1^r–p3^r (pp. 153–8, 2.1.76–3.2.1), p5^r (p. 162, 3.3.152–4.1.4), q1^r (p. 165,

4.3.41–4.6.15), and q4^r–q4^v (pp. 171–2, 5.5.44–5.7.46). A number of press variants affecting the text occur on the last page (see textual notes for 5.7, and Hinman, 1.275–6).

F1 and Q3 were both printed in the shop of William Jaggard and both were set into type, in part, by the same compositor (Blayney, 'Compositor B'). Although there are innumerable differences between the two versions, F1 and Q3 frequently agree against O and Q2 in small verbal details.[1] Greg noted that Q3's readings 'occasionally anticipate F' but dismissed most of these as 'chance coincidences arising through obvious emendation, normalization, and the like' (Greg, *Editorial Problem*, 133). But certain instances, such as 5.6.90 where F1 appears to follow the Q3 variants verbatim,[2] provocatively suggest that Q3 may have been used in some way by the Folio compositors.

Early English compositors had an absolute preference for printed copy over manuscript copy; Joseph Moxon's *Mechanic Exercises on the Whole Art of Printing* (1683) reveals that '*Printed Copy . . . is by Compositers* call'd *Good Copy, Light, Easie Work*', whereas '*Written Copy . . .* they call *Bad, Heavy, Hard Work*' (Moxon, 203). This preference apparently held true even when the printed copy was heavily annotated and corrected. In a seminal study of early modern printers' copy, J.K. Moore observes that 'despite the cramped pages that resulted, the printer may have asked for annotated copy because the ease of working from type would have compensated for slowness in setting manuscript additions and because a corrected copy also eliminated decisions about design' (Moore, 31).

1   Heauen (F, Q3) heauens (O, Q2); 1.1.78 my (F, Q3) mine (O, Q2); 1.1.196 an (F, Q3) thine (O, Q2); 2.2.46 ill (F, Q3) euill (O, Q2); 2.2.62 Lesson; (F, Q3) lesson boy, (O, Q2); 2.2.105 fly (F, Q3) flee (O, Q2); 2.2.107 droue (F, Q3) that droue (O, Q2); 2.6.24 out (F, Q3) our (O, Q2); 3.2.183 that which (F, Q3) that that (O, Q2); 3.3.233 SD *Exit Post* (F, Q3 *Exit Mes.*) (not in O, Q2); 3.3.243 Wedlocke (F, Q3) wedlockes (O, Q2); 4.1.22 pittie (F, Q3) a pittie (O, Q2); 4.1.29 mine (F, Q3) my (O, Q2); 4.1.47 Lord (F, Q3) the Lord (O, Q2); 4.1.135 neere (F, Q3) nearest (O, Q2); 5.1.75 if (F, Q3) and (O, Q2); 5.7.21 if (F, Q3) and (O, Q2).
2   O: '*Henry* and his sonne are gone, thou *Clarence* next' (sig. E7r8)
    Q3: 'King *Henry*, and the Prince his sonne are gone' (sig. Q3v35)
    F1: 'King *Henry*, and the Prince his Son are gone' (TLN 3165)

Perhaps as many as a third of the plays in the Shakespeare First Folio may have been set up from earlier printed quartos that had been annotated to varying extents; annotated copies of Jaggard's 1619 Pavier Quartos, for instance, may have served as copy for Folio *A Midsummer Night's Dream* and *King Lear* (see *TxC*, 145, 147). Cairncross argued that Folio *3 Henry VI* was likewise set up from an annotated quarto, but his thesis was weakened by the implausible suggestion that with 'a little use of scissors and paste' the Folio printers constructed a composite of Q2, Q3, and a manuscript (Ard², xxx–xxxii). The Oxford editors maintained that Shakespeare's holograph foul papers served as printer's copy but thought it probable that 'the F compositors had a copy of Q3 available for reference, and that they consulted it when they were unable to decipher a word or phrase in the manuscript' (*TxC*, 198).[1] In the absence of any typographic similarities between the two texts, which would provide bibliographic evidence that an annotated copy of Q3 served as primary printer's copy for the Folio, we are inclined to agree that Q3 was probably consulted only occasionally by the F compositors.

To summarize, then, the bibliographic stemma of textual descent is fairly straightforward: the first edition of 1595 (O) was reprinted with some minor changes in 1600; the second edition (Q2) was then reprinted with further revisions in 1619; this third edition (Q3) was then reprinted in a substantially revised form in 1623 (F1). The legendary difficulties associated with the texts of *The True Tragedy* and *3 Henry VI*, however, are due not to the moderate complexities of textual transmission but to the overwhelming uncertainties about textual origins. Does the order of publication reflect the order of composition? That is, does O represent the original version of the play and F a subsequently enlarged version? Or was F the original and O a shortened version? Were the changes made intentionally by a revising

---

1   This is essentially a restatement of McKerrow's theory that 'the MS was printed so far as it went, but when defective it was made good from the "bad" quartos' (McKerrow, 'Bad Quartos', 70).

playwright or accidentally by someone attempting to reconstruct the text from memory? Are the two texts versions of the same play (as we have been assuming in this discussion) or are they, in fact, different plays written by different dramatists?

Origins of The True Tragedy

The question of *The True Tragedy*'s origins was first addressed in print in the late seventeenth century. Gerard Langbaine's *New Catalogue of English Plays* (1688) included an entry for 'Contention between York and Lancaster, 2 Parts' under the 'Unknown Authors' section. Langbaine appended a footnote, '*Plot from the Second Part of* Shakespeare's Henry 6th, *Folio*', by which he probably wanted his readers to understand that *The Contention* and *The True Tragedy* were derivative texts that depended for their plots on *Henry VI Parts 2* and *3* (M. Jackson, 'Langbaine'). Alexander Pope (1725) asserted that the early Quartos – the Octavo itself was not discovered until late in the eighteenth century[1] – represented 'the first Sketch' of the play which was later 'vastly improved by the author' and 'greatly enlarged'. Pope moreover observed that 'the Poetry [was] improved' in the revised version although 'the Scenery was much the same' (Pope, 1.sig. B4ᵛ). Alternatively, Samuel Johnson (1765) maintained that:

> The old copies of the two latter parts of *Henry VI* . . . are so apparently imperfect and mutilated, that there is no reason for supposing them the first draughts of *Shakespeare*. I am inclined to believe them copies taken by some auditor who wrote down, during the representation, what the time would permit, then perhaps filled up some of his omissions at a second or third hearing, and

---

1 The 1595 Octavo was unknown to scholars until 1796, when the unique copy appeared at the estate sale of a Dr. Pegge (who had been 'unaware of its great value') and was purchased by George Chalmers for £5 15s. 6d. A manuscript note in the volume reveals that '[George] Steevens was enraged to find that it had gone for less than a fifth of what he would have given for it'. The British Library copy of Q2 belonged successively to Steevens and Malone.

when he had by this method formed something like a
play, sent it to the printer.

(Johnson, 5.225)

Edward Capell (1768) first articulated the difficulty of distinguishing between an authorial draft and an unauthorized
memorial reconstruction, noting that *The Contention* and *The
True Tragedy* are 'either first draughts, or mutilated and perhaps
surreptitious impressions of those plays, but whether of the two
is not easy to determine' (Capell, 1.2).

Edmond Malone (1790) refused to accept his predecessors' negative assessments of the early quartos. His 'Dissertation on the
Three Parts of King Henry VI' asserted that the 'old plays in quarto,
which have been hitherto supposed to be imperfect representations
of the second and third parts of *K. Henry VI*. are by no means mutilated and imperfect'. Malone argued for the legitimacy of these texts
(appropriating, perhaps unconsciously, the syntax of *Lear*'s
Edmund): 'the scenes are as well connected, and the versification as
correct, as that of most of the other dramas of that time' (Malone,
6.397) . Observing that 'no fraudulent copyist or short-hand writer
would invent circumstances *totally different* from those which appear
in Shakespeare's new-modelled draughts as exhibited in the first
folio; or insert *whole speeches*, of which scarcely a trace is found in
that edition', Malone concluded that 'the quarto plays were not spu-
rious and imperfect copies of Shakespeare's pieces, but elder dramas
on which he formed his *Second* and *Third* Part of *King Henry VI*'
(6.407). Malone initially suggested that these source plays were written by either Greene or Peele, but later attributed them to Marlowe.

The theory that was to dominate twentieth-century textual
scholarship emerged in the 1920s. In a note in *The Times Literary
Supplement* in 1924, Peter Alexander proposed that 'in the Folio
we have the earlier and original text of which the Quarto [*sic*] gives
only a stolen or surreptitious copy' (Alexander, *TLS*). In 1928,
Madeleine Doran argued that *The Contention* and *The True
Tragedy* 'appear to be shortened acting versions that have attained

160

their present form through reporting and rewriting' (Doran, 81). Doran maintained that during the plague of 1592–3 a large London acting company divided up, with some members travelling in the country; since the official playbooks would have been left in London, those who had acted in the *Henry VI* plays reconstructed them from memory, deliberately abridging the original plays and making some adjustments for a smaller cast. In 1994, Doran's theory was further refined by Kathleen Irace, who determined that the actors responsible for the reconstruction were probably those who played Warwick and Clifford.

The memorial reconstruction hypothesis is based – rather precariously, as we will argue – upon an interpretation of a single variant passage. In 1929, Alexander pointed out that the Octavo 'mangles history' in seven lines on signature D4^r which do not agree with Hall's *Chronicle* in the matter of matching the heiresses of Hungerford, Scales and Bonville to (respectively) Lord Hastings, the Queen's brother and the Queen's son, whereas the Folio accurately follows the source (4.1.47–57). Alexander concluded that 'Here at least we are dealing not with a transcript of Shakespeare's (or any other writer's) original, but only with a report of that original' (Alexander, *Shakespeare's*, 63–5). In 1986, the Oxford editors rightly characterized the Folio–Hall connection as the 'linch-pin' of Alexander's argument, and acknowledged that it has 'never' been 'plausibly refuted'. They further extrapolated that since Alexander 'established that part of O is clearly a report, it is natural to suppose that the rest of the text – which is open to alternative interpretations – is also a report' (*TxC*, 197).[1] Given

---

1 *TxC*'s practice of recycling paragraphs verbatim from the analysis of *The Contention* in the analysis of *Richard Duke of York* (*The True Tragedy*) implies that the textual situations are identical. Compare 'Once having established that part of Q [*Contention*] is clearly a report, it is natural to suppose that the rest of the text – which is open to alternative explanations – is also a report' (*TxC*, 175) and 'Once having established that part of O [*Richard Duke of York*] is clearly a report, it is natural to suppose that the rest of the text – which is open to alternative interpretations – is also a report' (197). We are far less certain that the transmission of the text of O is necessarily analogous to that of Q1 *The Contention*. See Ronald Knowles's Ard^3 *2H6* (106–41) for a textual analysis that is somewhat different from our own.

161

that F is apparently closer to Shakespeare's acknowledged source, and that O appears to be at several removes from that source, every editor of the play has chosen the Folio as control text.

Renewed attention to *The True Tragedy* and Hall's *Chronicle*, however, reveals significant orthographic correspondences between these two texts. The idiosyncratic spellings of 'Penbrooke', 'Norffolke', 'Fawconbridge' and 'Excester' are shared by O and Hall, whereas the Folio has 'Pembrooke', 'Norfolke', 'Falconbridge' and 'Exeter'.[1] Moreover, O and Hall agree in precise details of number and place: Warwick worries that his forces will only amount to 'five and twenty thousand' in F (2.1.180), but the '48. thousand' in O (B5ᵛ29), as Lucille King has observed, more closely approximates the figure of 48,660 given in Hall (see Hall, 255; L. King, 'Text', 717–18). So too, the length of Henry's reign at the time of Edward's accession is given as thirty-six years in the Folio (3.3.96) but as thirty-eight years in O (D1ʳ31) and in Hall (257). In the Folio, York retreats to a geographically unspecified place, 'I'll to my castle' (1.1.206); the parallel line in the Octavo situates York's castle in Wakefield, 'Ile to *Wakefield* | To my castell' (A5ᵛ25–6), and names it '*Sandall* castle' (A7ʳ17), as does Hall: 'The Duke by small jornies, came to his Castle of Sandall, beside Wakefield' (176).[2] In F, York recounts the battles he once won 'in France' (1.2.72); in O, York remembers his deeds 'In *Normandie*' (A7ᵛ9). In the parallel passage in Hall, York thinks back to when he was 'Regent of Normandy' (177).

In places, the Octavo text appears to derive its verbal texture from Hall. At 4.2.26–7, the Folio reads: 'You that will follow me to this attempt, / Applaud the name of Henry with your leader. *They all cry,* "Henry!"' The Octavo version of these lines, 'Courage my souldiers, now or neuer, / But follow me now, and *Edward* shall be ours. / *All.* A *Warwicke*, a *Warwicke*' (D5ᵛ10–12),

---

1   We are grateful to Jennifer Forsyth for bringing these orthographic links to our attention.

2   Other O passages reiterate this location: 'towards *Wakefield*, to disturbe the Duke' (A6ᵛ6), 'come to me to *Wakefield*' (A7ʳ12), 'marching towards *Wakefield*, | To besiedge you in your castell heere' (A7ʳ23–4), 'flie to *Wakefield*' (A7ᵛ16).

may indicate familiarity with Hall's account of Warwick's landing in 1470: 'all the towns and all the country adjacent was in a great roar . . . crying "King Henry! King Henry! A Warwick! A Warwick!"' (see Cam², 158n.). Moreover, as Geoffrey Bullough has observed, the sequence of scenes in the Octavo, which transposes 4.4 and 4.5, is more historically correct than the Folio ordering, since the events of 4.5 actually preceded those of 4.4 (Bullough, 3.164).

The idiosyncratic spellings of names, the number of Warwick's troops, the location of his castle, and York's regency in Normandy could not have been derived from the version of the play preserved in the Folio text. These connections in verbal detail between Hall's *Chronicle* and O call into question the prevailing view that *The True Tragedy* is a derivative text. This new evidence may be added to the growing number of recent challenges to the memorial reconstruction theory.[1] Paul Werstine, for instance, has effectively undermined the assumption that travelling troupes performed with an unauthorized book that they had memorially reconstructed by pointing to an entry in the Hall Book of Leicester dated 3 March 1583/4 which reads, 'No Play is to bee played, but such as is allowed by the sayd Edmund [Tilney], & his hand at the latter end of the said booke they doe play' (Werstine, 'Touring', 56). A basic tenet of the theory that O represents an abridgement made for a smaller number of actors has been weakened by David Bradley's calculation that *The True Tragedy* actually requires a cast of twenty-four; and Werstine observes that none of the recorded counts of travelling troupes before 1600 exceeds ten (D. Bradley, 51; Werstine, 'Touring', 58).

Many formerly 'bad quarto' texts have recently been reclassified as authorial first drafts – most famously in the rehabilitation

---

1 Laurie Maguire's extensive study of *Shakespearean Suspect Texts* (1996) concludes that whereas a strong case can be made for memorial reconstruction in *The Merry Wives of Windsor*, and a weaker case for *Hamlet* and *Pericles*, *The First Part of the Contention* and *The True Tragedy* do not show the symptoms which she uses to diagnose memorial reconstruction (Maguire, 324–5).

of the Quarto text of *King Lear* and the A-text of *Doctor Faustus*.[1] Steven Urkowitz has argued that *The True Tragedy* is a unified dramatic script which represents an early Shakespearean draft that was later revised to produce the version represented in the Folio (Urkowitz, 'If'). The links that we have established between the Octavo and Shakespeare's source might also be seen as evidence that O is an original authorial version, but we are cautious about advancing this conclusion since other explanations are certainly possible.[2] And the fact that the textual 'evidence' for memorial reconstruction can often suddenly become the evidence of authorial copy must give us pause. As Laurie Maguire has observed (Maguire, 93), the repetition of three of Warwick's lines in O may be compared with the repetitions in Q2 *Romeo and Juliet*:

> For strokes receiude, and manie blowes repaide,
> Hath robd my strong knit sinnews of their strength,
> And force perforce needes must I rest my selfe.
> (O *The True Tragedy*, sig. C1ʳ30–C1ᵛ2)

> For manie wounds receiu'd, and manie moe repaid,
> Hath robd my strong knit sinews of their strengh,
> And spite of spite needes must I yeeld to death.
> (O sig. E2ᵛ27–9)

> O true Appothecarie!
> Thy drugs are quicke. Thus with a kiss I die.
> (Q2 *Romeo and Juliet*, sig. L3ʳ24–5)

---

1   It should be noted that the textual editor of this volume has both criticized this trend and participated in it (see Rasmussen, 'Rehabilitating' and 'Textual studies').

2   The links between O and Hall that could not derive from F might suggest revision of the play between 1595 and 1623. Or, it could be argued that a group of actors attempting to reconstruct the play from memory might have turned to a copy of Hall's *Chronicle* for assistance in recalling specifics of the plot and spellings of certain names. Alternatively, Hattaway sees the direct consultation of the chronicles by the reporting actors as evidence of an authorial presence, suggesting that 'Shakespeare was at hand to tell the players what to do' (Cam, 203).

Heeres to my Loue. O true Appothecary:
Thy drugs are quicke. Thus with a kisse I die.
(Q2 sig. L3ʳ37–8)

The standard explanation for the repetition in *The True Tragedy*
is memorial error; the actor-reporter anticipated Warwick's lines
from the later passage and reproduced them in the earlier scene.
Such anticipations, according to Greg, are 'the most characteristic
mark of a reported text' (Greg, *Parallel Texts*, 54). And yet, the
similar repetition in Q2 *Romeo and Juliet* is not viewed as an
anticipation but as a 'false start', made by Shakespeare 'in the heat
of composition', and thus indicative of foul paper copy, which,
according to Greg, is 'characterized by textual duplications and
false starts' (Greg, *First Folio*, 479). Maguire has puckishly asked
'why does one "prove" indecisive authorial copy and the other
"prove" memorial reconstruction?' (Maguire, 93) – to which one
might reply, with Bottom, 'not so, neither'.

One salient feature of the Octavo suggests that memory may
have played a role in the transmission of that text. A number of
O/F textual variants appear to be the result of aural error: F's
'Wrath makes him deaf' (1.4.53) appears in O as 'Wrath makes
him death' (B1ʳ26); O has 'his adopted aire' (B2ʳ7) for F's 'his
adopted heir' (1.4.98); F's 'tigers of Hyrcania' (1.4.155) appear in
O as 'Tygers of *Arcadia*' (B3ʳ4); runners are 'Forespent with toil'
in F (2.3.1) but 'Sore spent' in O (C1ʳ29); for F's 'likeness of this
railer' (5.5.38), O reads 'litnes' (E5ʳ1); for F's 'Sicils' (5.7.39), O
has '*Cyssels*' (E7ᵛ30). Similar homonymic variants in Q1 and Q2
Hamlet ('ceasen' for 'season', 'right done' for 'writ down', 'impudent' for 'impotent', 'with tongue invenom'd speech' for 'with
tongue in venom steep'd') are frequently cited as evidence of Q1's
memorial origins. As Harold Jenkins observed, such instances in
which the sound of a word is retained while being associated with
a different meaning might be ascribed to 'an actor recalling what
he has heard recited but not seen written' (Jenkins, 23). Even those
who are inclined, as we are, to view the variants between *The True*

Tragedy and *3 Henry VI* as differences, rather than as errors in either text, would probably acknowledge that in the case of these homonyms the Folio reading invariably fits the context of the line better than does the Octavo variant. Although we are dubious about the theory of memorial reconstruction by touring actors, we do not believe that these homonymic errors are compatible with a theory of authorial copy behind O.

A more plausible scenario for the genesis of O is suggested by Blayney's innovative reading of Humphrey Moseley's preface to the 1647 Beaumont and Fletcher Folio in which Moseley implied that it was a common practice for actors to make copies of their play scripts for their friends: 'when private friends desir'd a Copy, they then (and justly too) transcribed what they *Acted*'. Blayney astutely observed that

> if the actor responsible was able to copy from the allowed book, dutifully omitting every passage marked for omission in the current performance version (which might itself vary from revival to revival), his text would be visibly shorter than most printed plays. If he had to copy it partly or wholly from memory, those parts of the performance he had least opportunity to observe might prove extremely difficult to reconstruct and might emerge noticeably garbled
>
> (Blayney, 'Publication', 393–4)

Blayney concludes that 'what Moseley has been trying to tell us since 1647 is, I believe, the commonplace and innocent origin of the kind of text that Pollard called a Bad Quarto – but we have been too busy chasing imaginary pirates to listen' (394). Perhaps *The True Tragedy* had its origins in just such a transcript, made by an early actor for his friends.

Origins of 3 Henry VI

The theory that the Folio text of *3 Henry VI* was set into type from an authorial manuscript rests largely upon the appearance in that text of three names – *Gabriel, Sinklo* and *Humfrey* – thought to refer to specific Elizabethan actors: Gabriel Spenser, John Sincler and Humphrey Jeffes. Greg's *The Shakespeare First Folio* (1955) lists 'the substitution of the name of an actor, when the part is written with a particular performer in view' as one of the key indicators that a playwright's rough draft manuscript was used as printer's copy (Greg, *First Folio*, 142).[1] In discussing the specific case of *Gabriel, Sinklo* and *Humfrey* in *3 Henry VI*, however, Greg asserts – in no uncertain terms – that the appearance of these names 'cannot possibly be attributed to the author' (183). Given this internal contradiction in the authoritative source to which editors of *3 Henry VI* continue to turn for information about the 'positive signs of authorial copy' (Cam², 206), it may be worth revisiting the issue.[2]

At the opening of 3.1, the Folio text reads: '*Enter Sinklo, and Humfrey, with Crosse-bowes | in their hands*' (TLN 1396–7). Their speech prefixes (SPs) appear as *Sinklo, Sink., Sin.* and *Hum.* in the scene that follows, in which these two gamekeepers capture the King. In the chronicles, Henry is 'known and taken of one Cantlow' (Holinshed, 282; Hall, 262). If we had no other information about the name '*Sinklo*', we might plausibly assume that it was a misreading of '*Cantlow*' given the graphic similarities between the two. But *Sinklo* appears in a number of the dramatic texts of the period: in a stage direction (SD) and an SP in Q1 (1600) *2 Henry IV* (5.4), in an SP in the Folio *The Taming of the Shrew* (TLN 98), and as a character in John Webster's Induction to John Marston's *The Malcontent* (1604). *John Sincler* is named in the manuscript Plot of *2 Seven Deadly Sins* (*c.* 1591) as the actor who plays, among other doubled roles, 'A Keeper' guarding King Henry VI – a remarkable coincidence given *Sinklo*'s role as a keeper who captures the King in *3 Henry VI*. Despite the absence

---

1 See also *TxC*: 'Such texts are often characterized by . . . the use of an actor's name (instead of a character's) in stage directions and speech-prefixes' (9).
2 Our discussion of this topic is indebted to Paul Werstine's unpublished essay, 'Actors' names in printed English Renaissance drama', presented at the Shakespeare Association of America meeting, 1988.

16 Folio sig. p3ᵛ from the First Folio, 1623, showing the opening of 3.1 with the entrance of 'Sinklo' and 'Humfrey'

of any other records pertaining to this individual, textual scholars have deduced that John Sincler or Sinklo was a long-time member of the King's Men; perhaps because he played bit parts, it is argued, his name does not appear in any of the formal lists of the 'principal actors' in the company such as those published in the Jonson Folio (1616) and the Shakespeare First Folio (1623). Since Sinklo apparently played the role of the Beadle in *2 Henry IV*, where much is made of the character's thinness, and similar jokes are made about Sinklo's meagre physique in the Induction to *The Malcontent*, it is further argued that Sinklo was generally typecast as a thin man and, as such, might have played the role of the Apothecary in *Romeo and Juliet*, of Robin Starveling in *A Midsummer Night's Dream* and of Robert Falconbridge in *King John* (Gaw, 'Sincklo').

The early editors who first remarked upon these actors' names in printed texts assumed that their appearance must have been accidental – they 'crept in' (Thomas Tyrwhitt, cited in Malone, 3.249) 'through negligence' (Malone, 6.249) – and, more importantly, that their presence signified 'in a clear and satisfactory manner' that a text had been 'printed from a play-house copy' (Furness, 230). In 1923, R. Crompton Rhodes first suggested that 'players' names may have been written by Shakespeare, who cast them in the parts mentally as he wrote them' (R.C. Rhodes, 57). Two years later, Allison Gaw similarly argued that Shakespeare wrote these small parts in *3 Henry VI* with particular actors in mind and that instead of inventing a fictional name for the character he simply put down the name of the actor: 'If two such characters have a dialogue, why write a colorless 1 Keeper and 2 Keeper? He writes the names of the actors, Sincklo and Humphrey, whom he wishes to play the parts' (Gaw, 'Actors' names', 538).

Gaw's hypothesis was immediately challenged by E.M. Albright, who pointed out that a shorthand reporter might well find it easier to remember the name of an actor rather than that of the character he played (Albright, 296); this might be especially true in the case at hand, where the keepers are not named in the dialogue. In 1931, Greg observed that Gaw's theory flies in the face of the empirical evidence:

> in every instance in which an actor's name appears in a manuscript play it is written in a different hand from the text, or at any rate in a different ink and style, showing it to be a later addition and not part of the original composition

> (Greg, *Dramatic Documents*, 216)

In 1942, however, while still insisting that Gaw's theory 'is not supported by any evidence in the extant manuscripts, in which all actors' names are added by the book-keeper', Greg argued that 'it is in the foul papers that the author's use of actors' names would appear, and they would probably be eliminated in the course of preparing the prompt-book' (Greg, *Editorial Problem*, 40). And yet, he continued to resist the notion that Shakespeare was responsible for the actors' names in F *3 Henry VI*: 'They are attached to subordinate parts that it is unlikely an author would write with a particular actor in mind. Most probably they were substituted for generic designations – Keepers and such – by the prompter' (Greg, *Editorial Problem*, 55).

T.H. Howard-Hill has suggested that in the manuscript of John Fletcher and Philip Massinger's *Sir John Van Olden Barnavelt* the assignments of specific actors to minor parts were probably entered in a playbook in order to instruct and guide the scribe who was charged with preparing the roles for each player (Howard-Hill, 'Promptbook'). Howard-Hill's suggestion that parts were prepared for specific actors rather than for characters has important implications. Preparing the actors' parts for the principal roles in *3 Henry VI* – King Henry, Warwick or Richard – would be a time-consuming but fairly straightforward task, a simple matter of transcribing that character's lines and his cue lines onto a strip of paper. However, the process of creating a part for an actor who was going to double in a number of roles would be much more complex. According to our calculations of the doubling possibilities inherent in the structure of *3 Henry VI* (see Appendix 2), the actor 'Gabriel' who played the messenger in 1.2 would play *ten* different speaking roles in the course of the play; his part would need to include the eleven lines of dialogue he speaks as Exeter in 1.1; the three lines as the same character in 2.5 and the two lines in 4.8; the four-line speech (as messenger to York) in 1.2; three lines as the tutor in 1.3; twenty-four lines as messenger to York in 2.1; six lines as messenger to Lancaster in 2.2; two lines as the Nobleman in 3.2; six lines as the Post in 3.3, eighteen lines as the same character in 4.1 and another seven lines in 4.6; eight lines as the Watch in 4.3; seven lines as Rivers in 4.4; five lines as the Mayor of York in 4.7; and five lines as Somerville in 5.1. It should surprise no one if, in the course of working out these intricate doubling possibilities, the book-holder found it necessary to note on the playbook which actor was to play which minor roles.

E.K. Chambers maintained that actors' names running through a series of SPs can be explained as instances in which 'probably Shakespeare wrote inadequate prefixes, in the form of mere numerals, and the book-keeper glossed them' (Chambers, *WS*, 1.237). Gaw had anticipated this argument and dismissed it out of hand: 'as for the theory that Shakespeare muddled his speech headings and someone else had to follow him in order to sort out the speeches among his characters, in the scene in *3 Henry VI* this supposition is demonstrably false' (Gaw, 'Actors' names', 536).[1] However, support for Chambers's position may be found in Shakespeare's 'Hand D' pages in the *Sir Thomas More* manuscript, in which the dramatist in three instances wrote simply

---

1   Gaw observed that King Henry's speech prefixes in the scene with Sinklo and
    Humfrey (fol. p3ᵛ) change from '*Hen.*' (in the first Folio column) to '*King.*' (in the
    second column) and argued that Shakespeare would have done this to avoid any con-
    fusion with '*Hum.*'. But Werstine points to a parallel instance on fol. p2ᵛ in which a
    similar change occurs, from '*Hen.*' in the first column to '*King.*' in the second; since
    both pages were set by Compositor B, we can be fairly confident that the change was
    compositorial rather than authorial, perhaps done because of a type shortage.

'*other*' as an SP; the names of the specific characters were later provided by a theatrical scribe.

The question of whether the playwright or book-keeper was responsible for these names is a fascinating one for all students of Shakespeare's texts, but it actually has little relevance to the editing process. In practice, all actors' names that appear in early texts – irrespective of how they got there – are systematically removed from modern editions; it is standard editorial procedure to 'substitute fictional names for those of actors' (*TxC*, 188). The real issue, then, is not one of agency but of fact and fiction. Do these names refer to someone who has an existence outside of the literary text or are they fictional?[1]

It would be difficult to imagine a more appropriate name for a fictional messenger than that of the divine messenger Gabriel. And yet, we know that Gabriel Spencer – before being killed by Ben Jonson in their famous duel in 1598 – was a member of the acting company that probably produced the play in the early 1590s. Does this fact tip the balance of probability in favour of the Folio's SD's referring to the actor? If so, the presence of this name indicates that the manuscript behind the Folio must have originated before the man's death in 1598.

Sinklo presents a more complex problem. In the Induction to *The Malcontent* it is possible that Sinklo appears *in propria persona* along with the other named members of the King's Men (Burbage, Condell, Lowin and Will Sly), although he plays a member of the audience. He may also have appeared in a cameo role as himself, the 'Player', in the Induction to *The Taming of the Shrew* – which raises the further issue of how the 'Sinklo' roles would have been cast and played when John Sincler was no longer with the company. It would no doubt strain credulity to argue that *Sinklo* in F *3 Henry VI* is simply the fictional name given to one

1 Richard Proudfoot has pointed out to us that Thomas L. Berger, William C. Bradford and Sidney L. Sondergard's *Index of Characters in Early Modern English Drama* (1998) provides an entry for Gabriel as a character in *3H6* but none for Sinklo or Humfrey.

of the gamekeepers, with no link to the actor, and we are not prepared to do so.

But this does not mean that F's *Humfrey*, appearing immediately after *Sinklo*, necessarily refers to the actor Humfrey Jeffes. The practice of mixing the names of roles and actors in SDs is well documented; the manuscript playbook of Massinger's *Believe as You List*, for instance, annotated by the book-keeper for the King's Men, contains such directions as 'Ent: flaminivs Mr Hobs: & Rowland' (fol. 10ʳ), referring to the character Flaminius (identified elsewhere in the manuscript as played by John Lowin) and the actors Hobbes and Rowland who played the roles of Calistus and Demetrius, respectively. *Humfrey* may refer to an actor or to a fictional character; we simply do not know. What we do know is that the appearance of this name, along with *Gabriel* and *Sinklo*, is of little use in helping us to understand the nature of the manuscript that may lie behind the Folio text of *3 Henry VI*.

The other textual feature that supposedly reveals 'foul papers' behind Folio *3 Henry VI* is the variety of names by which Lady Elizabeth Grey appears in SDs and SPs: she enters as '*Lady Gray*' in 3.2, but her SPs are invariably '*Wid.*' in the scene that follows; in 4.1 and 4.4 she is '*Lady Grey*' or '*Lady Gray*'; in 5.7 she is '*Queene*'. McKerrow famously suggested that Shakespeare's practice as he wrote was to distinguish his characters not only by their names but also 'by their functions (Goldsmith, not Angelo; Father, not Capulet) or their peculiarities (Braggart or Pedant, not Armado or Holophernes)' (McKerrow, 'Suggestion', 465). Such variation in names in a Folio text proved, to McKerrow and Greg's satisfaction, that 'the manuscript behind F was clearly the author's . . . since it is difficult to believe that the confusion in the character names and prefixes would have been tolerated in a prompt-book' (Greg, *First Folio*, 201–2). However, recent scholars have demonstrated that McKerrow's 'Suggestion' is undermined by the extant playbooks which, in fact, frequently show variation in characters' names; these inconsistencies may have originated in authorial manuscripts, but there is no indication that in preparing these scripts for use in the theatre anyone was concerned to regularize or clarify varying labels for the same character (Werstine, 'Suggestion'; S. Thomas; W. Long, 'Perspective'). Moreover, Richard Kennedy has argued that variant SPs in early printed texts may not be signs of an author after all, but are rather to be understood as indications of a compositor switching SPs because of a type shortage (R. Kennedy, 'Speech prefixes').

Should editors of *3 Henry VI* follow the traditional practice of normalizing and regularizing the Folio SPs to *Lady Grey* throughout? Or should the variant SPs be retained in a critical edition in the interest of preserving the indeterminacies in the early texts? Some of the variation is clearly compositorial. Compositor B has an absolute preference for the spelling *Gray* (TLN 1500, 2303, 2305, 2309, 2311, 2320, 2331) whereas Compositor A uses *Grey* (TLN 1502, 2026, 2094). Lady Grey's promotion to *Queene* (TLN 3170) in the final scene is a standard change found in dramatic texts in which the crown changes hands, analogous to the alteration in SDs and SPs of *Edward* (TLN 2952, 2971) to *King* (TLN 3170, 3171); one might wonder why the change from *Lady Grey* to *Queene* was not made earlier in the text, following Elizabeth's marriage to Edward, but perhaps an attempt was made to avoid confusion with Margaret, who continues to be referred to as *Queene* in SPs and SDs through TLN 3062.[1]

The *Lady Gray / Wid.* variation may have been due to a compositor change. The opening SD of 3.2, '*Enter K. Edward, Gloster, Clarence, Lady Gray*' (TLN 1500), and the scene's first line of dialogue appear at the foot of signature p3^v, set by Compositor B. The balance of the scene was set by Compositor A on sig. p4^r–p4^v, in which Lady Grey's twenty-four speech prefixes are invariably *Wid.* It is conceivable that the speech prefixes in the manuscript were unclear and that Compositor A, whose section of the

---

1 The French translation of the Oxford Shakespeare (Grivelet and Monsarrat) regularizes the SP KING HENRY to LE ROI throughout the play, which would not cause any difficulty were it not that it regularizes KING EDWARD to LE ROI as well. When a reader finds Henry's SP at 4.7.68 is LE ROI, and Edward's SP thirty lines later at 4.8.1 is also LE ROI, one suspects that, whoever is king, confusion will reign.

printer's copy did not include the page on which *Lady Gray* was named in the opening entrance direction, took his cue from the dialogue, in which she is referred to only as 'Widow' (TLN 1517, 1522, 1527, 1536, 1608, 1614, 1628, 1645); had he consulted the copy of Q3 that was apparently available to the Folio printers, he would have found her called *Lady Grey* in the SD and *La.* or *Lady.* in the SPs of the Q3 version of this scene.

Lady Grey is of interest to Edward in 3.2 specifically because she is a newly available widow. Theatre audiences know her only as 'Widow'. At some point in the transmission of the text – either when the play was originally written, when it was reinscribed to serve as the licensed playbook, or when it was set into type – someone codified her role in this scene by prefixing *Wid.* to each of her speeches. Every modern editor since Rowe has replaced the *Wid.* prefixes with *Lady Grey*, a process of regularization based on the belief that inconstancies in the early texts derive from confusions in Shakespeare's original papers which need to be clarified. But we are persuaded neither that the *Lady Grey / Wid.* variation necessarily points to 'foul paper' copy nor that the *Wid.* prefixes should be so easily discarded. In our view, preserving the potent ideological implications of Lady Elizabeth's functional identity as *Widow* in this scene far outweighs the need to iron out this anomaly in the text for the modern reader. We have therefore broken with three centuries of editorial tradition by retaining the WIDOW SPs in 3.2.

Conclusions

Our analysis of the Octavo text of *The True Tragedy* questions its origins in memorial reconstruction by touring actors and our analysis of the Folio text of *3 Henry VI* questions its 'foul paper' status. However, we are mindful that subjective editorial opinions about a text's origins – too often mistaken for bibliographic facts – can have a profound effect on a reader's interpretation of that text; we do not want to prejudice interpretation by pronouncing one text more authoritative than the other or even by attaching such labels as *original* and *revision*. After all, the continuing fascination of these texts derives largely from their refusal to fit snugly into any of the established textual categories. The complex relationship between *The True Tragedy* and *3 Henry VI* has challenged the ingenuity of generations of readers, students and scholars. We hope that the very inconclusiveness of our analysis will stimulate new ideas and fresh debate about these still enigmatic texts.

KING HENRY VI,

PART THREE,
WITH THE DEATH OF
THE DUKE OF YORK

LIST OF ROLES

YORKISTS

Richard Plantagenet, Duke of YORK	*leader of the Yorkist faction*
EDWARD, Earl of March	*eldest son of the Duke of York, later inheritor of the title and* KING EDWARD *the Fourth*
GEORGE, *later* Duke of CLARENCE	*second son of the Duke of York*
RICHARD, *later* Duke of GLOUCESTER	*third son of the Duke of York* 5
Earl of RUTLAND	*youngest son of the Duke of York*
SIR JOHN MORTIMER	*uncle of the Duke of York*
Sir Hugh Mortimer	*brother of Sir John*
LADY GREY (*also* WIDOW)	*later* QUEEN ELIZABETH, *wife of King Edward the Fourth*
Prince Edward of York	*the future King Edward the* 10 *Fifth*
Earl of WARWICK	*adherent of York, later of Lancaster*
Marquess of MONTAGUE	*brother of Warwick, adherent of York, later of Lancaster*
Duke of NORFOLK	
Lord HASTINGS	
Earl of Pembroke	15
Lord Stafford	
Sir William Stanley	
Lord RIVERS	*brother of Lady Grey, adherent first of Lancaster, then of York*
LIEUTENANT	*of the Tower of London*
MAYOR of York	20
Sir John MONTGOMERY	
TUTOR	*of Rutland*
Nurse	*of Prince Edward of York*
SON	*who has killed his father while fighting for York*
NOBLEMAN	25
Three WATCHMEN	

LANCASTRIANS

KING HENRY the Sixth	*leader of the Lancastrian faction*	
QUEEN MARGARET	*wife of King Henry*	
PRINCE EDWARD	*son of King Henry*	
Henry Tudor, Earl of Richmond	*the future King Henry the Seventh*	30
THIRD DUKE of Somerset	*adherent of both Lancaster and York*	
Fourth Duke of SOMERSET		
Duke of EXETER		
Lord CLIFFORD		
Earl of NORTHUMBERLAND		35
Earl of WESTMORLAND		
Earl of OXFORD		
Mayor of Coventry		
SOMERVILLE		
FATHER	*who has killed his son while fighting for Lancaster*	40
HUNTSMAN		

THE FRENCH

KING LEWIS the Eleventh	*of France*
LADY BONA	*sister-in-law of King Lewis*
Lord Bourbon	*French admiral*

OTHERS

Two KEEPERS   45
MESSENGERS
POSTS

*Soldiers, Aldermen of York, Citizens of Coventry,
Drummers, Trumpeters, Attendants*

LIST OF ROLES F contains no list; Rowe provided a partial one, with roles listed in order of customary social prominence (including all males before females).

1 **Duke of** YORK (1411–60) Richard Plantagenet, son of Richard, Earl of Cambridge, who is arrested and executed in *H5*, based his claim to the crown on his mother Anne's second marriage, to Edmund Mortimer, Fifth Earl of March, who was declared heir to the throne by the childless Richard II. (Mortimer was the great-grandson of Lionel, Duke of Clarence, third son of Edward III.) York is informed of his claim by the dying Mortimer in *1H6* 2.5 but bides his time in making it good, openly opposing Henry for the first time in *2H6* 5.1.

2 EDWARD (1442–83) First appearing in *2H6* 5.1, Edward comes into his own in *3H6*, inheriting the dukedom of York upon his father's death (when historically Edward was only eighteen) and declaring himself king shortly thereafter. Shakespeare elides his twenty-three-year reign (1460–83) between *3H6* 2.6 and *R3* 2.2, making it appear more troubled than it was and omitting Edward's many positive achievements.

3 GEORGE (1449–78) George Plantagenet was sixth son of Richard, Duke of York, created Duke of Clarence by his brother, King Edward IV, in 1461 (2.6). He joined Warwick's rebellion against Edward (4.1), married Warwick's elder daughter Isabella (see 4.1.118–22), but rejoined Edward before the battle of Barnet (5.1). His brother Richard has him murdered in *R3*.

4–5 RICHARD (1452–85) Eleventh child of Richard, Duke of York, Richard Plantagenet is comrade-in-arms with his brother Edward in *2H6* and *3H6*, though Edward was ten years older and Richard accordingly only eight when their father died in 1460. Richard was created Duke of Gloucester the following year. For discussion of Richard's character, see pp.

75–81. His succession to the throne after Edward is depicted in *R3*.

6 **Earl of** RUTLAND (1449–60) Edmund Plantagenet, second son of Richard Duke of York, killed by young Clifford at the battle of Wakefield when he was seventeen and lamented as a child by his historically younger brothers, George and Richard. This role could have been doubled by the boy who played Lady Bona, Richmond and the Nurse.

7, 8 SIR JOHN MORTIMER and **Sir Hugh Mortimer** Hall says that York's 'two bastard vncles, sir Ihon, & sir Hugh Mortimers' died with York at Wakefield (250). Cf. 1.2.61 and 1.4.2.

9 LADY GREY (1431–92) Daughter and wife of fierce Lancastrian partisans, Elizabeth Grey (*née* Woodville) was one of four ladies of the bedchamber to Queen Margaret until her husband, Sir John Grey (erroneously called 'Sir Richard' at 3.2.2), was killed at the second battle of St Albans. She and Queen Margaret were the founders of Queens' College, Cambridge. Successfully petitioning the new young Yorkist king for redress, she was 'the first subject raised to the throne of England as the wife of the reigning monarch' (W. Thomson, 100), and her promotion is the cause of much dissension among the Yorkists in both *3H6* and *R3*. This edition follows the varying SPs that are used for her in F, because they seem to embody a textual social prejudice against her. '*Wid.*', used in 3.2, where she first appears, denotes her marital situation, not her rank (on the situation of widows, see Stone, *Family*, 88–9, 195–6). In subsequent scenes F refers to her as 'Lady Grey' (4.1) and 'Grey' (4.4), even after she has become Edward's Queen. ('Richard' and 'George' are also used for the Dukes of Gloucester and Clarence, respectively, after their promotions, but the equivalent 'Elizabeth' is not used for the Queen.) Just once, in 5.7.0.2, she is properly styled '*Queene*', but her only SP in that scene (according to O) has been confused in

F with that of her brother-in-law, Clarence (5.7.30). This role could have been doubled by the boy who played Edmund Plantagenet, Prince Edward and Lady Bona.

10 **Prince Edward of York** born 1471 and crowned 1483. According to Shakespeare and his sources, Edward died two months later at the hand of his uncle, Richard Duke of Gloucester.

11 **Earl of WARWICK** (1428–71) Richard Neville, who earns his historical epithet 'kingmaker' in this play, first appears in *2H6* and remains a potent memory in *R3*. Despite his power and influence, he ranks, as earl, below the kings and dukes whom he assists and overthrows. He succeeded his father, Richard Neville, as Earl of Salisbury and inherited the title to the earldom of Warwick through his wife, Anne Beauchamp, only child of Richard Beauchamp, Earl of Warwick, who appears in *2H4* (where Shakespeare confuses him with Richard Neville), *1H6* and *H5*.

12 **Marquess of MONTAGUE** (d. 1471) John Neville, brother of Richard Neville (11n.), Earl of Warwick and son of the Earl of Salisbury in *2H6*. Montague switched sides along with his brother, and his death at the battle of Barnet is reported to the dying Warwick in *3H6* 5.2. Marquess is an aristocratic rank between duke and earl.

13 **Duke of NORFOLK** (1415–61) John Mowbray, third Duke of Norfolk, grandson of Thomas Mowbray, Duke of Norfolk in *R2*

14 **Lord HASTINGS** (1430–83) Sir William Hastings staunchly supported York in the Wars of the Roses, remaining in England to rally support when Edward fled to Holland after Warwick's invasion in 1470 and helping to persuade George, Duke of Clarence, to rejoin the clan. Richard Duke of Gloucester executes him in *R3* for resisting his rise to the throne.

15 **Earl of Pembroke** Sir William Herbert was created Earl of Pembroke

after the attainder, by the Yorkists, of Jasper Tudor, Earl of Pembroke, in 1468. Pembroke has no lines in *3H6*, though King Edward addresses him at 4.1.129, and an actor must therefore take his part.

16 **Lord Stafford** Sir Humphrey Stafford, cousin of the Staffords who were killed in Cade's rebellion (*2H6* 4.2–4.3) and whose property Humphrey inherited. Though a supporter of York, he was attainted and executed by King Edward in 1469 for failure to support Pembroke (15n.) in military action in Yorkshire, when he and Pembroke were quarrelling. Stafford has no lines in *3H6*, though King Edward addresses him at 4.1.129.

17 **Sir William Stanley** (1435–95) A loyal supporter of York during the Wars of the Roses, Stanley assists in the rescue of King Edward (4.5) and survives to oppose Richard III fatefully at the battle of Bosworth (*R3*). Despite this support for the future Henry VII, the first Tudor king eventually executed Stanley for joining the revolt of Perkin Warbeck.

18 **Lord RIVERS** (1442–83) Anthony Woodville, brother of Lady Grey (9n.) and an aristocrat of considerable education and ability, fought for Lancaster at Towton but joined the Yorkists after his sister's marriage to Edward IV. He rose rapidly at court but was displaced by Richard III, who executed him for treason (*R3*).

19 **LIEUTENANT** Though Shakespeare conflates them, two different men were lieutenants of the Tower in the two scenes where that officer appears. When Warwick released Henry in October 1470 (depicted in 4.6), the lieutenant was Sir John Tiptoft, Earl of Worcester (1427–70), who supported York in the Wars of the Roses and earned literary fame as the translator of Buonaccorso's *De vera nobilitate*, on which Henry Medwall based *Fulgens and Lucrece*, the earliest extant English secular play. Tiptoft was not present at Henry's release, however (4.6.0.3). When Henry was imprisoned a second

time (5.6), the lieutenant of the Tower was Sir John Sutton (1401–87).

20 MAYOR of York Thomas Beverly, merchant of the Staple, was mayor for the second time in 1471, when he protested against Edward's entry into the city (4.7).

21 Sir John MONTGOMERY (d. 1495) Historically this character was Sir Thomas Montgomery, whom Shakespeare mistook for his brother John. Despite his support of both Edward IV and Richard III, Thomas survived well into the reign of Henry VII.

22 TUTOR Hall identifies Rutland's tutor as Sir Robert Aspall, who was a younger son of the Aspalls of Norfolk.

27 KING HENRY the Sixth (1421–71) Henry Plantagenet, grandson of Henry Bolingbroke who seizes the throne from Richard II in *R2*, and only child of Henry V, the heroic king who rises to power in *1H4*, *2H4* and *H5*, and whose premature death is lamented in *1H6* 1.1. Henry VI's claim to the crown is through John of Gaunt, Duke of Lancaster, fourth son of Edward III and father of Henry Bolingbroke. Henry VI succeeded to the throne at the age of nine months, because of his father's untimely death (1.1.112n.).

28 QUEEN MARGARET (1430–82) One of the most imposing characters in the early histories, Margaret is also the only character who appears in all four of them, winning the heart of Henry VI in absentia at the end of *1H6* and surviving to curse the triumphant Yorkists memorably (but unhistorically) in *R3*. She was French, the daughter of René of Anjou (referred to as '*Reynold*' in F *1H6* at TLN 105, 'Reignier' in Ard³ *1H6* at 1.1.94, and '*Reynard*' in F *3H6* at TLN 3209 (see 5.7.38), and her marriage with Henry VI was arranged by the Duke of Suffolk, who stood as proxy for the king at her wedding in 1445. In *3H6* she loses both her husband and her son to the fury of Yorkist vengeance. 'Nothing but the untiring energy of his queen could have maintained

Henry on the throne for which he was quite unfitted, but which her dauntless courage so long upheld' (G. French, 178). If this role was originally played by a boy, as women's roles usually were, he must have been unusually experienced and forceful.

29 PRINCE EDWARD (1453–71) Edward Plantagenet, Prince of Wales, only child of Henry VI and Queen Margaret, appears only in *3H6*. He was knighted by his father at the age of eight, after the second battle of St Albans, but Shakespeare places it just before the battle of Towton (2.2). After Warwick's defection to Lancaster, Edward was betrothed to Warwick's younger daughter Anne (3.3), who later married Richard III (*R3* 1.2). Appendix 2 explains why this role was probably played by an actor who took no other roles.

30 Henry Tudor, Earl of Richmond (1457–1509) The future Henry VII based his claim to the throne on his mother, Margaret Beaufort, who was descended from John of Gaunt, fourth son of Edward III. Henry's paternal grandmother, Katherine, married Henry V, and after his death married Owen Tudor. Born after Owen's death, Henry Tudor had as his first guardian his uncle, Jasper Tudor, Earl of Pembroke, who was attainted and therefore lost his title to William Lord Herbert, Earl of Pembroke (15n.), who assumed guardianship of Henry. When he appears in 4.6, Henry is accompanied by his third guardian, Edmund, fourth Duke of Somerset (32n.), a Beaufort descended, like Henry's mother, from John of Gaunt. Richmond became head of the Lancastrians when Henry VI and his son died. He succeeded to the throne after defeating Richard III and forged an alliance between the warring families of York and Lancaster by marrying Edward IV's daughter, Elizabeth, grandmother of Elizabeth I.

31 THIRD DUKE of Somerset (1436–64) Henry Beaufort fought for Lancaster, was attainted by the Yorkists in 1461,

was restored to favour by Edward IV (which is why Somerset appears at Edward's court in 4.1), and was executed after again taking up arms for Lancaster at the battle of Hexham (not included by Shakespeare). When Richard, Duke of Gloucester, refers to two Dukes of Somerset who opposed York (5.1.73), he addresses his comments to Edmund, fourth Duke (32n.), but he means Edmund (father of the third and fourth Dukes, whose head Richard carries on stage in 1.1, and Henry, the third Duke.

32 **Fourth Duke of** SOMERSET (1438–71) Edmund Beaufort, younger brother of Henry (31n.), inherited the forfeited title after his brother's attainder and execution and was himself executed by the victorious Yorkists after the battle of Tewkesbury (5.5.3). Richard, Duke of Gloucester, addresses him as the third Duke of Somerset to oppose York (5.1.73–75; cf. King Edward at 5.7.5), thus distinguishing him from his elder brother, who had died seven years earlier, though neither O nor F distinguishes the roles in SDs or SPs.

33 **Duke of** EXETER (d. 1473) Henry Holland supported Lancaster, though he was married to Anne Plantagenet, sister of Edward IV. Surviving severe wounds at Towton, he was neglected by the triumphant Yorkists and died in dire poverty.

34 **Lord** CLIFFORD (1435–61) John, thirteenth Baron Clifford, is the son of Lord Clifford who is killed at the first battle of St Albans in *2H6* 5.2. Though Shakespeare presents him as an implacable foe of the Yorkists, he was in fact reconciled to them after his father's death and attainted by the Lancastrians in 1459. Nonetheless, he fought for Lancaster at the battle of Wakefield, as Shakespeare depicts in 1.3, and was killed at Towton. Baron is the lowest of aristocratic ranks.

35 **Earl of** NORTHUMBERLAND (1421–61) In 5.7.8 Edward IV honours the memory of 'two Northumberlands' who had opposed York. Both lived during the reign of Henry VI and died in the Wars of the Roses. They were father and son, both named Henry Percy, and were second and third Earls of Northumberland, respectively. The elder (1384–1455) was the son of Hotspur in *1H4*. Despite the Percys' opposition to Henry IV, depicted in *1H4* and *2H4*, Henry V restored Hotspur's son to the title, and he was killed fighting for Lancaster at the first battle of St Albans (*2H6* 5.1–5.2). His son, who appears in *3H6* 1.1 and assists in the capture of York in 1.4, succeeded to the title when his father died, and was killed at the battle of Towton in 1461.

36 **Earl of** WESTMORLAND (d. 1484) Ralph Neville, second Earl of Westmorland, was less active in Lancaster's defence than his younger brother, John, who died at the battle of Towton in 1461, though both Hall (256) and Holinshed (278) mistakenly record Ralph's death there as well.

37 **Earl of** OXFORD (1443–1513) John de Vere, thirteenth Earl, loyal Lancastrian, fought alongside Warwick at Barnet and later joined the Earl of Richmond's invasion, commanding the right wing at the battle of Bosworth in *R3* 5.3.

38 **Mayor of Coventry** John Brett was mayor of Coventry in 1471, when 5.1 takes place. After the battle of Barnet, Edward IV deprived him of his sword of state for supporting Lancaster, but years later he consented to be godfather to the mayor's newborn child.

39 SOMERVILLE an invented character, called simply 'Somerville' in F, but George Russell French identified a fifteenth-century knight, Sir Thomas Somerville, from Aston-Somerville, four miles south of Evesham, within twenty miles of Stratford (G. French, 199). For a possible topical identification of Somerville, see Martin and Cox.

42 KING LEWIS (1423–83) normally pronounced as a monosyllable rhyming with 'loose' (Cercignani, 282). Louis XI's reign (1460–83) coincided with that of Edward IV of England

183

(1461–83), and Louis' entire reign was almost as troubled as the first ten years of Edward's. Louis' abortive marriage negotiation with Edward and his subsequent alliance with Warwick (3.3) took place between 1464 and 1470.

43 LADY BONA Third daughter of Louis, Duke of Savoy, Lady Bona was related to Louis XI by marriage: her eldest sister, Charlotte, was his Queen. This role could have been doubled by the boy who played Rutland, Richmond and the Nurse.

44 **Lord Bourbon** Louis, Count of Rousillon, was the illegitimate son of Charles, Duke of Bourbon, whose father was Admiral of France.

45–6 KEEPERS, MESSENGERS See the discussion on pp. 167–73 of the names 'Gabriel', 'Sinklo' and 'Humfrey' used in F. A 'keeper' is 'an officer who has charge of a forest, woods, or grounds' (*OED* I.1d).

KING HENRY VI, PART THREE,

WITH THE DEATH OF THE DUKE OF YORK

1.1   *Alarum. Enter* [Richard] Plantagenet[, *the* Duke
of YORK], EDWARD, RICHARD, NORFOLK, MONTAGUE,
WARWICK [,*with white roses in their hats,*] *and Soldiers.*

WARWICK
I wonder how the King escaped our hands.

1.1 Straining the resources of Shakespeare's acting company, the scene required at least twenty-one adult actors to enter and confront each other as the opposing Yorkists and Lancastrians (see Appendix 2). Anonymous '*Soldiers*' who enter at 1.1.0.3 have no lines and were likely hired extras, like '*the rest*' at 49.3. Two boy actors who enter at 210.1 have speaking parts and nearly filled out the full complement of the company on stage at one time. The imagined location, parliament, is identified at lines 25, 35, 39, 64, 71. In 1592, as in 1460 (when the scene is imagined to have taken place), this would have been part of the palace of Westminster (25) (Sugden, 562). The Yorkists have just won a battle, and the date of the imagined action (York's invasion of Parliament) suggests it was Northampton (fought on 10 July 1460), but details are also included from the first battle of St Albans, five years earlier. A throne was required on stage (26, 51), and it was somehow elevated (32 SD).

Shakespeare invented the confrontation, but York's occupation of the throne is recorded by both Hall (245) and Holinshed (262).

0.1 *Alarum* 'any noise – bells, trumpet blasts, or drum rolls – which would serve to indicate an enemy attack' (J. Long, 8). This SD, which is not in O, may be explained by the Yorkists' breaking in *by force* (29), but it also complements the dripping swords and fresh battle trophies, even though such details are literally incompatible with the distance between either St Albans or Northampton and the palace of Westminster.

0.2–3 O's SD indicates that these noblemen were dressed in Elizabethan costumes, which required officers to wear hats rather than steel helmets (illustrated in Ard³ *H5*, 4). The white rose was a Yorkist emblem; see *1H6* 2.4 and King Henry's comment at 2.5.97–102.

1   **the King escaped** For dramatic purposes, the scene is imagined to follow immediately after the first battle of St Albans on 22 May 1455 (Hall, 232–3;

TITLE] The third Part of Henry the Sixt, with the death of the Duke of YORKE. *F;* The true Tragedie of Richard *Duke of Yorke, and the death of* good King Henrie the Sixt, *with the whole contention betweene* the two Houses Lancaster and Yorke, as it was sundrie times acted by the Right Honourable the Earle of Pembroke his seruants *O.*   1.1] *Actus Primus. Scœna Prima. F*   0.1 Richard] *O*   0.1–2 *the* Duke of YORK] *O*   0.3 *with . . . hats*] *O*

YORK

While we pursued the horsemen of the north,
He slyly stole away, and left his men;
Whereat the great Lord of Northumberland,
Whose warlike ears could never brook retreat,   5
Cheered up the drooping army; and himself,
Lord Clifford and Lord Stafford, all abreast,
Charged our main battle's front, and breaking in,
Were by the swords of common soldiers slain.

EDWARD

Lord Stafford's father, Duke of Buckingham,   10
Is either slain or wounded dangerous.
I cleft his beaver with a downright blow.
That this is true, father, behold his blood.

MONTAGUE

And, brother, here's the Earl of Wiltshire's blood,

Holinshed, 240–2), which concludes *2H6*, but Henry did not flee that battle, and York was not declared heir apparent until 7 October 1460, three months after the battle of Northampton, which Shakespeare does not depict.

4   **Lord of Northumberland** See List of Roles, 35n.; Northumberland enters at 49.1.

5   **brook** put up with
    retreat a trumpet call to signal retreat in battle. *3H6* is unusual, among Shakespeare's plays, in starting with such offstage noise.

7   **Lord Stafford** Humphrey, eldest surviving son of Humphrey, first Duke of Buckingham (see 10n.). He was wounded at the first battle of St Albans and died soon after.

8   **main battle's** belonging to the principal body of the army, as opposed to van, rear, or wings (*OED* battle 9)

9   **by ... slain** York kills Clifford himself in *2H6* 5.2.13–30, and other references

to Clifford's death in *3H6* are consistent with that depiction (1.1.55, 162; 1.3.47; 1.4.31–32, 175). We may imagine York thinking of Stafford's death and inadvertently conflating Clifford's with it.

10   **Duke of Buckingham** Humphrey Stafford, first Duke of Buckingham (1402–60), killed at the battle of Northampton

11   **dangerous** O has 'dangerouslie', but such uninflected adverbs are common in Shakespeare, and F preserves the metre (see Abbott, 1).

12   **beaver** the lower portion of the face-guard of a helmet, when worn with a visor, but occasionally serving the purposes of both (*OED sb.*[2] 1)

13, 14   **blood** Edward and Montague presumably display weapons dripping with blood.

14   **brother** Montague could be addressing his brother Warwick (see List of Roles, 12n.), but Montague and York

2+ SP YORK] *O subst.; Pl. or Plan. or Plant. in F throughout the scene except for Yorke. at 76, 78 and 85*

Whom I encountered as the battles joined. 15
RICHARD [*Shows the head of Somerset.*]
Speak thou for me, and tell them what I did.
YORK
Richard hath best deserved of all my sons.
But is your grace dead, my Lord of Somerset?
NORFOLK
Such hope have all the line of John of Gaunt.
RICHARD
Thus do I hope to shake King Henry's head. 20
WARWICK
And so do I. Victorious Prince of York,
Before I see thee seated in that throne
Which now the house of Lancaster usurps,
I vow by heaven these eyes shall never close.
This is the palace of the fearful King, 25

also call one another *brother* at 1.2.4, 35, 54, and 59, whereas in fact they were nephew and uncle, since York was married to Cicely Neville, sister to Richard Neville, father of Warwick and Montague. F thus confuses Warwick with his father (both called Richard Neville), whereas O correctly has 'cousen' (in the general sense of a relation more distant than brother or sister) for F's ' brother'. *TxC* suggests that *brother* means 'brother-in-law', on the assumption that Shakespeare assumed York and Montague to be related that way. F correctly identifies Warwick and Montague as brothers at 2.1.166 and following.
Earl of Wiltshire James Butler, who was wounded at the first battle of St Albans but survived to fight at Wakefield, Mortimer's Cross and Towton, where he was taken prisoner and executed in 1461

15 **battles** troops in battle array (*OED sb.* 8a)

16 SD F's silence about Richard's action allows the actor a great deal of latitude, but he must do something to display Somerset's head and evoke the cruel mockery of York (18).

16 **Speak thou** Richard addresses the head of Somerset, which he carries (20). For Somerset, see List of Roles, 31n. and 32n.. Richard fought neither at Northampton, on 10 July 1460, when he was only eight years old, nor at the first battle of St Albans (imagined here), when he was three.

18 **your grace** York follows his son's example in mocking the dead man.

19 **Such hope** i.e. of death
   the . . . Gaunt York's rival in the Wars of the Roses was 'the house of Lancaster' (23), whose progenitor was John of Gaunt, Duke of Lancaster, fourth son of Edward III.

20 **shake** Richard presumably shakes Somerset's head, perhaps holding it by the hair.

16 SD] *Theobald subst.* 19 hope] hap *Dyce²*

And this the regal seat. Possess it, York,
For this is thine and not King Henry's heirs'.

YORK

Assist me then, sweet Warwick, and I will,
For hither we have broken in by force.

NORFOLK

We'll all assist you; he that flies shall die.   30

YORK

Thanks, gentle Norfolk. Stay by me, my lords,
And soldiers, stay and lodge by me this night.
    They go up [*to the chair of state*].

WARWICK

And when the King comes, offer him no violence,
Unless he seek to thrust you out perforce.

YORK

The Queen this day here holds her parliament,   35
But little thinks we shall be of her council.
By words or blows here let us win our right.

---

26 **regal seat** Holinshed's phrase (262); not in Hall (Boswell-Stone, 291). Already speaking in character as the 'kingmaker', Warwick gestures toward the *chair of state* (51) as he urges York to occupy it.

29 York 'broke vp the lockes and doores' of the palace 'and so lodged himselfe therein' (Holinshed, 262; not in Hall).

32 **soldiers, stay** The soldiers who entered with York at 1.1.0.3 must re-enter in a surprise move at 169 SD, and their exit for that re-entry could be York's command to remain *by me*, i.e. close by.

32 SD *They go up* York must go up, because he is later on the throne (50), which was probably on a movable platform. Cam[1] compares the staging in *Tit* 1.1, and notes that 'the dialogue, which allows no time for "going up" by the stair in the tiring-house',

implies a platform on the main stage. As many of York's allies may join him as the platform can hold and decorum permits.

35 **parliament** used here to describe a council of nobles (*OED sb.*[1] 2) rather than the Great Council of the nation (*OED sb.*[1] 3), which *parliament* connoted in the late sixteenth century. On the history plays' attention to Elizabethan constitutional issues, see p. 111.

36 **council** The king's privy council was a selected group of trusted noble advisors who together constituted the executive branch of government. York's reference to the council as belonging to the Queen reflects late sixteenth-century historical fact but in context is a disparagement of Henry's power and authority.

---

32 SD *to . . . state*] *Oxf subst.*   36 council] *Pope;* counsaile *F*

RICHARD

Armed as we are, let's stay within this house.

WARWICK

The 'Bloody Parliament' shall this be called,

Unless Plantagenet, Duke of York, be king,   40

And bashful Henry deposed, whose cowardice

Hath made us bywords to our enemies.

YORK

Then leave me not; my lords, be resolute.

I mean to take possession of my right.

WARWICK

Neither the King, nor he that loves him best,   45

The proudest bird that holds up Lancaster,

Dares stir a wing if Warwick shake his bells.

I'll plant Plantagenet; root him up who dares.

Resolve thee, Richard; claim the English crown.

Flourish. Enter KING HENRY, CLIFFORD, NORTHUMBERLAND,
WESTMORLAND, EXETER [, *with red roses in their hats,*]
and the rest.

40, 48 **Plantagenet** a family name, first
adopted as such by Richard Planagenet
(see List of Roles, 1n.) but originating
as a nickname for Geoffrey of Anjou
(1158–86), whose emblem was 'a sprig
(*planta*) of broom (*genesta*, a white or
yellow-flowered shrub)' (Saccio,
Shakespeare's, 244). This is another
remark that Warwick makes in character as 'kingmaker'. He again puns on
'plant' at 3.3.198.
41, 81, 107, 131, etc. **Henry** possibly trisyllabic (Cercignani, 358)
42 **Hath ... enemies** biblical: 'Thou
makest vs to be a byworde among the
Heathen' (Psalm 44.14) (Shaheen, 63)
46–7 The bells that enabled falconers to
locate a bird were an incidental means

to alarm the falcon's prey as well. Cf.
Luc 511.
49.1 *Flourish* a trumpet fanfare sig-
nalling ceremonial royal movement. J.
Long (27–8) points out that the flourish here highlights political ambiguity:
is it for York, who has just seated himself in the throne, or for Henry, who
has just entered?
49.2 *with ... hats* O's SD complements
the one at 1.1.0.3. Red roses were an
emblem of the house of Lancaster.
49.3 *and the rest* O's equivalent phrase
is '*with soldiers*', indicating followers of
Clifford, Northumberland and
Westmorland, with whom they leave
the stage at 188 SD.

46 bird] *O (burd);* hee *F*   49.2 *with ... hats*] *O*

KING HENRY

My lords, look where the sturdy rebel sits 50
Even in the chair of state. Belike he means,
Backed by the power of Warwick, that false peer,
To aspire unto the crown and reign as king.
Earl of Northumberland, he slew thy father,
And thine, Lord Clifford, and you both have
vowed revenge 55
On him, his sons, his favourites and his friends.

NORTHUMBERLAND

If I be not, heavens be revenged on me.

CLIFFORD

The hope thereof makes Clifford mourn in steel.

WESTMORLAND

What, shall we suffer this? Let's pluck him down.
My heart for anger burns; I cannot brook it. 60

KING HENRY

Be patient, gentle Earl of Westmorland.

CLIFFORD

Patience is for poltroons, such as he.
He durst not sit there had your father lived.
My gracious lord, here in the Parliament

---

50 **sturdy** intractable, hard to manage (*OED a.* 5). Ard² compares the common phrase 'sturdy beggar'.
  sturdy rebel sits York has seated himself by this time, perhaps at 44 or more climactically at 48. The latter would reinforce the ambiguity of '*Flourish*' (49.1n.).
51 **chair of state** 'the trone royall, vnder the clothe of estate (whiche is the kynges peculiar seate)' (Hall, 245) For *state*, see *1H4* 2.4.374.
  Belike probably
54 **he . . . father** See List of Roles, 35n.
55 **revenge** Among Shakespeare's plays, *3H6* is second only to *Tit* in the number of words with the root *venge*, just

as the two plays are comparable in depictions of anger, studied hate and stage violence.
56 **friends** used here, and most often throughout the play, to denote a network of aristocratic male relatives, allies and retainers. See Stone, *Family*, 97–8.
58 **mourn in steel** grieve without removing his armour
60 **brook** put up with
61 **gentle** noble
62 **Patience** three syllables (Cercignani, 309)
  poltroons cowards. The word was emphasized on the first syllable until the late seventeenth century.

Let us assail the family of York.   65
NORTHUMBERLAND
Well hast thou spoken, cousin. Be it so.
KING HENRY
Ah, know you not the city favours them,
And they have troops of soldiers at their beck?
EXETER
But when the Duke is slain, they'll quickly fly.
KING HENRY
Far be the thought of this from Henry's heart,   70
To make a shambles of the Parliament House.
Cousin of Exeter, frowns, words and threats
Shall be the war that Henry means to use. –
Thou, factious Duke of York, descend my throne
And kneel for grace and mercy at my feet.   75
I am thy sovereign.
YORK   I am thine.
EXETER
For shame, come down. He made thee Duke of York.
YORK
It was my inheritance, as the earldom was.
EXETER
Thy father was a traitor to the crown.

---

65 **family of York** Hall's phrase (245)
67 **the . . . them** Hall reports that in 1457
Margaret dared not attack the Duke of
York near 'the citie of London,
because she well perceyued the duke of
Yorke to be had in more estimacion
emonge the citezens & communaltie,
then the kyng her husband or her awn
person' (236).
71 **shambles** slaughter-house
77 **He . . . York.** See *1H6* 3.1.
78 **my inheritance** York inherited both
the duchy of York and the earldom of
Cambridge from his grandfather,
Edmund Langley, Duke of York, fifth
son of Edward III. The title descended
to York's uncle, Edward, called
Aumerle in *R2*, who was killed at
Agincourt (*H5* 4.8.104). The earldom
was given to York's father, Richard,
Aumerle's younger brother, who was
arrested and executed for treason by
Henry V, as Exeter points out (79; cf.
H5 2.2). York discovers his inheritance
for the first time in *1H6* 2.5, and he
explains it again to Warwick in *2H6*
2.2. For York's claim to the throne, see
List of Roles, 1n.

69 SP EXETER] *O; Westm. F*

WARWICK

    Exeter, thou art a traitor to the crown,   80

    In following this usurping Henry.

CLIFFORD

    Whom should he follow but his natural king?

WARWICK

    True, Clifford, and that's Richard, Duke of York.

KING HENRY

    And shall I stand, and thou sit in my throne?

YORK

    It must and shall be so. Content thyself.   85

WARWICK [*to Henry*]

    Be Duke of Lancaster. Let him be King.

WESTMORLAND

    He is both King and Duke of Lancaster,

    And that the Lord of Westmorland shall maintain.

WARWICK

    And Warwick shall disprove it. You forget

    That we are those which chased you from the field   90

    And slew your fathers, and with colours spread

    Marched through the city to the palace gates.

NORTHUMBERLAND

    Yes, Warwick, I remember it to my grief;

    And by his soul, thou and thy house shall rue it.

WESTMORLAND

    Plantagenet, of thee and these thy sons,   95

    Thy kinsmen and thy friends, I'll have more lives

    Than drops of blood were in my father's veins.

---

82 **natural** rightful, duly succeeded. The adjective begs the question being debated.

87 For Henry's claim to the throne, see List of Roles, 27n.

91 **fathers** Hall notes that Henry's council 'committed the gouernaunce of the armye to the duke of Somerset, the erle of Northumberland, and ye lord Clifford, as men desiring to reuenge ye death of their parentes slayn at the first battayle of sainct Albons' (254).

94 **rue** regret, be sorry for

83 and that's] *Q3;* and that is *O, Q2;* that's *F;* that is *(RP)*   86 SD] *Oxf*   93 Yes] *F;* No *O*

CLIFFORD

> Urge it no more, lest that instead of words
> I send thee, Warwick, such a messenger
> As shall revenge his death before I stir.   100

WARWICK

> Poor Clifford, how I scorn his worthless threats!

YORK

> Will you we show our title to the crown?
> If not, our swords shall plead it in the field.

KING HENRY

> What title hast thou, traitor, to the crown?
> Thy father was, as thou art, Duke of York,   105
> Thy grandfather, Roger Mortimer, Earl of March.
> I am the son of Henry the Fifth,
> Who made the Dauphin and the French to stoop
> And seized upon their towns and provinces.

WARWICK

> Talk not of France, sith thou hast lost it all.   110

KING HENRY

> The Lord Protector lost it and not I.
> When I was crowned, I was but nine months old.

99 **such a messenger** a fatal blow. Clifford proposes to move from words to violent deeds.

101 Warwick is 'disrespecting' Clifford, and the remark comes back to haunt the Yorkists in Clifford's savage treatment of York and Rutland.

102 **title** claim, legal right, entitlement

106 **Thy grandfather** What Henry leaves unsaid is that York's principal claim to the throne was the childless Richard II's declaration of Mortimer as his heir to the throne (*1H6* 2.5). Here, as in *1H4*, Shakespeare follows his sources in mistaking Roger, fourth Earl of March, for Edmund, fifth Earl, who was Richard's heir.

108 **Dauphin** the French heir, pronounced 'dolphin'(Cercignani, 354), as indicated in the spelling in Ard³ *1H6*

111 **Protector** one in charge of the kingdom during the minority, absence or incapacity of the sovereign (*OED sb.* 2a). Henry refers to his uncle, Humphrey, Duke of Gloucester, who was appointed Lord Protector after the death of Henry V, his elder brother (Hall, 115).

112 Henry V died on 31 August 1422, and his son, born on 6 December 1421, was named his heir on 1 September, thus succeeding to the throne at the age of nine months. Henry VI was crowned on 6 November 1429, at the age of seven. Cf. 3.1.76.

105 Thy] *O;* My *F*   108 Dauphin] *(Dolphin)*

RICHARD

> You are old enough now and yet methinks you lose.
> Father, tear the crown from the usurper's head.

EDWARD

> Sweet father, do so; set it on your head.　　　　　　　115

MONTAGUE

> Good brother, as thou lov'st and honourest arms,
> Let's fight it out and not stand cavilling thus.

RICHARD

> Sound drums and trumpets and the King will fly.

YORK

> Sons, peace.

KING HENRY

> Peace thou, and give King Henry leave to speak.　　　　120

WARWICK

> Plantagenet shall speak first; hear him, lords,
> And be you silent and attentive too,
> For he that interrupts him shall not live.

KING HENRY

> Think'st thou that I will leave my kingly throne,
> Wherein my grandsire and my father sat?　　　　　　125
> No, first shall war unpeople this my realm.
> Ay, and their colours, often borne in France,
> And now in England to our heart's great sorrow,
> Shall be my winding-sheet. Why faint you, lords?
> My title's good, and better far than his.　　　　　　130

---

113 The metre suggests elision of *You are* to *You're*, with consequent stress on *now* and *yet* (RP).
116 **brother** See 14n.
117 **cavilling** raising captious objections (*OED v.* 1)
120–4 O assigns 120 to Northumberland, deletes Warwick's command in 121–3, and gives Henry the following lines:

'Ah *Plantagenet*, why seekest thou to depose me? / Are we not both both [*sic*] *Plantagenets* by birth, / And from two brothers lineallie discent? / Suppose by right and equitie thou be king, / Thinkst thou that I will leaue my kinglie seate'.
129 **winding-sheet** burial cloth, shroud

113] *Pope; F lines* now, / loose: /　　116] *Pope; F lines* Brother, / Armes, /

194

WARWICK

    Prove it, Henry, and thou shalt be king.

KING HENRY

    Henry the Fourth by conquest got the crown.

YORK

    'Twas by rebellion against his King.

KING HENRY [*aside*]

    I know not what to say. My title's weak. –

    Tell me, may not a king adopt an heir?   135

YORK

    What then?

KING HENRY

    An if he may, then am I lawful king:

    For Richard, in the view of many lords,

    Resigned the crown to Henry the Fourth,

    Whose heir my father was, and I am his.   140

YORK

    He rose against him, being his sovereign,

    And made him to resign his crown perforce.

WARWICK

    Suppose, my lords, he did it unconstrained,

    Think you 'twere prejudicial to his crown?

EXETER

    No, for he could not so resign his crown,   145

    But that the next heir should succeed and reign.

---

133 **rebellion** four syllables
137 **An if** if. See Abbott, 103, on intensi-
    fication of the subjunctive.
139 **Resigned the crown** What Henry
    again leaves unsaid is that Richard
    declared Edmund Mortimer, not
    Henry Bolingbroke, to be his heir.
    Henry possibly trisyllabic (Cercignani,
    358)
143 **he** Richard II
143–6 Warwick argues that even a volun-
    tary (as opposed to coerced) surrender

of power on Richard's part would not
have invalidated his *right* to power, and
the argument persuades Exeter, who
states the corollary: that Richard's heir
(i.e. Mortimer) also had the right.
Hence Henry's question to Exeter
(147), who is a Lancastrian.
145–8, 150–3 York's question at 149 is an
implicit SD, indicating that the
Lancastrians confer among themselves. Cf. 165.

134 SD] *Capell subst.*

KING HENRY

Art thou against us, Duke of Exeter?

EXETER

His is the right, and therefore pardon me.

YORK

Why whisper you, my lords, and answer not?

EXETER

My conscience tells me he is lawful king.   150

KING HENRY

All will revolt from me and turn to him.

NORTHUMBERLAND [*to York*]

Plantagenet, for all the claim thou lay'st,

Think not that Henry shall be so deposed.

WARWICK

Deposed he shall be, in despite of all.

NORTHUMBERLAND

Thou art deceived. 'Tis not thy southern power   155

Of Essex, Norfolk, Suffolk nor of Kent,

Which makes thee thus presumptuous and proud,

Can set the Duke up in despite of me.

CLIFFORD

King Henry, be thy title right or wrong,

Lord Clifford vows to fight in thy defence.   160

May that ground gape and swallow me alive

Where I shall kneel to him that slew my father.

KING HENRY

O Clifford, how thy words revive my heart!

---

148 **His** York's
158 **Can** that can
159–62 Clifford's express allowance of a
doubt about Henry's title may indicate
that these lines are again meant only
for Lancastrian ears. On the other
hand, Clifford's declaration moves the
basis of action importantly from ques-

tions of right to questions of personal
vengeance, and Clifford is in no mood
to conceal his motive from anyone.
161 biblical: 'And the earth opened her
mouthe, and swalowed them vp . . . So
thei & all that thei had, went downe
aliue into the pit' (Numbers, 16.32–3)
(Shaheen, 64)

152 SD] *Oxf*   155] *Pope; F lines* decciu'd: / power /

YORK

    Henry of Lancaster, resign thy crown.

    What mutter you, or what conspire you, lords?   165

WARWICK

    Do right unto this princely Duke of York,

    Or I will fill the house with armed men

    And over the chair of state where now he sits

    Write up his title with usurping blood.

        He stamps with his foot, and the Soldiers show
        themselves.

KING HENRY

    My Lord of Warwick, hear me but one word: 170

    Let me for this my lifetime reign as king.

YORK

    Confirm the crown to me and to mine heirs,

    And thou shalt reign in quiet while thou liv'st.

KING HENRY

    I am content. Richard Plantagenet,

    Enjoy the kingdom after my decease.   175

CLIFFORD

    What wrong is this unto the Prince, your son!

WARWICK

    What good is this to England, and himself!

---

167 **armed** armèd

169 SD *Soldiers . . . themselves* For the concealing of the soldiers, see 32n.

170 **hear** possibly two syllables (Cercignani, 146). O has 'heare me speake', but the line is four syllables short. If *hear* is treated as a reflexive verb, *hear me*, the line is metrically perfect.

171 The suggestion made by Henry is, in Hall, the conclusion of 'long argumentes made, & deliberate consultacion had among the peeres, prelates, and commons of the realme' (249).

172–3 York's quick acceptance of Henry's suggestion in 171 indicates a keen awareness of political reality, in contrast to Henry, whose suggestion puts him in a position of damaging weakness to himself and his son, as his followers indignantly point out, especially Margaret (230–7).

174 **I am content.** O's Henry is less compliant: he refuses to concede under immediate threat, demanding that the soldiers who have just been summoned be dismissed, and Warwick dismisses them.

170 hear me] *F3;* heare *F1*

WESTMORLAND

Base, fearful and despairing Henry!

CLIFFORD

How hast thou injured both thyself and us.

WESTMORLAND

I cannot stay to hear these articles.   180

NORTHUMBERLAND

Nor I.

CLIFFORD [*to Northumberland*]

Come, cousin, let us tell the Queen these news.

WESTMORLAND

Farewell, faint-hearted and degenerate King,

In whose cold blood no spark of honour bides.

NORTHUMBERLAND

Be thou a prey unto the house of York   185

And die in bands for this unmanly deed.

CLIFFORD

In dreadful war mayst thou be overcome,

Or live in peace abandoned and despised.

> [*Exeunt Westmorland, Northumberland
> and Clifford, with their Soldiers.*]

WARWICK

Turn this way, Henry, and regard them not.

EXETER

They seek revenge and therefore will not yield.   190

---

178 **Henry** possibly trisyllabic (Cercignani, 358)
182 **cousin** Clifford's grandfather, John,
  married Elizabeth Percy, daughter of
  Hotspur in *1H4*. For Northumberland's relationship to Hotspur (and
  therefore to Clifford), see List of
  Roles, 35n.
  news frequently a plural noun in
  the sixteenth century, equivalent to

'new things'
184 **cold blood** the opposite of hot-
  blooded honour, quick in its own
  defence
186 **bands** whatever might be used to
  bind and imprison him
188 SD **with their Soldiers** These are
  '*the rest*' (49.3), who now leave with
  their lords.

182 SD] *this edn*   188 SD] *this edn; exits after 184, 186 and 188 O*

KING HENRY

   Ah, Exeter.

WARWICK   Why should you sigh, my lord?

KING HENRY

   Not for myself, Lord Warwick, but my son,

   Whom I unnaturally shall disinherit.

   But be it as it may. [*to York*] I here entail

   The crown to thee and to thine heirs forever,   195

   Conditionally, that here thou take an oath

   To cease this civil war and, whilst I live,

   To honour me as thy King and sovereign,

   And neither by treason nor hostility

   To seek to put me down and reign thyself.   200

YORK

   This oath I willingly take, and will perform.

WARWICK

   Long live King Henry! Plantagenet, embrace him.

KING HENRY

   And long live thou, and these thy forward sons.

YORK

   Now York and Lancaster are reconciled.

EXETER

   Accursed be he that seeks to make them foes.   205

                  Sennet. Here they come down.

YORK

   Farewell my gracious lord, I'll to my castle.

           [*Exeunt York, his sons and their Soldiers.*]

---

194 **entail** cause to descend to a designated series of possessors (*OED v.*² 2). Henry addresses the comment to York.

196 **oath** Holinshed prints a legal agreement between York and Henry (265–8), which includes an oath by York (266).

202 **embrace** perhaps an implicit SD. The SD at 205 suggests that York waits for Henry to ascend for the

embrace; if so, his waiting is as fraught with the symbolism of power as the fact that Warwick gives the command (202), and a duke and king obey him.

203 **forward** ready, prompt, eager (*OED a.* 6a)

205 SD *Sennet* music to accompany formal processions

206 **my castle** Sandal Castle, near Wakefield, also mentioned at 1.2.49, 62

194 SD] *Collier MS*   206, 207, 208, 209 SDs] *O subst.*

199

WARWICK
And I'll keep London with my soldiers.   [*Exit.*]
NORFOLK
And I to Norfolk with my followers.   [*Exit.*]
MONTAGUE
And I unto the sea, from whence I came.   [*Exit.*]
KING HENRY
And I with grief and sorrow to the court.   210

Enter QUEEN [MARGARET *and* PRINCE EDWARD].

EXETER
Here comes the Queen, whose looks bewray her anger.
I'll steal away.   [*Offers to leave.*]
KING HENRY   Exeter, so will I.
QUEEN MARGARET
Nay, go not from me; I will follow thee.
KING HENRY
Be patient, gentle Queen, and I will stay.
QUEEN MARGARET
Who can be patient in such extremes?   215
Ah, wretched man, would I had died a maid
And never seen thee, never borne thee son,

---

207 **soldiers** three syllables, as at 1.2.41
and in *JC* 4.1.28 (Cercignani, 309)
207–9 SD Soldiers presumably accompany Warwick, Norfolk and
Montague as each departs.
209 Montague had no connection with
the sea. Shakespeare may have
momentarily confused him with
Falconbridge. See 239.
211 an implicit SD to the actor playing
Margaret. Margaret's confrontation
with Henry at this point is Shakespeare's invention, but Hall describes
her angry looks: 'whose countenaunce

was so fearfull [i.e. frightening], and
whose looke was so terrible, that to al
men, against whom she toke a small
displeasure, her frounyng was their
vndoyng, & her indignacion, was their
death' (241).
bewray reveal, disclose (*OED*)
212 Exeter and Henry presumably head
toward another exit than the one
through which Margaret is entering.
214 **gentle** noble (as at 61); tender (with
evident dramatic irony)
215 **patient** three syllables (see 62n.)

210.1 MARGARET . . . EDWARD] and the *Prince. O*   211] *Pope subst.; F lines* Queene, / anger: /   212
SD] *Capell subst.*

Seeing thou hast proved so unnatural a father.
Hath he deserved to lose his birthright thus?
Hadst thou but loved him half so well as I,   220
Or felt that pain which I did for him once,
Or nourished him, as I did with my blood,
Thou wouldst have left thy dearest heart-blood there,
Rather than have made that savage Duke thine heir
And disinherited thine only son.   225

PRINCE EDWARD
Father, you cannot disinherit me.
If you be king, why should not I succeed?

KING HENRY
Pardon me, Margaret; pardon me, sweet son;
The Earl of Warwick and the Duke enforced me.

QUEEN MARGARET
Enforced thee? Art thou king, and wilt be forced?   230
I shame to hear thee speak. Ah, timorous wretch,
Thou hast undone thyself, thy son and me,
And given unto the house of York such head
As thou shalt reign but by their sufferance.
To entail him and his heirs unto the crown,   235
What is it, but to make thy sepulchre
And creep into it far before thy time?
Warwick is Chancellor and the lord of Calais;
Stern Falconbridge commands the narrow seas;

---

218 **thou hast** possibly elided to 'thou'st' (RP)

222 **blood** perhaps a compositor's anticipation of the next line, because a mother's nourishing milk (not blood) follows the pain of birth (GWW)

230–7 'The Queen's reproach is founded on a position long received among politicians, that the loss of a king's power is soon followed by loss of life' (S. Johnson, 8.598).

233 **head** freedom (from giving a horse its head, or relaxing the reins) (*OED sb.* 57)

239 **Falconbridge** William Neville (d. 1463) became Baron Falconbridge by marrying Joan, only child of the previous baron. He was the son of Ralph Neville, first Earl of Westmorland, half brother of Ralph Neville, second Earl, and uncle to Richard Neville, Earl of Warwick (for these two, see List of Roles, 11n. and 36n.). Falconbridge was given command of a fleet at

---

222 blood] milk *(GWW)*   238 Calais] *(Callice)*

The Duke is made Protector of the realm;   240
And yet shalt thou be safe? Such safety finds
The trembling lamb environed with wolves.
Had I been there, which am a silly woman,
The soldiers should have tossed me on their pikes
Before I would have granted to that act.   245
But thou preferr'st thy life before thine honour.
And seeing thou dost, I here divorce myself
Both from thy table, Henry, and thy bed,
Until that act of Parliament be repealed
Whereby my son is disinherited.   250
The northern lords, that have forsworn thy colours,
Will follow mine if once they see them spread:
And spread they shall be, to thy foul disgrace,
And utter ruin of the house of York.
Thus do I leave thee. Come, son, let's away.   255
Our army is ready; come, we'll after them.

KING HENRY
Stay, gentle Margaret, and hear me speak.

QUEEN MARGARET
Thou hast spoke too much already. Get thee gone.

KING HENRY
Gentle son Edward, thou wilt stay with me?

QUEEN MARGARET
Ay, to be murdered by his enemies.   260

PRINCE EDWARD
When I return with victory from the field

Southampton in 1457 and appointed
admiral of England in 1462.

240 The agreement drawn up by Henry
and York provided that York would
serve as Lord Protector until Henry's
death (Hall, 249).

242 **environed** environèd

243 **silly** helpless, defenceless (*OED adj.*

1b)

247–50 With this declaration, Margaret
becomes *de facto* leader of the Lancastrian party. Cf. Prince Edward at
261–2 and Northumberland's deference to Margaret at 1.4.65.

258 **Thou hast** See 218n.

259 with] *O; not in F*   261 from] *O; to F*

I'll see your grace; till then, I'll follow her.

QUEEN MARGARET

Come, son, away. We may not linger thus.

[Exit with Prince Edward.]

KING HENRY

Poor Queen, how love to me and to her son
Hath made her break out into terms of rage.   265
Revenged may she be on that hateful Duke,
Whose haughty spirit, wingèd with desire,
Will coast my crown and, like an empty eagle,
Tire on the flesh of me and of my son.
The loss of those three lords torments my heart.   270
I'll write unto them and entreat them fair.
Come, cousin, you shall be the messenger.

EXETER

And I, I hope, shall reconcile them all.   *Flourish. Exeunt.*

[1.2]   *Enter* RICHARD, EDWARD *and* MONTAGUE.

263 **may** must
267 **wingèd** wingèd
268 **coast** a falcon's deviation from a straight course in order to cut off the prey when it doubles (*OED v.* 10)
269 **Tire** feed greedily upon (from falconry) (*OED sb.* II 2b)
272 **cousin** used to describe virtually any family relationship not specifiable by some other term. Exeter was married to Anne Plantagenet, sister of Edward, Richard and George; Exeter was therefore related to Henry by marriage, through Henry's and Anne's common descent from Edward III. See List of Roles, 33n.
273 SD *Flourish.* F places this SD in TLN 307 (i.e. at 1.2.0), because the compositor had no room for it at the end of TLN 306, where it would more clearly accompany Henry's departure (GWW). J. Long points out that the

flourish again sounds ambiguously – not only for Henry's exit but also close to York's entrance, 'one who is losing his grip on the scepter, and the other who is being urged to seize it' (28).
1.2 The Messenger identifies the scene as York's castle (49), where York said he intended to go in 1.1.206. This was Sandal Castle (62), near Wakefield, which York reached on Christmas Eve, 1460, having left London on 2 December (Hall, 250). The battle of Wakefield, which occupies the rest of Act 1, was fought nearby on 30 December.
0.1 Edward was not present at the battle of Wakefield, having been ordered to the Welsh border. Hall reports that a servant urged York to wait for Edward and the forces he had with him, in order to even the odds against the Lancastrians, but the Duke refused

263 SD] *Rowe subst.*   264–5] *Pope subst.; F lines* Queene, / Sonne, /   268 coast] *(cost)*   273 SD] *Wilson subst.; Exit. / Flourish. (as part of 1.2.0.1) F*   1.2] *Capell*

RICHARD

    Brother, though I be youngest, give me leave.

EDWARD

    No, I can better play the orator.

MONTAGUE

    But I have reasons strong and forcible.

Enter the Duke of YORK.

YORK

    Why, how now, sons and brother, at a strife?

    What is your quarrel? How began it first?   5

EDWARD

    No quarrel, but a slight contention.

YORK   About what?

RICHARD

    About that which concerns your grace and us:

    The crown of England, father, which is yours.

YORK

    Mine, boy? Not till King Henry be dead.

RICHARD

    Your right depends not on his life or death.   10

EDWARD

    Now you are heir; therefore enjoy it now.

    By giving the house of Lancaster leave to breathe,

    It will outrun you, father, in the end.

YORK

    I took an oath that he should quietly reign.

EDWARD

    But for a kingdom any oath may be broken.   15

---

(250). Historically, Richard was too young to have fought at Wakefield (see 1.1.16n.).

1   Richard's assertiveness complements his ghoulishness (1.1.16), irony (1.2.17), sophistry (21–4), and ambition (27–30) as vicious aspects of his character in this play. See pp. 75–81.

4   **brother** See 1.1.14n.

9   **Henry** possibly trisyllabic (Cercignani, 358)

15 proverbial. Ard[1] cites Cicero, 'If the law must be violated, it must be violated in order to govern' (*De officiis,*

I would break a thousand oaths to reign one year.
RICHARD
No. God forbid your grace should be forsworn.
YORK
I shall be, if I claim by open war.
RICHARD
I'll prove the contrary, if you'll hear me speak.
YORK
Thou canst not, son; it is impossible.   20
RICHARD
An oath is of no moment, being not took
Before a true and lawful magistrate
That hath authority over him that swears.
Henry had none, but did usurp the place.
Then, seeing 'twas he that made you to depose,   25
Your oath, my lord, is vain and frivolous.
Therefore, to arms. And, father, do but think
How sweet a thing it is to wear a crown,
Within whose circuit is Elysium
And all that poets feign of bliss and joy.   30
Why do we linger thus? I cannot rest
Until the white rose that I wear be dyed
Even in the lukewarm blood of Henry's heart.
YORK
Richard, enough. I will be king or die.
Brother, thou shalt to London presently   35
And whet on Warwick to this enterprise.

3.83). Compare, 'For a kingdom any law may be broken' (Tilley, K90).

21–4 'The obligation of an oath is here eluded by very despicable sophistry. A lawful magistrate alone has the power to exact an oath, but the oath derives no part of its force from the magistrate' (S. Johnson, 8.598–9).

25 **depose** promise formally upon oath (*OED v.* 5b)

26 **frivolous** manifestly insufficient or futile (*OED a.* 1b), another legal term

27–30 an echo of *1 Tamburlaine*, 2.6.863–80, implicitly identifying Richard with Christopher Marlowe's overweening hero

35 **Brother** See 1.1.14n.
   presently immediately

Thou, Richard, shalt to the Duke of Norfolk
And tell him privily of our intent.
You, Edward, shall unto my Lord Cobham,
With whom the Kentishmen will willingly rise.   40
In them I trust, for they are soldiers
Witty, courteous, liberal, full of spirit.
While you are thus employed, what resteth more,
But that I seek occasion how to rise,
And yet the King not privy to my drift,   45
Nor any of the house of Lancaster.

Enter a Messenger.

But stay, what news? Why com'st thou in such post?
MESSENGER
        The Queen with all the northern earls and lords
        Intend here to besiege you in your castle.
        She is hard by with twenty thousand men,   50
        And therefore fortify your hold, my lord.   [*Exit.*]
YORK
        Ay, with my sword. What, think'st thou that we fear
            them?
        Edward and Richard, you shall stay with me.
        My brother Montague shall post to London.
        Let noble Warwick, Cobham and the rest,   55
        Whom we have left protectors of the King,

---

41 **soldiers** three syllables. See 1.1.207n.
42 **Witty** intelligent
43–4 York has consistently sought 'occa-
    sion how to rise' since discovering his
    claim to the throne in *1H6*. In this, he
    anticipates his son Richard.
43 **resteth** remains
45 **drift** scheme, plot (*OED sb.* 5)
46.1 **Messenger** See List of Roles,
    45–6n.

50 **twenty thousand** Hall has: 'eightene
    thousande men, or as some write,
    twentie and twoo thousande' (250).
54 **brother Montague** See 1.1.14n.
56 **protectors** York uses the word as
    defined at 1.1.111n., but context sug-
    gests ironic inconsistency with the pri-
    mary definition: 'One who protects,
    defends, or shields from injury or
    harm' (*OED* 1a).

46.1 *a* Messenger] *O; Gabriel F*   48 SP MESSENGER] *O subst.; Gabriel F*   48] *Pope subst.; F lines*
Queene, / Lords, /   51 SD] *this edn*   52] *Pope subst.; F lines* Sword. / them? /

206

With powerful policy strengthen themselves
And trust not simple Henry nor his oaths.

MONTAGUE

Brother, I go; I'll win them, fear it not.   59
And thus most humbly I do take my leave.   *Exit.*

Enter [SIR JOHN] MORTIMER *and his brother*
[*Sir Hugh Mortimer*].

YORK

Sir John and Sir Hugh Mortimer, mine uncles,
You are come to Sandal in a happy hour.
The army of the Queen mean to besiege us.

SIR JOHN MORTIMER

She shall not need; we'll meet her in the field.

YORK

What, with five thousand men?   65

RICHARD

Ay, with five hundred, father, for a need.
A woman's general. What should we fear?

A march afar off.

EDWARD

I hear their drums. Let's set our men in order,
And issue forth and bid them battle straight.

YORK

Five men to twenty: though the odds be great,   70

---

57 **policy** political dissimulation. For the
significance of this word in sixteenth-
century drama, see Bawcutt.
58 **simple** stupid, half-witted (*OED a.*
10a). As York has just broken his own
oath to Henry, his denigration of
Henry's intelligence where oath-
keeping is concerned seems particularly self-serving.
59 **Brother** See 1.1.14n.
65 'he hauing with him not fully fiue

thousande persones' (Hall, 250).
66–7 Richard takes the lead in bravado, as
in misogyny, whereas in Hall, the
aggression is all York's (250).
67.1 *march* Elizabethan theatres replicat-
ed the same marches, played on drum
and fife, that were used to signal troop
movements in actual battles (J. Long,
4–6) and sometimes hired royal musi-
cians for the purpose (J. Long, 11–12).
afar off i.e. off-stage

60.1 SIR JOHN] O   60.2 *Sir Hugh Mortimer*] O   68] *Pope; F lines* Drummes: / order, /

I doubt not, uncle, of our victory.
Many a battle have I won in France,
When as the enemy hath been ten to one.
Why should I not now have the like success?   *Alarum. Exeunt.*

[1.3]   *Enter* RUTLAND *and his* Tutor.

RUTLAND
  Ah, whither shall I fly to scape their hands?

                  Enter CLIFFORD [*with Soldiers*].

  Ah, tutor, look where bloody Clifford comes!
CLIFFORD
  Chaplain, away, thy priesthood saves thy life.
  As for the brat of the accursed Duke,
  Whose father slew my father, he shall die.   5
TUTOR
  And I, my lord, will bear him company.
CLIFFORD
  Soldiers, away with him.
TUTOR
  Ah, Clifford, murder not this innocent child,

---

73 **When as** when. See Abbott, 116.
1.3 Rutland, aged seventeen (though
    imagined here to be much younger),
    fled the battle of Wakefield, which
    begins at the end of 1.2, but was over-
    taken and murdered by Clifford. The
    scene follows Hall's description
    (250–1).
0.1 O includes 'Alarmes' in its SD. In
    Elizabethan staging, the '*Alarum*' in F
    at 1.2.74 SD would have been continu-
    ous with the beginning of 1.3.
2 **bloody Clifford** Rutland's epithet
    anticipates the deed for which Hall

describes Clifford as a *deadly bloudsup-
per* (251).
4 **accursed** accursèd
5 **Whose . . . father** York kills Clifford's
    father in *2H6* 5.2.
7 O gives Clifford additional lines that
    suggest a struggle: 'Soldiers awaie and
    drag him hence perforce: / Awaie with
    the villaine', but not all of Clifford's
    soldiers need leave with the Tutor. See
    9 SDn.
8 **this innocent child** Shakespeare
    reduces Rutland's age for effect. See
    1.3n.

---

74 SD *Exeunt*] *Q2; Exit. F*   **1.3**] *Capell*   1.1] *O; after 2 F*   *with Soldiers*] *Theobald*

Lest thou be hated both of God and man.   *Exit [guarded]*.
CLIFFORD

How now, is he dead already? Or is it fear   10
That makes him close his eyes? I'll open them.
RUTLAND

So looks the pent-up lion o'er the wretch
That trembles under his devouring paws;
And so he walks, insulting o'er his prey,
And so he comes to rend his limbs asunder.   15
Ah, gentle Clifford, kill me with thy sword
And not with such a cruel threat'ning look.
Sweet Clifford, hear me speak before I die:
I am too mean a subject for thy wrath;
Be thou revenged on men and let me live.   20
CLIFFORD

In vain thou speak'st, poor boy; my father's blood
Hath stopped the passage where thy words should enter.
RUTLAND

Then let my father's blood open it again.

---

9   **hated . . . man** Ard[2] compares *FQ*,
1.1.13, 'whom God and man does hate',
and 1.5.48, 'scorned of God and man'.
9 SD The soldiers mentioned in 7 may all
exit with the Tutor in custody, thus
clearing the stage for the unequal confrontation that follows. On the other
hand, to have some of them attend
Clifford while he kills Rutland – perhaps holding and threatening the child
– would strengthen comparison with
the death of Prince Edward in 5.5,
where several adults surround and
destroy a child.
12–15 suggested by Hall: 'for the prop-
ertie of the Lyon, which is a furious
and an vnreasonable beaste, is to be
cruell to them that withstande hym,

and gentle to such as prostrate or
humiliate them selfes before him'
(Hall, 251). Cf. 2.2.11–12.
12 **pent-up** 'That is, the lion that hath
long been "confined" without food,
and is let out to devour a man condemned' (S. Johnson, 8.599).
14 **insulting** exulting proudly or contemptuously (*OED v.* 1.)
16 Cam[1] compares Lavinia's plea: 'O
Tamora, be called a gentle queen, /
And with thine own hands kill me in
this place!'(*Tit* 2.2.168–9).
    gentle noble
19 **mean** inferior in social rank or senior-
ity (*OED a.* 2a.), here used by Rutland
to suggest that he is not a worthy
opponent for Clifford

---

9 SD *guarded*] *Theobald subst.*   10–11] *Pope; F lines* alrcadic? / eyes? / them.   21–2] *Pope; F lines*
Boy: / passage / enter. /

He is a man and, Clifford, cope with him.

CLIFFORD

Had I thy brethren here, their lives and thine   25
Were not revenge sufficient for me.
No, if I digged up thy forefathers' graves
And hung their rotten coffins up in chains,
It could not slake mine ire nor ease my heart.
The sight of any of the house of York   30
Is as a Fury to torment my soul:
And till I root out their accursed line
And leave not one alive, I live in hell.
Therefore –

RUTLAND

O, let me pray before I take my death;   35
To thee I pray: sweet Clifford, pity me!

CLIFFORD

Such pity as my rapier's point affords.

RUTLAND

I never did thee harm; why wilt thou slay me?

CLIFFORD

Thy father hath.

RUTLAND   But 'twas ere I was born.
Thou hast one son, for his sake pity me,   40
Lest in revenge thereof, sith God is just,
He be as miserably slain as I.

---

24 **cope** come to blows with, engage
(*OED v.*² 2)
26 **sufficient** four syllables (Cercignani,
309)
31 **Fury** one of the classical demonic
goddesses who torment the guilty
32 **accursed** accursèd
34 With this word, Clifford appears ready
to deliver the final blow. Cf. 47.
36 **I pray** Rutland may kneel, as reported
by both Hall (251) and Holinshed
(269).
37 **rapier's point** an anachronism, as at

1.4.80. The rapier was first introduced
into England in the second half of the
sixteenth century, when it became the
aristocratic weapon of choice. See
Stone, *Crisis*, 242–50.
39 **ere . . . born** In alluding to York's
killing of Old Clifford at the first battle of St Albans, only five years earlier,
Rutland may be exaggerating his own
youth for effect.
40–2 Rutland's hope for God's vengeance
against Clifford's son is not realized in
Shakespeare.

Ah, let me live in prison all my days,
And when I give occasion of offence
Then let me die, for now thou hast no cause.   45
CLIFFORD
No cause?
Thy father slew my father; therefore die. [*Stabs him.*]
RUTLAND
Di faciant laudis summa sit ista tuae. [*Dies.*]
CLIFFORD
Plantagenet, I come, Plantagenet!
And this thy son's blood, cleaving to my blade,   50
Shall rust upon my weapon till thy blood
Congealed with this do make me wipe off both.

Exit [*with Rutland's body*].

[**1.4**]   *Alarum. Enter* Richard, Duke of YORK.

YORK
The army of the Queen hath got the field.
My uncles both are slain in rescuing me,
And all my followers to the eager foe
Turn back and fly like ships before the wind,

---

45 **no cause** Cf. *KL* 4.7.75.
48 'The gods grant that this may be the
height of your glory' (Ovid, *Heroides*,
2.66). The line is spoken by Phyllis
after Demophoön has abandoned her,
and its bitter irony is therefore heightened in a play where so many people
break their promises as soon as they
make them. With this line Rutland
presumably dies.
50 **cleaving** clinging
52 SD Either Clifford alone or the soldiers with him (see 9 SD) clear the
stage by removing Rutland's body as
they leave.

1.4 The scene imagines another part of
the battle of Wakefield, near Sandal
Castle (1.2.62). Shakespeare used both
Hall and Holinshed in staging the capture and death of York, as indicated
below, but he invented such details as
the cloth steeped in Rutland's blood
and Margaret's making a game out of
her torment of York.
2 **My uncles** Sir John and Sir Hugh
Mortimer, whom York welcomes to the
battle at 1.2.61. See List of Roles,
7–8n.
4 **Turn back** turn their backs (as at
2.1.184)

46–7] *Pope; one line F*   47 SD] *Rowe*   48 *Di] (Dij)*   SD] *Theobald*   52 SD *with Rutland's body] Oxf*
1.4] *Capell*

Or lambs pursued by hunger-starved wolves.   5
My sons, God knows what hath bechanced them;
But this I know, they have demeaned themselves
Like men born to renown, by life or death.
Three times did Richard make a lane to me
And thrice cried, 'Courage, father, fight it out!'   10
And full as oft came Edward to my side,
With purple falchion painted to the hilt
In blood of those that had encountered him;
And when the hardiest warriors did retire,
Richard cried, 'Charge, and give no foot of ground!'   15
And cried, 'A crown, or else a glorious tomb,
A sceptre, or an earthly sepulchre!'
With this we charged again, but, out, alas,
We budged again, as I have seen a swan
With bootless labour swim against the tide   20
And spend her strength with overmatching waves.

                                   A short alarum within.

Ah, hark, the fatal followers do pursue,
And I am faint and cannot fly their fury;
And were I strong, I would not shun their fury.
The sands are numbered that makes up my life: 25
Here must I stay, and here my life must end.

            Enter QUEEN [MARGARET], CLIFFORD,
NORTHUMBERLAND, *young* PRINCE [EDWARD] *and Soldiers.*

---

5 **hunger-starved** hunger-starvèd
6 **bechanced** bechancèd
7 **demeaned** behaved, conducted or comported themselves (*OED v.*¹ 6)
12 **falchion** sword
14 **retire** retreat
18 **out, alas** expression of indignant reproach (*OED int.* 2)
20 **bootless** useless, unavailing
21 **with** as a result of, by the action of

(*OED* 39a), i.e. 'expend all her energy by competing with the current (as if she were on a treadmill)'. Cf. *TS* 3.2.241, *TN* 3.4.333.
24 **And were I** If I were
25 **sands . . . makes** See Abbott, 333, on third-person plural in *-s*.
26.2 *young* PRINCE Historically Edward was eight years old in 1460, when the battle of Wakefield was fought.

19 budged] (bodg'd)

212

Come bloody Clifford, rough Northumberland,
I dare your quenchless fury to more rage;
I am your butt and I abide your shot.

NORTHUMBERLAND

Yield to our mercy, proud Plantagenet!   30

CLIFFORD

Ay, to such mercy as his ruthless arm
With downright payment showed unto my father.
Now Phaëton hath tumbled from his car
And made an evening at the noontide prick.

YORK

My ashes, as the phoenix, may bring forth   35
A bird that will revenge upon you all,
And in that hope I throw mine eyes to heaven,
Scorning whate'er you can afflict me with.
Why come you not? What, multitudes, and fear?

CLIFFORD

So cowards fight when they can fly no further,   40
So doves do peck the falcon's piercing talons,
So desperate thieves, all hopeless of their lives,
Breathe out invectives 'gainst the officers.

---

29 **butt** target
  abide stand to receive
32 **downright** Cam¹ suggests wordplay:
  (1) immediate and full; (2) with a
  downward sweep of the arm (comparing 1.1.12).
33 **Phaëton** Attempting to drive his
  father's chariot (the sun), Phaëton lost
  control, and Jove had to destroy him
  with a thunderbolt (*Metamorphoses*, 2).
  Clifford may allude to Phaëton
  because the sun was York's emblem,
  but he applies it to Henry at 2.6.12,
  and it was a favourite for the young
  Shakespeare. See *TGV* 3.1.153, *R2*
  3.3.178, *RJ* 3.2.3.
34 **prick** a mark on a dial (*OED sb.* 3).
35 **phoenix** 'A certaine byrd of whose
  kinde is neuer but one at ones. He

liueth aboue 600 yeres, and then
makyng his neast in the toppe of an
high mountayne with swete spices, by
the heate of the sunne and labour of
his wynges kindleth fiar wherwith he is
consumed: then of his ashes riseth an
other like birde' (Cooper). See
Metamorphoses, 15.392–407.
36 York's prediction is fulfilled both in
  Edward, who defeated the Lancastrians, and in Richard, who extin-
  guished the Lancastrian male line.
40 proverbial: 'Despair makes cowards
  courageous' (Tilley, D216)
41 Ard¹ compares 2.2.18 and *AC*
  3.13.201–2, 'in that mood / The dove
  will peck the estridge'.
43 **Breathe** say vehemently or passion-
  ately (*OED v.* 12b)

YORK

O Clifford, but bethink thee once again,
An in thy thought o'errun my former time: 45
An, if thou canst for blushing, view this face
And bite thy tongue that slanders him with cowardice
Whose frown hath made thee faint and fly ere this.

CLIFFORD

I will not bandy with thee word for word,
But buckler with thee blows twice two for one.   50

QUEEN MARGARET

Hold, valiant Clifford, for a thousand causes
I would prolong awhile the traitor's life.
Wrath makes him deaf: speak thou, Northumberland.

NORTHUMBERLAND

Hold, Clifford, do not honour him so much
To prick thy finger, though to wound his heart.   55
What valour were it when a cur doth grin
For one to thrust his hand between his teeth,
When he might spurn him with his foot away?
It is war's prize to take all vantages,
And ten to one is no impeach of valour.   60

[*They fight and take York.*]

---

44 **bethink thee** reflect, consider (*OED v. refl.* 8)
45 **o'errun** look over, review
46 **if . . . blushing** if you are not ashamed **for** in spite of
47 **bite** control, discipline. The phrase is proverbial (Dent, T400.1). York uses it in *2H6* 1.1.227, and it appears once again in *Tit* 3.1.132.
49 **bandy** go to and fro, rally (metaphor from tennis)
50 **buckler** (1) ward or catch blows with the shield (*OED v.* 2), though this is the only instance; (2) perhaps 'buckle',

as in O, grapple with in combat (*OED* 3b). Cf. *1H6* 1.2.95 and 5.2.49.
53 **him** Clifford
55 **prick . . . heart** proverbial: 'The pricking of thy finger is the piercing of his heart' (Dent, P571.1)
56 **grin** bare its teeth (*OED v.* 1a)
59 **prize** privilege (*OED sb.*[1] 3b)
60 **ten . . . valour** The patent falseness of Northumberland's bluster illustrates the extent to which civil war has eroded civil conduct.
impeach impairment

45, 46 An] *(And)*   60 SD] *O subst.*

CLIFFORD

Ay, ay, so strives the woodcock with the gin.

NORTHUMBERLAND

So doth the cony struggle in the net.

YORK

So triumph thieves upon their conquered booty;

So true men yield, with robbers so o'ermatched.

NORTHUMBERLAND

What would your grace have done unto him now?　　　　65

QUEEN MARGARET

Brave warriors, Clifford and Northumberland,

Come, make him stand upon this molehill here

That raught at mountains with outstretched arms,

Yet parted but the shadow with his hand.

What, was it you that would be England's king?　　　　70

Was't you that revelled in our Parliament

And made a preachment of your high descent?

Where are your mess of sons to back you now?

The wanton Edward and the lusty George?

And where's that valiant crookback prodigy,　　　　75

---

61 **gin** snare, trap. 'He was enuironed on euery side, like a fish in a net, or a deere in a buckestall' (Hall, 250).

62 **cony** rabbit (*OED sb.* 1a.); dupe, gull (*OED* 6)

67 **molehill** Holinshed describes York being mocked on a 'molehill' (269). The actor may indicate a platform on stage (perhaps the same one used for the dais at 1.1.32 SD), but Margaret is primarily interested in the contrast with *mountains* (68), as in 'Of a mole-hill he makes a mountain' (Tilley, M1035).

68 **raught at** reached for
outstretched outstretchèd

69 **parted** divided. Margaret implies a contrast between reality or substance and appearance or shadow.

71 **revelled** 'led your party of riotous masquers' (Cam¹). Cf. 2.2.150 and 3.3.224–5.

72 **made a preachment** preached a (wearying) sermon

73 **mess** set of four (Onions), i.e. Edward, Rutland, George and Richard

74 **wanton** This is the first indication of Edward's weakness for women, which he manifests in 3.2.

75 **crookback** hunchback. Following Thomas More's *Life of Richard III* (1513–18), Hall calls Richard 'croke backed' (342), and the word appears only in this play (see 2.2.96, 5.5.30), though Clifford calls Richard 'crooked in . . . shape' in *2H6* 5.1.158.
prodigy monster. See p. 58.

215

Dickie, your boy, that with his grumbling voice
Was wont to cheer his dad in mutinies?
Or with the rest, where is your darling, Rutland?
Look, York, I stained this napkin with the blood
That valiant Clifford with his rapier's point   80
Made issue from the bosom of the boy;
And if thine eyes can water for his death,
I give thee this to dry thy cheeks withal.
Alas, poor York, but that I hate thee deadly
I should lament thy miserable state.   85
I prithee grieve to make me merry, York.
What, hath thy fiery heart so parched thine entrails
That not a tear can fall for Rutland's death?
Why art thou patient, man? Thou shouldst be mad;
And I to make thee mad do mock thee thus.   90
Stamp, rave and fret, that I may sing and dance.
Thou wouldst be fee'd, I see, to make me sport:
York cannot speak unless he wear a crown.
A crown for York, and, lords, bow low to him.
Hold you his hands whilst I do set it on.   95
Ay, marry, sir, now looks he like a king;
Ay, this is he that took King Henry's chair,
And this is he was his adopted heir.
But how is it that great Plantagenet
Is crowned so soon and broke his solemn oath?   100
As I bethink me, you should not be king

---

80 **rapier's point** See 1.3.37n.
86 Holinshed compares the mocking of York to the mocking of Christ (269), and Margaret's determination to make a game out of her cruelty to York, while not in the chronicles, has a precedent in the buffeting and scourging of Christ in the mystery plays. See Kolve, 175–206.
87 **entrails** 'inward parts regarded as the seat of the emotions, thoughts, etc.; = "heart", "soul"' (*OED sb.*[1] 4)

92 **fee'd** paid a fee. Margaret mocks York by imagining him to be a common paid performer.
95 an implicit SD. In different versions of York's death, Holinshed mentions both 'a crowne of paper' and 'a crowne ... made of sedges or bulrushes' (269). Richard accuses Margaret of using a paper crown in *R3* 1.3.17; see Introduction p.19.
96 **marry** attenuated oath, 'by the Virgin Mary'

Till our King Henry had shook hands with death.
And will you pale your head in Henry's glory
And rob his temples of the diadem
Now, in his life, against your holy oath?   105
O, 'tis a fault too too unpardonable.
Off with the crown, and with the crown, his head,
And whilst we breathe take time to do him dead!

CLIFFORD
That is my office, for my father's sake.

QUEEN MARGARET
Nay, stay, let's hear the orisons he makes.   110

YORK
She-wolf of France, but worse than wolves of France,
Whose tongue more poisons than the adder's tooth!
How ill-beseeming is it in thy sex
To triumph like an Amazonian trull,
Upon their woes whom Fortune captivates.   115
But that thy face is vizard-like, unchanging,
Made impudent with use of evil deeds,
I would assay, proud Queen, to make thee blush.
To tell thee whence thou cam'st, of whom derived,
Were shame enough to shame thee, were thou
    not shameless.   120

---

102 **shook hands with** greeted, met. Proverbial (Dent, SS6).
103 **pale** surround. Ard[2] compares *impale* at 3.2.171 and 3.3.189.
107 Since Margaret does not behead York at this point, she may not remove the crown either. He seems to shake it off himself at 164.
108 While there is a break in the battle, let's take the opportunity to kill him.
109 **office** obligation, service
110 **orisons** prayers
111 **She-wolf** Cooper defines *lupa* (she-wolf) as 'An harlotte'. Cf. *trull* (114).
114 **Amazonian** belonging to the

Amazons, whom Cooper describes as 'Women of Scythia, whiche wanne a great parte of Asia. They slew all the men children, and kepte the women children, of whome they bourned the right pappe, because it shoulde not let them to throw their jauelins, or to shoote'.
trull prostitute
115 **captivates** captures
116 **vizard-like** mask-like, expressing no emotion
117 **impudent** shameless (*OED a.* 1)
use habitual practice

111] *Pope; F lines* France, / France, /   120] *Pope; F lines* thee, / shamelesse. /

217

Thy father bears the type of King of Naples,
Of both the Sicils and Jerusalem,
Yet not so wealthy as an English yeoman.
Hath that poor monarch taught thee to insult?
It needs not, nor it boots thee not, proud Queen,   125
Unless the adage must be verified
That beggars mounted run their horse to death.
'Tis beauty that doth oft make women proud,
But God he knows thy share thereof is small.
'Tis virtue that doth make them most admired,   130
The contrary doth make thee wondered at.
'Tis government that makes them seem divine,
The want thereof makes thee abominable.
Thou art as opposite to every good
As the Antipodes are unto us,   135
Or as the south to the Septentrion.
O, tiger's heart wrapped in a woman's hide,
How couldst thou drain the lifeblood of the child
To bid the father wipe his eyes withal,

121 **bears the type** carries the distinguishing mark or sign (*OED* type *sb.* 3)
122 **Sicils** Sicily and Naples, the titular kingdom of Margaret's father (*2H6* 1.1.47)
123 **yeoman** freeholder, small landowner
124 **insult** exult proudly or contemptuously (as at 1.3.14)
125 **boots** profits, avails
126 **adage** proverb
127 proverbial: 'Set a beggar on horseback and he will run his horse out of breath' (Tilley, B238)
132 **government** becoming conduct (*OED sb.* 2b)
133 **abominable** odious, detestable, but with a suggestion of 'inhuman', as indicated by F's spelling, 'abhominable', which reflects a false etymology *ab homine* (*OED*). See 154n.
135 **Antipodes** *Anti* against; *podes* feet, i.e. those who live on the opposite side

of the globe. 'People goyng directly agaynst vs, foote to foote' (Cooper). Four syllables, accent on the second.
136 **Septentrion** 'The North coaste: the North pole' (Cooper), from *sepentriones*, the seven stars of the Great Bear or Big Dipper
137 Robert Greene adapts this line in *Greene's Groatsworth of Wit* (1592) to refer to Shakespeare as 'an vpstart Crow, beautified with our feathers, that with his *Tygers hart wrapt in a Players hyde*, supposes he is as well able to bombast out a blanke verse as the best of you: and beeing an absolute *Iohannes fac totum*, is in his owne conceit the onely Shake-scene in a countrey' (F). It is the first known allusion to Shakespeare as a playwright (see p. 6).
139 **withal** therewith, with it

And yet be seen to bear a woman's face?
Women are soft, mild, pitiful and flexible;
Thou stern, obdurate, flinty, rough, remorseless
Bidd'st thou me rage? Why, now thou hast thy wis
Wouldst have me weep? Why, now thou hast thy will.
For raging wind blows up incessant showers,
And when the rage allays, the rain begins:
These tears are my sweet Rutland's obsequies,
And every drop cries vengeance for his death
'Gainst thee, fell Clifford, and thee, false
      Frenchwoman!

NORTHUMBERLAND

Beshrew me, but his passions moves me so   150
That hardly can I check my eyes from tears.

YORK

That face of his the hungry cannibals
Would not have touched, would not have stained with
      blood;
But you are more inhuman, more inexorable,
O, ten times more than tigers of Hyrcania.   155

---

140 **bear . . . face** Cam[1] notes that the phrase is also used of Tamora in *Tit* 2.3.136, where Tamora too is compared to a tiger (2.3.142).
141 **pitiful** compassionate, tender (*OED a.* 2)
   flexible tractable (*OED a.* 3)
142 **obdurate** emphasis on second syllable. O has 'indurate', perhaps echoing the Vulgate phrase, '*induratum est cor Pharaonis*' (Exodus, 7.13, 22) (Ard[2]).
   rough violent, harsh (*OED a.* 7a)
145–6 **raging . . . begins** proverbial: 'Little rain allays great winds' (Tilley, R16) and 'After wind comes rain' (Tilley, T275)
147 **obsequies** funeral rites
149 **fell** cruel
150–1 Northumberland's comments may

be asides, since no one responds to them; see also 169–71 and n.
150 **Beshrew me** Literally 'Curse me', the expression here has the force of 'Heaven help me'.
   passions moves usually emended to 'passion moves', on the argument that Shakespeare nowhere else uses *passion* in this sense in the plural. He does, however, use -*s* as a third-person plural inflection regularly. See 1.4.25, 2.1.54–5, 83, 2.5.27, etc., and Abbott, 333.154.
154 **inhuman** inhumane. See 133n.
155 **tigers of Hyrcania** from *Aeneid*, 4.366–7, where Dido accuses Aeneas of emotional cruelty by claiming that tigresses from Hyrcania nursed him. O's meaningless *Arcadia* (for

152–3] *O; F lines* his, / toucht, / blood: /

219

See, ruthless Queen, a hapless father's tears.
This cloth thou dipp'd'st in blood of my sweet boy,
And I with tears do wash the blood away.
Keep thou the napkin and go boast of this,
And if thou tell'st the heavy story right,   160
Upon my soul the hearers will shed tears.
Yea, even my foes will shed fast-falling tears
And say, 'Alas, it was a piteous deed!'
There, take the crown, and with the crown my curse,
And in thy need such comfort come to thee   165
As now I reap at thy too cruel hand.
Hard-hearted Clifford, take me from the world,
My soul to heaven, my blood upon your heads!

NORTHUMBERLAND

Had he been slaughter-man to all my kin,
I should not for my life but weep with him   170
To see how inly sorrow gripes his soul.

QUEEN MARGARET

What, weeping-ripe, my Lord Northumberland?
Think but upon the wrong he did us all,
And that will quickly dry thy melting tears.

CLIFFORD [*Stabs York twice.*]

Here's for my oath; here's for my father's death!   175

QUEEN MARGARET [*Stabs York.*]

And here's to right our gentle-hearted King!

Hyrcania) has been taken as evidence
of possible memorial reconstruction of
O, but see Maguire on 'aural error'
(196–8).
156 **hapless** unfortunate. Used by
Shakespeare exclusively in early
works: *CE*, *1H6*, *2H6*, *3H6*, *Luc*, *TGV*
159 **napkin** handkerchief
160 **heavy** in the Latin sense of *gravis*,
defined by Cooper as 'heauy, greeuous,
peinfull'
164 If York's hands are being held (95),

this line may indicate that he shakes
his head to remove the mocking paper
crown.
169–71 As at 150–1, Northumberland
may keep this comment to himself,
Margaret seeing only his tears (172).
171 **inly** inward, heartfelt (*OED a.*)
gripes grips, seizes (*OED v.* 3a);
grieves, afflicts (*OED v.* 7)
172 **weeping-ripe** tearful, ready to weep
176 **gentle-hearted** tender-hearted,
compassionate

175 SD] *Pope subst.*   176 SD] *Rowe subst.*

YORK

Open thy gate of mercy, gracious God,
My soul flies through these wounds to seek out thee!   [*Dies.*]

QUEEN MARGARET

Off with his head and set it on York gates,
So York may overlook the town of York.   180

Flourish. Exeunt [with the body].

[2.1] *A march. Enter* EDWARD, RICHARD *and their power.*

EDWARD

I wonder how our princely father scaped,
Or whether he be scaped away or no
From Clifford's and Northumberland's pursuit.
Had he been ta'en, we should have heard the news;
Had he been slain, we should have heard the news;   5
Or had he scaped, methinks we should have heard
The happy tidings of his good escape.
How fares my brother? Why is he so sad?

RICHARD

I cannot joy until I be resolved
Where our right valiant father is become.   10

179 Margaret repeats the order to behead York (see 107). In Hall (251), Clifford beheads York and presents the trophy to Margaret.

2.1 Historically Edward was not at the battle of Wakefield, depicted in 1.3 and 1.4, because he was engaged in fighting on the Welsh border, or *marches* (139), and it was near there that the battle of Mortimer's Cross was fought on 'Candelmas day in the morning' (Hall, 251), i.e. 2 February 1461. York's sons have not heard of their father's death two weeks earlier, and when Warwick enters, he says that he heard it *ten days ago* (104) and reports the Yorkist defeat at the second battle

of St Albans (119–36), fought on 17 February 1461. Hall says that Edward met Warwick 'at Chippyng Norton' (253), a village on the road between London and Stratford-upon-Avon.

0.1 *A march* See 1.2.67.1n.
power army, i.e. accompanying soldiers. O adds 'with drum and Souldiers', but it is not clear that the phrase adds anything not included in '*A march*' and '*their power*'.

4 ta'en taken, captured; pronounced as one syllable, 'tane' (here with internal rhyme with *slain*, 5)

9 resolved satisfied (by being informed)

10 Where . . . is become what has become of . . .

178 SD] *Rowe*   180 SD *Exeunt] O; Exit. F   with the body] Oxf subst.*   2.1] *Rowe*

221

I saw him in the battle range about
And watched him how he singled Clifford forth.
Methought he bore him in the thickest troop
As doth a lion in a herd of neat,
Or as a bear encompassed round with dogs,   15
Who having pinched a few and made them cry,
The rest stand all aloof and bark at him.
So fared our father with his enemies;
So fled his enemies my warlike father;
Methinks 'tis prize enough to be his son.   20
    [*Three suns appear in the air.*]
See how the morning opes her golden gates
And takes her farewell of the glorious sun.
How well resembles it the prime of youth,
Trimmed like a younker prancing to his love.

EDWARD
    Dazzle mine eyes, or do I see three suns?   25

---

12 **watched him how** observed how
13, 20 **Methought, Methinks** it seemed to me
13 **him** himself
14 **neat** cattle
16 **pinched** seized with the teeth, bitten (*OED v.* 4)
17 **stand all aloof** stay at a distance
20 **prize** privilege (as at 1.4.59)
21–4 biblical: 'in them hathe he set a tabernacle for the sunne. Which commeth forth as a bridegrome out of his chambre, and *reioyceth* as a Gyant to runne *his* course' (Psalm 19.4–5). Shaheen also compares *FQ*, 1.5.2.1–4 (66). O gives a shorter version of this speech to Edward.
21–2 The morning is personified as the goddess Aurora, bidding the sun god farewell as he begins his course across the sky.
21 an implicit SD, as at 25 and 29–31. For

Walter Hodges' illustration of how the three suns might have been staged mechanically, see Cam², 20. Hodges imagines three 'suns', each at the end of a separate mechanical arm and all falling from a central suspended axle. When this device is lowered through a hole in the 'heavens', two of the suns are swung outward by means of a line attached to them, held by technicians above. The three suns collapse into one again as the device is withdrawn. The incident is mentioned in Hall, 251.
24 **Trimmed** dressed up
younker young man. Often used by Spenser in *FQ*.
prancing dancing, gambolling, capering (*OED* 3b)
25 **Dazzle mine eyes** have my eyes lost vision (*OED* dazzle *v.* 1 *intr.*), i.e. are my eyes dazzled?

20 SD] *O; after 24 Ard²*

RICHARD

Three glorious suns, each one a perfect sun,
Not separated with the racking clouds
But severed in a pale clear-shining sky.
See, see, they join, embrace and seem to kiss,
As if they vowed some league inviolable. 30
Now are they but one lamp, one light, one sun:
In this, the heaven figures some event.

EDWARD

'Tis wondrous strange, the like yet never heard of.
I think it cites us, brother, to the field,
That we, the sons of brave Plantagenet, 35
Each one already blazing by our meeds,
Should, notwithstanding, join our lights together
And over-shine the earth, as this the world.
Whate'er it bodes, henceforward will I bear
Upon my target three fair-shining suns. 40

RICHARD

Nay, bear three daughters: by your leave, I speak it,
You love the breeder better than the male.

Enter [a Messenger] *blowing.*

27 **with** by
  racking driving before the wind (*OED* rack *ppl. a¹*)
32 **heaven** Use of the definite article with *heaven* is unusual but not unparalleled. See *TGV* 4.2.41.
  figures prefigures, foreshows (*OED v.* 5, citing this as the only instance)
34 **cites** summons, calls (*OED v.* 2)
36 **meeds** reward, prize awarded for excellence or achievement (*OED sb.* 1b)
39–40 'for which cause, men imagined, that he gaue the sunne in his full brightnes for his cognisaunce or badge' (Hall, 251)

40 **target** shield
41–2 Richard's mocking remark, simultaneously characterizing both himself and his brother, may be an aside. Hall says that Edward 'loved well both to loke and to fele fayre dammosels' (265).
42 **breeder** female, mother
  male Cf. 5.6.15, where *male* is used, as here, in the sense of 'begetter'.
42.1 *blowing* This could mean either 'blowing a horn', as at 3.3.161 SD, or 'panting heavily', as in *MW* 3.3.80. Hall uses it in the second sense when he says that Warwick 'like a man desperate, mounted on his Hackeney, and

33] *Pope; F lines* strange, / of. / 41] *Pope; F lines* Daughters: / it, / 42.1 *a* Messenger] *Q3; one* F

But what art thou whose heavy looks foretell
Some dreadful story hanging on thy tongue?

MESSENGER
    Ah, one that was a woeful looker-on   45
    When as the noble Duke of York was slain,
    Your princely father and my loving lord!

EDWARD
    O, speak no more, for I have heard too much.

RICHARD
    Say how he died, for I will hear it all.

MESSENGER
    Environed he was with many foes   50
    And stood against them, as the hope of Troy
    Against the Greeks that would have entered Troy.
    But Hercules himself must yield to odds:
    And many strokes, though with a little axe,
    Hews down and fells the hardest-timbered oak.   55
    By many hands your father was subdued,
    But only slaughtered by the ireful arm
    Of unrelenting Clifford and the Queen,
    Who crowned the gracious Duke in high despite,
    Laughed in his face, and when with grief he wept,   60
    The ruthless Queen gave him to dry his cheeks
    A napkin steeped in the harmless blood
    Of sweet young Rutland, by rough Clifford slain.
    And after many scorns, many foul taunts,
    They took his head and on the gates of York   65

---

came blowying to kyng Edward' (253).
Holinshed has 'puffing and blowing' in
the corresponding passage (277).
43 **heavy** See 1.4.160n.
46 **When as** when
50 **Environed** environèd
51 **hope of Troy** Hector, greatest of
Trojan warriors, killed in combat by
the Greek Achilles (echoing *Aeneid*,
2.281). Shakespeare uses the phrase

again of Warwick, another key military
leader killed in combat (4.8.25).
54–5 proverbial: 'Many strokes fell great
oaks' (Tilley, S941)
    strokes . . . Hews On the verb ending
in *-s*, see 1.4.150n.
59 **high despite** extreme contempt,
scorn, disdain
62 **steeped** steepèd, soaked

They set the same, and there it doth remain,
The saddest spectacle that e'er I viewed.   [*Exit.*]
EDWARD

Sweet Duke of York, our prop to lean upon,
Now thou art gone we have no staff, no stay.
O Clifford, boist'rous Clifford, thou hast slain   70
The flower of Europe for his chivalry;
And treacherously hast thou vanquished him,
For hand to hand he would have vanquished thee.
Now my soul's palace is become a prison;
Ah, would she break from hence, that this my body   75
Might in the ground be closed up in rest,
For never henceforth shall I joy again.
Never, O never, shall I see more joy!
RICHARD

I cannot weep, for all my body's moisture
Scarce serves to quench my furnace-burning heart;   80
Nor can my tongue unload my heart's great burden,
For selfsame wind that I should speak withal
Is kindling coals that fires all my breast
And burns me up with flames that tears would quench.
To weep is to make less the depth of grief: 85
Tears then for babes; blows and revenge for me.
Richard, I bear thy name, I'll venge thy death
Or die renowned by attempting it.
EDWARD

His name that valiant Duke hath left with thee;

69 **stay** support (*OED sb.*²)
70 **boist'rous** full of rough violence to others (*OED a.* 9a)
71 **chivalry** bravery or prowess in war (*OED* 3b)
74 **soul's palace** the body (75), inhabited by the soul
75 **she** the soul, whose departure from the body results in death
76 **closed** closèd

79 **moisture** liquid part, 'humours' (*OED sb.* 2c)
80 **furnace-burning heart** Anger was thought of as literal heat emanating from the heart. See 1.4.87n.
83 **coals that fires** See 1.4.150n.
87 **Richard . . . name** addressed to his father, Richard Duke of York. See 89.
88 **renowned** renownèd

67 SD] *this edn*

His dukedom and his chair with me is left.   90

RICHARD
    Nay, if thou be that princely eagle's bird,
    Show thy descent by gazing 'gainst the sun;
    For chair and dukedom, throne and kingdom 'ssay,
    Either that is thine or else thou wert not his.

March. Enter WARWICK, Marquess [of] MONTAGUE *and their army.*

WARWICK
    How now, fair lords? What fare, what news abroad?   95
RICHARD
    Great lord of Warwick, if we should recount
    Our baleful news, and at each word's deliverance
    Stab poniards in our flesh till all were told,
    The words would add more anguish than the wounds.
    O valiant lord, the Duke of York is slain!   100
EDWARD
    O Warwick, Warwick, that Planagenet
    Which held thee dearly as his soul's redemption

90, 93   **chair** seat of authority, state, or dignity (*OED* 2). Cf. 1.1.51, 1.4.97.
91–2   **princely . . . sun** proverbial: 'Only the eagle can gaze at the sun' (Tilley, E3)
91   **bird** offspring
93   *'**ssay** make a successful attempt to gain. The emendation makes sense of the following line in which Richard proposes that success in the attempt is the only proof of Edward's legitimacy as York's son. Although the F reading 'say' could be defended as meaning 'say that the titles are yours or say you are no legitimate son of your father', *For* would then, rather awkwardly, have to mean 'in respect of'.

94.1   **O** adds 'drum, ancient, and souldiers'. An 'ancient' was an 'ensign' or standard-bearer, in this case probably carrying Warwick's heraldic emblem of a bear and ragged staff (*2H6* 5.1.203).
95   **What fare** What is the state of things? 'What's happening?'
97   **baleful** full of pain or suffering, painful (*OED a.* 2a)
98   **poniards** daggers
102   **dearly as** as dearly as. See Abbott, 276, on omission of the first 'as'. Comparison with 109 shows that omission or retention is dictated by metre (JH).

---

93 'ssay] *this edn (RP);* say *F*   94.1 MONTAGUE] *O; Mountacute F*   96 recount] *F3;* tecompt *F1;* recompt *F2;* report *O*

Is by the stern Lord Clifford done to death!
WARWICK

Ten days ago I drowned these news in tears,
And now to add more measure to your woes,   105
I come to tell you things sith then befall'n.
After the bloody fray at Wakefield fought,
Where your brave father breathed his latest gasp,
Tidings, as swiftly as the posts could run,
Were brought me of your loss and his depart.   110
I, then in London, keeper of the King,
Mustered my soldiers, gathered flocks of friends,
Marched toward Saint Albans to intercept the Queen,
Bearing the King in my behalf along;
For by my scouts I was advertised   115
That she was coming with a full intent
To dash our late decree in Parliament
Touching King Henry's oath and your succession.
Short tale to make, we at Saint Albans met,
Our battles joined, and both sides fiercely fought.   120

---

104 **Ten days ago** The phrase tells us
how much time is imagined to have
elapsed in the few minutes since York's
death was depicted on stage. Though
common in Shakespeare, such disjunc-
tions between imagined and real time
became increasingly worrying to critics in his own day, to the point that in
WT he asks his auditors to 'Impute it
not a crime / To me or my swift passage, that I slide / O'er sixteen years'
(4.1.4–6).
  news See 1.1.182n.
105 **add . . . to** increase
106 **sith** since
108 **latest** last
109 **posts** messengers
110 **depart** departure (i.e. death), as at
4.1.92. See Abbott, 451, on omission
of the suffix.

111–40 Warwick's description of the second battle of St Albans on 17 February
1461 follows Hall, who mentions the
death that day of 'syr Ihon Gray,
which thesame day was made knight'
(252). Grey's widow approaches
Edward for redress in 3.2.
114 **in my behalf** in my interest, for my
benefit (*OED behalf a.* 2b)
115 **advertised** advertisèd, i.e. informed
(accented on the second syllable; see
Cercignani, 41)
117 **dash** overturn, defeat
  late recent
118 **Touching** in reference or relation to
(*OED prep.* 2)
119 **Short . . . make** proverbial (Dent,
SS8)
120 **battles** troops in battle array (*OED
sb.* 8a)

112–13 friends, / Marched] friends, / And verie well appointed as I thought, / Marcht *O*

But whether 'twas the coldness of the King,
Who looked full gently on his warlike Queen,
That robbed my soldiers of their heated spleen,
Or whether 'twas report of her success,
Or more than common fear of Clifford's rigour,   125
Who thunders to his captives blood and death,
I cannot judge; but to conclude with truth,
Their weapons like to lightning came and went;
Our soldiers', like the night-owl's lazy flight,
Or like an idle thresher with a flail,   130
Fell gently down as if they struck their friends.
I cheered them up with justice of our cause,
With promise of high pay and great rewards;
But all in vain, they had no heart to fight,
And we, in them, no hope to win the day,   135
So that we fled, the King unto the Queen;
Lord George your brother, Norfolk and myself,
In haste, post-haste, are come to join with you,
For in the marches here we heard you were,
Making another head to fight again.   140

EDWARD

Where is the Duke of Norfolk, gentle Warwick?
And when came George from Burgundy to England?

---

121 **coldness . . . King** Both Hall (252) and Holinshed (270) report that Henry's presence was discouraging to his own side, but neither one draws Warwick's odd inference that Henry's *coldness* discouraged his enemies. Warwick's excuse may explain Richard's caustic response in 147–9.

123 **spleen** high spirit, courage (*OED sb.* 5a)

125 **rigour** harsh or severe action (*OED* 1b)

126 **captives** O reads 'captaines', 'in which case we should read "Blood and death", Clifford's war-cry' (Cam²).

128 **weapons . . . lightning** proverbial: 'as swift as lightning' (Tilley, L279)

130 **idle** F's repetition of 'lazie' from 129 is a clear case of compositorial recollection.

139 **marches** frontier, border, especially referring to Scotland and Wales (*OED sb.³*)

140 **Making another head** raising troops (*OED* head *sb.* 52b)

141 **gentle** noble

130 an idle] *O;* a lazie *F*

WARWICK

Some six miles off the Duke is with the soldiers;
And for your brother, he was lately sent
From your kind aunt, Duchess of Burgundy,   145
With aid of soldiers to this needful war.

RICHARD

'Twas odds, belike, when valiant Warwick fled.
Oft have I heard his praises in pursuit,
But ne'er till now his scandal of retire.

WARWICK

Nor now my scandal, Richard, dost thou hear;   150
For thou shalt know this strong right hand of mine
Can pluck the diadem from faint Henry's head
And wring the awful sceptre from his fist,
Were he as famous and as bold in war
As he is famed for mildness, peace and prayer.   155

RICHARD

I know it well, Lord Warwick; blame me not.
'Tis love I bear thy glories makes me speak.
But in this troublous time, what's to be done?
Shall we go throw away our coats of steel
And wrap our bodies in black mourning gowns,   160

---

144 **for** as for
144–5 **your . . . Burgundy** Hall reports
    the duchess's sending her two younger
    sons to 'Philippe duke of Bourgoyne',
    but adds that 'there thei remayned, till
    their brother Edwarde had obteyned
    the Realme, and gotten the regiment'
    (253). Neither Hall nor Holinshed
    mentions the Yorkist tie to the duchess
    of Burgundy, who was in fact a distant
    cousin to Richard and George, not their
    aunt, since she was a granddaughter of
    John of Gaunt (Boswell-Stone, 303).
146 **needful** full of need, needy, requir-
    ing assistance (*OED a.* 2a)

147–9 Richard may genuinely be making
    excuses for Warwick, a potent ally of
    York, but belligerent irony would be
    more typical of the character
    Shakespeare creates for him in this
    play and *R3*.
147 **'Twas odds** things turned against us
    belike probably, in all likelihood (*OED
    adv.* A), 'no doubt'
149 **scandal of retire** being defamed for
    retreating
151–5 Warwick speaks in character as the
    'kingmaker'. Cf. 1.1.48.
152 **faint** faint-hearted
153 **awful** awe-inspiring

157 makes] *Q2;* make *O*

229

Numb'ring our Ave-Maries with our beads?
Or shall we on the helmets of our foes
Tell our devotion with revengeful arms?
If for the last, say 'Ay', and to it, lords.

WARWICK

Why, therefore Warwick came to seek you out,   165
And therefore comes my brother Montague.
Attend me, lords. The proud insulting Queen,
With Clifford and the haught Northumberland,
And of their feather many moe proud birds,
Have wrought the easy-melting King like wax.   170
He swore consent to your succession,
His oath enrolled in the Parliament;
And now to London all the crew are gone
To frustrate both his oath and what beside
May make against the house of Lancaster.   175
Their power, I think, is thirty thousand strong.
Now, if the help of Norfolk and myself,
With all the friends that thou, brave Earl of March,
Amongst the loving Welshmen canst procure,

161 A close variant of this line appears in *2H6* 1.3.57, where Margaret uses it to describe her husband disdainfully. Elizabethan anti-popery is not relevant in either case, despite reference to a distinctively Catholic devotion.
   Numb'ring counting
   Ave-Maries recitations of the 'Hail Mary'
163 **Tell** disclose, reveal (*OED v.* 5a); 'tell one's beads or rosary' (*OED v.* 21c)
166 **brother** See List of Roles, 12n., and 1.1.14n.
167 **insulting** scornfully triumphant (*OED vbl. sb.*)
168 **haught** haughty
169 **feather . . . birds** proverbial: 'Birds of a feather flock together' (Tilley, B393)
   moe (also 'mo') plural of 'more'
170 **wrought . . . wax** proverbial: 'to

work (upon one) (anything) like wax' (Dent, W138)
172 **enrolled** enrollèd, i.e. entered among the rolls, or the records (*OED v.* 5)
173 **crew** used derogatorily, as in *2H6* 2.2.72 (*OED* crew[1] 4)
174 **frustrate** annul, abrogate (*OED v.* 2b)
   what beside whatever else
175 **make against** be unfavourable to, militate against (*OED* make *v.* 76)
176–80 The numbers cited in O ('fifty thousand' and '48.thousand') are closer to Hall's numbers (60,000 and 48,660) than those cited in F. Though Warwick here estimates the Yorkist strength at 25,000, a messenger later estimates it at 30,000 (2.2.68).
178 **Earl of March** Edward's title before inheriting his father's title, Duke of York. See 191 and List of Roles, 2n.

Will but amount to five and twenty thousand,   180
Why, *via*, to London will we march,
And once again bestride our foaming steeds,
And once again cry 'Charge!' upon our foes,
But never once again turn back and fly.

RICHARD

Ay, now methinks I hear great Warwick speak.   185
Ne'er may he live to see a sunshine day
That cries 'Retire!' if Warwick bid him stay.

EDWARD

Lord Warwick, on thy shoulder will I lean;
And when thou fail'st, as God forbid the hour,
Must Edward fall, which peril heaven forfend!   190

WARWICK

No longer Earl of March, but Duke of York;
The next degree is England's royal throne.
For King of England shalt thou be proclaimed
In every borough as we pass along;
And he that throws not up his cap for joy   195
Shall for the fault make forfeit of his head.
King Edward, valiant Richard, Montague,
Stay we no longer dreaming of renown,
But sound the trumpets and about our task.

RICHARD

Then, Clifford, were thy heart as hard as steel,   200
As thou hast shown it flinty by thy deeds,

---

181 *via* onward, forward (Italian)
184 Warwick seems to be making up for his *scandal of retire*. During the battle of Ferrybridge (partially depicted in 2.2) he declared, 'let him flie that wil, for surely I wil tary with him that wil tary with me' (Hall, 255).
185–7 Though Richard agrees with Warwick and echoes his encouragement of the Yorkists, he may also be gratuitously reminding Warwick of the latter's earlier admission of having

retreated (121–40), thus rubbing salt in a fresh wound (cf. 147–9).
191–4 Hall describes Edward's ascent to the throne as 'incontinent' (253), that is, over-hasty, but it was not as incontinent as Shakespeare makes it, being deliberated by parliament, popularly supported, and accompanied by a coronation at Westminster, all of which Shakespeare eliminates.
200–1 **heart . . . steel . . . flinty** proverbial (Dent, H310.1, 311)

I come to pierce it or to give thee mine.

EDWARD

Then strike up drums! God and Saint George for us!

Enter a Messenger.

WARWICK

How now, what news?

MESSENGER

The Duke of Norfolk sends you word by me,   205
The Queen is coming with a puissant host
And craves your company for speedy counsel.

WARWICK

Why, then, it sorts. Brave warriors, let's away.   *Exeunt omnes.*

[**2.2**] *Flourish. Enter* KING [HENRY], QUEEN [MARGARET],
             CLIFFORD, NORTHUMBERLAND *and young*
             PRINCE [EDWARD], *with Drum and Trumpets.*
             [*York's head is set above the gates.*]

QUEEN MARGARET

Welcome, my lord, to this brave town of York.
Yonder's the head of that arch-enemy
That sought to be encompassed with your crown.

---

206 **puissant** powerful
208 **it sorts** it is fitting (*OED* sort *v.* 18b),
   'all right'
2.2 The scene is set in York (1). A messenger has announced Margaret's
   coming in 2.1.206, though that scene is
   not located in York but either in the
   marches (2.1.139), where the battle of
   Mortimer's Cross was fought, or at
   Chipping Norton (see 2.1n.). Historically, the two opposing parties did
   not formally confront each other
   before the battle of Towton, but in
   3H6 their meeting this way parallels a

similar confrontation before the battle
of Wakefield (1.1). Reinforcing the
parallel between the two scenes is the
requirement in 2.2 for at least twelve
adult actors and two boys (assuming
Margaret was played by a boy) to be on
stage together.
0.2–3 *young* PRINCE On Prince Edward's
   age, see 1.4.26.2n.
2 **head ... arch-enemy** an implicit SD,
   indicating Margaret's gesture to York's
   head, presumably mounted in the
   upper acting area. See 54–5 and
   1.4.179.

2.2] *Capell*   0.4] *Oxf subst.*

Doth not the object cheer your heart, my lord?
KING HENRY

    Ay, as the rocks cheer them that fear their wrack, 5
    To see this sight it irks my very soul.
    Withhold revenge, dear God. 'Tis not my fault,
    Nor wittingly have I infringed my vow.
CLIFFORD

    My gracious liege, this too much lenity
    And harmful pity must be laid aside. 10
    To whom do lions cast their gentle looks?
    Not to the beast that would usurp their den.
    Whose hand is that the forest bear doth lick?
    Not his that spoils her young before her face.
    Who scapes the lurking serpent's mortal sting? 15
    Not he that sets his foot upon her back.
    The smallest worm will turn, being trodden on,
    And doves will peck in safeguard of their brood.
    Ambitious York did level at thy crown,
    Thou smiling while he knit his angry brows; 20
    He, but a duke, would have his son a king

4 **object** i.e. object of sight
5 **wrack** shipwreck (*OED sb.*² 2)
7 **Withhold revenge** 'Henry is the only opponent of the revenge principle in the play, which is a kind of inclusive revenge tragedy – father for son (Clifford), as in *The Spanish Tragedy*; and son for father (Richard, 2.1.87, 163), as in *Hamlet*' (Ard²).
8 **infringed my vow** Henry is conscience-stricken about having broken the impolitic promise he made in 1.1.194–5.
9 **lenity** lenience
11–18 Ard¹ points to a precedent in Hall, ironically spoken by Warwick in attempting to sway his brother against Edward IV: 'What worme is touched, and will not once turne again? What beast is striken, that will not rore or sound? What innocent child is hurt that will not crye? If the poore and vnreasonable beastes: If the sely babes that lacketh discrecion, grone against harme to them proffered, How ought an honest man to be angery, when thynges that touche his honestie, be daily against him attempted?' (270).
11–12 The supposed gentleness of lions is proverbial: 'The lion spares the suppliant' (Tilley, L316). See 1.3.12–15n.
13 **forest** wild (as opposed to trained performing bears)
14 **spoils** steals, takes away as spoil
15 Ard¹ compares *Luc* 362–4.
17 **worm . . . turn** proverbial: 'Tread on a worm and it will turn' (Tilley, W909)
18 On the pecking dove, see 1.4.41n.
19 **level** aim

And raise his issue like a loving sire;
Thou, being a king, blest with a goodly son,
Didst yield consent to disinherit him,
Which argued thee a most unloving father.   25
Unreasonable creatures feed their young;
And though man's face be fearful to their eyes,
Yet in protection of their tender ones,
Who hath not seen them, even with those wings
Which sometime they have used with fearful flight,   30
Make war with him that climbed unto their nest,
Offering their own lives in their young's defence?
For shame, my liege, make them your precedent.
Were it not pity that this goodly boy
Should lose his birthright by his father's fault?   35
And long hereafter say unto his child,
'What my great-grandfather and grandsire got,
My careless father fondly gave away'?
Ah, what a shame were this. Look on the boy,
And let his manly face, which promiseth   40
Successful fortune, steel thy melting heart
To hold thine own and leave thine own with him.

KING HENRY
Full well hath Clifford played the orator,
Inferring arguments of mighty force.
But, Clifford, tell me, didst thou never hear   45
That things ill got had ever bad success?

22 **raise his issue** train up his children
  conscientiously; advance his offspring
25 **argued** made an argument for, proved
26 **Unreasonable creatures** those not
  endowed with reason, i.e. all but the
  human race
27 **fearful** frightening
28 **tender** young; precious, beloved
30 **fearful** frightened, full of fear
37 **great-grandfather ... grandsire**
  Prince Edward's great-grandfather

was Henry IV; his grandfather, Henry
V.
38 **fondly** foolishly
43 **played the orator** proverbial (Dent,
  O74.1)
44 **Inferring** bringing in, introducing
  (*OED v.* 2)
46 **things ... success** proverbial: 'Evil-
  gotten goods never prove well' (Tilley,
  G301)
  success result

37 great-grandfather] *Capell;* great Grandfather *F*

And happy always was it for that son
Whose father for his hoarding went to hell?
I'll leave my son my virtuous deeds behind,
And would my father had left me no more.   50
For all the rest is held at such a rate
As brings a thousandfold more care to keep
Than in possession any jot of pleasure.
Ah, cousin York, would thy best friends did know
How it doth grieve me that thy head is here.   55

QUEEN MARGARET

My lord, cheer up your spirits: our foes are nigh,
And this soft courage makes your followers faint.
You promised knighthood to our forward son.
Unsheathe your sword and dub him presently.
Edward, kneel down.   60

KING HENRY

Edward Plantagenet, arise a knight,
And learn this lesson: draw thy sword in right.

PRINCE EDWARD

My gracious father, by your kingly leave,

47–8   **happy . . . hell** proverbial: 'Happy
is the child whose father goes to the
devil' (Tilley, C305)
50   Henry alludes to the guilty legacy of
the Lancastrians, springing from
Henry IV's seizing of Richard II's
throne, a matter of concern to the present king's father, Henry V, as well (*H5*
4.1.289–302). Cf. York's charge at
1.1.133, which also abashes Henry.
54   **cousin York** For Henry VI's relation-
.   ship to Richard, Duke of York, see
List of Roles, 1n. and 27n.
friends See 1.1.56n.
55   **thy . . . here** an implicit SD. Cf. 2.
56   **spirits** monosyllable: 'sp'rits'
57   **courage** heart, disposition (*OED sb.* 1)
faint lose heart (*OED v.* 1)
58   **forward** ready, prompt, eager (*OED a.*
6a); ardent, zealous (*OED* 6c); precocious (*OED* 7). Prince Edward was

only eight in 1461, but if anyone is forward on this occasion, it would appear
to be Margaret, who orders her son to
kneel and her husband to knight him;
Prince Edward himself has accomplished nothing apart from watching
silently while York was killed in 1.4. In
Hall (252), Prince Edward is knighted
immediately after the second battle of
St Albans, fought on 17 February 1461
and described by Warwick at
2.1.111–40.
59   **dub** 'confer the rank of knighthood by
the ceremony of striking the shoulder
with a sword' (*OED*)
presently immediately
62   **in right** in justice. The phrase
inevitably rings hollow, given the oath-
breaking and motives of power and
vengeance on both sides.

I'll draw it as apparent to the crown
And in that quarrel use it to the death.   65

CLIFFORD

Why, that is spoken like a toward prince.

Enter a Messenger.

MESSENGER

Royal commanders, be in readiness,
For with a band of thirty thousand men
Comes Warwick, backing of the Duke of York,
And in the towns as they do march along,   70
Proclaims him king, and many fly to him.
Deraign your battle, for they are at hand.   [*Exit.*]

CLIFFORD

I would your highness would depart the field.
The Queen hath best success when you are absent.

QUEEN MARGARET

Ay, good my lord, and leave us to our fortune.   75

KING HENRY

Why that's my fortune too; therefore, I'll stay.

NORTHUMBERLAND

Be it with resolution, then, to fight.

PRINCE EDWARD

My royal father, cheer these noble lords
And hearten those that fight in your defence.
Unsheathe your sword, good father, cry 'Saint George!'   80

---

64 **apparent** heir apparent
65 **quarrel** cause (*OED sb.*[2] 2d)
66 **toward** promising, apt (of young persons) (*OED a.* 3)
68 **thirty thousand** See 2.1.176–80n.
69 **backing of** backing up, supporting
72 **Deraign** dispose troops in battle array (*OED v.*[1] 4c)
73–4 Describing the second battle of St

Albans, Hall says, 'Happy was the quene in her two battayls, but vnfortunate was the kyng in all his enterprises, for where his person was present, ther victory fled euer from him to the other parte, and he commonly was subdued and vanqueshed' (252).
74 **success** result

72 SD] *this edn*

March. Enter EDWARD, WARWICK, RICHARD, GEORGE,
     NORFOLK, MONTAGUE *and Soldiers.*

EDWARD

Now, perjured Henry, wilt thou kneel for grace
And set thy diadem upon my head,
Or bide the mortal fortune of the field?

QUEEN MARGARET

Go rate thy minions, proud insulting boy.
Becomes it thee to be thus bold in terms   85
Before thy sovereign and thy lawful King?

EDWARD

I am his king, and he should bow his knee.
I was adopted heir by his consent.
Since when his oath is broke; for as I hear,
You that are king, though he do wear the crown,   90
Have caused him, by new act of Parliament,
To blot out me and put his own son in.

CLIFFORD

And reason too;
Who should succeed the father but the son?

RICHARD

Are you there, butcher? O, I cannot speak!   95

CLIFFORD

Ay, crookback, here I stand to answer thee,
Or any he, the proudest of thy sort.

80.1 GEORGE F has '*Clarence*', though
     Edward does not promote George to
     the title 'Duke of Clarence' until
     2.6.104.
81 **perjured** See 8n. The Yorkists also
     have perjured themselves; see
     1.2.21–45n.
83 **bide** await, wait for (*OED* 1); endure,
     suffer, bear (*OED* 6)
84 **rate** chide, scold

minions favourites
86–7 The stalemate produced by com-
     peting claims to the throne repeats the
     stalemate in 1.1. See 2.2n.
90 **You** addressed to Margaret
93 **reason** with good reason, 'quite right'
97 **he** man. See Abbott, 224, on 'he' and
     'she' for 'man' and 'woman'.
     proudest . . . sort proverbial: 'the
     proudest of them all' (Dent, P614.1)

80.1 GEORGE] *Clarence F*   89 Since] *F2; Cla.* Since *F1 (assigning 89–92 to George)*

RICHARD

    'Twas you that killed young Rutland, was it not?

CLIFFORD

    Ay, and old York, and yet not satisfied.

RICHARD

    For God's sake, lords, give signal to the fight.   100

WARWICK

    What sayst thou, Henry, wilt thou yield the crown?

QUEEN MARGARET

    Why, how now, long-tongued Warwick, dare you
        speak?

    When you and I met at Saint Albans last,

    Your legs did better service than your hands.

WARWICK

    Then 'twas my turn to fly, and now 'tis thine.   105

CLIFFORD

    You said so much before and yet you fled.

WARWICK

    'Twas not your valour, Clifford, drove me thence.

NORTHUMBERLAND

    No, nor your manhood that durst make you stay.

RICHARD

    Northumberland, I hold thee reverently.

    Break off the parley, for scarce I can refrain   110

    The execution of my big-swoll'n heart

    Upon that Clifford, that cruel child-killer.

---

    sort band, crowd (*OED sb.* 17a)

102 **long-tongued** having much to say.
The phrase is proverbial (Dent, LL6),
also used in *Tit* 4.2.152, the only other
occurrence in Shakespeare.

104 **legs … hands** proverbial: 'One pair
of heels is worth two pair of hands'
(Dent, P34)

109 **hold** respect

110 **refrain** restrain (*OED v. trans.* 1)

111 **execution** action (of putting the
heart's feelings into deeds)
big-swoll'n used only once more by
Shakespeare, in *Tit* 3.1.224

112 **child-killer** Richard says this
despite the fact that he himself will
soon kill young Prince Edward.
Historically Rutland was older than
Richard, who was the same age as
Prince Edward. The reduction of

101] *Pope; F lines Henry,* / Crowne? /

CLIFFORD

I slew thy father: call'st thou him a child?

RICHARD

Ay, like a dastard and a treacherous coward,

As thou didst kill our tender brother Rutland.   115

But ere sunset I'll make thee curse the deed.

KING HENRY

Have done with words, my lords, and hear me speak.

QUEEN MARGARET

Defy them, then, or else hold close thy lips.

KING HENRY

I prithee, give no limits to my tongue:

I am a king and privileged to speak.   120

CLIFFORD

My liege, the wound that bred this meeting here

Cannot be cured by words; therefore, be still.

RICHARD

Then, executioner, unsheathe thy sword.

By him that made us all, I am resolved

That Clifford's manhood lies upon his tongue.   125

EDWARD

Say, Henry, shall I have my right or no?

A thousand men have broke their fasts today

That ne'er shall dine unless thou yield the crown.

WARWICK

If thou deny, their blood upon thy head,

For York in justice puts his armour on.   130

Rutland's age and the increase of Richard's reinforce the parallel between Rutland and the Lancastrian prince.

114 **dastard** mean, base, or despicable coward (*OED*)

115 **tender** young

121–5 Clifford's brusque order to Henry and Richard's interruption before the King can reply are telling indications of Henry's ineffective and retiring character.

121 **wound** Clifford myopically interprets the whole conflict in terms of his personal loss (*2H6* 5.2).

129 **upon** be upon

PRINCE EDWARD

If that be right which Warwick says is right,
There is no wrong, but everything is right.

RICHARD

Whoever got thee, there thy mother stands,
For well I wot thou hast thy mother's tongue.

QUEEN MARGARET

But thou art neither like thy sire nor dam,   135
But like a foul misshapen stigmatic,
Marked by the Destinies to be avoided,
As venom toads or lizards' dreadful stings.

RICHARD

Iron of Naples hid with English gilt,
Whose father bears the title of a king,   140
As if a channel should be called the sea,
Sham'st thou not, knowing whence thou art
    extraught,
To let thy tongue detect thy baseborn heart?

EDWARD

A wisp of straw were worth a thousand crowns

---

133 **Whoever got thee** In *1H6* and *2H6*, Margaret establishes a close, possibly sexual, alliance with Suffolk, and Richard may allude to a rumour reported by Hall that when Prince Edward was conceived, Margaret 'susteyned not a litle slaunder and obloquye of the common people, saiyng [*sic*] that the kyng was not able to get a chyld, and that this was not his sonne' (230; Boswell-Stone, 304).
got begat, fathered
134 **wot** know
135 **dam** mother (contemptuous) (*OED*)
136 **stigmatic** person marked by a physical deformity (*OED*). Cf. *2H6* 5.1.215.
137 **Destinies** the three Fates of classical mythology
138 **venom** venomous (*OED* B *adj.*)

lizards' . . . stings also at *2H6* 3.2.325, the only two instances in Shakespeare
139 **gilt** gilding. Richard insults Margaret for her poor nobility: her father was styled king but was impoverished when she married Henry. See *2H6* 1.1. Richard also puns on 'guilt', as in *H5* 2.0.26, again alluding to Margaret's affair with Suffolk.
141 **channel** rivulet (*OED sb.* 2); gutter (*OED sb.* 3)
142 **extraught** derived, descended (*OED*)
143 **detect** find out a secret quality in (*OED v.* 3)
144 **wisp of straw** figure for scolds to rail at (as a punishment) (*OED sb.*[1] 2b)

133 SP RICHARD] *O; War. F*

To make this shameless callet know herself.   145
Helen of Greece was fairer far than thou,
Although thy husband may be Menelaus;
And ne'er was Agamemnon's brother wronged
By that false woman, as this king by thee.
His father revelled in the heart of France,   150
And tamed the King and made the Dauphin stoop;
And had he matched according to his state,
He might have kept that glory to this day.
But when he took a beggar to his bed
And graced thy poor sire with his bridal day,   155
Even then that sunshine brewed a shower for him
That washed his father's fortunes forth of France
And heaped sedition on his crown at home.
For what hath broached this tumult but thy pride?
Hadst thou been meek, our title still had slept,   160
And we, in pity of the gentle King,
Had slipped our claim until another age.

---

145 **callet** lewd woman, strumpet, scold (*OED*)

146–7 The Trojan war was fought to retrieve Helen, Greek wife of Menelaus, 'Agamemnon's brother' (148), from Paris, the Trojan prince. Edward's intent is to insult Margaret by comparing her to the adulteress Helen. Cf. *1H6* 5.4.103–8.

150 **His father** Henry V, father of Henry VI

revelled made merry, took pleasure (used boastfully to describe Henry V's victorious military campaigns in France)

151 **Dauphin** official title of the French heir apparent

152 **had he matched** had Henry VI married

state condition as regards riches or possessions (*OED sb.* 1e)

155 **graced . . . day** 'enriched your [Margaret's] father with his [Henry VI's] wedding'. Henry received no dowry from Margaret's father, as was customary, but instead was obliged to pay for her passage and reception (*2H6* 1.1.57–9).

156 **that sunshine** either the *glory* won by Henry V (153) or the sunshine of Henry VI's wedding day (155) or both

159 **broached** set on foot, started, introduced (*OED*)

160–2 Edward rationalizes the Yorkist rebellion in order to insult Margaret. In *1H6* his father already determines to gain the crown before Henry marries Margaret.

160 **still** quietly; now, as formerly

160, 162 **had, Had** would have

162 **slipped** passed over, avoided mention or consideration of (*OED v.*[1] *trans.*[21])

151 Dauphin] *(Dolphin)*

GEORGE

But when we saw our sunshine made thy spring,
And that thy summer bred us no increase,
We set the axe to thy usurping root;   165
And though the edge hath something hit ourselves,
Yet know thou, since we have begun to strike,
We'll never leave till we have hewn thee down
Or bathed thy growing with our heated bloods.

EDWARD

And in this resolution, I defy thee,   170
Not willing any longer conference,
Since thou denied'st the gentle King to speak.
Sound trumpets! Let our bloody colours wave;
And either victory or else a grave!

QUEEN MARGARET

Stay Edward.   175

EDWARD

No, wrangling woman, we'll no longer stay.
These words will cost ten thousand lives this day.

Exeunt omnes.

---

163 **our sunshine** George uses Edward's
image in 156 and also alludes to the
emblem Edward adopts in 2.1.21–40.
163–9 'When our success helped you to
flourish but your flourishing was no
benefit to us, we opposed you with some
loss to ourselves, but now that we have
started, we will not stop until we have
destroyed you, or watered you with our
hot blood (shed in battle).' The ornate
imagery conceals the bare power politics
of George's motives and reasoning.
165–8 biblical: 'Now also is the axe laid
vnto the roote of the trees: therefore
euerie tre which bringeth not forthe
food frute, shalbe hewen downe and
cast into the fyre' (Luke, 3.10;
Shaheen, 66)
165 **usurping** George alludes to Henry

Bolingbroke's (Henry IV's) deposition
of Richard II.
166 **something** somewhat
169 **heated** angry
170 **resolution** conviction, certainty.
(*OED* 13b)
171 **conference** conferring or taking
counsel (*OED sb.* 4a)
172 **denied'st ... speak** O has 'deniest',
making the action continuous and
therefore another affront to Margaret,
but the past tense points to a specific
instance, which would appear to be
118, though Richard also prevents the
king's reply (123) – a fact Edward
seems to have forgotten.
177 SD Oxf specifies that the two contending parties exit by different doors.
Cf. 2.5.54.1–2.

163 SP GEORGE] *O subst.; Cla. F*

[**2.3**]   *Alarum. Excursions. Enter* WARWICK.

WARWICK

Forespent with toil, as runners with a race,
I lay me down a little while to breathe;
For strokes received and many blows repaid
Have robbed my strong-knit sinews of their strength,
And, spite of spite, needs must I rest awhile.   5

Enter EDWARD *running.*

EDWARD

Smile, gentle heaven, or strike, ungentle death!
For this world frowns, and Edward's sun is clouded.

Enter GEORGE.

WARWICK

How now, my lord, what hap? What hope of good?
GEORGE

Our hap is loss, our hope but sad despair,
Our ranks are broke, and ruin follows us.   10
What counsel give you? Whither shall we fly?

2.3 to **2.6** stage the battle of Towton, fought near York on 29 March 1461. The Yorkist setback that opens the scene was the result of preliminary action near Ferrybridge on 28 March, where Warwick's brother was killed (Hall, 255).

2.3.0.1 *Excursions* issuing forth against an enemy, presumably from both stage doors

1 **Forespent** worn out

5 **spite of spite** in spite of difficulties (*OED sb.* 5c)

5.1 *running* Richard is also 'running' as he enters in O (13.1), but neither F nor O specifies the speed of George's entry. Cf. *E3* 3.4, opening SD: '*After them* Prince Edward, *running*' (RP).

6 **ungentle** ignoble

7 **Edward's sun** The sun was Edward's emblem. See 2.1.21–40.

8 **hap** chance or fortune. Warwick presumably addresses his question to Edward, who has just arrived, not to George, who is arriving.

2.3] *Capell*   7.1] *after 8 F*   GEORGE] *O; Clarence F*   9+ SP GEORGE] *O subst.; Cla. F*

EDWARD

    Bootless is flight: they follow us with wings,
    And weak we are and cannot shun pursuit.

Enter RICHARD.

RICHARD

    Ah, Warwick, why hast thou withdrawn thyself?
    Thy brother's blood the thirsty earth hath drunk,   15
    Broached with the steely point of Clifford's lance;
    And in the very pangs of death he cried,
    Like to a dismal clangour heard from far,
    'Warwick, revenge! Brother, revenge my death!'
    So underneath the belly of their steeds,   20
    That stained their fetlocks in his smoking blood,
    The noble gentleman gave up the ghost.

WARWICK

    Then let the earth be drunken with our blood.
    I'll kill my horse, because I will not fly.
    Why stand we like soft-hearted women here,   25
    Wailing our losses whiles the foe doth rage,
    And look upon, as if the tragedy
    Were played in jest by counterfeiting actors?
    Here on my knee I vow to God above:
    I'll never pause again, never stand still,   30
    Till either death hath closed these eyes of mine
    Or Fortune given me measure of revenge.

12 **Bootless** to no purpose, unavailing **with wings** flying. A pun on *flight* and *fly* (11).

15 **brother's blood** This is not Montague, who appears in 1.1, but 'the Bastard of Salisbury' (Hall, 255).

21 **smoking** giving out vapour or fine spray (*OED ppl. a.* 2a)

23 biblical: 'their mountaines shalbe drunken with their blood' (Judith, 6.4) (Shaheen, 67)

24 **kill my horse** In Hall (255), Warwick actually does what he merely threatens to do here, presumably limited by the constraints of staging such a deed. **because** so that, in order that

27 **look upon** observe, be lookers on

29 **Here . . . knee** an implicit SD, indicating that Warwick either kneels at this point or has knelt by this point. See 25.

EDWARD

O Warwick, I do bend my knee with thine,
And in this vow do chain my soul to thine.
And, ere my knee rise from the earth's cold face,   35
I throw my hands, mine eyes, my heart to Thee,
Thou setter-up and plucker-down of kings,
Beseeching Thee, if with Thy will it stands
That to my foes this body must be prey,
Yet that Thy brazen gates of heaven may ope   40
And give sweet passage to my sinful soul.
Now, lords, take leave until we meet again,
Where'er it be, in heaven or in earth.

RICHARD

Brother, give me thy hand; and, gentle Warwick,
Let me embrace thee in my weary arms.   45
I, that did never weep, now melt with woe
That winter should cut off our springtime so.

WARWICK

Away, away! Once more, sweet lords, farewell.

GEORGE

Yet let us all together to our troops
And give them leave to fly that will not stay,   50

33 **I . . . knee** an implicit SD, indicating
that Edward kneels with Warwick.
37 'Having fashioned his "*regum creator*"
from the facts, [Shakespeare] seems to
have had difficulty in distinguishing
him (at least in the minds of his characters) from the God of the Book of
Daniel of whom it is said, "he taketh
away kings, hee setteth vp kinges"
[2.21]: the words are twice almost
repeated, once when Warwick and
Edward kneel together in prayer
[2.3.37], and once when Margaret uses
them of Warwick himself [3.3.157]'
(Brockbank, 'Shakespeare's', 188).

40 **brazen** strong (referring to defensive
quality rather than the actual material)
(*OED a.* 1b)
44–6 **hand . . . embrace . . . melt with
woe** implicit SDs for the actor playing
Richard
46 **that . . . weep** 'a point to be noted in
the building up of Richard's character'
(Ard²)
47 **winter . . . springtime** Edward's
emblem of the sun gives rise to season-
al metaphors from time to time. See
also 2.2.163–4 and *R3* 1.1.1–4.
49–55 In Hall, George's suggestion is
made more viciously by Edward, when

44] *Pope; F lines* Brother, / Warwicke, /   47 springtime] *(Spring-time)*   48] *O; F lines* away: /
farwell. /   49 all together] *Rowe;* altogether *F*

And call them pillars that will stand to us;
And, if we thrive, promise them such rewards
As victors wear at the Olympian games.
This may plant courage in their quailing breasts,
For yet is hope of life and victory.   55
Forslow no longer; make we hence amain.   *Exeunt.*

[2.4]   *Excursions. Enter* RICHARD [*at one door*] *and*
                        CLIFFORD [*at the other*].

RICHARD

Now, Clifford, I have singled thee alone.
Suppose this arm is for the Duke of York,
And this for Rutland, both bound to revenge,
Wert thou environed with a brazen wall.

CLIFFORD

Now, Richard, I am with thee here alone.   5
This is the hand that stabbed thy father York,
And this the hand that slew thy brother Rutland,
And here's the heart that triumphs in their death
And cheers these hands that slew thy sire and brother
To execute the like upon thyself.   10

he promises double wages to any soldier who kills another who flees after
having agreed to remain (255).
51 **stand to** stand by, take the side of (not
noted in *OED*)
53 **Olympian games** The classical eru-
dition of the early plays is evident in
this allusion, the only use of the phrase
in Shakespeare, though the games may
be alluded to again in *TC* 4.5.195. 'For
an odd and garbled allusion to the
Olympic Games, see *A Knack to Know
a Knave*, MSR, 1304–5' (RP).
54 **quailing** losing hope or courage (*OED
ppl.* 1a)
56 **Forslow** be slow or dilatory
make . . . amain let us leave at once,

without delay
2.4 Imagining another part of the battle
of Towton, the action is continuous
with the previous scene, but it has no
authority in the chronicles.
2.4.0.1–2 O specifies 'enter *Richard* at one
dore and *Clifford* at the other', each
voicing a war-cry: 'A *Clifford* a
Clifford', 'A *Richard* a *Richard*'.
1 **singled** picked out and chased separately (from hunting) (*OED v.*[1] 2).
Richard continues the hunting
imagery in 12–13.
4 **Wert thou environed** if you were
surrounded, i.e. protected
brazen strong. See 2.3.40n.

2.4] *Capell*   0.1 *at one door*] O   0.2 *at the other*] O

And so, have at thee!

[*Alarums.*] *They fight.* WARWICK *comes* [*and rescues Richard*].
Clifford flies.

RICHARD
Nay, Warwick, single out some other chase,
For I myself will hunt this wolf to death.   *Exeunt.*

[**2.5**]   *Alarum. Enter* KING HENRY *alone.*

KING HENRY
This battle fares like to the morning's war,
When dying clouds contend with growing light,
What time the shepherd, blowing of his nails,
Can neither call it perfect day nor night.
Now sways it this way, like a mighty sea   5
Forced by the tide to combat with the wind.
Now sways it that way, like the selfsame sea
Forced to retire by fury of the wind.
Sometime the flood prevails, and then the wind;
Now one the better, then another best,   10

11.1 O's SD clarifies that Clifford is getting the better of Richard until Warwick arrives: 'They fight, and then enters *Warwike* and rescues *Richard*, & then *exeunt omnes*'.

12 **chase** hunted animal (*OED sb.*[1] 4a)

2.5 The action is imagined near the battle of Towton, from which the King has withdrawn. His opening soliloquy is invented, but the lamenting son and father have a precedent in Hall's comment that 'This conflict was in maner vnnaturall, for in it the sonne fought against the father, the brother against the brother, the nephew against the vncle, and the tenaunt against his lord' (256). Ard[2] points to parallel comments in *Gorboduc* (1561), 5.2.180, and

the *Homily against Disobedience and Wilful Rebellion* (1569). Cam[2] adds a parallel from Tacitus.

1 **fares** goes on impetuously, rages (*OED v.*[1] 4b)

3 **What time** that time when (circumlocution for 'when'). Used elsewhere in Shakespeare only in *Tit* 4.3.19 and *TN* 4.3.30.

3 **blowing . . . nails** blowing on his hands to warm them in the cold before sunrise

5–12 The image is suggested by Hall: 'This deadly battayle and bloudy conflicte, continued .x. houres in doubtfull victorie. The one parte some time flowyng, and sometime ebbyng . . .' (256).

11.1 *Alarums*] O   *and rescues Richard*] O   2.5] *Capell*

Both tugging to be victors, breast to breast,
Yet neither conqueror nor conquered:
So is the equal poise of this fell war.
Here on this molehill will I sit me down.
To whom God will, there be the victory.   15
For Margaret, my Queen, and Clifford too,
Have chid me from the battle, swearing both
They prosper best of all when I am thence.
Would I were dead, if God's good will were so.
For what is in this world but grief and woe?   20
O God! Methinks it were a happy life
To be no better than a homely swain,
To sit upon a hill, as I do now,
To carve out dials quaintly, point by point,
Thereby to see the minutes how they run: 25
How many makes the hour full complete,
How many hours brings about the day,
How many days will finish up the year,
How many years a mortal man may live.
When this is known, then to divide the times: 30
So many hours must I tend my flock,

---

11 The image suggests combatants straining against each other, as boxers do in a clinch.
tugging contending, striving in opposition
12 **conquered** conquerèd
13 **fell** fierce, savage, cruel
14 **molehill** Henry alludes to a *hill* again in 23. For staging suggestions, see 1.4.67, where York is killed on a *molehill*.
16–19 See 2.2.73–6, where Henry obstinately refuses to heed Clifford's and Margaret's urging.
17 **chid** scolded
19 **Would . . . dead** perhaps suggested by *Mirror*, 'Woulde god the day of birth had brought me to my beere' (213)
20 **grief** pain, which gives rise to *woe*

22 **homely swain** unsophisticated, simple shepherd. For *homely* see *Mac* 4.2.69.
24 **dials** sundials. Ard[1] suggests 'a shepherd's device of cutting sun-dials on grassy plots, with an erection of a slate or board as a device for a gnomon'.
quaintly with ingenious art (*OED a.* 2)
25–6 **minutes . . . makes** See Abbott, 333, on third-person plural in *-s*. Cf. *hours brings* (27).
26, 27, 31–4, 38 **hour, hours** two syllables (Cercignani, 228)
27 **brings about** causes to come round, makes a complete revolution; completes (*OED* bring 11b). Cf. *LLL* 5.2.792.

So many hours must I take my rest,
So many hours must I contemplate,
So many hours must I sport myself,
So many days my ewes have been with young,   35
So many weeks ere the poor fools will ean,
So many years ere I shall shear the fleece.
So minutes, hours, days, weeks, months and years,
Passed over to the end they were created,
Would bring white hairs unto a quiet grave.   40
Ah! What a life were this, how sweet, how lovely!
Gives not the hawthorn bush a sweeter shade
To shepherds looking on their silly sheep
Than doth a rich embroidered canopy
To kings that fear their subjects' treachery?   45
O yes, it doth, a thousandfold it doth.
And to conclude, the shepherd's homely curds,
His cold thin drink out of his leather bottle,
His wonted sleep under a fresh tree's shade,
All which secure and sweetly he enjoys,   50
Is far beyond a prince's delicates;
His viands sparkling in a golden cup,

---

34 **sport** divert
36 **fools** those destitute of reason and hence of language. Cf. 'dumb animals'. **ean** yean, give birth (to lambs)
38 ***weeks** Rowe's emendation replaces the necessary element of the timeline catalogue mentioned at 36 and fills out the metre.
39 **end** purpose
40 biblical: 'ye shal bring my graie head with sorowe vnto the graue' (Genesis, 42.38; Shaheen, 67)
42–54 A similar contrast between kings and commoners, again preferring the latter, is twice made by Henry's father in later plays (*2H4* 4.5.23–8, *H5*

4.1.254–81). Ard² suggests a biblical precedent: 'The slepe of him that trauaileth, *is* swete, whether he eat litle or muche: but the sa[t]ietie of the riche wil not suffer him to slepe' (Ecclesiastes, 5.11).
44 **canopy** cloth carried above a monarch on formal occasions. Ard² suggests also the covering over a four-poster bed, pointing to 49 and 53.
48 **thin** weak (*OED a.* 4c)
49 **wonted** accustomed
50 **secure** without cares
51 **delicates** choice, dainty foods (*OED sb.* 2b)
52 **viands** items of sustenance

38 weeks] *Rowe; not in F*

249

His body couched in a curious bed,
When care, mistrust and treason waits on him.

Alarum. Enter a Son *that hath killed his father at one door, and a*
Father *that hath killed his son at another door* [*with their bodies*].

SON

Ill blows the wind that profits nobody.   55
This man, whom hand to hand I slew in fight,
May be possessed with some store of crowns,
And I, that haply take them from him now,
May yet ere night yield both my life and them
To some man else, as this dead man doth me.   60
Who's this? O God! It is my father's face,
Whom in this conflict I unwares have killed.
O heavy times, begetting such events!
From London by the King was I pressed forth.
My father, being the Earl of Warwick's man,   65
Came on the part of York, pressed by his master.
And I, who at his hands received my life,
Have by my hands of life bereaved him.
Pardon me, God, I knew not what I did;
And pardon, father, for I knew not thee.   70
My tears shall wipe away these bloody marks,

---

53 **couched** couchèd, i.e. laid down
   curious made with care (*OED a.* 7a)
54 **care** mental suffering, sorrow, grief
54.1–2 F requires the Son and Father to
   enter simultaneously, and the Father to
   enter again at 78 SD. O requires a separate entry for each. Either they enter
   separately or the Father remains 'aloof'
   until the Son has finished speaking.
55 proverbial: 'It is an ill wind that blows
   no man good' (Tilley, W421)
57 **possessed** possessèd
   crowns coins

58 **haply** by chance, maybe
62 **unwares** unaware, unknowingly
63 **heavy** grievous, painful, as at 1.4.160
64 **pressed** forced to serve in the army
68 **bereaved** bereavèd
69 biblical: 'Then said Iesus, Father,
   forgiue them: for they knowe not what
   thei do' (Luke, 23.24; Shaheen, 67).
   See 1.4.86n.
71 The line contains two implicit SDs:
   weeping for the Son (cf. 76 and 85) and
   bloody marks on the Father.

54.2 *with their bodies*] O (*subst.*)

And no more words, till they have flowed their fill.

KING HENRY

O piteous spectacle! O bloody times!
While lions war and battle for their dens,
Poor harmless lambs abide their enmity.   75
Weep, wretched man; I'll aid thee tear for tear,
And let our hearts and eyes, like civil war,
Be blind with tears and break o'ercharged with grief.

[*The*] *Father* [*comes forward,*] *bearing of his son.*

FATHER

Thou that so stoutly hath resisted me,
Give me thy gold, if thou hast any gold,   80
For I have bought it with an hundred blows.
But let me see: is this our foeman's face?
Ah, no, no, no, it is mine only son!
Ah, boy, if any life be left in thee,
Throw up thine eye! See, see what showers arise,   85
Blown with the windy tempest of my heart,
Upon thy wounds, that kills mine eye and heart!
O pity, God, this miserable age!
What stratagems, how fell, how butcherly,
Erroneous, mutinous and unnatural,   90
This deadly quarrel daily doth beget!
O boy, thy father gave thee life too soon,

---

75 **abide** endure, suffer (*OED v. trans.* 16)
77–8 The verbs, *be blind . . . and break,* reverse the sequence of their subjects, *hearts and eyes,* a rhetorical figure called 'chiasmus', or the cross.
79 **stoutly** bravely, strongly
85 **Throw up** raise quickly (*OED v.* 48c)
87 **wounds, that kills** See Abbott, 333, on third-person plural in -*s*.
89 **stratagems** deeds of blood or violence (*OED* 3)

fell harsh, cruel
90 **Erroneous** morally faulty, criminal (*OED* 2)
mutinous subverting hierarchy
unnatural 'This conflict was in maner vnnatural' (Hall, 256). ·
92–3 **thy . . . late** 'Thy father exposed thee to danger by "giving thee life too soon," and hath "bereft thee of life" by living himself too long' (S. Johnson, 8.603).

---

78 SD] *this edn; Enter Father, bearing of his Sonne. F*   82 our] *F;* a *Collier*   89 stratagems] *F3;* Stragems *F1*   90 Erroneous] *F2;* Erreoneous *F1*

And hath bereft thee of thy life too late!

KING HENRY

Woe above woe! Grief more than common grief!

O that my death would stay these ruthful deeds!   95

O pity, pity, gentle heaven, pity!

The red rose and the white are on his face,

The fatal colours of our striving houses:

The one his purple blood right well resembles,

The other his pale cheeks methinks presenteth.   100

Wither one rose, and let the other flourish;

If you contend, a thousand lives must wither.

SON

How will my mother for a father's death

Take on with me, and ne'er be satisfied!

FATHER

How will my wife for slaughter of my son   105

Shed seas of tears, and ne'er be satisfied!

KING HENRY

How will the country for these woeful chances

Misthink the King, and not be satisfied!

SON

Was ever son so rued a father's death?

FATHER

Was ever father so bemoaned his son?   110

KING HENRY

Was ever king so grieved for subjects' woe?

Much is your sorrow; mine, ten times so much.

---

93 **late** lately, recently

95 **stay** stop, put an end to
   ruthful lamentable, piteous (*OED a.*
   2)

100 **presenteth** See Abbott, 334, on
   third person plural in *-th*.

101–2 The Tudors claimed to have *united*
   the two roses of Lancaster and York.
   See List of Roles, 30n.

104 **Take on with** rage against, distress

herself greatly (*OED* take *v.* 86j)

106 **seas of tears** proverbial (Dent,
   T82.1)

108 **Misthink** misjudge, think ill of.
   Used only once more in Shakespeare
   ('misthought') in *AC* 5.2.175.

109 **Was ever son** was there ever a son
   who
   rued regretted, wished it had never
   taken place

SON

I'll bear thee hence, where I may weep my fill.

[Exit bearing his father.]

FATHER

These arms of mine shall be thy winding-sheet;
My heart, sweet boy, shall be thy sepulchre,   115
For from my heart thine image ne'er shall go;
My sighing breast shall be thy funeral bell;
And so obsequious will thy father be
E'en for the loss of thee, having no more,
As Priam was for all his valiant sons.   120
I'll bear thee hence, and let them fight that will,
For I have murdered where I should not kill.

Exit [bearing his son].

KING HENRY

Sad-hearted men, much overgone with care,
Here sits a king more woeful than you are.

Alarums. Excursions. Enter QUEEN [MARGARET],
PRINCE [EDWARD] *and* EXETER.

PRINCE EDWARD

Fly, father, fly! For all your friends are fled,   125
And Warwick rages like a chafed bull:
Away, for Death doth hold us in pursuit.

---

113 **I'll . . . hence** an implicit SD, as at 121, to indicate how the bodies were to be cleared from the stage
114 **winding-sheet** burial cloth, shroud
118 **obsequious** attentive to funeral obsequies (*OED a.* 1b)
119 *****E'en** The F reading 'Men' no doubt derives from a 'foul case' error (the 'E' and 'M' sort-boxes were adjacent in seventeenth-century type-cases).
120 **Priam** King of Troy, reputed to have fifty sons
123 **overgone** overcome, overwhelmed (*OED v.* 5a)
126 **chafed** chafèd i.e. angered, irritated
127 **hold . . . pursuit** puts us to flight (*OED* pursuit 2b)

---

113 SD] *O subst.* 119 E'en] *Capell (Even); Men F1; Man F4; Sad Rowe; Mean Hulme; Mad (GWW)* 122 SD *bearing his son] O subst.* 127 Death] *(death)*

QUEEN MARGARET

Mount you, my lord; towards Berwick post amain.
Edward and Richard, like a brace of greyhounds
Having the fearful flying hare in sight,   130
With fiery eyes sparkling for very wrath,
And bloody steel grasped in their ireful hands,
Are at our backs, and therefore hence amain.

EXETER

Away, for Vengeance comes along with them.
Nay, stay not to expostulate, make speed;   135
Or else come after. I'll away before.

KING HENRY

Nay, take me with thee, good sweet Exeter:
Not that I fear to stay, but love to go
Whither the Queen intends. Forward, away!   *Exeunt.*

[2.6]   *A loud alarum. Enter* CLIFFORD
            wounded[, with an arrow in his neck].

CLIFFORD

Here burns my candle out; ay, here it dies.

---

128 **towards Berwick** Henry 'departed
   incontinent with his wife and sonne, to
   the towne of Barwycke' (Hall, 256).
128, 133 **post amain, hence amain**
   move (1) with all one's might, vehemently (*OED adv.* 1); (2) at full speed
   (*OED* 2); (3) at once, immediately
   (*OED* 2b)
129 **brace** pair
135 **expostulate** complain, discourse,
   discuss (*OED v. intr.* a and b)
139 **intends** directs her way (*OED v.* 6)
2.6 The scene imagines another part of
   the battle of Towton, though Hall and
   Holinshed report that Clifford died in
   the preliminary skirmish near
   Ferrybridge (see 2.3n.). Postponing
   Clifford's death enhances the sense

that the tide is turning in York's favour
(3–10). Clifford's fatal wound is
explained in Hall: 'For the lord
Clifforde, either for heat or payne,
putting of his gorget, sodainly with an
arrowe (as some say) without an hedde,
was striken into the throte, and incontinent rendered hys spirite' (255); it is
also reported in Holinshed (277) and
Mirror (191). O specifies Clifford's
wound, 'with an arrow in his necke',
suggesting that O's SD was written
either with the sources in mind or
from memory of the scene in performance. For arrow wounds in the skull
of a warrior slain at Towton, see Fig. 5.
1 **Here . . . out** Cam[2] compares biblical
   Job, 21.17 ('How oft shal the candel of

134 Vengeance] *(vengeance)*   139 Whither] *(Whether)*   2.6] Capell   0.2 *with . . . neck*] O

Which whiles it lasted gave King Henry light.
O Lancaster, I fear thy overthrow
More than my body's parting with my soul!
My love and fear glued many friends to thee,   5
And now I fall. Thy tough commixtures melts,
Impairing Henry, strength'ning misproud York.
The common people swarm like summer flies,
And whither fly the gnats but to the sun?
And who shines now but Henry's enemies?   10
O Phoebus, hadst thou never given consent
That Phaëton should check thy fiery steeds,
Thy burning car never had scorched the earth!
And Henry, hadst thou swayed as kings should do,
Or as thy father and his father did,   15
Giving no ground unto the house of York,
They never then had sprung like summer flies;
I and ten thousand in this luckless realm
Had left no mourning widows for our death,
And thou this day hadst kept thy chair in peace.   20
For what doth cherish weeds but gentle air?

the wicked be put out?') and the proverbial 'candle of life' (Dent, CC1). Cf.
Mac 5.5.23.
5 **My . . . glued** others' love and fear of
me attracted
5–6 **thee . . . Thy** The first pronoun
refers to Lancaster (3), whose alliance
(*commixtures*) Clifford fears will come
apart (*melt*) because of his own (*Thy*)
death.
6 **tough** sticky, tenacious (*OED a.* 2),
continuing the metaphor suggested by
glued (5)
   commixtures melts See Abbott,
333, on third-person plural in *-s*.
7 **misproud** wrongly proud, arrogant
9–10 The image suggests Edward's
emblem, the sun. See 2.1.21–40.
11–13 Phoebus is an epithet of Apollo,
god of the sun. For Phaëton, see

1.4.33n. The mythology of the sun in
this allusion is incongruent with
immediately preceding allusions to the
sun as York's emblem, since in this
case Phaëton clearly alludes to
Lancaster (specifically to Henry), not
to York, as at 1.4.33.
12 **check** rein, control (*OED v.* 14b)
13 **car** chariot
13, 17, 19 **had** would have
14 **swayed** ruled
17 **sprung** reproduced
19 **mourning widows** widows mourning. See Abbott, 419a, on the transposition of adjectival phrases.
20 **kept thy chair** Ard[2] notes wordplay
on (1) lived to old age (citing *2H6*
5.2.48) and (2) retained your throne.
21 **gentle air** proverbial: 'as gentle as air'
(Dent, A88.1). Cf. *AC* 5.2.310.

8] *O; not in F*   9 whither] *(whether)*

And what makes robbers bold but too much lenity?
Bootless are plaints, and cureless are my wounds:
No way to fly, nor strength to hold out fight.
The foe is merciless and will not pity,   25
For at their hands I have deserved no pity.
The air hath got into my deadly wounds,
And much effuse of blood doth make me faint.
Come, York and Richard, Warwick and the rest:
I stabbed your fathers' bosoms; split my breast.   30

Alarum and retreat. Enter EDWARD, WARWICK, RICHARD *and*
Soldiers, MONTAGUE *and* GEORGE.

EDWARD

Now breathe we, lords; good fortune bids us pause
And smooth the frowns of war with peaceful looks.
Some troops pursue the bloody-minded Queen,
That led calm Henry, though he were a king,
As doth a sail filled with a fretting gust   35
Command an argosy to stem the waves.
But think you, lords, that Clifford fled with them?

WARWICK

No, 'tis impossible he should escape,
For, though before his face I speak the words,
Your brother Richard marked him for the grave,   40

---

23 **Bootless** useless, unavailing
   plaints laments, grieving
24 **hold out** keep up, maintain (*OED v.*
   41f)
28 **effuse of blood** effusion of blood,
   bloodshed, slaughter
30.1 *retreat* a trumpet call to signal
   retreat in battle
31 **Now breathe we** now we have a
   chance to breathe

35 **fretting gust** gusting wind. *Fretting* is
   appropriate both to the wind and to
   scolding (with an allusion to 'the
   bloody-minded Queen') (Cam[1]).
36 **Command** compel (with continuing
   allusion to Margaret's domination of
   Henry)
   argosy large merchant ship
   stem contend with
39 **his** Richard's

24 out] *Q3, F;* our *O*   fight] *(Johnson);* flight *F*   30.2 GEORGE] *Clarence F*

And wheresoe'er he is, he's surely dead.   *Clifford groans.*

RICHARD

Whose soul is that which takes her heavy leave?
A deadly groan, like life and death's departing.

EDWARD

See who it is; and now the battle's ended,
If friend or foe, let him be gently used.   45

RICHARD

Revoke that doom of mercy, for 'tis Clifford,
Who not contented that he lopped the branch
In hewing Rutland when his leaves put forth,
But set his murd'ring knife unto the root
From whence that tender spray did sweetly spring,   50
I mean our princely father, Duke of York.

WARWICK

From off the gates of York fetch down the head,
Your father's head, which Clifford placed there;
Instead whereof let this supply the room:

---

41 SD *Clifford groans.* Clifford may die
with this groan, as O suggests
('*Clifford* grones and then dies'), but F
specifies no moment of death, and the
Yorkists later seem to abuse Clifford
physically, as well as verbally (see 68-
86n.). If he were to die in the midst of
such savagery, his death would be
more pitiable, in addition to recalling
the death of York in 1.4.

43 **departing** separation, sundering.
Ard² compares the *BCP* liturgy for
matrimony, 'Till death us depart'.

44–5 Shakespeare makes Edward more
gracious here than in the chronicles
(see 2.3.49–55n.), perhaps to create a
contrast between Edward and Richard
(2.6.46n.).

45 **If** whether
gently nobly, as befits a nobleman

46 **doom** decree, sentence. Richard's savage exclamation, and his brothers'

instant assent to it, measure how far
aristocratic behaviour has departed
from its own code under the pressure
of fratricidal civil war.

47–9 **Who ... set** 'who was not contented merely that he lopped ... but also
set ...'. The primary reference is to a
genealogical tree, as at 2.2.163–9, but
Cam¹ compares *Tit* 2.4.17–18 as well,
where the human body is compared to
a tree: 'Hath lopped and hewed and
made thy body bare / Of her two
branches'.

50 **spray** twig, shoot

52–3 In Hall, this order is given by
Edward, not by Warwick (256), and
Shakespeare invents the order (repeated by Warwick in 85–6) that Clifford's
head be put in place of York's.

53 **placed** placèd

54 **this** Clifford's head
supply the room take the place

44 SP] *O subst.; See who it is continued to Richard F*

257

Measure for measure must be answered.   55

EDWARD

Bring forth that fatal screech-owl to our house
That nothing sung but death to us and ours:
Now death shall stop his dismal threat'ning sound,
And his ill-boding tongue no more shall speak.

WARWICK

I think his understanding is bereft.   60
Speak, Clifford, dost thou know who speaks to thee?
Dark cloudy death o'ershades his beams of life,
And he nor sees, nor hears us what we say.

RICHARD

O would he did, and so perhaps he doth.
'Tis but his policy to counterfeit,   65
Because he would avoid such bitter taunts
Which in the time of death he gave our father.

GEORGE

If so thou think'st, vex him with eager words.

RICHARD

Clifford, ask mercy and obtain no grace.

EDWARD

Clifford, repent in bootless penitence.   70

---

55 **Measure for measure** biblical (Mark, 4.24) and proverbial (Tilley, M800)
answered answerèd i.e. paid back, requited
56 **fatal . . . house** the screech-owl fatal to our house. See Abbott, 419a, on the transposition of adjectival phrases. The semiotic screech-owl is proverbial: 'The croaking raven (screeching owl) bodes misfortune' (Dent, R33). Cf. 5.6.44, where Richard is referred to in the same way.
58 **dismal** unlucky, malign (*OED adj.* 2)

60–3 Warwick's address to Clifford recalls Richard's to Somerset at 1.1.16.
60 **bereft** taken from him; deficient
65 **policy** See 1.2.57n.
counterfeit deceive
66 **taunts** Cooper defines *sarcasmos* as 'A bitinge taunte or scoffe' (Ard²).
68–86 The 'eager words' may be accompanied by physical abuse of Clifford, as suggested by George at 72, culminating in Warwick's order to decapitate him.
68 **eager** sharp, biting (*OED a.* 1c)

60 his] *O;* is *F*   68] *O; F lines* think'st, / Words. /

WARWICK

    Clifford, devise excuses for thy faults.

GEORGE

    While we devise fell tortures for thy faults.

RICHARD

    Thou didst love York, and I am son to York.

EDWARD

    Thou pitied'st Rutland; I will pity thee.

GEORGE

    Where's Captain Margaret to fence you now?   75

WARWICK

    They mock thee, Clifford: swear as thou wast wont.

RICHARD

    What, not an oath? Nay, then the world goes hard

    When Clifford cannot spare his friends an oath.

    I know by that he's dead, and, by my soul,

    If this right hand would buy two hours' life,   80

    That I in all despite might rail at him,

    This hand should chop it off, and with the issuing blood

    Stifle the villain whose unstaunched thirst

    York and young Rutland could not satisfy.

WARWICK

    Ay, but he's dead. Off with the traitor's head,   85

    And rear it in the place your father's stands.

---

72 **fell** cruel
75 **fence** protect, defend
77 **world goes hard** proverbial: 'It is a hard world' (Dent, W877.1)
81 **despite** contempt, scorn (*OED sb.* 1)
82 **This hand** my left hand. Richard regrets not having killed Clifford himself and wishes him alive again that he might cut off his own right hand with his left and drown Clifford 'with the issuing blood'. Cf. Rutland's epithet *bloody Clifford* at 1.3.2.
83 **Stifle** choke by pouring (blood) down

his throat (*OED v.*[1] 3)
unstaunched unstaunchèd
85–98 Warwick speaks as kingmaker to Edward, announcing plans for Edward's coronation and marriage and also anticipating the major plot development of the play's second half, which will include (though he does not know it) his own defection to Lancaster and eventual destruction in that cause.
86 **rear** put up, raise

76] O; F lines Clifford, / wont. /

And now to London with triumphant march,
There to be crowned England's royal king:
From whence shall Warwick cut the sea to France
And ask the Lady Bona for thy queen.   90
So shalt thou sinew both these lands together;
And having France thy friend thou shalt not dread
The scattered foe that hopes to rise again,
For though they cannot greatly sting to hurt,
Yet look to have them buzz to offend thine ears.   95
First will I see the coronation;
And then to Brittany I'll cross the sea
To effect this marriage, so it please my lord.

EDWARD

Even as thou wilt, sweet Warwick, let it be;
For in thy shoulder do I build my seat,   100
And never will I undertake the thing
Wherein thy counsel and consent is wanting.
Richard, I will create thee Duke of Gloucester,
And George, of Clarence. Warwick as ourself

---

88 **crowned** crownèd
89 **cut the sea** The phrase may be
Virgilian. Cooper translates *sulcare
maria* as 'To cut the seas' (Ard²).
91 **sinew** bind together, as with sinews
93 **scattered** thrown down (in defeat), as
seed is scattered in planting
95 **buzz** the sound of insects (from *sting*
at 94); spread rumours (cf. 5.6.86)
96 **coronation** five syllables. Edward was
crowned at Westminster on 29 June
1461 (Hall, 257).
100 **in thy shoulder** depending on your
strength. The comment reflects
Warwick's reputation as kingmaker,
though ironically Edward will shortly
cease to lean on Warwick, and Warwick
will lend his shoulder to the other side.
seat (1) throne, authority (*OED sb.* 8a):
cf. 1.1.26; (2) basis, foundation, sup-

port (*OED* IV)
103–4 Richard's and George's promotions are recorded in Hall (258), but
Shakespeare remembered Richard's
superstition about the title of Gloucester from an earlier passage, where
Hall attributes it to 'many men', not to
Richard: 'the name and title of
Gloucester, hath been vnfortunate and
vnluckie to diuerse, whiche for their
honor, haue been erected by creacion
of princes, to that stile and dignitie, as
Hugh   Spencer,   Thomas   of
Woodstocke, sonne to kyng Edward
the third, and this duke Humfrey,
which thre persones, by miserable
death finished their daies, and after
them kyng Richard the .iii. also, duke
of Glucester, in ciuill warre was slain
and confounded' (209).

91 sinew] *(sinow)*   100 in] on *(RP)*

Shall do and undo as him pleaseth best.   105

RICHARD

Let me be Duke of Clarence, George of Gloucester;
For Gloucester's dukedom is too ominous.

WARWICK

Tut, that's a foolish observation.
Richard, be Duke of Gloucester. Now to London,   109
To see these honours in possession.   *Exeunt.*

[3.1]   *Enter two* Keepers *with crossbows in their hands.*

1 KEEPER

Under this thick-grown brake we'll shroud ourselves,
For through this laund anon the deer will come;
And in this covert will we make our stand,
Culling the principal of all the deer.

---

105 **him pleaseth** he thinks
108 **observation** remark (five syllables)
110 **to possess these honours**
     possession four syllables
3.1 During the battle of Towton, Margaret orders Henry to Berwick, a town on the Scottish border (2.5.128). Hall says Henry went on to 'the kynges court of Scotland' (256), and in this scene the king says he has left Scotland to come back into England (13–14). An indefinite amount of time has elapsed since the battle of Towton on 29 March 1461. Henry, who has heard of Warwick's mission to France (29–31), was in fact captured four years after Towton, on 29 June 1465 (Boswell-Stone, 309). The play thus omits the battle of Hexham on 15 May 1464, when Montague defeated the Lancastrians after attacking their camp, and Henry was again compelled to flee (Hall, 260; Holinshed, 281). The method of Henry's capture in the

scene is invented; Hall says simply that 'he was· knowen and taken of one Cantlowe' (261; Holinshed, 281).
3.1.0.1 *two* **Keepers** See List of Roles, 45–6n.
     crossbows This weapon, favoured more on the Continent than in England, appears only here, among all of Shakespeare's plays, and has no warrant in the sources, but it is used precisely. The sporting crossbow was reserved principally for hunting deer in dense cover where a longbow would be difficult to draw, and the weapon was relatively noisy, as the First Keeper points out (6). See Payne-Gallwey, 11–12.
1 **brake** brushwood, thicket
   shroud hide, conceal
2 **laund** glade, pasture
3 **covert** protected spot, shelter
   stand place of concealment (*OED sb.* 3)
4 **Culling** selecting

3.1] *Rowe*   0.1 *two* Keepers] *O; Sinklo, and Humfrey F*   1+ SP] *Malone; Sink. F*   1 thick-grown] *Pope;* thicke growne *F*

2 KEEPER

   I'll stay above the hill, so both may shoot.   5

1 KEEPER

   That cannot be; the noise of thy crossbow

   Will scare the herd, and so my shoot is lost.

   Here stand we both, and aim we at the best,

   And, for the time shall not seem tedious,

   I'll tell thee what befell me on a day   10

   In this self place where now we mean to stand.

2 KEEPER

   Here comes a man; let's stay till he be past.

      Enter KING [HENRY, *disguised,*] *with a prayer book.*

KING HENRY

   From Scotland am I stol'n, even of pure love,

   To greet mine own land with my wishful sight.

   No, Harry, Harry, 'tis no land of thine;   15

   Thy place is filled, thy sceptre wrung from thee,

   Thy balm washed off wherewith thou wast anointed.

   No bending knee will call thee Caesar now,

   No humble suitors press to speak for right,

   No, not a man comes for redress of thee.   20

   For how can I help them, an not myself?

---

7 **my . . . lost** I would lose my chance to
shoot; my shot would be wasted

9 **for** so, in order that

11 **self** same

12 **stay** wait, hold up

12.1 O adds that Henry is 'disguised',
either following Hall's comment that
Henry entered England 'in a disguysed
apparell' (261), or recalling performance of the scene.

17 The line anticipates *R2*, 'wash the

balm off from an anointed king'
(3.2.55). Henry refers to the perfumed
oil that is poured on the monarch's
head in a coronation as a symbol for
the charisma of kingship conferred on
an individual by the ceremony.

18–20 Ard[2] points to echoes of these lines
in *JC* 3.1.27–75.

20 **of** from

21 **an** if

5+ SP] *Malone; Hum. F*   11 **self place**] *(selfe-place)*   12.1 *disguised*] *O*   17 wast] *F3;* was *F1*
19 press] *(prease)*

1 KEEPER

    Ay, here's a deer whose skin's a keeper's fee!

    This is the quondam king; let's seize upon him.

KING HENRY

    Let me embrace the sour adversaries,

    For wise men say it is the wisest course.   25

2 KEEPER

    Why linger we? Let us lay hands upon him.

1 KEEPER

    Forbear awhile; we'll hear a little more.

KING HENRY

    My Queen and son are gone to France for aid;

    And, as I hear, the great commanding Warwick

    Is thither gone, to crave the French King's sister   30

    To wife for Edward. If this news be true,

    Poor Queen and son, your labour is but lost,

    For Warwick is a subtle orator,

    And Lewis a prince soon won with moving words.

    By this account, then, Margaret may win him,   35

    For she's a woman to be pitied much:

    Her sighs will make a batt'ry in his breast;

---

22 **keeper's** due to an officer who has charge of a forest, woods, or grounds (*OED* 1d)

    fee Ard[1] cites William Harrison's *Description of England* (1577) as authority for the keeper's fee being the head and hide of the deer.

23 **quondam** sometime, used-to-be

24 **the sour adversaries** usually emended to 'thee, sour Adversity' with various references cited. However, polysyllabic words often vary in emphasis in Shakespeare (Cercignani, 42–4), as *adversaries* does in this case, where

emphasis is on the second syllable. See also 25n.

25 **wise men say** biblical: 'Agre with thine aduersarie quickely' (Matthew, 5.25). Henry is reading a prayer book (12 SD), and this text occurs in *BCP*, 186. See Fig. 12. Henry is presumably in a mood for making peace.

31 **To wife** as wife. See Abbott, 189, on 'to' for 'as'.

32 **labour . . . lost** proverbial (Dent, L9)

34 **Lewis** For the pronunciation of this name, see List of Roles, 42n.

37 **batt'ry** bombardment

---

24 the sour adversaries] *F;* these sour adversities *Pope;* thee, sour adversity *Singer (Dyce)*
30 Is] *F2;* I: *F1*

Her tears will pierce into a marble heart;
The tiger will be mild whiles she doth mourn;
And Nero will be tainted with remorse,   40
To hear and see her plaints, her brinish tears.
Ay, but she's come to beg, Warwick to give:
She on his left side, craving aid for Henry;
He on his right, asking a wife for Edward.
She weeps, and says her Henry is deposed;   45
He smiles, and says his Edward is installed:
That she, poor wretch, for grief can speak no more,
Whiles Warwick tells his title, smooths the wrong,
Inferreth arguments of mighty strength,
And in conclusion wins the King from her   50
With promise of his sister, and what else,
To strengthen and support King Edward's place.
O Margaret, thus 'twill be; and thou, poor soul,
Art then forsaken, as thou went'st forlorn.

2 KEEPER
    Say, what art thou that talk'st of kings and queens?   55

---

38 **tears . . . heart** proverbial: 'Constant
dropping will wear the stone' (Tilley,
D618) and 'a heart of stone' (Dent,
H311)

39 York sees Margaret's relation to the
tiger very differently, in a line that has
become famous as an allusion to
Shakespeare. See 1.4.137n.

40 **Nero** Roman emperor famous for
sadistic cruelty
    will Pope emended to 'would', but if
Henry is thinking of Nero in the afterlife (i.e. in hell), the line is more powerful as it stands.
    tainted violated (i.e. Nero's character
will experience something foreign to
it)

41 **brinish** briny, salty

43–4 **left . . . right** Henry's point is that
the left side is disadvantageous (cf.

MW 2.2.22–3, *JC* 5.1.17–18), and his
comment may suggest a way of staging
3.3.0.1–3 and 3.3.42.1.

46 **installed** on the throne

48 **tells his title** formally declares
Edward's claim to the throne (*OED* tell
v. B3b)

49 **Inferreth** brings in, introduces (*OED
v.* 2). Henry uses *inferring* the same
way at 2.2.44.

50–1 **wins . . . sister** wins the King
from Margaret with a promise to
marry Lady Bona to Edward

51 **what else** what not, other things

52 **place** social rank, dignity (*OED sb.*
9a), in this case referring to Edward's
claim to be king

55 **what** The Second Keeper is asking
about Henry's rank. See Abbott, 254.

55 that talk'st] that talkes *O;* talk'st *F*

KING HENRY

    More than I seem, and less than I was born to:
    A man at least, for less I should not be;
    And men may talk of kings, and why not I?

2 KEEPER

    Ay, but thou talk'st as if thou wert a king.

KING HENRY

    Why so I am, in mind, and that's enough.   60

2 KEEPER

    But if thou be a king where is thy crown?

KING HENRY

    My crown is in my heart, not on my head:
    Not decked with diamonds and Indian stones,
    Nor to be seen. My crown is called content,
    A crown it is that seldom kings enjoy.   65

2 KEEPER

    Well, if you be a king crowned with content,
    Your crown content and you must be contented
    To go along with us, for, as we think,
    You are the king King Edward hath deposed;
    And we his subjects sworn in all allegiance   70
    Will apprehend you as his enemy.

KING HENRY

    But did you never swear and break an oath?

2 KEEPER

    No, never such an oath, nor will not now.

KING HENRY

    Where did you dwell when I was King of England?

2 KEEPER

    Here in this country, where we now remain.   75

---

63 **diamonds** three syllables
64 **crown . . . content** proverbial: 'A mind content is as a crown' (Tilley, C623)

71 **apprehend** seize, arrest
75 **this country** this region, this part of England

KING HENRY

 I was anointed king at nine months old.

 My father and my grandfather were kings,

 And you were sworn true subjects unto me:

 And tell me, then, have you not broke your oaths?

1 KEEPER

 No, for we were subjects but while you were king. 80

KING HENRY

 Why, am I dead? Do I not breathe a man?

 Ah, simple men, you know not what you sware.

 Look, as I blow this feather from my face,

 And as the air blows it to me again,

 Obeying with my wind when I do blow, 85

 And yielding to another when it blows,

 Commanded always by the greater gust,

 Such is the lightness of you common men.

 But do not break your oaths: for of that sin

 My mild entreaty shall not make you guilty. 90

 Go where you will, the King shall be commanded;

 And be you kings: command, and I'll obey.

1 KEEPER

 We are true subjects to the King, King Edward.

KING HENRY

 So would you be again to Henry,

 If he were seated as King Edward is. 95

---

76 **anointed . . . old** See 1.1.112.
80 The First Keeper's position is an inference drawn from strict Tudor political orthodoxy regarding passive obedience, which is explored at greater length and with deeper irony in the Duke of York in *R2*.
82 **simple** foolish
 sware archaic form of 'swore'

83 **feather** The same image is used of commoners in *2H6* 4.8.55–64.
85 **Obeying . . . wind** compelled by my breath
87 **Commanded** compelled, forced (also at 2.6.36)
94 **Henry** possibly trisyllabic (Cercignani, 358)

80 No, for we] *F*; No, we *Pope* 82 sware] *Ard²* *(Delius);* sweare *F* 93] *Pope; F lines* king, / Edward. /

1 KEEPER

We charge you, in God's name and the King's,
To go with us unto the officers.

KING HENRY

In God's name lead; your King's name be obeyed,
And what God will, that let your King perform;   99
And what he will, I humbly yield unto.   *Exeunt.*

[**3.2**]   *Enter* KING EDWARD, [RICHARD, Duke OF]
          GLOUCESTER, [GEORGE, Duke OF] CLARENCE,
                 [*and the* WIDOW,] Lady Grey.

KING EDWARD

Brother of Gloucester, at Saint Albans field
This lady's husband, Sir Richard Grey, was slain,
His lands then seized on by the conqueror.

3.2 The scene offers no hint of a particular location, but Hall says that Edward met Elizabeth Grey in 1563 at 'the mannor of Grafton' when he was hunting 'in the forest of Wychwood besyde Stonnystratforde' in Northamptonshire, and later married her 'where he first phantasied her visage' (264). Though Elizabeth's strategy for winning the King's hand is described by Hall, Shakespeare invented the King's brothers' choric comments, which make her strategy clear in the play, and he added Richard's anticipatory and seemingly gratuitous remark at 2.1.41–2. The anonymous *Edward III* has a similar wooing scene, but it 'moves off the political level', as Brockbank says ('Shakespeare's', 171), in a way Shakespeare's does not.

1–7 Edward is mistaken on two counts: (1) Grey was a Lancastrian, so his land was not seized by 'the conqueror' at the second battle of St Albans, which was won by Lancaster; (2) Grey was not fighting

for York (6–7) but for Lancaster, so the Yorkists owe his widow nothing on that account. Grey's lands were more likely seized by York after Henry's capture and Margaret's departure for France, as Hall suggests: 'folowying the old auncient adage which saith, that the husbandman ought first to tast of the new growen frute: [Edward] distributed the possessions, of such as toke parte with kyng Henry the .vi. to his souldiors and capitaines, which he thought well deserued it' (262; cf. Holinshed, 282). Ard[2] suggests that the errors arose from Hall's confusing account (252) of rewards issued after the second battle of St Albans. In *R3* 1.3.127–30 Richard describes Lady Grey's situation accurately.

2   **Sir Richard Grey** error for Sir John Grey, perhaps occasioned by Elizabeth's father's name, Sir Richard Woodville, which appears in the line before her husband's in Hall (264), as noted in Cam[2]

3.2] *Pope*   0.1–3] *(Enter K.Edward, Gloster, Clarence, Lady Gray.)*   0.3 WIDOW] *this edn*   3 lands] *O;* Land *F*

Her suit is now to repossess those lands,
Which we in justice cannot well deny,   5
Because in quarrel of the house of York
The worthy gentleman did lose his life.

RICHARD OF GLOUCESTER
Your highness shall do well to grant her suit:
It were dishonour to deny it her.

KING EDWARD
It were no less, but yet I'll make a pause.   10

RICHARD OF GLOUCESTER [*aside to George*]
Yea, is it so?
I see the lady hath a thing to grant,
Before the King will grant her humble suit.

GEORGE OF CLARENCE [*aside to Richard*]
He knows the game: how true he keeps the wind!

RICHARD OF GLOUCESTER [*aside to George*]
Silence!   15

KING EDWARD
Widow, we will consider of your suit;
And come some other time to know our mind.

WIDOW
Right gracious lord, I cannot brook delay.
May it please your highness to resolve me now,
And what your pleasure is shall satisfy me.   20

---

4 **repossess** regain legal title to
6 **in quarrel of** in the quarrel of, i.e. on behalf of. See Abbott, 82, 89, 90, on omission of the definite article (probably determined here by the metre) (JH).
12 **thing** bawdy wordplay on Elizabeth's sexual submission (Partridge, 199)
   grant yield, give up (*OED v.* 6)
13 **grant** accede to, concede to fulfil (*OED v.* 3)
14 **game . . . keeps the wind** The language is from hunting, a metaphor for courtship and seduction that is at least as old as Latin elegy. 'To keep the wind' is to remain downwind of the prey.
18 **brook** tolerate, put up with
19 **resolve** i.e. resolve my doubt, give me your answer
20 **pleasure . . . satisfy** Elizabeth is deferential and correct, but *doubles entendres* inevitably suggest themselves, especially since Richard construes her

11, 14, 15, 21, 24, 25, 27, 28, 30, 34, 50, 51, 57, 82, 83, 84, 107, 108 SDs] *Capell subst.*

RICHARD OF GLOUCESTER [*aside to George*]

    Ay, widow? Then I'll warrant you all your lands,

    An if what pleases him shall pleasure you.

    Fight closer, or good faith, you'll catch a blow.

GEORGE OF CLARENCE [*aside to Richard*]

    I fear her not, unless she chance to fall.

RICHARD OF GLOUCESTER [*aside to George*]

    God forbid that, for he'll take vantages.   25

KING EDWARD

    How many children hast thou, widow, tell me?

GEORGE OF CLARENCE [*aside to Richard*]

    I think he means to beg a child of her.

RICHARD OF GLOUCESTER [*aside to George*]

    Nay, then whip me: he'll rather give her two.

WIDOW

    Three, my most gracious lord.

RICHARD OF GLOUCESTER [*aside to George*]

    You shall have four, if you'll be ruled by him.   30

KING EDWARD

    'Twere pity they should lose their father's lands.

---

language equivocally in 22, and Edward addresses the issue of interpretation openly in 60. Hall's description of Elizabeth serves as an extended SD to the actor: 'her sober demeanure, louely lokyng, and femynyne smylyng (neither to wanton nor to humble) besyde her toungue so eloquent and her wit so pregnant . . . . she so wisely, and with so couert speache aunswered and repugned . . .'. (254).

21 **warrant** assure, guarantee; probably monosyllabic: 'warr'nt' (Cercignani, 275). Spoken as if to the widow, with *doubles entendres*: 'I guarantee you the return of all your lands if you derive pleasure from his wish (to seduce you)'.

22 **An if** if

23 **Fight closer** close with your enemy to

avoid his swinging blow; become more intimate

catch a blow be struck; have sexual intercourse (Partridge, 67). O makes the equivocation stronger with the phrase 'catch a clap', i.e. contract venereal disease.

24 **I . . . not** I am not afraid for her

fall fall down (continuing Richard's military metaphor in 23); surrender to Edward sexually (Partridge, 103)

25 **vantages** position likely to give superiority; advantage (of her)

27 **beg a child** petition the Court of Wards for custody of a minor (*OED* beg *v.* 5a); persuade her to conceive a child by him

28 **whip** 'confound', 'hang' (mild execration)

30 if you'll] *F;* and you wil *O*

WIDOW

    Be pitiful, dread lord, and grant it then.

KING EDWARD

    Lords, give us leave; I'll try this widow's wit.

    [*George and Richard stand aside.*]

RICHARD OF GLOUCESTER [*aside to George*]

    Ay, good leave have you, for you will have leave,

    Till youth take leave and leave you to the crutch.   35

KING EDWARD

    Now tell me, madam, do you love your children?

WIDOW

    Ay, full as dearly as I love myself.

KING EDWARD

    And would you not do much to do them good?

WIDOW

    To do them good, I would sustain some harm.

KING EDWARD

    Then get your husband's lands, to do them good.   40

WIDOW

    Therefore I came unto your majesty.

KING EDWARD

    I'll tell you how these lands are to be got.

WIDOW

    So shall you bind me to your highness' service.

KING EDWARD

    What service wilt thou do me, if I give them?

---

32 **pitiful** merciful, compassionate
33 **give us leave** allow, permit us; 'excuse us'
    try test
    wit mental capacity, understanding, intelligence
34–5 'We shall stand aside, as requested, for you will take liberties till youth bid farewell and you can walk only with support.'

34 **good leave have you** you have the permission you need
    have leave have freedom
35 **take leave** bid farewell
    leave you abandon you
    crutch support in old age; crotch, i.e. Elizabeth's
43 **service** as subject to liege; as sexual partner (44)

33 SD] *Johnson subst.*

WIDOW
> What you command, that rests in me to do. 45

KING EDWARD
> But you will take exceptions to my boon.

WIDOW
> No, gracious lord, except I cannot do it.

KING EDWARD
> Ay, but thou canst do what I mean to ask.

WIDOW
> Why, then I will do what your grace commands.

RICHARD OF GLOUCESTER [*aside to George*]
> He plies her hard, and much rain wears the marble. 50

GEORGE OF CLARENCE [*aside to Richard*]
> As red as fire! Nay, then her wax must melt.

WIDOW
> Why stops my lord? Shall I not hear my task?

KING EDWARD
> An easy task: 'tis but to love a king.

WIDOW
> That's soon performed, because I am a subject.

KING EDWARD
> Why then, thy husband's lands I freely give thee. 55

WIDOW
> I take my leave with many thousand thanks.

---

45 **rests in me** is in my power
46 **boon** order expressed as a request (*OED sb.*[1] 2)
47 **except** unless
48 **thou** Edward's shift to the familiar form of address signals his intention more clearly, and Elizabeth responds accordingly, using *your grace* for the first time (49) (RP).
49 Elizabeth's response seems to overwhelm Edward momentarily with increased ardour, as suggested at 50 and 51. She had said the same thing very differently at 45.
50 **much . . . marble** proverbial, as at

3.1.38
51 **As . . . fire** possibly suggested by Hall's comment: 'where he was a littell before heated with the darte of Cupido, he was nowe set all on a hote burnyng fyre' (254). Holinshed also refers to 'his affections fiered with the flames of loue' (284). The saying is proverbial (Tilley, F248). It is also possible, of course, that Elizabeth is blushing as well.
wax must melt Edward's ardour must overcome Elizabeth's reticence. Proverbial: 'to melt like wax against the fire' (Dent, W137.1).

RICHARD OF GLOUCESTER [*aside to George*]

　The match is made; she seals it with a curtsy.

KING EDWARD

　But stay thee, 'tis the fruits of love I mean.

WIDOW

　The fruits of love I mean, my loving liege.

KING EDWARD

　Ay, but I fear me, in another sense. 60

　What love, think'st thou, I sue so much to get?

WIDOW

　My love till death, my humble thanks, my prayers;

　That love which virtue begs and virtue grants.

KING EDWARD

　No, by my troth, I did not mean such love.

WIDOW

　Why then, you mean not as I thought you did. 65

KING EDWARD

　But now you partly may perceive my mind.

WIDOW

　My mind will never grant what I perceive

　Your highness aims at, if I aim aright.

KING EDWARD

　To tell thee plain, I aim to lie with thee.

WIDOW

　To tell you plain, I had rather lie in prison. 70

KING EDWARD

　Why then, thou shalt not have thy husband's lands.

WIDOW

　Why then, mine honesty shall be my dower,

　For by that loss I will not purchase them.

---

58 **stay thee** wait a moment
　fruits of love sexual satisfaction;
　pregnancy
59 **fruits of love** deeds appropriate to a

　loyal subject
72 **honesty** chastity
73 **that loss** the loss of my sexual mod-
　esty

KING EDWARD

    Therein thou wrong'st thy children mightily.

WIDOW

    Herein your highness wrongs both them and me.   75

    But, mighty lord, this merry inclination

    Accords not with the sadness of my suit.

    Please you dismiss me either with ay or no.

KING EDWARD

    Ay, if thou wilt say 'ay' to my request;

    No, if thou dost say 'no' to my demand.   80

WIDOW

    Then 'no', my lord; my suit is at an end.

RICHARD OF GLOUCESTER [*aside to George*]

    The widow likes him not: she knits her brows.

GEORGE OF CLARENCE [*aside to Richard*]

    He is the bluntest wooer in Christendom.

KING EDWARD [*aside*]

    Her looks doth argue her replete with modesty,

    Her words doth show her wit incomparable;   85

    All her perfections challenge sovereignty:

    One way or other, she is for a king,

    And she shall be my love, or else my queen. –

    Say that King Edward take thee for his queen?

WIDOW

    'Tis better said than done, my gracious lord: 90

    I am a subject fit to jest withal,

    But far unfit to be a sovereign.

KING EDWARD

    Sweet widow, by my state I swear to thee,

---

77 **sadness** seriousness, soberness

84 **looks doth** See Abbott, 334, on third person plural in *-th*; also *words doth* (85).

85 **wit** See 33n.

86 **challenge sovereignty** have a natural right or claim to (*OED* challenge *v.* 6a *fig.*)

88 **love** lover

90 **'Tis ... done** proverbial (Tilley, S116)

91 **subject** subject matter; one subject to the monarch

    jest disport or amuse oneself, make merry (*OED v.* 4b)

93 **state** high rank, greatness, power (*OED sb.* 16b). Cf. 1.1.51.

I speak no more than what my soul intends,
And that is to enjoy thee for my love. 95

WIDOW
And that is more than I will yield unto.
I know I am too mean to be your queen
And yet too good to be your concubine.

KING EDWARD
You cavil, widow: I did mean my queen.

WIDOW
'Twill grieve your grace my sons should call you father. 100

KING EDWARD
No more than when my daughters call thee mother.
Thou art a widow and thou hast some children,
And, by God's mother, I, being but a bachelor,
Have other some. Why, 'tis a happy thing
To be the father unto many sons. 105

97–8 The lines are adapted from Elizabeth's response as recorded by both Hall (366) and Holinshed (387) during the reign of Edward V: 'And in conclusion she shewed him plain, that as she wist her self to simple to be his wife, so thought her self to good to be his concubine' (Boswell-Stone, 311).

97 **mean** inferior in rank or quality. Elizabeth was daughter of Sir Richard Woodville, Lord Rivers, and Jacquetta of Luxemburg, widow of John, Duke of Bedford. Neither connection was sufficiently elevated to make her an appropriate royal spouse, and Edward already possessed, by right of conquest, the lands she owned as a result of her husband's death, so he stood to gain nothing materially from the marriage. In this respect, and in rejecting a more profitable arrangement, Edward's imprudence parallels that of Henry VI in marrying Margaret of Anjou.

99 **cavil** object, dispute unfairly
100 Elizabeth is aware of political risks in her potential elevation, and she wants to be certain she has the King's full support, not only for herself but for her children by her previous marriage.
101 **my daughters** Edward is referring to his illegitimate children, as he goes on to make clear.
102–4 also adapted from Shakespeare's sources for the reign of Edward V, where Edward defends his choice of Elizabeth to his mother, the Duchess of York: 'That she is a widdowe and hath already children: By god his blessed lady, I am a bacheler and haue some to' (Hall, 367; Holinshed, 388)
103 **by God's mother** by the Virgin Mary, a mild oath, retained from Hall (see 102–4n.), particularly ironic in context
104 **other some** other children

101] *Pope; F lines* Daughters / Mother. /

Answer no more, for thou shalt be my queen.

RICHARD OF GLOUCESTER [*aside to George*]

The ghostly father now hath done his shrift.

GEORGE OF CLARENCE [*aside to Richard*]

When he was made a shriver, 'twas for shift.

KING EDWARD

Brothers, you muse what chat we two have had.

RICHARD OF GLOUCESTER

The widow likes it not, for she looks very sad.   110

KING EDWARD

You'd think it strange if I should marry her.

GEORGE OF CLARENCE

To who, my lord?

KING EDWARD   Why, Clarence, to myself.

RICHARD OF GLOUCESTER

That would be ten days' wonder at the least.

GEORGE OF CLARENCE

That's a day longer than a wonder lasts.

RICHARD OF GLOUCESTER

By so much is the wonder in extremes.   115

KING EDWARD

Well, jest on, brothers; I can tell you both,

---

106 **shalt** connoting command, promise, determination. Cf. *Cor* 5.3.122–4.

107 **ghostly father** spiritual adviser, priest. Richard alludes caustically to 103–5.

shrift shriving, confession

108 **shriver** confessor

for shift in an emergency

109 For the first time since asking them to move further away (33), Edward acknowledges his brothers' presence and turns from Elizabeth to them. Hall comments that after deciding to marry Elizabeth, Edward asked 'counsaill of them, whiche he knewe neither woulde nor once durst impugne his concluded purpose' (254).

muse wonder, ask yourselves

112 **who** On 'who' for 'whom', see Abbott, 274. O has 'whom', thus illustrating the variation possible in Early Modern English (and indeed still today). O is consistently more 'standard' in grammatical choices than F: at 3.2.84 O avoids third-person plural with *-th*; at 2.5.27 and 2.6.6 O avoids third-person plural with *-s* (JH).

113 **ten days' wonder** proverbial: 'A wonder lasts but nine days' (Tilley, W728)

115 **in extremes** close to expiring (*in extremis*) (*OED sb.* 2b); to the utmost imaginable degree (*OED sb.* 4)

116 **jest on** Edward's remark makes clear that the brothers' teasing in 113–15 is

---

Her suit is granted for her husband's lands.

Enter a Nobleman.

NOBLEMAN

My gracious lord, Henry, your foe, is taken
And brought your prisoner to your palace gate.

KING EDWARD

See that he be conveyed unto the Tower,   120
And go we, brothers, to the man that took him
To question of his apprehension.
Widow, go you along; lords, use her honourably.

                              Exeunt [all but] Richard.

RICHARD OF GLOUCESTER

Ay, Edward will use women honourably.
Would he were wasted, marrow, bones and all,   125
That from his loins no hopeful branch may spring
To cross me from the golden time I look for.
And yet, between my soul's desire and me,
The lustful Edward's title buried,

not aside but direct, unlike their previous comments in the scene.

120 'By the kynges commaundement' Henry was brought 'through London, to the toure' (Hall, 261).

121 **go we, brothers** Despite Edward's command, Richard remains behind, his passive resistance perhaps hinting at the subversion he makes explicit in the following lines.

122 **apprehension** five syllables

123 **go you along** accompany us

124–95 This extraordinary soliloquy, placed at the midpoint of the action, is Richard's first open statement of his own ambition, though he earlier says something similar in encouraging his father to claim the crown (1.2.27–30). The way Richard begins and the placement of the soliloquy immediately following Edward's courtship of Lady Grey suggest a connection between Edward's easy way with women and Richard's determination to go his own way despite the disadvantages he faces.

124 **use** deal with; have sexual intercourse with
    honourably uprightly; 'on-her-ably' (Partridge, 122)

125 **wasted** sterile from venereal disease
    marrow Cam² compares *VA* 142 and *AW* 2.3.282 as examples of *marrow* expended in sexual intercourse.

127 **cross** prevent
    golden time used for 'golden age', a time of imagined perfection (as at 3.3.7), but Richard seemingly alludes to seizing the crown. Cf. 1.2.27–30 and 3.2.152.

129 i.e. once Edward's claim is buried

123 honourably] *O;* honourable *F*   123 SD *all but*] *Capell; Manet F*

Is Clarence, Henry and his son, young Edward,   130
And all the unlooked-for issue of their bodies
To take their rooms, ere I can place myself.
A cold premeditation for my purpose.
Why then, I do but dream on sovereignty
Like one that stands upon a promontory   135
And spies a far-off shore where he would tread,
Wishing his foot were equal with his eye,
And chides the sea that sunders him from thence,
Saying he'll lade it dry to have his way:
So do I wish the crown, being so far off,   140
And so I chide the means that keeps me from it,
And so, I say, I'll cut the causes off,
Flattering me with impossibilities;
My eye's too quick, my heart o'erweens too much,
Unless my hand and strength could equal them.   145
Well, say there is no kingdom then for Richard:
What other pleasure can the world afford?
I'll make my heaven in a lady's lap,
And deck my body in gay ornaments
And witch sweet ladies with my words and looks.   150
O miserable thought, and more unlikely

with his children. The veiled murderous threat is realized in *R3*.
    buried burièd
131 **unlooked-for** unpredictable, unwant-
ed (by Richard)
132 **rooms** places
    place O has 'plant', which involves a
sexual innuendo and continues the
imagery of 126.
133 'A thought that cools my purpose'
135 **promontory** hill
137 i.e. wishing his foot could traverse the
distance as easily as his eye
139 **lade** empty by baling or scooping
(*OED v.* 6)

140–2 **wish . . . chide . . . cut** The verbs
parallel those in 137–9, as Richard
concludes his comparison between
himself and one who sees *a far-off
shore* (136). Cutting down those who
stand in his way thus becomes a task as
impossible as scooping the sea dry.
143 **me** myself
144 **quick** alive; fast (i.e. takes in too
much)
    o'erweens presumptuously longs for
(not in *OED*)
148–64 Richard pursues this train of
thought again in *R3* 1.1.14–31.
150 **witch** bewitch

144 eye's] *Rowe;* Eyes *F*   150 witch] *Capell;* 'witch *F*

Than to accomplish twenty golden crowns!
Why, Love forswore me in my mother's womb,
And, for I should not deal in her soft laws,
She did corrupt frail Nature with some bribe   155
To shrink mine arm up like a withered shrub;
To make an envious mountain on my back,
Where sits deformity to mock my body;
To shape my legs of an unequal size;
To disproportion me in every part,   160
Like to a chaos or an unlicked bear whelp,
That carries no impression like the dam.
And am I then a man to be beloved?
O monstrous fault to harbour such a thought!
Then, since this earth affords no joy to me   165
But to command, to check, to o'erbear such
As are of better person than myself,
I'll make my heaven to dream upon the crown
And whiles I live t'account this world but hell,
Until my misshaped trunk that bears this head   170
Be round impaled with a glorious crown.
And yet I know not how to get the crown,
For many lives stand between me and home,

---

152 **accomplish** acquire
153 **Love** the goddess of love
154 **for** so, in order that (as at 3.1.9)
161 **chaos** amorphous mass or lump
(*OED* 4)
  unlicked bear whelp Ard[1] cites
  Arthur Golding's translation (1567) of
  Metamorphoses, 15.416–19: 'The
  Bearwhelp . . . like an euill fauored
  lump of flesh alyue dooth lye. / The
  dam by licking shapeth out his members orderly'.
162 **dam** mother (especially of animals,
  hence the contemptuous use at
  2.2.135)
164 **monstrous fault** huge mistake;
  unnatural vagina (Rubinstein, 98, and

Astington). Cf. *KL* 1.1.15.
165–71 Richard states a similar motive
  again at 5.6.78–9.
166 **check** rebuke, reprove (*OED v.* 11)
167 **person** bodily figure or appearance
  (*OED sb.* 4b)
170 often variously emended to make the
  head, rather than the trunk, impaled
  with the crown. Richard is so focused
  on his deformity, however, that it is not
  nonsensical for him to describe his
  body incongruously as crowned,
  rather than his head.
171 **round impaled** round impalèd, i.e.
  encircled, as with a fence
173 **between . . . home** proverbial:
  'between one and home'(Dent, H533.1)

And I, like one lost in a thorny wood,
That rents the thorns and is rent with the thorns,   175
Seeking a way and straying from the way,
Not knowing how to find the open air,
But toiling desperately to find it out,
Torment myself to catch the English crown:
And from that torment I will free myself,   180
Or hew my way out with a bloody axe.
Why, I can smile, and murder whiles I smile,
And cry 'Content!' to that which grieves my heart,
And wet my cheeks with artificial tears,
And frame my face to all occasions.   185
I'll drown more sailors than the mermaid shall,
I'll slay more gazers than the basilisk,
I'll play the orator as well as Nestor,
Deceive more slyly than Ulysses could,
And, like a Sinon, take another Troy.   190
I can add colours to the chameleon,
Change shapes with Proteus for advantages,

175 **rents** rends, tears
182–93 After determining to be violent in order to gain his end, Richard determines also to be subtle. Here he is most like the traditional stage Vice. See pp. 78–81.
182 **murder . . . smile** proverbial: 'To smile in one's face and cut one's throat' (Tilley, F16). Cam[1] also compares Chaucer, *Knight's Tale*, 1141: 'The smylere with the knyf under the cloke'.
185 **frame** shape, compose, give expression (*OED v.* 5b)
occasions four syllables
186 **mermaid** Mermaids were sometimes identified with the sirens of classical legend. Cf. *CE* 3.2.45–6.
187 **basilisk** 'A serpent, killyng man and beast, with his breath and sight' (Cooper). Proverbial: 'The basilisk's eye is fatal' (Tilley, B99).

188 **play the orator** proverbial (Dent, O74.1); cf. 2.2.43
Nestor aged but eloquent Greek hero in Homer's *Iliad*, depicted humorously in *TC*
189 **Ulysses** 'a man excellynge all other Greekes, whiche came againste Troy, in eloquence and subtiltie of wytte' (Cooper), hero of Homer's *Odyssey*, depicted in *TC*
190 **Sinon** a clever Greek, selected by Ulysses in Virgil's *Aeneid* to tell a deceptive story that persuaded the Trojans to bring the wooden horse within the walls of Troy, described in *Luc* 1501–66
191 **chameleon** proverbial for its ability to match its colour to its environment: 'The chameleon can change to all colours save white' (Tilley, C222)
192 **Proteus** god of the sea in Homer's *Odyssey* 4, who 'tourned himselfe into

And set the murderous Machiavel to school.
Can I do this, and cannot get a crown?   194
Tut, were it farther off, I'll pluck it down.   *Exit.*

[3.3]   *Flourish. Enter* LEWIS, *the French King; his sister,*
[the LADY*]* BONA; *[and] his Admiral, called Bourbon;*
PRINCE EDWARD, QUEEN MARGARET *and the* Earl of OXFORD.
Lewis sits and riseth up again.

KING LEWIS
Fair Queen of England, worthy Margaret,

sundry fygures, sometyme beynge like
a flame of fire, sometyme lyke a bull,
an other tyme lyke a terrible serpente'
(Cooper). Proverbial: 'as many shapes
as Proteus' (Tilley, S285).
  for advantages to gain advantage
193 **set . . . school** proverbial: 'set
Machiavel to school' (Dent, M1.1)
  Machiavel Shakespeare perpetuates
the Elizabethan demonic caricature of
Machiavelli, the sixteenth-century
political theorist, whose real insights
about power and influence are in fact
often embodied in Shakespeare's history plays, including *3H6*.
3.3 The only scene in *3H6* that is imagined outside of England is, ironically,
an extension of the English fratricide
to the French court, with each side
appealing to King Lewis for his assistance against the other. The scene
therefore offers a striking contrast with
1H6, which is set predominantly in
France, because the English are fighting to retain and extend their French
claim. The scene also contrasts with
3H6 1.1, where a quarrel breaks out
over literal possession of the English
throne. 3.3 compresses seven years
into a single scene. Margaret sought
assistance at the French court in 1462,
soon after the Lancastrian defeat at
Towton, as Henry reports at 3.1.28,
when he proceeds to imagine accur-

ately what will happen at 3.3.1–161.
Warwick announces his intention to
visit Lewis at 2.6.89–90. His first mission to France occurred in 1463 (Hall,
263–4), but he did not openly switch
allegiance from York to Lancaster until
after his second visit in 1470, here conflated with the first. Shakespeare
reverses the order of the chronicle narratives, thus lending dramatic irony to
3.3, since we already know of Edward's
courting Elizabeth Grey at the time
Warwick is negotiating with Lewis.
0.1 *Flourish* The ceremonious fanfare for
a royal entry or exit is ambiguous here,
as at 1.1.49.1 and 273 (J. Long, 29). In
continuous staging, the flourish is
associated both with Richard's stirring
but perversely ambitious couplet at
3.2.194–5 and with Lewis's entry at
3.3.0.1.
  sister i.e. sister-in-law. See List of
Roles, 43n.
0.4 The flourish and Lewis's attendants
indicate that his entry was probably
treated processionally as a state occasion in order to emphasize the courtly
setting. The King would therefore
presumably have been seated ceremo-
nially on a stage throne, probably on a
platform, as indicated at 46 SD, and
this is the place from which he
explains his rising in 1–3.

3.3] *Capell*

Sit down with us. It ill befits thy state
And birth that thou shouldst stand while Lewis doth sit.

QUEEN MARGARET

No, mighty King of France: now Margaret
Must strike her sail and learn awhile to serve 5
Where kings command. I was, I must confess,
Great Albion's Queen in former golden days,
But now mischance hath trod my title down
And with dishonour laid me on the ground,
Where I must take like seat unto my fortune 10
And to my humble seat conform myself.

KING LEWIS

Why say, fair Queen, whence springs this deep
despair?

QUEEN MARGARET

From such a cause as fills mine eyes with tears
And stops my tongue, while heart is drowned in cares.

KING LEWIS

Whate'er it be, be thou still like thyself 15
And sit thee by our side. (*Seats her by him.*)
                                       Yield not thy neck
To Fortune's yoke, but let thy dauntless mind

---

2   **state** See 3.2.93n.
3   **thou . . . sit** implicit SDs to the actors playing Margaret and Lewis. A ceremonial seat for Margaret has been prepared beside Lewis, as indicated by 16 SD.
    while if. Lewis is standing (0.4), so his reference to *sit* describes a hypothetical situation, not the actual one.
    Lewis See List of Roles, 42n.
5   **strike her sail** proverbial: 'strike a sail' (Dent, S24.3). Lowering the topsail was a salute or sign of surrender (*OED* strike *v.* 17), here referring to a sign of deference.

7   **Albion's** England's, as at 49
10–11 **seat . . . seat** Margaret may respond to Lewis's comment about her standing by sinking at this point to the floor (9–10) and twice referring to her *seat*, dramatic gestures that Lewis correctly reads at 12. Henry anticipates this kind of melodrama on Margaret's part at 3.1.35–41.
11   **humble** low-lying, not elevated (*OED* a^1. 2b)
15   **like thyself** i.e. as becomes the dignity of your social standing. Cf. 122 and 4.7.67.
17   **dauntless** undaunted

16–18] *Theobald; F lines* side. / yoake, / triumph, / mischance. /

Still ride in triumph over all mischance.
Be plain, Queen Margaret, and tell thy grief:
It shall be eased, if France can yield relief.   20

QUEEN MARGARET

Those gracious words revive my drooping thoughts
And give my tongue-tied sorrows leave to speak.
Now therefore be it known to noble Lewis
That Henry, sole possessor of my love,
Is, of a king, become a banished man   25
And forced to live in Scotland a forlorn;
While proud ambitious Edward, Duke of York,
Usurps the regal title and the seat
Of England's true-anointed lawful King.
This is the cause that I, poor Margaret,   30
With this my son, Prince Edward, Henry's heir,
Am come to crave thy just and lawful aid.
An if thou fail us, all our hope is done.
Scotland hath will to help, but cannot help;
Our people and our peers are both misled,   35
Our treasure seized, our soldiers put to flight,
And, as thou seest, ourselves in heavy plight.

KING LEWIS

Renowned Queen, with patience calm the storm

---

18 **Still** nonetheless
20 **France** metonymy for the King of France
24–6 Margaret does not know of Henry's capture, depicted in 3.1.
24 Margaret's claim ironically exaggerates her fidelity for effect, since she showed a clear preference for Suffolk over Henry in *2H6*.
25 **of a king** from being a king
26 **forlorn** either an adjective (with *man*

understood from 25) or a forlorn person (*OED* B *sb. Obs.*)
27–9 Margaret introduces the issue of who legally belongs on the English throne, and she subsequently debates it vigorously but inconclusively for the third time in the play. See 1.1 and 2.2.
33 **An if** if indeed. See Abbott, 105.
36 **treasure** treasury (*OED sb.* 3)
37 **heavy** sad, sorrowful
38 **Renowned** renownèd

21] *Rowe; F lines* words / thoughts, /   38] *Rowe; F lines* Queene, / Storme, /

While we bethink a means to break it off.

QUEEN MARGARET

The more we stay, the stronger grows our foe.   40

KING LEWIS

The more I stay, the more I'll succour thee.

QUEEN MARGARET

O, but impatience waiteth on true sorrow.

Enter WARWICK.

And see where comes the breeder of my sorrow.

KING LEWIS

What's he approacheth boldly to our presence?

QUEEN MARGARET

Our Earl of Warwick, Edward's greatest friend.   45

KING LEWIS

Welcome, brave Warwick. What brings thee to France?

He descends. She ariseth.

QUEEN MARGARET

Ay, now begins a second storm to rise,

For this is he that moves both wind and tide.

---

39 **bethink** devise, plan, contrive (*OED v.* 4)

break it off stop it for the time being, suspend it (*OED v.* 28a)

40 **stay** tarry, linger, delay (*OED v.*[1] 7)

41 **stay** as in 40n.; support, sustain, hold up (*OED v.*[2]). Using elegant diplomatic wordplay, Lewis plays for time and promises nothing.

succour help, assist, aid (*OED v. trans.* 1); furnish with military assistance (*OED v. trans.* 2)

42 **waiteth on** attends. Margaret infers that Lewis's *stay* means 'tarry', 'delay' (as hers does at 40) and frankly voices her frustration.

44 **What's he** Lewis is asking about

Warwick's social rank. See 3.1.55n.

47–8 Here and at 58 Margaret indicates her fear of Warwick and his possible effect on Lewis. Her plaintive remarks may be asides, but if they are not, everyone's determination to ignore them would be a potent rejection of her and an effective indication of her helplessness, not unlike Lear's when he is rejected by Goneril and Regan in *KL* 2.2.

48 **he . . . tide** Ard[2] notes a similar image used of Warwick by Hall: 'whiche waie he bowed, that waie ranne the streame, and what part he auaunced, that side gat the superioritie' (232).

42.1] *after 43 F*

WARWICK

    From worthy Edward, King of Albion,

    My lord and sovereign and thy vowed friend,   50

    I come in kindness and unfeigned love,

    First, to do greetings to thy royal person,

    And then to crave a league of amity,

    And, lastly, to confirm that amity

    With nuptial knot, if thou vouchsafe to grant   55

    That virtuous Lady Bona, thy fair sister,

    To England's King in lawful marriage.

QUEEN MARGARET

    If that go forward, Henry's hope is done.

WARWICK (*speaking to [Lady] Bona*)

    And, gracious madam, in our King's behalf,

    I am commanded, with your leave and favour,   60

    Humbly to kiss your hand, and with my tongue

    To tell the passion of my sovereign's heart,

    Where Fame, late ent'ring at his heedful ears,

    Hath placed thy beauty's image and thy virtue.

QUEEN MARGARET

    King Lewis and Lady Bona, hear me speak   65

    Before you answer Warwick. His demand

    Springs not from Edward's well-meant honest love

---

50 **vowed** vowèd

51 **kindness . . . love** biblical: *BCP* Epistle for first Sunday in Lent: 'In kindnesse, in the holy Ghost, in loue vnfained', closer than Geneva's 'By kindnes, by the holy Ghost, by loue vnfained' (2 Corinthians, 6.6) (Shaheen, 69)
    unfeigned unfeignèd

56 **That** Warwick may recognize Lady Bona with a deferential gesture such as a bow, or he may use *that* analogously to Latin *illa*, in the sense 'the renowned', or both (RP).

57 **marriage** three syllables

59] *Rowe; F lines* Madame, / behalfe, /

58 See 47–8n.

62 **passion** The word as used here is closer to 'suffering' (for love, in the manner of a Petrarchan lover) than to 'amorous feeling or desire', but either meaning would be an empty cliché in a formal marriage arrangement whose irony is heightened by what we know of Edward's real desire for Elizabeth Grey. Cf. 128.

63 **Fame** Virgil's Fama (*Aeneid*, 4), 'Fame or brute of a thynge: a rumour or noyse of a thyng' (Cooper)
    late of late, recently

But from deceit, bred by necessity:
For how can tyrants safely govern home
Unless abroad they purchase great alliance?   70
To prove him tyrant, this reason may suffice:
That Henry liveth still; but were he dead,
Yet here Prince Edward stands, King Henry's son.
Look, therefore, Lewis, that by this league and marriage
Thou draw not on thy danger and dishonour,   75
For though usurpers sway the rule awhile,
Yet heavens are just, and Time suppresseth wrongs.

WARWICK

Injurious Margaret.

PRINCE EDWARD   And why not 'Queen'?

WARWICK

Because thy father Henry did usurp,
And thou no more art prince than she is queen.   80

OXFORD

Then Warwick disannuls great John of Gaunt,
Which did subdue the greatest part of Spain;
And after John of Gaunt, Henry the Fourth,
Whose wisdom was a mirror to the wisest;
And after that wise prince, Henry the Fifth,   85

---

69 **tyrants** usurpers (also at 71 and 206).

70 **purchase** procure, bring about (*OED* 1 *Obs.*)

73 **Prince Edward stands** Margaret rose from her place beside Lewis at Warwick's entry (46 SD), and while there is no indication how the Prince responded to her dramatic gestures earlier, he seems at this point to be standing with her.

76 **sway** possess, wield

78 **Injurious** offensive in language, insulting (*OED a.* 2)

81 **disannuls** deprives by annulling his title (*OED v.* 2)

81–2 Oxford exaggerates Gaunt's achieve-

ment. Gaunt's second wife was Blanche of Castile, a Spanish princess, and he invaded Spain to claim her inheritance but with little success. The popularity of his attempt is attested by a 1601 play bought by Henslowe but not extant, called *The Conquest of Spain by John of Gaunt* (Boswell-Stone, 313). Ard¹ also cites Thomas Kyd's *Spanish Tragedy* (1592): 'Brave John of Gaunt . . . with a puisant armie came to Spaine, / And tooke our King of Castile prisoner' (1.6.48–52).

82 **Which** who. See Abbott, 265. Early Modern English allowed the use of *which* with a personal antecedent (JH).

Who by his prowess conquered all France:
From these, our Henry lineally descends.

WARWICK

Oxford, how haps it in this smooth discourse
You told not how Henry the Sixth hath lost
All that which Henry the Fifth had gotten?   90
Methinks these peers of France should smile at that.
But, for the rest: you tell a pedigree
Of threescore and two years, a silly time
To make prescription for a kingdom's worth.

OXFORD

Why, Warwick, canst thou speak against thy liege   95
Whom thou obeyed'st six and thirty years
And not bewray thy treason with a blush?

WARWICK

Can Oxford, that did ever fence the right,
Now buckler falsehood with a pedigree?
For shame, leave Henry and call Edward king.   100

---

86 This allusion to Henry V's conquest of France is a diplomatic blunder occasioned by Oxford's forgetting where he is. Warwick exploits the lapse at 91.
conquered conquerèd

88–91 Warwick resorts to an argument of mere power and success, ignoring the argument made by the Yorkists in 1.1 concerning Henry IV's deposition of Richard II, presumably because the Yorkists themselves are now vulnerable to the counter-charge of having deposed a king.

88 **haps it** does it happen
smooth rhetorically adept

92 **tell** recount, narrate; count (cf. 'bank teller') (Ard²)

93 **threescore and two years** the time of Lancastrian ascendancy, following Henry IV's deposition of Richard II in

1399. This dates the scene to 1461, but see 3.3n.
silly scanty, meagre (*OED a.* 2d, citing this line)

94 **prescription** possession giving title or right (*OED* 4b)

96 ***six and thirty** 'Thirty and six' does not scan and may well have been set by the compositor from a numeral in the manuscript. In any case, the number is an unexplained error for 'five and thirty' or 1463, the date of Warwick's first visit to France. Warwick was born in 1428, making the date of this remark 1464. O has 'thirty and eight'.

97 **bewray** reveal, expose the existence of (*OED v.* 6)

98 **ever** always
fence defend

99 **buckler** shield

96 six and thirty] *this edn (RP);* thirtie and six *F*

OXFORD

Call him my king by whose injurious doom
My elder brother, the lord Aubrey Vere,
Was done to death? And more than so, my father,
Even in the downfall of his mellowed years
When nature brought him to the door of death?   105
No, Warwick, no: while life upholds this arm,
This arm upholds the house of Lancaster.

WARWICK

And I the house of York.

KING LEWIS

Queen Margaret, Prince Edward and Oxford,
Vouchsafe at our request to stand aside   110
While I use further conference with Warwick.

They stand aloof.

QUEEN MARGARET

Heavens grant that Warwick's words bewitch him not.

KING LEWIS

Now, Warwick, tell me, even upon thy conscience,
Is Edward your true king? For I were loath
To link with him that were not lawful chosen.   115

101–5 Oxford would seem to be included in this fictitious scene for the sole purpose of stating his motive of personal revenge, which is little better than Warwick's or Richard's motive of mere power. Hall reports that the Yorkists executed Oxford's father and his brother, Lord Aubrey Vere, in 1461, 'whiche caused Ihon erle of Oxford, euer after to rebell' (258). Cf. 1.1.91n.

103 **And . . . so** This phrase occurs in Shakespeare only here and in *Tit* (1.1.297 and 4.2.33) and *VA* 661.

104 **downfall** used in this sense by Shakespeare only here and in *Tit* 5.2.57, referring to the sun's 'downfall in the sea'

105 **door of death** proverbial: 'to be at death's door' (Tilley, D162)

110 **Vouchsafe** show a gracious willingness (*OED v.* 6)

111 **use further conference** speak further

111 SD **aloof** away, at some distance

112 Margaret's line may be an aside or meant only for her allies on stage, but see 47–8n.

113–15 The issue of establishing a rightful claim according to the conscience of someone else reappears in *H5* 1.2.29–32. Hall specifies the details of Edward's claim in the context of his coronation (254).

115 **lawful** lawfully. On the uninflected adverb see 1.1.11n.

WARWICK

Thereon I pawn my credit and mine honour.

KING LEWIS

But is he gracious in the people's eye?

WARWICK

The more that Henry was unfortunate.

KING LEWIS

Then further: all dissembling set aside,

Tell me for truth the measure of his love   120

Unto our sister Bona.

WARWICK   Such it seems

As may beseem a monarch like himself.

Myself have often heard him say and swear

That this his love was an eternal plant

Whereof the root was fixed in virtue's ground,   125

The leaves and fruit maintained with beauty's sun,

Exempt from envy, but not from disdain,

Unless the Lady Bona quit his pain.

KING LEWIS

Now, sister, let us hear your firm resolve.

LADY BONA

Your grant or your denial shall be mine.   130

(*Speaks to Warwick.*) Yet I confess that often ere this day,

When I have heard your King's desert recounted,

Mine ear hath tempted judgement to desire.

---

116 **pawn** give (with the understanding that the assurance will be made good), stake
  credit credibility, reputation
117 Hall describes 'the louing consent which the commons frankelie and freelie had giuen' at the time of Edward's coronation (254).
118 **unfortunate** Warwick sees Edward's success as enhanced by Henry's mis-

fortune. Cf. 146 and 4.3.46–7n.
127 'exempt from malice on his part but not from [fear of] rejection on hers'
  envy malice, enmity
  disdain scorn, contemptuous rejection
128 **quit** remove, take away (*OED v.* 9 *trans.*). O has 'quite', i.e. requite, reward. Cf. 4.5.23.

---

117 eye] *F; cies O*   124 eternal] *O; externall F*   131 SD] *opp. 131 F*

KING LEWIS

    Then, Warwick, thus: our sister shall be Edward's.
    And now forthwith shall articles be drawn   135
    Touching the jointure that your King must make,
    Which with her dowry shall be counterpoised. –
    Draw near, Queen Margaret, and be a witness
    That Bona shall be wife to the English King.

PRINCE EDWARD

    To Edward, but not to the English King.   140

QUEEN MARGARET

    Deceitful Warwick, it was thy device
    By this alliance to make void my suit.
    Before thy coming, Lewis was Henry's friend.

KING LEWIS

    And still is friend to him and Margaret.
    But if your title to the crown be weak,   145
    As may appear by Edward's good success,
    Then 'tis but reason that I be released
    From giving aid, which late I promised.
    Yet shall you have all kindness at my hand
    That your estate requires and mine can yield.   150

WARWICK

    Henry now lives in Scotland at his ease,
    Where, having nothing, nothing can he lose.

---

136 **jointure** portion of an estate allotted to a wife in the event of her husband's death (*OED sb.* 4b), in this case presumably equivalent to (*counterpoised with*) the dowry to be paid by Lewis
138 Having asked the Lancastrians to *stand aside* (110), Lewis now invites Margaret to return.
141, 143 **thy** Margaret's use of the familiar form of address is contemptuous. Cf. Warwick to Prince Edward (80).
142 **make . . . suit** make my errand fruitless

145–6 Lewis emphasizes Warwick's claim that the Yorkists are right merely because they are successful (88–90). Warwick has not responded to Lewis's request (113–14) to declare Edward's right to the throne.
146 **success** result (as at 2.2.46)
148 **late** of late, recently (as at 63)
    promised promisèd
152 **having . . . lose** proverbial: 'They that have nothing need fear to lose nothing' (Dent, N331)

134] *Pope; F lines thus: / Edwards. /*

And as for you yourself, our quondam Queen,
You have a father able to maintain you,
And better 'twere you troubled him than France.   155

QUEEN MARGARET

Peace, impudent and shameless Warwick,
Proud setter-up and puller-down of kings!
I will not hence till with my talk and tears,
Both full of truth, I make King Lewis behold
Thy sly conveyance and thy lord's false love,   160
For both of you are birds of selfsame feather.

Post blowing a horn within.

KING LEWIS

Warwick, this is some post to us or thee.

Enter the Post.

POST (*Speaks to Warwick.*)

My lord ambassador, these letters are for you,
Sent from your brother, Marquess Montague.
(*to Lewis*) These from our King unto your majesty.   165
(*to Margaret*) And, madam, these for you; from
    whom, I know not. *They all read their letters.*

---

153 **quondam** sometime, used-to-be (as at 3.1.23)

154–5 Warwick insults Margaret by alluding to her father's poverty. See 2.2.154–5.

156 The line is trochaic; its strong emphases on *peace, impudent* and *shameless* make it clear and effective.

157 biblical. See 2.3.37n.

160 **conveyance** cunning management or contrivance (*OED* 11b). Cf. *1H6* 1.3.2.

161 **birds . . . feather** proverbial, as at 2.1.169

161 SD *Post* express letter-carrier (*OED*

sb. 1)

163 Although the line has two extra feet, only *My lord* seems superfluous, and it is hard to imagine a messenger not addressing Warwick honorifically.

167–70 presumably spoken apart or aside. The lines contain implicit SDs to the actors playing Margaret, Warwick and Lewis. Holinshed says, 'The French king was not well pleased to be thus dallied with' (284), but his particular gesture is invented.

---

157 setter-up] (setter vp) puller-down] (puller downe)   161 SD] *after 160 F*   163] *Pope; F lines* Ambassador, / you. /   SD] *opp. 163 F*   165 SD] *opp. 165 F*   166] *O; F lines* you: / not. /   SD *to Margaret*] *after* for you: *F*

OXFORD

    I like it well that our fair Queen and mistress

    Smiles at her news, while Warwick frowns at his.

PRINCE EDWARD

    Nay, mark how Lewis stamps as he were nettled.

    I hope all's for the best.   170

KING LEWIS

    Warwick, what are thy news? And yours, fair Queen?

QUEEN MARGARET

    Mine, such as fill my heart with unhoped joys.

WARWICK

    Mine, full of sorrow and heart's discontent.

KING LEWIS

    What? Has your King married the Lady Grey,

    And now, to soothe your forgery and his,   175

    Sends me a paper to persuade me patience?

    Is this th'alliance that he seeks with France?

    Dare he presume to scorn us in this manner?

QUEEN MARGARET

    I told your majesty as much before:

    This proveth Edward's love and Warwick's honesty.   180

WARWICK

    King Lewis, I here protest, in sight of heaven

    And by the hope I have of heavenly bliss,

    That I am clear from this misdeed of Edward's;

    No more my King, for he dishonours me –

169 **as** as if
    nettled irritated, vexed, provoked
    (*OED* 2b *v.* in *pa. pple.*)
170 **all's . . . best** proverbial (Dent,
    A136.1)
171 **news** See 1.1.182n.
175 **soothe** smooth or gloss over (*OED v.*
    6a)
    forgery lie
180 **proveth** tests, challenges; makes

good, establishes (said satirically)
183 **clear from** not responsible for
184 Warwick's switch of allegiance is not
so precipitate in the chronicles. Hall
says, 'lest in his fury, his purpose
might be espied and broughte to
nought, [Warwick] determined him
self, couertly dissimulyng, so longe to
suffer all such wronges & iniuries . . .
til he might spye a tyme conuenient, &

169–70] *Rowe; F lines as prose*   171] *Pope; F lines* Newes? / Queene. /

But most himself, if he could see his shame.   185
Did I forget that by the house of York
My father came untimely to his death?
Did I let pass th'abuse done to my niece?
Did I impale him with the regal crown?
Did I put Henry from his native right?   190
And am I guerdoned at the last with shame?
Shame on himself, for my desert is honour!
And, to repair my honour lost for him,
I here renounce him and return to Henry.
My noble Queen, let former grudges pass   195
And henceforth I am thy true servitor.
I will revenge his wrong to Lady Bona
And replant Henry in his former state.

QUEEN MARGARET
Warwick, these words have turned my hate to love,
And I forgive and quite forget old faults,   200
And joy that thou becom'st King Henry's friend.

---

a world after his awn appetite, for the setting furth of his enterprise' (265–6). These are tactics favoured by Richard in *3H6* and by his father in *1* and *2H6*, but never by Warwick. Dramatically the change emphasises Warwick's arrogance and self-importance.

186–8 Warwick's resentment against York surfaces so quickly as to be almost farcical, perhaps emphasising the sorry state into which public life has declined. His father, Richard Neville, Earl of Salisbury, appears in *2H6* and is described by Hall as being wounded and captured at the battle of Wakefield, and soon thereafter beheaded by the Lancastrians (250–1). Warwick's point about his father seems to be that he would not have died had the Yorkists not rebelled, but the reasoning is far-fetched, and Hall does not mention Salisbury's death as a

motive for Warwick's rebellion when he describes Edward's sexual assault on Warwick's 'doughter or his nece' (265). Since Warwick's nieces 'were both quite children it is supposed that the lady was one of his own daughters and . . . (as Isabel was the wife of Clarence) . . . it was his younger daughter, Anne, then in the flower of her youth' (W. Thomson, 300).

189 **impale** encircle, as with a fence (as at 3.2.171)

191 **guerdoned** rewarded, recompensed

192 **my desert** what I deserve

196 **servitor** servant (with connotations of extreme humility and politeness)

198 **replant . . . state** restore Henry to his former rank. For *state* see 3.2.93n. Ironically, Warwick had pledged to *plant Plantagenet* at 1.1.48.

200 **forgive . . . forget** proverbial: 'forgive and forget' (Tilley, F597)

199] *Pope; F lines* Warwicke, / Loue,

WARWICK

So much his friend, ay, his unfeigned friend,
That if King Lewis vouchsafe to furnish us
With some few bands of chosen soldiers,
I'll undertake to land them on our coast   205
And force the tyrant from his seat by war.
'Tis not his new-made bride shall succour him;
And as for Clarence, as my letters tell me,
He's very likely now to fall from him
For matching more for wanton lust than honour,   210
Or than for strength and safety of our country.

LADY BONA

Dear brother, how shall Bona be revenged
But by thy help to this distressed Queen?

QUEEN MARGARET

Renowned prince, how shall poor Henry live
Unless thou rescue him from foul despair?   215

LADY BONA

My quarrel and this English Queen's are one.

WARWICK

And mine, fair Lady Bona, joins with yours.

KING LEWIS

And mine with hers, and thine, and Margaret's.
Therefore, at last, I firmly am resolved
You shall have aid.   220

QUEEN MARGARET

Let me give humble thanks for all at once.

---

202 **unfeigned** unfeignèd
204 **soldiers** three syllables
206 **tyrant** See 69n.
208–9 Clarence's defection from Edward actually came a good deal later, and he returned with Warwick to France in 1470 to forge an alliance with Margaret (Hall, 280; Holinshed, 290).

212–13, 216 The infection of vengeance spreads from England to the French court.
213 **distressed** distressèd. The phrase *this distressed queen* occurs only once more in Shakespeare, in *Tit* 1.1.106.
214 **Renowned** renownèd

221 all at once] *Rowe;* all, at once *F*

KING LEWIS

Then, England's messenger, return in post
And tell false Edward, thy supposed king,
That Lewis of France is sending over masquers
To revel it with him and his new bride.   225
Thou seest what's passed; go fear thy King withal.

LADY BONA

Tell him in hope he'll prove a widower shortly
I wear the willow garland for his sake.

QUEEN MARGARET

Tell him my mourning weeds are laid aside,
And I am ready to put armour on.   230

WARWICK

Tell him from me that he hath done me wrong,
And therefore I'll uncrown him ere't be long.
There's thy reward; be gone.   *Exit Post.*

KING LEWIS   But, Warwick,
Thou and Oxford with five thousand men
Shall cross the seas and bid false Edward battle;   235
And, as occasion serves, this noble Queen
And Prince shall follow with a fresh supply.
Yet, ere thou go, but answer me one doubt:
What pledge have we of thy firm loyalty?

WARWICK

This shall assure my constant loyalty: 240
That, if our Queen and this young Prince agree,

---

222 **in post** with haste, at full speed
(*OED* post *sb.*² 8d)
223 **supposed** supposèd
224 **masquers** those in a masquerade.
Lewis reverses the image used earlier,
when Edward says Henry V 'revelled
in the heart of France' (2.2.150).
226 **fear . . . withal** make your King
afraid with that
228 **willow garland** symbol of mourning and the scorned lover. Proverbial:

'to wear the willow' (Tilley, W403).
229 **weeds** clothes. The phrase may indicate something about Margaret's costume. Aside from an almost exact repetition of these lines in the next scene
(4.1.104–5), the phrase *thy mourning
weeds* occurs only once more in
Shakespeare, in *Tit* 1.1.73.
233 **There's thy reward** Warwick may
give the Post something tangible.

I'll join mine eldest daughter and my joy
To him forthwith in holy wedlock bands.

QUEEN MARGARET

Yes, I agree, and thank you for your motion.
Son Edward, she is fair and virtuous;   245
Therefore, delay not: give thy hand to Warwick,
And, with thy hand, thy faith irrevocable
That only Warwick's daughter shall be thine.

PRINCE EDWARD

Yes, I accept her, for she well deserves it;
And here, to pledge my vow, I give my hand.   250
He gives his hand to Warwick.

KING LEWIS

Why stay we now? These soldiers shall be levied,
And thou, Lord Bourbon, our High Admiral,
Shall waft them over with our royal fleet.
I long till Edward fall by war's mischance
For mocking marriage with a dame of France.   255
Exeunt [all but] Warwick.

WARWICK

I came from Edward as ambassador,
But I return his sworn and mortal foe:
Matter of marriage was the charge he gave me,

242–3 Time is telescoped here. Hall reports that 'a league and a treatie' between Margaret and Warwick were concluded in 1470, and 'for the more sure foundacion of the newe amitie, Edward Prince of Wales, wedded Anne second daughter to therle of Warwicke, which Lady came with her mother into Fraunce' (281). In fact, the two were betrothed but not married (Edward was only seventeen in 1570), and Edward's bride-to-be was Warwick's younger daughter, not his elder, a mistake repeated at 4.1.118 and in O but corrected in *R3* 1.1.153.

244 **motion** proposal, suggestion (*OED sb.* 7a)
251 **levied** enlisted, mustered
252–3 Lewis 'appointed the bastard of Burbon, admerall of Fraunce, with a greate nauie to defend them against the nauie of the duke of Burgognie' (Holinshed, 296, differing in significant details from Hall, 281). Lewis's command explains Bourbon's presence from the beginning of the scene, since Bourbon has no lines.
253 **waft** transport over water
254 **long till** am in longing until

255 SD *all but*] *Capell; Manet F*

But dreadful war shall answer his demand.
Had he none else to make a stale but me?   260
Then none but I shall turn his jest to sorrow.
I was the chief that raised him to the crown,
And I'll be chief to bring him down again;
Not that I pity Henry's misery,   264
But seek revenge on Edward's mockery.   *Exit.*

[**4.1**]   *Enter* RICHARD [OF GLOUCESTER],
                   [GEORGE OF] CLARENCE, [THIRD DUKE of]
                              Somerset *and* MONTAGUE.

RICHARD OF GLOUCESTER
Now tell me, brother Clarence, what think you
Of this new marriage with the Lady Grey?
Hath not our brother made a worthy choice?
GEORGE OF CLARENCE
Alas, you know, 'tis far from hence to France;
How could he stay till Warwick made return?   5

---

260 **stale** person used as a means for inducing some effect (*OED sb.*² 5)

4.1 The dissension caused by Edward's dalliance with Lady Grey (3.2) flares into the open in this scene: the King now has a lower-ranking English noblewoman for his bride, and the implications work themselves out rapidly. Drawing primarily on an interview between Warwick and Clarence in Hall (271), Shakespeare omits Hall's compelling description of Warwick's dissimulation and indirection, preferring another character for Warwick entirely. See 3.3.184n. On stage, the confrontation is reminiscent of 1.1, 2.2 and 3.3, but in those instances it occurs between rival houses; here, between rival factions in the house of York.

0.2–3 THIRD . . . **Somerset** Henry Beaufort. According to the chronicles,

he was executed after the battle of Hexham in 1464, about a year after the events depicted here (Hall, 260; Holinshed, 281). He is the only Somerset to have sided with York, and his presence in this scene on the Yorkist side therefore distinguishes him from his brother, the fourth Duke. At the same time, his reversion to Lancaster allows Shakespeare to conflate him and his brother as 'Somerset' in SPs and SDs in F, though action and dialogue clearly distinguish them. See List of Roles, 31n. and 32n.

1–3 Richard's sarcasm here and at 7 is consistent with the thoughts he expresses at 3.2.124–95. He may be needling George into opposing Edward for precisely the motives he earlier voices.

5 **stay** wait (said sarcastically)

4.1] *Rowe*   0.2 THIRD DUKE of] *this edn*

THIRD DUKE

My lords, forbear this talk;
Here comes the King.

Flourish. Enter KING EDWARD, LADY GREY
[*now* Queen Elizabeth], *Pembroke, Stafford,* HASTINGS:
four stand on one side and four on the other.

RICHARD OF GLOUCESTER And his well-chosen bride.
GEORGE OF CLARENCE

I mind to tell him plainly what I think.

KING EDWARD

Now, brother of Clarence, how like you our choice,
That you stand pensive, as half malcontent?   10

GEORGE OF CLARENCE

As well as Lewis of France, or the Earl of Warwick,
Which are so weak of courage and in judgement
That they'll take no offence at our abuse.

KING EDWARD

Suppose they take offence without a cause:
They are but Lewis and Warwick; I am Edward,   15
Your King and Warwick's, and must have my will.

7.1 LADY GREY Edward has now married
    Lady Elizabeth Grey (2, 7, 67–8), so
    she should rightly be styled 'Queen
    Elizabeth' or 'the *Queene*', as in O. For
    discussion of her anomalous titles in
    SDs and SPs, see List of Roles, 9n.,
    and pp. 173–5.
7.2 *Pembroke, Stafford* non-speaking
    roles
7.3 Since nine actors are on stage at this
    point, Edward presumably stands
    alone, with four on either side of him.

8 **mind** intend
9 **choice** Edward unconsciously echoes
    Richard at 3 and 7.
10 **pensive** gloomy, sad
11 **As well as** i.e. 'I like your choice as
    well as Lewis and Warwick do'
13 **abuse** injury, wrong (*OED sb.* 5)
16 Here and at 50 Edward ironically
    expresses the sentiments of Suffolk,
    one of York's most hated enemies, in
    1H6 2.4.7–9.

---

6 SP THIRD DUKE] *this edn; Som. F* 6–7] *this edn (RP); F lines* King. / Bride. / 7.2 *now* Queen
Elizabeth] *Rowe subst. Pembroke* (Penbrooke) 9] *Pope; F lines* Clarence, / Choyce, / 11] *Pope; F
lines* France, / Warwicke, /

RICHARD OF GLOUCESTER

And shall have your will, because our King;
Yet hasty marriage seldom proveth well.

KING EDWARD

Yea, brother Richard, are you offended too?

RICHARD OF GLOUCESTER

Not I, no!   20
God forbid that I should wish them severed,
Whom God hath joined together! Ay, and 'twere pity
To sunder them that yoke so well together.

KING EDWARD

Setting your scorns and your mislike aside,
Tell me some reason why the Lady Grey   25
Should not become my wife and England's queen?
And you too, Somerset and Montague,
Speak freely what you think.

GEORGE OF CLARENCE

Then this is mine opinion: that King Lewis
Becomes your enemy for mocking him   30
About the marriage of the Lady Bona.

RICHARD OF GLOUCESTER

And Warwick, doing what you gave in charge,

17 Unlike George, Richard does not openly rebel against Edward, yet he appears to fall back one step here, in order to gain two elsewhere. See 124–5.
18 **hasty . . . well** proverbial: 'Marry in haste and repent in leisure' (Tilley, H196)
21–2 Richard echoes the Bible on marriage, with deliberate irony, as Edward recognizes (24): 'Let not man therefore put a sundre that, which God hathe coupled together' (Matthew, 19.6) (Shaheen, 69).

23 **yoke** are joined in marriage; have sexual intercourse (Partridge, 223)
24 **mislike** dislike (of his marriage choice), unhappiness
32 **gave in charge** ordered, charged him to do. Ironically, Edward never orders Warwick to make a marriage treaty with France; Warwick proposes the match himself (2.6.89–90) and then carries it out. Shakespeare never hints that Edward resents Warwick's overbearing manner, but the manner itself is part of Shakespeare's portrait of the 'kingmaker'.

17 And shall] *F, O*; And you shall *Rowe*   20 Not I, no!] Not I: no: *F*; Not I my Lord, no, *O*; Not I; no: *Rowe*   22–3] *Capell; F lines* together: / them, / together. /   29–31] *Pope; F lines* opinion: / Enemie, / Marriage / Bona. /

Is now dishonoured by this new marriage.
KING EDWARD

What if both Lewis and Warwick be appeased
By such invention as I can devise?   35
MONTAGUE

Yet to have joined with France in such alliance
Would more have strengthened this our
    commonwealth
'Gainst foreign storms than any home-bred marriage.
HASTINGS

Why, knows not Montague that of itself
England is safe, if true within itself?   40
MONTAGUE

But the safer when 'tis backed with France.
HASTINGS

'Tis better using France than trusting France:
Let us be backed with God and with the seas,
Which he hath given for fence impregnable,
And with their helps only defend ourselves.   45
In them, and in ourselves, our safety lies.
GEORGE OF CLARENCE

For this one speech, Lord Hastings well deserves
To have the heir of the Lord Hungerford.

---

33 **dishonoured** dishonourèd
35 **invention** solution to the problem
    (*OED* I 1c)
40 Shakespeare's history plays are a major
    source of English nationalism.
    Hastings's sentiment also appears in
    KJ 5.7.117–18 and *R2* 2.1.61–6 (where
    it is expressed negatively).
42 **using** often emended to 'losing', to
    improve the sense implied in O's read-
    ing: 'We need not France nor any
    alliance with them'
43–4 The image of the sea as England's
    defensive 'wall' appears again at 4.8.20

and is common in Shakespeare. See *KJ*
2.1.26–7 and *R2* 2.1.46–8, 61–3.
45 **only** alone
47–8 taken directly from Hall (271), who
    mistakes the marriage of Hastings's
    son for that of his father (W.
    Thomson, 148). George's point is that
    Hastings has profited from Edward's
    English marriage. Johnson notes dis-
    approvingly that unmarried heiresses
    were royal wards, and their marriage
    partners were therefore chosen by the
    monarch (S. Johnson, 8.606).

41 But] Yes, but *F2*

KING EDWARD

Ay, what of that? It was my will and grant,
And for this once my will shall stand for law.   50

RICHARD OF GLOUCESTER

And yet methinks your grace hath not done well
To give the heir and daughter of Lord Scales
Unto the brother of your loving bride.
She better would have fitted me, or Clarence;
But in your bride you bury brotherhood.   55

GEORGE OF CLARENCE

Or else you would not have bestowed the heir
Of the Lord Bonville on your new wife's son,
And leave your brothers to go speed elsewhere.

KING EDWARD

Alas, poor Clarence, is it for a wife
That thou art malcontent? I will provide thee.   60

GEORGE OF CLARENCE

In choosing for yourself, you showed your judgement,
Which being shallow, you shall give me leave
To play the broker in mine own behalf.
And, to that end, I shortly mind to leave you.

KING EDWARD

Leave me, or tarry, Edward will be king   65
And not be tied unto his brother's will.

---

50 **my will** See 16n. Cf. *2H6* 4.7.5–13.
51–5 See Hall, 271. Richard complains
  that Edward has awarded one of the
  best marriage prospects to his new
  Queen's brother, Anthony Woodville,
  thus depriving his own brothers of an
  opportunity for significant material
  benefit.
55 **in . . . brotherhood** you destroy
  brotherhood by marrying Elizabeth;
  you prefer sexual intercourse with

your wife to your relationship with
your brothers
56–8 taken from Hall, 271. Elizabeth's
  son was Sir Thomas Grey, 'sonne to
  syr Ihon Grey, the quenes fyrst husband . . . created Marques Dorset, and
  maried to Cicilie, heyre to the lord
  Bonuile' (Hall, 264).
58 **speed** succeed, prosper
63 **play the broker** negotiate a marriage
64 **mind** intend (as at 8)

61] *Pope; F lines* selfe, / iudgement: /

LADY GREY

My lords, before it pleased his majesty
To raise my state to title of a queen,
Do me but right, and you must all confess
That I was not ignoble of descent,   70
And meaner than myself have had like fortune.
But as this title honours me and mine,
So your dislikes, to whom I would be pleasing,
Doth cloud my joys with danger and with sorrow.

KING EDWARD

My love, forbear to fawn upon their frowns.   75
What danger or what sorrow can befall thee
So long as Edward is thy constant friend
And their true sovereign, whom they must obey?
Nay, whom they shall obey, and love thee too,
Unless they seek for hatred at my hands;   80
Which if they do, yet will I keep thee safe,
And they shall feel the vengeance of my wrath.

RICHARD OF GLOUCESTER [*aside*]

I hear, yet say not much, but think the more.

Enter a Post.

KING EDWARD

Now, messenger, what letters, or what news
From France?   85

POST

My sovereign liege, no letters, and few words,
But such as I without your special pardon

70–1 Elizabeth is right about her nobility:
her father was Sir Richard Woodville,
Earl Rivers, and Hall says she was
'borne of noble bloude' (365), but she
is mistaken about precedents for her
elevation.
71 **meaner** those of lower social rank

73 **dislikes** displeasure, disapproval. The
antecedent of *whom* is 'you' implied:
'dislikes of you'.
83 proverbial: 'Though he said little, he
thought the more' (Tilley, L367)
83.1 **Post** See 3.3.161 SDn.

67 SP LADY GREY] *F; Queen. O*   83 SD] *Johnson*   84–5] *verse Capell; prose F*

Dare not relate.

KING EDWARD

Go to, we pardon thee. Therefore, in brief,
Tell me their words as near as thou canst guess them.   90
What answer makes King Lewis unto our letters?

POST

At my depart, these were his very words:
'Go tell false Edward, thy supposed king,
That Lewis of France is sending over masquers,
To revel it with him and his new bride.'   95

KING EDWARD

Is Lewis so brave? Belike he thinks me Henry.
But what said Lady Bona to my marriage?

POST

These were her words, uttered with mild disdain:
'Tell him, in hope he'll prove a widower shortly,
I'll wear the willow garland for his sake.'   100

KING EDWARD

I blame not her; she could say little less;
She had the wrong. But what said Henry's Queen?
For I have heard that she was there in place.

POST

'Tell him', quoth she, 'my mourning weeds are done,
And I am ready to put armour on.'   105

KING EDWARD

Belike she minds to play the Amazon.
But what said Warwick to these injuries?

---

89 **Go to** expression of impatience
90 **guess** approximate (*OED v. trans.* 1a)
92 **depart** departure. See Abbott, 451, on omission of the suffix.
93 **supposed** supposèd
98 **disdain** scorn, contemptuous rejection, as at 3.3.127n.
103 **in place** present, at hand (*OED* place

sb. 19b)
104 **done** Margaret says *laid aside* (3.3.229) with the same meaning.
106 'Perhaps she intends to play the role of a woman warrior.' See 1.4.114n.
107 **injuries** offensive words, insults (*OED sb.* 2)

89–90] *Capell; F lines* thee: / words, / them. /   93 thy] *O, Rowe; the F*   104] *Pope; F lines* she) / done, /

POST

> He, more incensed against your majesty
> Than all the rest, discharged me with these words:
> 'Tell him from me that he hath done me wrong,   110
> And therefore I'll uncrown him ere't be long.'

KING EDWARD

> Ha! Durst the traitor breathe out so proud words?
> Well, I will arm me, being thus forewarned.
> They shall have wars and pay for their presumption.
> But say, is Warwick friends with Margaret?   115

POST

> Ay, gracious sovereign, they are so linked in friendship
> That young Prince Edward marries Warwick's
>   daughter.

GEORGE OF CLARENCE [*aside*]

> Belike, the elder; Clarence will have the younger. –
> Now, brother king, farewell, and sit you fast,
> For I will hence to Warwick's other daughter,   120
> That, though I want a kingdom, yet in marriage
> I may not prove inferior to yourself.
> You that love me and Warwick, follow me.

> > *Exit Clarence, and Somerset follows.*

RICHARD OF GLOUCESTER [*aside*]

> Not I. My thoughts aim at a further matter:
> I stay not for the love of Edward, but the crown.   125

KING EDWARD

> Clarence and Somerset both gone to Warwick?
> Yet am I armed against the worst can happen,

---

113 proverbial: 'forewarned is forearmed'
(Tilley, H54). Shakespeare deliberately departs from the chronicles, where
forewarning Edward is just what
Warwick aims to avoid doing.

118 Clarence actually married Isabel,
Warwick's elder daughter. See
3.3.242–3n.
121 **want** lack

116] *Pope subst.; F lines* Soueraigne, / friendship, /   118 SD] *this edn (GWW)*   118] *Pope; F lines*
elder; / younger. /   124] *Pope; F lines* Not I: / matter: /   SD] *Rowe; after* Not I *Oxf*   125 the love]
love *Pope*

And haste is needful in this desp'rate case.
Pembroke and Stafford, you in our behalf
Go levy men and make prepare for war.   130
They are already, or quickly will be, landed.
Myself in person will straight follow you.

Exeunt Pembroke and Stafford.

But ere I go, Hastings and Montague,
Resolve my doubt. You twain, of all the rest,
Are near to Warwick, by blood and by alliance.   135
Tell me if you love Warwick more than me.
If it be so, then both depart to him;
I rather wish you foes than hollow friends.
But if you mind to hold your true obedience,
Give me assurance with some friendly vow,   140
That I may never have you in suspect.

MONTAGUE

So God help Montague, as he proves true.

HASTINGS

And Hastings, as he favours Edward's cause.

KING EDWARD

Now, brother Richard, will you stand by us?

RICHARD OF GLOUCESTER

Ay, in despite of all that shall withstand you.   145

KING EDWARD

Why, so. Then am I sure of victory.
Now therefore let us hence, and lose no hour
Till we meet Warwick, with his foreign power.   *Exeunt.*

130 **prepare** preparation. See 92n.
132 **straight** immediately
133–5 Montague is Warwick's brother; Hastings was sheriff of Warwickshire (W. Thomson, 147) but a loyal Yorkist, despite Edward's expressed misgivings here. See List of Roles, 14n.
138 **wish . . . friends** proverbial: 'It is better to have an open foe than a dissembling friend' (Dent, F410)
142 Montague's 'truth' was more apparent than real, according to the chronicles. He joined Warwick only reluctantly and with strong inducements, and he remained non-committal to both his brother and Edward, 'whiche lukewarme harte, and double dissimulacion, wer bothe the destruccion of him and his brethren' (Hall, 271). Shakespeare transfers Montague's dissimulation to Richard (145).

304

[4.2]   *Enter* WARWICK *and* OXFORD *in England,*
with French Soldiers.

WARWICK

Trust me, my lord, all hitherto goes well.
The common people by numbers swarm to us.

Enter [GEORGE OF] CLARENCE *and* SOMERSET.

But see where Somerset and Clarence comes.
Speak suddenly, my lords, are we all friends?

GEORGE OF CLARENCE

Fear not that, my lord.   5

WARWICK

Then, gentle Clarence, welcome unto Warwick.

4.2 The scene conflates events in the summer of 1469 with Warwick's and Margaret's return from France in the late summer of 1470, bringing French reinforcements with them, as promised by King Lewis in 3.3. Shakespeare passes over agitations in Yorkshire that produced an invasion of northerners into the south in support of Warwick, culminating in the battle of Edgcote, near Banbury, on 26 July 1469, which the northerners won (Hall, 274–5). Warwick and Clarence then joined forces and entered into negotiations with Edward, whom they captured while the negotiations were going on (Hall, 275).

0.1–2 *in . . . Soldiers* Specifying a location in a SD is unusual in Shakespeare, and seems to be prompted in this case by reflection about French soldiers fighting in England under English command. 'This S.D. almost suggests patriotic indignation' (Cam¹). The soldiers would have been identified on stage as *French* by heraldic markings on their tabards and banners (Scott-

Giles, 163–7).

2 Compare Hall's comment when Warwick landed in 'August or September, 1470' (Boswell-Stone, 322): 'It is almost incredible to thinke how sone the fame of the erles landing was blowen ouer, and thorow all the whole Realme, and how many thousand men of warre, at the very first tidings of his landyng, were sodaynly assembled and set forwarde to welcome him' (282).

2.1 SOMERSET As 'Somerset' Shakespeare in F conflates Edmund Beaufort, fourth Duke, with his older brother, Henry Beaufort, third Duke, who appears in 4.1 (see 4.1.0.2–3n.), and who had been executed in 1564. See List of Roles, 32n.

3 comes See 1.4.150n. and Abbott, 336.

4 suddenly immediately, without premeditation

6 gentle noble

6–7 welcome . . . welcome implicit SDs: Warwick greets Clarence and Somerset, possibly shaking hands or embracing them, after noting their entry in 3.

4.2] *Capell*   **2** common people by numbers swarm to us] *F, O, Rowe;* common people swarm by numbers to us *Pope;* common people swarm to us by numbers *Hudson;* common sort by numbers swarm to us *Oxf;* common men by numbers swarm to us *Cam²;* commoners by number swarm to us *(GWW)*

And welcome, Somerset. I hold it cowardice
To rest mistrustful where a noble heart
Hath pawned an open hand in sign of love;
Else might I think that Clarence, Edward's brother,   10
Were but a feigned friend to our proceedings.
But welcome, sweet Clarence, my daughter shall be
    thine.
And now what rests but in night's coverture,
Thy brother being carelessly encamped,
His soldiers lurking in the towns about,   15
And but attended by a simple guard,
We may surprise and take him at our pleasure?
Our scouts have found the adventure very easy;
That as Ulysses and stout Diomed

8 **rest** remain
8–11 **mistrustful . . . love . . . feigned
friend** Warwick's words are remarkably hollow: Warwick has just switched sides, as has Clarence, who will shortly switch sides yet again, despite his oath and marriage alliance with Warwick.
9 **pawned** given (as at 3.3.116)
11 **feigned** feignèd
12 **welcome** Since Warwick has already welcomed Clarence (6), this welcome seems redundant. O reads simply 'come', which is more rhythmic. If Warwick were again to shake Clarence's hand, however, or embrace him, it would reinforce Warwick's attempt to overcome the sense of awkwardness between him and Clarence that is implied by Warwick's exaggerated affirmation of trust between them (7–11). In that case, an arhythmic line would help to imply the awkwardness.
my daughter See 4.1.118n. Clarence had in fact married Isabel, Warwick's elder daughter, in 1469, when he 'had sworne on the Sacrament to kepe his promise and pacte inviolate made and concluded with the erle of Warwicke' (Hall, 272).

13–17 Holinshed is the source for Warwick's initiative in this case (293); Hall says the idea of capturing Edward was thought of and executed on his own initiative by 'a wyse and politique Capitayne entendyng not to lese so great an auauntage to hym geuen' (275).
13 **rests** remains (as at 8)
in night's coverture under cover of darkness
14–15 During negotiations with Warwick after the battle of Edgcote, 'the king (bicause they were entered into termes by waie of communication to haue a pece) tooke small heed to himselfe, nothing doubting anie outward attempt of his enimies' (Holinshed, 293, clarifying Hall's account, 275).
15 **lurking** idling (*OED v.* 1b)
16 **simple** small, weak (*OED a.* 7a)
18 **adventure** venture, risk
19–21 In the *Iliad*, 10, Homer tells how Ulysses and Diomedes killed Rhesus and stole his horses as soon as he arrived, because of a prophecy that if the horses grazed on Trojan grass or drank from the river Xanthus, Troy would not fall to the Greeks.
19 **stout** brave

15 towns] *Theobald (Thirlby);* Towne *F;* towne *O*

With sleight and manhood stole to Rhesus' tents   20
And brought from thence the Thracian fatal steeds,
So we, well covered with the night's black mantle,
At unawares may beat down Edward's guard
And seize himself. I say not 'slaughter him',
For I intend but only to surprise him.   25
You that will follow me to this attempt,
Applaud the name of Henry with your leader.
    They all cry 'Henry!'
Why then, let's on our way in silent sort,
For Warwick and his friends, God and Saint George!   *Exeunt.*

[**4.3**]   *Enter three* Watchmen *to guard the King's tent.*

1 WATCHMAN

Come on, my masters, each man take his stand.
The King by this is set him down to sleep.

---

20 **sleight and manhood** cleverness and courage, attributed as dominant characteristics to Ulysses and Diomedes, respectively. Cooper says that 'next to Achilles and Ajax [Diomedes] was compted the most valiaunt' of the Greek heroes at Troy. For Ulysses, see 3.2.189n.

21 **fatal** destined

23 **At unawares** without their being aware of us

27 Warwick 'made a Proclamation in the name of kyng Henry th. vi.' (Hall, 282). The soldiers' loyalty to Henry is clearer in F than in O, where no one responds to this line, but after Warwick urges 'follow me now' the SD reads, '*All*, A *Warwike*, a *Warwike*', perhaps recalling Hall's report of mixed acclaim when Warwick landed: 'kynge Henry, kyng Henry, a Warwycke a Warwycke' (283).

4.3 The imagined location, outside

Edward's '*tent*', is prepared for in 4.2, where Warwick prepares to capture Edward. He succeeded in doing so on 26 July 1469 (Boswell-Stone, 323).

0.1 **three Watchmen** These three and their conversation are invented, briefly offering a characteristically Shakespearean view of political events from the perspective of those not involved in making events happen.

tent An actual tent may have been erected on stage, as in *R3* 5.3, but the fact that Edward is carried out '*sitting in a chair*' (27.6) suggests that in this case the opening of the '*tent*' was the curtained discovery space or a door in the tiring-house façade.

2 **set him down** Edward is later captured '*sitting in a chair*' (27.6), and the first watchman says he knows why the King prefers to sit rather than lie down (4–6). Cf. *H8* 4.2.3 and 81 (RP).

2 WATCHMAN

What, will he not to bed?

1 WATCHMAN

Why, no, for he hath made a solemn vow
Never to lie and take his natural rest   5
Till Warwick or himself be quite suppressed.

2 WATCHMAN

Tomorrow, then, belike shall be the day,
If Warwick be so near as men report.

3 WATCHMAN

But say, I pray, what nobleman is that,
That with the King here resteth in his tent?   10

1 WATCHMAN

'Tis the Lord Hastings, the King's chiefest friend.

3 WATCHMAN

O, is it so? But why commands the King
That his chief followers lodge in towns about him,
While he himself keeps in the cold field?

2 WATCHMAN

'Tis the more honour, because more dangerous.   15

3 WATCHMAN

Ay, but give me worship and quietness;
I like it better than a dangerous honour.
If Warwick knew in what estate he stands,
'Tis to be doubted he would waken him.

4–6 This motive is not in the chronicles nor in 4.2. It would appear to be ascribed to Edward by the speaker, in order to counterpoint the Third Watchman's scepticism about it, in an effective evocation of enlisted soldiers' conversation.

11 **Hastings . . . friend** possibly influenced by Hall's comment about 'the lord Hastynges his Chamberleyn, which had maried the Erles sister, &

yet was euer trew to the kyng his Master' (283)

14 **keeps** watches (*OED v.* 4b)

15 proverbial: 'the more danger the more honour' (Tilley, D35)

16 **worship** honour, deference (i.e. in court rather than on the battlefield)

18 'if Warwick knew the King's situation' **estate** state, condition, situation

19 **doubted** feared

---

14 keeps] keeps here *Hanmer;* keeps out *(Vaughan);* keeps thus *(RP)*

1 WATCHMAN

Unless our halberds did shut up his passage.   20

2 WATCHMAN

Ay, wherefore else guard we his royal tent
But to defend his person from night-foes?

Enter WARWICK, [GEORGE OF] CLARENCE, OXFORD,
SOMERSET *and French Soldiers, silent all.*

WARWICK

This is his tent, and see where stand his guard.
Courage, my masters; honour now or never.
But follow me, and Edward shall be ours.   25

1 WATCHMAN

Who goes there?

2 WATCHMAN

Stay or thou diest!

Warwick and the rest cry all 'A Warwick! A Warwick!'
and set upon the guard, who fly, crying 'Arm! Arm!',
Warwick and the rest following them.

The drum playing and trumpet sounding, enter WARWICK,
SOMERSET *and the rest, bringing* KING [EDWARD] *out in his gown,
sitting in a chair.* RICHARD [OF GLOUCESTER] *and* HASTINGS
fly over the stage.

20 **halberds** weapons combining a spear and a battle-axe (*OED sb.* 1); soldiers carrying halberds (*OED sb.* 2). The word seems to be an implicit SD for how these soldiers were armed, but it could be their reference to another line of defence.
did . . . his barred or prevented Warwick's
22.2 *French Soldiers* See 4.2.0.1–2n.

silent all 'as secretly as was possible' (Hall, 275)
27.2 *the . . . fly* Contrast Hall, where the watch are killed (275). The guards' flight is ironic in view of their declarations at 20–2. Cf. *1H6* 1.2.20–1 and SD.
27.4 *drum . . . sounding* J.Long suggests a 'simple cavalquot' (Appendix 1).
27.5 *gown* nightgown

27.1 A Warwick! A Warwick!] *this edn;* A Warwike, a Warwike. O; Warwicke, Warwicke, F; Warwick! Warwick! Pope   27.7 *fly*] (flyes)

SOMERSET

What are they that fly there?

WARWICK

Richard and Hastings. Let them go. Here is

The Duke.

KING EDWARD   The Duke? Why, Warwick, when we parted,   30

Thou called'st me King.

WARWICK   Ay, but the case is altered.

When you disgraced me in my embassade,

Then I degraded you from being King

And come now to create you Duke of York.

Alas, how should you govern any kingdom,   35

That know not how to use ambassadors,

Nor how to be contented with one wife,

Nor how to use your brothers brotherly,

Nor how to study for the people's welfare,

Nor how to shroud yourself from enemies?   40

KING EDWARD

Yea, brother of Clarence, art thou here too?

Nay, then I see that Edward needs must down.

Yet, Warwick, in despite of all mischance,

Of thee thyself and all thy complices,

Edward will always bear himself as King.   45

29–31 Warwick charged all men 'to prepare them selfs to fight against Edward
duke of Yorke, which contrarye to al
right, Iustice and law, had vntrewly
vsurped the Croune and Imperial dig-
nite of this realme' (Hall, 282).

31 **case is altered** proverbial (Tilley,
C111)

32 **embassade** mission or function of an
ambassador (*OED*). Cam[1] notes that
Hall uses this word to describe

Warwick's mission (278), and that it is
the only instance of *embassade* in
Shakespeare.

34 Warwick betrays his overweening self-
conception: in presuming to alter
Edward's noble rank, Warwick usurps
a right that is reserved to monarchs.

40 **shroud** protect (*OED v.*[1] 2b *refl.*)

42 **down** fall (anticipating his image in
46–7)

44 **complices** accomplices, allies

29–30 Richard . . . The Duke] *Capell; as prose F*   30] *Pope; F lines* Duke? / . . .parted, /   32 embas-
sade] *F;* embassage *O;* Ambassade *Pope*   41] *Steevens; F lines* Clarence, / too? /

Though Fortune's malice overthrow my state,
My mind exceeds the compass of her wheel.

WARWICK

Then, for his mind, be Edward England's King,
   Takes off his crown.
But Henry now shall wear the English crown,
And be true king indeed, thou but the shadow. 50
My Lord of Somerset, at my request,
See that, forthwith, Duke Edward be conveyed
Unto my brother, Archbishop of York.
When I have fought with Pembroke and his fellows,
I'll follow you, and tell what answer 55
Lewis and the Lady Bona send to him.
Now for a while farewell, good Duke of York.
                          They lead him out forcibly.

KING EDWARD

What fates impose, that men must needs abide;
It boots not to resist both wind and tide.
         Exeunt [King Edward, Somerset and Soldiers].

OXFORD

What now remains, my lords, for us to do, 60
But march to London with our soldiers?

WARWICK

Ay, that's the first thing that we have to do,

46–7 The goddess Fortune was imagined to turn a wheel to which people were bound, sometimes rising toward her, sometimes declining away. Cf. *H5* 3.6.26–8, *Luc* 952. Edward stoically determines to ignore his misfortune.

48 **for** with regard to. See Abbott, 149.

52–3 Warwick 'caused [Edward] by secret iorneys in the nyght to be conueyed to Myddelham Castell in Yorkeshire, &

there to be kept vnder the custody of the Archebishop of Yorke his brother', i.e. Warwick's brother, George Neville (Hall, 275).

55 The line is metrically defective. O has *and come and tell.*

59 **boots** profits, avails
   resist . . . tide proverbial: 'to sail against wind and tide' (Dent, W435.1)

61 **soldiers** three syllables

---

55 tell] come and tell *O;* I'll tell him *(RP)*   59 SD] *Capell subst.; Exeunt. F; Exeunt* some with *Edward. O*

To free King Henry from imprisonment
And see him seated in the regal throne.   *Exeunt.*

[**4.4**]   *Enter* RIVERS *and* LADY GREY
                          [*now* Queen Elizabeth].

RIVERS
    Madam, what makes in you this sudden change?
LADY GREY
    Why, brother Rivers, are you yet to learn
    What late misfortune is befallen King Edward?
RIVERS
    What? Loss of some pitched battle against Warwick?
LADY GREY
    No, but the loss of his own royal person.   5
RIVERS
    Then is my sovereign slain?
LADY GREY
    Ay, almost slain, for he is taken prisoner,
    Either betrayed by falsehood of his guard,
    Or by his foe surprised at unawares.

4.4 The scene dramatizes the plight of the Queen as if it resulted from Edward's capture in July 1469, not, as in the chronicles, from his flight overseas in the autumn of 1470, when Warwick landed with French support, and Yorkist adherents were forced to seek sanctuary. 'Emongest other, Quene Elizabeth his wyfe, all moste desperate of all comfort, toke sentuarye at Westmynster, & their in great penurie forsaken of all her frendes, was deliuered of a fayre sonne called Edwarde' (Hall, 285; Holinshed, 300).

0.1 LADY GREY another instance of this character's textual demotion in F, also evident in her SPs in this scene. She should properly have been styled 'Queen Elizabeth' or 'Queen', as in O, since the end of 3.2.

1 **what . . . change?** What makes you change so suddenly?
   *in you Collier's suggestion, followed by Ard², citing a possible slip by F's compositor. The grammar of F's wording has not been adequately explained.

2 **brother Rivers** Anthony Woodville, Lord Rivers. See List of Roles, 18n.

64 SD *Exeunt*] *Exeunt Omnes. O; Exeunt. Rowe; exit. F*   **4.4**] *Capell*   0.2 *now* Queen Elizabeth] *Theobald subst.*   1 in you] *Collier MS;* you in *F*   2+ SP LADY GREY] *F (subst.); Queen. O*   4] *Pope; F lines* battell / *Warwicke* / What? Loss] *O;* What losse *F;* What, loss *Capell*

And as I further have to understand,   10
Is new committed to the Bishop of York,
Fell Warwick's brother and by that our foe.

RIVERS

These news I must confess are full of grief,
Yet, gracious madam, bear it as you may;
Warwick may lose, that now hath won the day.   15

LADY GREY

Till then fair hope must hinder life's decay.
And I the rather wean me from despair
For love of Edward's offspring in my womb.
This is it that makes me bridle passion
And bear with mildness my misfortune's cross.   20
Ay, ay, for this I draw in many a tear
And stop the rising of blood-sucking sighs,
Lest with my sighs or tears I blast or drown
King Edward's fruit, true heir to th'English crown.

RIVERS

But madam, where is Warwick then become?   25

LADY GREY

I am informed that he comes towards London

---

10 **have to** am given to
11 **Bishop** Archbishop (as at 4.3.53)
12 **Fell** cruel
 by that therefore, for that reason
13 **news** See 1.1.182n.
18 **Edward's offspring** the future Edward V, 1470–83. In *R3* his death is ordered by his uncle, Richard Duke of Gloucester.
19 **bridle passion** restrain my emotions (as one uses a bridle to restrain a horse)
20 **bear . . . cross** endure . . . affliction (*OED* cross *sb*.10) (with a biblical echo: Luke, 14.27, 'Whosoeuer beareth not his crosse . . . can not be my disciple' (Shaheen, 70))

21 **draw in** restrain (cf. 19n.). Cf. Macbeth's 'I pull in resolution' (5.5.22) (RP).
22 **blood-sucking sighs** Sighs were thought to rob the heart of its blood. Cf. *2H6* 3.2.60–3.
23–4 Elizabeth's concern is more poetic than medical, even by the standards of contemporary gynaecology: sighs blast, and tears drown.
23 **blast** blow on perniciously, blight (*OED v.* II 7 *trans.*)
25 **where . . . become?** What has become of Warwick? (*OED* become I 1b)
26 **informed** informèd

17 wean] *(waine)*   25] *Pope subst.; F lines* Madam, / become? /

To set the crown once more on Henry's head.
Guess thou the rest: King Edward's friends must down.
But to prevent the tyrant's violence –
For trust not him that hath once broken faith –   30
I'll hence forthwith unto the sanctuary,
To save at least the heir of Edward's right.
There shall I rest secure from force and fraud.
Come, therefore, let us fly, while we may fly;   34
If Warwick take us, we are sure to die.   *Exeunt.*

[4.5]   *Enter* RICHARD [OF GLOUCESTER],
        Lord HASTINGS *and Sir William Stanley*[, *with Soldiers*].

RICHARD OF GLOUCESTER
Now, my Lord Hastings and Sir William Stanley,
Leave off to wonder why I drew you hither,
Into this chiefest thicket of the park.
Thus stands the case: you know our King, my brother,
Is prisoner to the bishop here, at whose hands   5

28 **down** fall (as at 4.3.42)
30 **trust . . . faith** proverbial: 'He that
once deceives is ever suspected'
(Tilley, D180)
31 **I'll hence forthwith** I'll go from here
immediately
sanctuary i.e. Westminster (see 4.4n.)
4.5 Edward remained Warwick's prisoner
for about three months, from early July
to early October 1469 (Boswell-Stone,
324). He was ostensibly imprisoned at
Middleham Castle, Yorkshire, under
the oversight of the Archbishop of
York (4.3.52–34n.), but he 'spake euer
fayre to the Archebishop and to the
other kepers, (but whether he corrupt-
ed them with money or fayre promises) he had libertie diuers dayes to go on
huntynge' (Hall, 275). Richard identi-

fies the location as a 'thicket of the
park' (3).
0.2 *Soldiers* Though neither F nor O
specifies soldiers in an SD, they are
indicated as *the rest* at 16. Hall says
they had 'suche a great bend of men,
that neither his kepers woulde, nor
once durst moue him to retorne to
prison agayn' (275).
2 **Leave . . . wonder** cease wondering.
See Abbott, 355, on the infinitive used
as a noun.
3 **park** aristocratic hunting preserve. Cf.
the bishop's deer (17).
4 **Thus . . . case** Here is the situation.
Cf. *case* at 18.
5 **bishop** the Archbishop of York, who
had imprisoned Edward (4.3.52–3).
Cf. *Bishop of York* (4.4.11).

4.5] *Capell*   0.2 *with Soldiers*] *Capell subst.*   4 stands] *Rowe;* stand *F*

He hath good usage and great liberty,
And, often but attended with weak guard,
Comes hunting this way to disport himself.
I have advertised him by secret means,
That, if about this hour he make this way   10
Under the colour of his usual game,
He shall here find his friends, with horse and men,
To set him free from his captivity.

Enter KING EDWARD *and a* Huntsman *with him.*

HUNTSMAN
This way, my lord, for this way lies the game.
KING EDWARD
Nay, this way, man. See where the huntsmen stand.   15
Now, brother of Gloucester, Lord Hastings and the rest,
Stand you thus close to steal the bishop's deer?
RICHARD OF GLOUCESTER
Brother, the time and case requireth haste.
Your horse stands ready at the park corner.
KING EDWARD
But whither shall we then?   20
HASTINGS
To Lynn, my lord, and shipped from thence to
    Flanders.

---

8 **disport** amuse or enjoy (*OED v.* 2 *refl.*)
9 **advertised** informed (accented on
   second syllable, as at 2.1.115)
10 **make this way** come this way, make
   his way here
11 on the pretence of hunting as usual
   colour semblance, pretence (*OED* III
   11a)
14 **game** quarry, object of the hunt
15 **huntsmen** Edward may indicate that
   the rescue party is disguised, or he

   may simply be playing with words.
17 **close** concealed
18 **requireth** See Abbott, 334, on third-
   person plural in *-th*.
19 **corner** distant or secluded part (*OED
   sb.*[1] 7)
21 Edward's escape from Middleham
   Castle in October 1469 is conflated
   with his escape to Flanders in
   September 1470, after Warwick landed
   with French assistance. 'With all hast

8 Comes] *Rowe;* Come *F*   14–15] *Pope; F lines* Lord, / Game. / man, / stand. /   21] *this edn; F lines*
Lord, / Flanders. /

RICHARD OF GLOUCESTER

Well guessed, believe me, for that was my meaning.

KING EDWARD

Stanley, I will requite thy forwardness.

RICHARD OF GLOUCESTER

But wherefore stay we? 'Tis no time to talk.

KING EDWARD

Huntsman, what sayst thou? Wilt thou go along?   25

HUNTSMAN

Better do so than tarry and be hanged.

RICHARD OF GLOUCESTER

Come then, away; let's ha' no more ado.

KING EDWARD

Bishop, farewell; shield thee from Warwick's frown,

And pray that I may repossess the crown.   *Exeunt.*

[**4.6**]   *Flourish. Enter* KING HENRY the Sixth, [GEORGE
          OF] CLARENCE, WARWICK, SOMERSET, *young Henry*
          [*of Richmond*], OXFORD, MONTAGUE *and* Lieutenant.

possible [Edward] passed the wasshes
(in greater ieopardye then it besemed a
Prince to be in) & came to the towne of
Lynne' (Hall, 283), i.e. King's Lynn,
Norfolk.
  shipped take ship, be shipped
22 **meaning** intention. Richard momentarily reveals his penchant for double
  meanings.
23 **requite** reward
  forwardness promptness, eagerness,
  zeal
28 **thee** yourself
4.6 In early October 1470 Warwick
  released Henry from the Tower, where
  Edward had imprisoned him after his
  capture (3.1) (Boswell-Stone, 326). A
  ceremonial liberation followed on 25
  October, when Warwick and Clarence
  accompanied the King 'with great

pompe . . . appareled in a longe gowne
of blew veluet' from the Tower to St
Paul's, and he 'offered as kynges vse to
do' (Hall, 285). Henry summoned parliament the next day. Events in the
scene are reported in substantially the
same way by Hall (286–7) and by
Holinshed (300–2), with particular
details selected from each.
0.1 *Flourish* another of this play's
  ambiguous fanfares, pointing both to
  Edward's hope for reinstatement
  (4.5.29) and to Henry's release from
  the Tower (J.Long, 29–30). O omits
  the flourish, puts Warwick first in the
  entry, adds 'with the Crowne' after
  Clarence, and has Henry enter just
  ahead of Richmond.
0.3 **Lieutenant** He would be distinguished from others on stage by an

25] *Pope; F lines* say'st thou? / along? /   28] *Pope; F lines* farwell, / frowne, /   **4.6**] *Capell*

KING HENRY

Master Lieutenant, now that God and friends
Have shaken Edward from the regal seat
And turned my captive state to liberty,
My fear to hope, my sorrows unto joys
At our enlargement, what are thy due fees?   5

LIEUTENANT

Subjects may challenge nothing of their sov'reigns,
But if an humble prayer may prevail,
I then crave pardon of your majesty.

KING HENRY

For what, lieutenant, for well using me?
Nay, be thou sure, I'll well requite thy kindness,   10
For that it made my imprisonment a pleasure.
Ay, such a pleasure as encagèd birds
Conceive, when after many moody thoughts,

---

official costume. In October, 1470, the Lieutenant of the Tower was Sir John Tiptoft. See List of Roles, 19n. However, Tiptoft was also Lord Lieutenant of Ireland, 'exercising there more extreme crueltie than princelie pietie', and he was not present at Henry's release, having fled as an adherent of King Edward. (*Mirror* blames him for all the official crimes sanctioned by Edward.) Captured 'in the top of an high tree, in the forest of Waibridge', he was attainted and beheaded (Holinshed, 301).

1–15 Henry's conversation with the Lieutenant is invented, as is the Lieutenant's presence in the scene. The effect is to emphasize the piety of Henry's character.

2 **regal seat** also used at 1.1.26

5 **enlargement** release
due fees the fees a prisoner was expected to pay for costs associated with imprisonment. Cam[2] compares Thomas Heywood's *Woman Killed with Kindness* (1607), 2.2.10ff.

6 **challenge nothing of** make no claim on

7 **prayer** one who prays (two syllables), not what is prayed

10 **requite** repay

11 **For that** because
my imprisonment Pope omitted *my* to improve the meter. Ard[2] emended *imprisonment* to 'prisonment' for the same reason, citing *KJ* 3.4.161. Eliding *my* with the first syllable of *imprisonment* ('my'mprisonment') achieves the same effect (GWW).

12 **encaged** encagèd. Ard[1] notes that the same idea, using the image of the caged bird, also appears in *Cym* 3.3.42–4, though its expression there is more felicitous.

13 **Conceive** engender

---

1 Master] *Capell;* M. *F;* Mr. *Rowe*

At last, by notes of household harmony,
They quite forget their loss of liberty.   15
But Warwick, after God thou set'st me free,
And chiefly, therefore, I thank God and thee.
He was the author, thou the instrument.
Therefore, that I may conquer Fortune's spite
By living low where Fortune cannot hurt me,   20
And that the people of this blessed land
May not be punished with my thwarting stars,
Warwick, although my head still wear the crown,
I here resign my government to thee,
For thou art fortunate in all thy deeds.   25

WARWICK

Your grace hath still been famed for virtuous
And now may seem as wise as virtuous
By spying and avoiding Fortune's malice,
For few men rightly temper with the stars.
Yet, in this one thing let me blame your grace,   30
For choosing me when Clarence is in place.

GEORGE OF CLARENCE

No, Warwick, thou art worthy of the sway,

---

14 **household** familiar, homely (*OED* 6
    adj. c)
18 **author** originator
   instrument means
19–20 On the goddess Fortune, see
    4.3.46–7n.
20 **living low** Henry expresses a wish to
    live beneath his social rank at
    2.5.21–54; he now uses his restored
    power to make his wish come true.
21 **blessed** blessèd
22 **thwarting** adverse, untoward (a figure
    from astrology)
23–5 '[T]he erle of Warwycke as one to
    whome the common welthe was much
    beholden, was made Ruler, &
    Gouernor of the Realm, with whom as
    felow and compaignion was associated,

George duke of Clarence his sonne in
law' (Hall, 286).
25 **fortunate** lucky, favoured by Fortune
    (19, 20)
26 **still** always
   virtuous being virtuous
28 **spying** discerning
29 **temper with** regulate, control (them-
    selves), i.e. adjust their attitude or dis-
    position. Following Henry's allusion to
    astrological influence (22), Warwick
    observes that few people are able to
    adjust appropriately to what destiny
    sends them, though Henry has done so
    by anticipating the worst and acting to
    avoid it.
31 **in place** in this place, here
32 **sway** rule

To whom the heavens in thy nativity
Adjudged an olive branch and laurel crown
As likely to be blest in peace and war. 35
And therefore I yield thee my free consent.

WARWICK

And I choose Clarence only for Protector.

KING HENRY

Warwick and Clarence, give me both your hands.
Now join your hands, and with your hands your hearts,
That no dissension hinder government. 40
I make you both Protectors of this land,
While I myself will lead a private life
And in devotion spend my latter days,
To sin's rebuke and my Creator's praise.

WARWICK

What answers Clarence to his sovereign's will? 45

GEORGE OF CLARENCE

That he consents, if Warwick yield consent;
For on thy fortune I repose myself.

WARWICK

Why then, though loath, yet must I be content.
We'll yoke together, like a double shadow
To Henry's body, and supply his place, 50

---

33 **heavens . . . nativity** Clarence continues the astrological imagery, alluding to the constellations that prevailed at Warwick's birth.

34–5 The second line explains the first: the olive branch represents peaceful accomplishment; the laurel, deeds in war.

37 **only** alone
Protector See 1.1.111n.

38–40 Henry's gesture of attempted conciliation is yet another false start toward peace in this play: Clarence will shortly defect to Edward, and Warwick will be defeated and killed at Barnet.

39 **join . . . hearts** proverbial: 'with heart and hand' (Dent, H339)

43 **latter** final

47 **repose myself** rely

50 **Henry's body** The manifest instability of the political arrangement worked out here is suggested by the awkwardness of Warwick's image. In Elizabethan political thinking, the king had two 'bodies', one legal and one physical (Kantorowicz). Since Henry has resigned the crown, the king, in effect, no longer has a 'body' – either legal or physical – for anything to be a shadow of, let alone to be a 'double shadow' of.
supply fill

I mean, in bearing weight of government,
While he enjoys the honour and his ease.
And Clarence, now then it is more than needful
Forthwith that Edward be pronounced a traitor
And all his lands and goods be confiscate.   55

GEORGE OF CLARENCE
What else? And that succession be determined.

WARWICK
Ay, therein Clarence shall not want his part.

KING HENRY
But with the first of all your chief affairs
Let me entreat, for I command no more,
That Margaret your Queen and my son Edward   60
Be sent for, to return from France with speed.
For till I see them here, by doubtful fear
My joy of liberty is half eclipsed.

GEORGE OF CLARENCE
It shall be done, my sovereign, with all speed.

KING HENRY
My Lord of Somerset, what youth is that   65
Of whom you seem to have so tender care?

SOMERSET
My liege, it is young Henry, Earl of Richmond.

54–5 '[K]yng Edwarde was declared a
traytor to his country, & vsurpor of the
Realme, because he had vniustly taken
on him, the Croune & Scepter, & all
his goodes were confiscate & adjudged,
forfayted' (Hall, 286).

55 **confiscate** On the omission of *-ed*
after *d* and *t*, see Abbott, 342.

56–7 In Hall, parliament decides what is
decided here among three noblemen:
Henry's heirs were to succeed him
unless the line failed, in which case the
crown would revert to Clarence's heirs

(286).

56 **What else?** not 'what next?' but 'I
concur'

57 **want** lack

62 **doubtful** filled with doubt. Since
'doubt' usually means 'fear' in
Elizabethan English, rather than
'question', the effect of this adjective is
to intensify Henry's concern.

67 **Richmond** See List of Roles, 30n.
young Richmond was born in 1457,
making him thirteen in October 1470,
when this scene is set.

55 be confiscate] *Malone;* confiscate *F*

320

KING HENRY

    Come hither, England's hope.

    Lays his hand on Richmond's head.

                               If secret powers

    Suggest but truth to my divining thoughts,

    This pretty lad will prove our country's bliss.   70

    His looks are full of peaceful majesty,

    His head by nature framed to wear a crown,

    His hand to wield a sceptre, and himself

    Likely in time to bless a regal throne.

    Make much of him, my lords, for this is he   75

    Must help you more than you are hurt by me.

Enter a Post.

WARWICK

    What news, my friend?

POST

    That Edward is escaped from your brother

    And fled, as he hears since, to Burgundy.

WARWICK

    Unsavoury news! But how made he escape?   80

68–76 Henry's prophecy is accorded a special place in Hall, as it is in Shakespeare. Hall frequently treats providential interpretations sceptically, but in Richmond's case he says: 'This lorde Henry was he . . . whom wee ought to beleue, to be sent from God, and of hym onely to be prouided a kyng, for to extinguish bothe the faccions and partes, of kyng Henry the .vi. and kyng Edwarde the .iiii. . . . when the kyng had a good space by himself, secretly beholden and marked, both [Richmond's] wit and his likely towardnes, he said to suche princes, as were then with hym: Lo surely this is he, to whom both wee and our aduersaries leuyng the possession of all thynges, shall hereafter geue rome and place. So this holy man shewed before, the chaunce that should happen, that this erle Henry so ordeined by God, should in tyme to come (as he did in deede) haue and enioye the kyndome, and the whole rule of the realme' (287).

69 **divining thoughts** Ard² compares Ovid's phrase, 'divinante animo', from *Tristia*, 4.6.29.

76.1 **Post** See 3.3.161 SDn.

78–9 On the conflation of two escapes by Edward, see 4.5.21n.

78 **escaped** escapèd.

68–9] *Pope; F lines* Hope: / truth / thoughts, / 68 SD *Richmond's*] *Oxf; his* F

POST

He was conveyed by Richard, Duke of Gloucester,
And the Lord Hastings, who attended him
In secret ambush on the forest side
And from the bishop's huntsmen rescued him,
For hunting was his daily exercise.   85

WARWICK

My brother was too careless of his charge.
But let us hence, my sovereign, to provide
A salve for any sore that may betide.
                    Exeunt [all but] Somerset, Richmond and Oxford.

SOMERSET

My lord, I like not of this flight of Edward's,
For doubtless Burgundy will yield him help,   90
And we shall have more wars before't be long.
As Henry's late presaging prophecy
Did glad my heart with hope of this young
    Richmond,
So doth my heart misgive me, in these conflicts,
What may befall him to his harm and ours.   95
Therefore, Lord Oxford, to prevent the worst,
Forthwith we'll send him hence to Brittany,
Till storms be past of civil enmity.

OXFORD

Ay, for if Edward repossess the crown,
'Tis like that Richmond, with the rest, shall down.   100

---

81 **conveyed** taken away, removed (*OED*
    v. 5)
82 **attended** waited for
83 **forest side** side of the forest
88 **salve . . . sore** proverbial: 'There is a
    salve for every sore' (Tilley, S84)
    betide occur, come to pass
89 **like not of** do not like. See Abbott,

177.
92 **late** recent. See 68–76.
    presaging portentous, that has pre-
    sentiment or prevision (a redundant
    adjective for emphasis)
93 **glad my heart** make my heart glad
100 **like** likely
    down fall

88 SD *all but*] F (*Manet*)

SOMERSET

It shall be so: he shall to Brittany.

Come, therefore, let's about it speedily.   *Exeunt.*

[**4.7**]   *Flourish. Enter* [KING] EDWARD,
RICHARD [OF GLOUCESTER], HASTINGS *and Soldiers.*

KING EDWARD

Now, brother Richard, Lord Hastings, and the rest:

Yet thus far Fortune maketh us amends,

And says that once more I shall interchange

My waned state for Henry's regal crown.

Well have we passed, and now repassed, the seas,   5

And brought desired help from Burgundy.

What then remains, we being thus arrived

From Ravenspurgh Haven before the gates of York,

But that we enter as into our dukedom? [*Hastings knocks.*]

---

101 Hall says Richmond was removed to Brittany after the battle of Tewkesbury in May 1471 (303).

4.7 When Edward returned from Flanders on 14 March 1471 he landed at Ravenspurgh and moved on to York, where this scene takes place (8). Both the compromise with the aldermen of York and Montgomery's determination to follow Edward only as king, not as duke, are recorded in the chronicles (Hall, 290–2; Holinshed, 302–6).

0.2 *and Soldiers* O omits this phrase but adds 'with a troope of Hollanders', presumably to clarify that Edward's assistance came from the Duke of Burgundy, whose territory included Holland. F mentions 'desired help from Burgundy' (6) and 'blunt Hollanders' (4.8.2), but it may follow sources more closely in omitting O's SD, since Hall specifies that Burgundy openly forbade anyone to assist Edward while doing so secretly himself by lending money and ships (290). For

Hollanders to be identifiable on stage, they would have had to wear distinctive costumes.

3 **interchange** exchange

4 **waned state** wanèd, reduced condition or power

6 **desired** desirèd

8 **Ravenspurgh Haven** harbour at the mouth of the Humber, in north-eastern England. Pope deleted *Haven* to smooth the metre.

9 **as . . . dukedom** Edward quickly discovered that he won more support by claiming that he came only for his duchy than by claiming the kingdom (Hall, 290–1). Holinshed notes that Edward landed at the same place 'where Henrie erle of Derbie, after called king Henrie the fourth landed, when he came to depriue king Richard the second of the crowne, and to vsurpe it to himselfe' (303). In *R2* Bolingbroke also claims to have come 'but for mine own' (3.3.196).

4.7] *Capell* 8 Ravenspurgh] *(Rauensperre)* 9 SD] *Cam²*

RICHARD OF GLOUCESTER

The gates made fast? Brother, I like not this.   10
For many men that stumble at the threshold
Are well foretold that danger lurks within.

KING EDWARD

Tush, man, abodements must not now affright us.
By fair or foul means we must enter in,
For hither will our friends repair to us.   15

HASTINGS

My liege, I'll knock once more to summon them. [*Knocks.*]

Enter on the walls the Mayor of York *and his brethren.*

MAYOR

My lords, we were forewarned of your coming,
And shut the gates for safety of ourselves,
For now we owe allegiance unto Henry.

KING EDWARD

But, master mayor, if Henry be your king,   20
Yet Edward, at the least, is Duke of York.

10 **gates made fast** Richard presumably infers that the gates are locked when someone knocks on them. A prior knock is implied at 16. O omits a knock and has Richard order, 'Sound vp the drum and call them to the wals'. The *gates* may be one of the doors at the back of the stage.

11–12 **men . . . within** proverbial: 'to stumble at the threshold' (Tilley, T259)

12 **foretold** forewarned (construing the stumbling as a bad omen)

13 **abodements** omens

15 **friends** See 1.1.56n.
   repair make their way

16 Hastings's line indicates a second knock on the gate and possibly a second drum roll (see 10n.).

16.1 **on the walls** on the upper level of

the tiring-house façade (as at 5.1.0.2 and n.)

Mayor of York No mayor is mentioned in the chronicles. Holinshed specifies 'the recorder of Yorke, whose name was Thomas Coniers (one knowne in deed not to beare [Edward] anie faithfull good will)' (305). For the historical Mayor of York in 1470, see List of Roles, 20n.

and his brethren Hall says the citizens of York sent 'two of the chiefest Aldermen of the citie' (291) The brethren are designated as '*two Aldermen*' at 34.1.

17 **forewarned of** forewarnèd, warned about (Abbott, 174)

21 Edward has already hinted at the policy of claiming that he comes only for his dukedom (9). When Edward

MAYOR

True, my good lord, I know you for no less.

KING EDWARD

Why, and I challenge nothing but my dukedom,
As being well content with that alone.

RICHARD OF GLOUCESTER [*aside*]

But when the fox hath once got in his nose,   25
He'll soon find means to make the body follow.

HASTINGS

Why, master mayor, why stand you in a doubt?
Open the gates, we are King Henry's friends.

MAYOR

Ay, say you so? The gates shall then be opened.
He descends [with his brethren].

RICHARD OF GLOUCESTER

A wise stout captain, and soon persuaded.   30

HASTINGS

The good old man would fain that all were well,
So 'twere not long of him. But being entered,
I doubt not, I, but we shall soon persuade
Both him and all his brothers unto reason.

---

announced this policy publicly, 'It was almost incredible to se what effect this new imaginacion (all thoughe it were but fayned) sorted and toke immediatly vpon the fyrst opening (Such a power hath Iustice euer emongest all men) when it was blowen abrode that Kyng Edwardes desyer was farther from nothyng, then from the couetyng for desyre of the kyngdome and royall dominion, and that he no erthely promocion desyred before hys iust patrimony, and lyneall enheritance' (Hall, 291).

23 **challenge** claim

25–6 proverbial (Tilley, F655). Richard's

lines would seem to be an aside or spoken to Edward and Hastings out of the Mayor's hearing. Hall describes Edward's negotiations as 'fayre wordes and flatterynge speche' (290).

29 SD The Mayor leaves the upper level with the aldermen (16.1n.).

30 **stout** brave (sneering at the Mayor's easy capitulation)

31–2 **would . . . him** 'would be glad to cause no problems, as long as he is not blamed for anything'

31 **fain** gladly

32 **long of** owing to, on account of (*OED* long *a.*[2])

---

25 SD] *Rowe*[2]   29 SD *with his brethren*] *Dyce subst.*

Enter the Mayor *and two Aldermen.*

KING EDWARD

So, master mayor, these gates must not be shut   35
But in the night or in the time of war.
What, fear not, man, but yield me up the keys.
   Takes his keys.
For Edward will defend the town and thee,
And all those friends that deign to follow me.

March. Enter MONTGOMERY *with Drum and Soldiers.*

RICHARD OF GLOUCESTER

Brother, this is Sir John Montgomery,   40
Our trusty friend, unless I be deceived.

KING EDWARD

Welcome, Sir John; but why come you in arms?

MONTGOMERY

To help King Edward in his time of storm,
As every loyal subject ought to do.

KING EDWARD

Thanks, good Montgomery, but we now forget   45
Our title to the crown, and only claim
Our dukedom, till God please to send the rest.

MONTGOMERY

Then fare you well, for I will hence again.
I came to serve a king and not a duke.

---

37 If the Mayor does not have 'the keies in his hand' (O), then he must have them hanging at his belt, or wherever mayors carry keys, so he can yield them up at this point. Edward's taking the keys (not mentioned in the chronicles) suggests that he intends to back up his claim to justice with force.

39 **deign** think fit

39.1 MONTGOMERY See List of Roles, 21n.
48–9 Hall says Edward met Montgomery 'and diuers other of hys assured frendes with their aydes, which caused hym at the fyrst coming to make Proclamacion in hys owne name, kyng Edward the .iiij. boldely sayng to hym, that they would serue no man but a kynge' (292).

45–7] *Pope; F lines Mountgomerie: / Crowne, / Dukedome, / rest. /*

Drummer, strike up, and let us march away.   50

The Drum begins to march.

KING EDWARD

Nay, stay, Sir John, awhile, and we'll debate

By what safe means the crown may be recovered.

MONTGOMERY

What talk you of debating? In few words,

If you'll not here proclaim yourself our king,

I'll leave you to your fortune and be gone   55

To keep them back that come to succour you.

Why shall we fight, if you pretend no title?

RICHARD OF GLOUCESTER

Why brother, wherefore stand you on nice points?

KING EDWARD

When we grow stronger, then we'll make our claim.

Till then 'tis wisdom to conceal our meaning.   60

HASTINGS

Away with scrupulous wit, now arms must rule.

RICHARD OF GLOUCESTER

And fearless minds climb soonest unto crowns.

Brother, we will proclaim you out of hand.

The bruit thereof will bring you many friends.

KING EDWARD

Then be it as you will, for 'tis my right,   65

And Henry but usurps the diadem.

---

50 SD *begins to march* strikes up a march beat

51 **stay** wait, hold up
   debate discuss

57 **shall** must
   pretend claim

58 After this line O adds, 'Resolue your selfe, and let vs claime the crowne'.
   wherefore . . . points? 'Why insist on niceties?' Cf. *RJ* 5.2.18, *JC* 4.3.8.
   nice unimportant, trivial

61 **scrupulous wit** reasoning that is too meticulous in matters of right and wrong (*OED* scrupulous *a*. 1)
   now . . . rule This is the principle that has come increasingly to dominate the action throughout the three *H6* plays.

63 **out of hand** at once, immediately (*OED* hand *sb*. 33a). Proverbial (Dent, HH1).

64 **bruit** report, news

59] *Pope; F lines* stronger, / Clayme: /

MONTGOMERY

Ay, now my sovereign speaketh like himself,
And now will I be Edward's champion.

HASTINGS

Sound trumpet, Edward shall be here proclaimed.
Come, fellow soldier, make thou proclamation.   70

Flourish. Sound.

SOLDIER [*Reads.*]   *Edward the Fourth, by the Grace of God,*
King of England and France, and Lord of Ireland, etc.

MONTGOMERY

And whosoe'er gainsays King Edward's right,
By this I challenge him to single fight.

Throws down his gauntlet.

ALL

Long live Edward the Fourth!   75

KING EDWARD

Thanks, brave Montgomery, and thanks unto you all.

---

67 **like himself** like the king he is. See 3.3.15n.
68 **champion** The monarch's champion is the one who represents the monarch in ceremonial displays of power, such as tournaments.
69 **proclaimed** i.e. proclaimed king
69–74 F is inferior to O in this passage but not incomprehensible, and we follow Ard² in letting F stand. O assigns 69–74 to Montgomery, omitting 70. Oxf eliminates the soldier, arguing that at some stage in putting F together, *Come, fellow soldier* was misread as 'Come fellow, soldier', from which misreading an SP for the soldier was invented, with confusing results. See 72n. Oxf therefore specifies that 70 is addressed to Montgomery, who then reads 71–4, as in O. The rationale is that Montgomery has just stirringly declared himself to be the royal champion (68). In grateful response,

Hastings gives him a proclamation that he had presumably prepared to read himself, and as Montgomery finishes reading, he throws down his gauntlet in character as the King's champion.
72 *etc.* The abbreviation may indicate material the actor should supply himself, according to the known formula. It is difficult to imagine a common soldier challenging anyone in King Edward's right, however, and F therefore gives that much of the soldier's speech to Montgomery. What else the soldier may be supposed to have said is difficult to know. The problem is to explain why Hastings would give the proclamation to a common soldier in the first place, knowing both what it says and that Montgomery is standing by, having just proclaimed himself the King's champion.
73 **gainsays** denies

71 SD] *Capell*   76] *Steevens; F lines Mountgomery, / all: /*

If fortune serve me, I'll requite this kindness.
Now, for this night, let's harbour here in York,
And when the morning sun shall raise his car
Above the border of this horizon,   80
We'll forward towards Warwick and his mates;
For well I wot that Henry is no soldier.
Ah, froward Clarence, how evil it beseems thee
To flatter Henry and forsake thy brother!
Yet, as we may, we'll meet both thee and Warwick.   85
Come on, brave soldiers, doubt not of the day,
And that once gotten, doubt not of large pay.   *Exeunt.*

[4.8]   *Flourish. Enter* KING [HENRY], WARWICK,
MONTAGUE, [GEORGE OF] CLARENCE, OXFORD
and EXETER.

77 **serve** favour
78 **harbour** lodge, take shelter, encamp (*OED v.* II *intr.*)
79 **his car** the imagined chariot of the sun. See 1.4.33n.
80 **horizon** accent on first syllable (Cercignani, 40). This is the only time the word is used by Shakespeare.
82 **wot** know
83 **froward** perverse, hard to please
   evil ill
   beseems becomes, suits
86 **doubt not of** have no fear concerning
   the day the day of victory
4.8 After landing in March 1471 (4.7), Edward quickly seized the initiative. Avoiding battle with Warwick at Coventry, he was reconciled to Clarence (depicted in 5.1), and by 11 April he had arrived in London and captured Henry (Hall, 294). The Lancastrians were so surprised by Edward's speed and the size of his force that Warwick was unable to hold the Lancastrian alliance together: 'When the duke of Somerset and other of kynge Henryes frendes, saw the

world thus sodaynly chaunged euery man fled, and in hast shifted for hym selfe, leuyng kyng Henry alone, as an host that should be sacrificed' (Hall, 294). This scene is imagined 'in the bishops palace of London', as indicated at 22 and 33, where Henry was captured (Hall, 294). It begins before Warwick's departure from London to confront Edward.
0.1 *Flourish* The royal fanfare sounds ambiguously both for Edward, as he leaves the stage, and for Henry, as he enters (J. Long, 29–30).
   WARWICK Warwick may be holding a letter he has just received, as suggested by the opening SD in O ('Enter one with a letter to *Warwike.*'), which reverses the order of 4.7 and 4.8.
0.2 CLARENCE Clarence was not with Warwick in London. Hall says Clarence's dilatory movement toward London made Warwick suspect his loyalty, and he therefore hurried to Coventry to encounter Edward before Clarence could join his brother (293).
0.3 *EXETER Somerset, though named in

4.8] *Capell*   0.3 EXETER] *Capell subst.; Somerset F*

WARWICK

What counsel, lords? Edward from Belgia,
With hasty Germans and blunt Hollanders,
Hath passed in safety through the narrow seas
And with his troops doth march amain to London,
And many giddy people flock to him.   5

KING HENRY

Let's levy men and beat him back again.

GEORGE OF CLARENCE

A little fire is quickly trodden out,
Which, being suffered, rivers cannot quench.

WARWICK

In Warwickshire I have true-hearted friends,
Not mutinous in peace, yet bold in war.   10
Those will I muster up, and thou, son Clarence,
Shalt stir up in Suffolk, Norfolk and in Kent,
The knights and gentlemen to come with thee.
Thou, brother Montague, in Buckingham,
Northampton and in Leicestershire shalt find   15
Men well inclined to hear what thou command'st.
And thou, brave Oxford, wondrous well beloved
In Oxfordshire, shalt muster up thy friends.
My sovereign, with the loving citizens,
Like to his island girt in with the ocean   20
Or modest Dian circled with her nymphs,

F, has no lines in the scene, and he is not referred to again in SDs. Exeter, on the other hand, is given no entrance, but the King addresses him at 34, and he replies at 37. It would appear that *Somerset* was somehow substituted for *Exeter*.

1 **Belgia** Belgium
2 **hasty** precipitate, rash (*OED adj.* 3)
   blunt abrupt of speech or manner, curt (*OED* A. *adj.* 5)
4 **amain** at once, without delay. See 2.5.128, 133n.

5 **giddy** frivolous, flighty, inconstant (*OED a.* 3a)
6 **levy** enlist, muster
7–8 **fire . . . quench** proverbial: 'of a little spark a great fire' (Tilley, S714)
8 **being suffered** permitted to grow
11 **son** son-in-law. See 4.1.118n.
12 **up** omitted by Pope to make the line metrical. *Stir up* can mean 'set in motion, agitate' (*OED v.* 16a).
20 **island . . . ocean** See 4.1.43–4n.
21 **Dian** Diana (Dian, stressed on the first syllable) was the goddess of the

Shall rest in London till we come to him.
Fair lords, take leave, and stand not to reply.
Farewell, my sovereign.

KING HENRY

Farewell, my Hector, and my Troy's true hope.   25

GEORGE OF CLARENCE

In sign of truth, I kiss your highness' hand.

KING HENRY

Well-minded Clarence, be thou fortunate.

MONTAGUE

Comfort, my lord; and so I take my leave.

OXFORD

And thus I seal my truth and bid adieu.

KING HENRY

Sweet Oxford, and my loving Montague,   30
And all at once, once more a happy farewell.

WARWICK

Farewell, sweet lords, let's meet at Coventry.

Exeunt [all but King Henry and Exeter].

KING HENRY

Here at the palace will I rest awhile.
Cousin of Exeter, what thinks your lordship?
Methinks the power that Edward hath in field   35

---

moon and of chastity; cf. 4.8.52, where
Henry is called *shamefaced*, and *Tit*
1.1.321–2 (Phoebe was another name
for Diana).
circled Ard² notes a parallel with
Ovid's description of Diana in
Metamorphoses, 2.441: '*suo comitata
choro*'.
23 **stand not** do not wait
25 **Hector** A messenger calls York 'the
hope of Troy' after his death (2.1.51
and n.). Cf. *Tit* 4.1.88.
26 **In ... truth** another of the many empty

gestures and words in this play
kiss ... hand an implicit SD, as at 28
and 29
27 **Well-minded** Ard¹ notes that Hall
(295) uses 'well mynded' of Montague
shortly after his image of Edward as a
swelling river (see 54–6n.).
33 **palace** See 4.8n. The Bishop's Palace
'stood at the N.W. corner of the
precinct of St. Paul's' (Sugden, 62).
35 **Methinks** it seems to me
in field in the field, in fighting readiness

32 SD *all . . . Exeter*] *Capell subst.*

Should not be able to encounter mine.

EXETER

The doubt is that he will seduce the rest.

KING HENRY

That's not my fear. My meed hath got me fame.
I have not stopped mine ears to their demands,
Nor posted off their suits with slow delays.   40
My pity hath been balm to heal their wounds.
My mildness hath allayed their swelling griefs.
My mercy dried their water-flowing tears.
I have not been desirous of their wealth
Nor much oppressed them with great subsidies,   45
Nor forward of revenge, though they much erred.
Then why should they love Edward more than me?
No, Exeter, these graces challenge grace,
And when the lion fawns upon the lamb,
The lamb will never cease to follow him.   50
       Shout within, 'A Lancaster! A Lancaster!'

EXETER

Hark, hark, my lord. What shouts are these?

---

36 **encounter** meet as an adversary, do battle with

37 **doubt** fear, concern (as at 4.3.19)
    seduce lead astray (the Latin sense)

38 **meed** merit, excellence, worth (*OED sb.* 3)

40 **posted off** put off, deferred (*OED v.* IV 7b)
    suits petitions, supplications, entreaties (*OED sb.* 11a)

41 **balm** healing ointment

42 **griefs** hardships, sufferings (*OED sb.* 1 *Obs.*)

45 **subsidies** taxes granted to the crown by parliament to meet special needs (*OED sb.* 2). See *2H6* 4.7.18-20.

46 **forward of** inclined to (*OED a.* 6b)

48 **challenge grace** lay claim to favour (presumably both divine and human)

49 **fawns upon** shows delight in the presence of, caresses (*OED v.*[1] 1b)

50 SD Johnson was puzzled as to why the Yorkists raise a cry for Lancaster. It is possible that the Yorkists give a Lancastrian shout to confuse their opponents, or that the Lancastrians shout as they defend their King, but a shout for York would more clearly signal what is happening to those watching the play. Hall reports that on the very day Edward reached London, the Archbishop of York 'caused [Henry] to ryde about London, apparelled in a gowne of blewe veluet, with a great company cryeng kyng Henry, king Henry' (294).

51.1 O says 'Enter *Edward* and his train.' Gloucester at least must accompany him and the soldiers.

Enter [KING] EDWARD [*with* RICHARD OF GLOUCESTER]
and his Soldiers.

KING EDWARD

Seize on the shamefaced Henry. Bear him hence,
And once again proclaim us King of England.
You are the fount that makes small brooks to flow:
Now stops thy spring, my sea shall suck them dry   55
And swell so much the higher by their ebb.
Hence with him to the Tower. Let him not speak.

[Some Soldiers] exeunt with King Henry.

And lords, towards Coventry bend we our course,
Where peremptory Warwick now remains.
The sun shines hot, and if we use delay,   60
Cold biting winter mars our hoped-for hay.

RICHARD OF GLOUCESTER

Away betimes, before his forces join,
And take the great-grown traitor unawares.
Brave warriors, march amain towards Coventry.   *Exeunt.*

[**5.1**]   *Enter* WARWICK, *the Mayor of Coventry,*
two Messengers *and others upon the walls.*

---

52 **shamefaced** modest, bashful (a mis-
construction of 'shamefast' or
'immovably attached to shame'). Ard¹
notes that Grafton says of Henry, 'In
hym reigned shamefastnesse', followed
by Hall (208). Shakespeare uses the
word only once more, in *R3* 1.4.140.

53 **us** Edward signals his claim by assuming the royal 'we'.

54–6 Edward's image may be suggested
by Hall: 'Edward did dayly encrease
hys power (as a runnyng ryuer by
goyng more & more augmenteth'
(Hall, 293).

59 **peremptory** sure of himself, over-
confident (*OED a.* 4), stressed on first
syllable

60–1 proverbial: 'Make hay while the sun
shines' (Tilley, H235)

62 **betimes** soon, forthwith (*OED adv.* 4)

63 **take** attack, capture

64 **amain** at once, immediately

5.1 The closeness of F and O is evident in
the way they treat this scene: both take
advantage of the Elizabethan stage by
moving Clarence's defection to
Edward from 'a playne by the citie'
(Hall, 293) to the walls of Coventry
itself. Moreover, they rearrange
chronology, placing Edward's capture
of Henry on 11 April (4.8) before
Clarence's defection on 29 March
(5.1), thus suggesting a crescendo of
events in Edward's favour, from the

51.1 *with* RICHARD OF GLOUCESTER] *Hanmer*   57.1 *Some Soldiers*] *Capell subst.*   **5.1**] *Pope*

WARWICK

> Where is the post that came from valiant Oxford?
> How far hence is thy lord, mine honest fellow?

1 MESSENGER

> By this at Dunsmore, marching hitherward.   [*Exit.*]

WARWICK

> How far off is our brother Montague?
> Where is the post that came from Montague?   5

2 MESSENGER

> By this at Daintry, with a puissant troop.   [*Exit.*]

Enter SOMERVILLE.

WARWICK

> Say, Somerville, what says my loving son?
> And by thy guess how nigh is Clarence now?

SOMERVILLE

> At Southam I did leave him with his forces

symbolic victory of Henry's capture to the real victory of Clarence's revolt. Both Hall and Holinshed record the events staged in this scene, but it follows Hall more closely.

0.1 Warwick has left London (4.8), marched north, and garrisoned in Coventry, where he waits for reinforcements to arrive, including Clarence's army, before issuing to fight Edward.

0.2 *the walls* the upper level in the tiring-house façade, used for the same purpose in 4.7. O has simply 'Enter *Warwike* on the walles', with no entries for those Warwick speaks to.

1–2 Warwick addresses l.1 to both Messengers; l.2 to the one who silently identifies himself – perhaps by stepping forward – as coming from Oxford.

1 **Oxford** John de Vere, Earl of Oxford. See List of Roles, 37n.

3, 6 **By this** by this time

3 **Dunsmore** 'heath on the N.W. road between Coventry and Daventry, about 10 miles from each' (Sugden). On this and other local references in this scene, see Martin and Cox (341–2).

6 **Daintry** local pronunciation of Daventry, a town in Northamptonshire, about twenty miles south-east of Coventry.
  puissant troop powerful force

6.1 *Enter* SOMERVILLE. Somerville is not in the chronicles and may be another indication of Shakespeare's familiarity with his native region (Martin and Cox).

7 **son** son-in-law, George Duke of Clarence, married to Warwick's daughter Isabel. See 4.1.118n. Hall says Warwick suspected Clarence's loyalty and resolved not to leave Coventry until he had determined where Clarence stood (293).

9, 12 **Southam** a town in Warwickshire, about ten miles south-east of Coventry

3, 6 SDs] *this edn*

And do expect him here some two hours hence.   10

[*A march afar off.*]

WARWICK

Then Clarence is at hand, I hear his drum.

SOMERVILLE

It is not his, my lord, here Southam lies.
The drum your honour hears marcheth from
    Warwick.

WARWICK

Who should that be? Belike unlooked-for friends.

SOMERVILLE

They are at hand, and you shall quickly know.   15

[*Exit into the city.*]

March. Flourish. Enter [KING] EDWARD,
RICHARD [OF GLOUCESTER] *and Soldiers.*

KING EDWARD

Go, trumpet, to the walls and sound a parle.

RICHARD OF GLOUCESTER

See how the surly Warwick mans the wall.

WARWICK

O, unbid spite, is sportful Edward come?

---

10 **two hours** Shakespeare well knew the
country described in these lines, and
the time estimate is based on steady
travel, either on foot or horseback, of
about five miles per hour.
11 See 1.2.68 SD.
12 **here** Somerville indicates a different
direction from the one where Warwick
looks and the sound of the drum is
coming. His correction of Warwick
indicates Somerville's better knowledge of the locale.
14 **Belike** probably
15.2–3 This is a main stage entry, as if
outside the walls of Coventry. Edward

first confronted Warwick near
Coventry on 29 March 1471, before
capturing Henry in London.
16 **trumpet . . . sound** an implicit SD for
a different trumpet call from the one
designated as '*Flourish*' in 15.1, which
was reserved exclusively for significant
royal movements.
parle meeting to discuss terms of a
truce
17 **surly** haughty, arrogant (*OED a.* 2a)
18 **unbid spite** unasked-for outrage,
injury
sportful sportive, playful. Cf. playboy.

10 SD] *Oxf*   15 SD *Exit into the city*] *this edn*

Where slept our scouts, or how are they seduced,
That we could hear no news of his repair?   20

KING EDWARD

Now Warwick, wilt thou ope the city gates,
Speak gentle words, and humbly bend thy knee?
Call Edward king and at his hands beg mercy,
And he shall pardon thee these outrages.

WARWICK

Nay, rather wilt thou draw thy forces hence,   25
Confess who set thee up and plucked thee down?
Call Warwick patron and be penitent,
And thou shalt still remain the Duke of York.

RICHARD OF GLOUCESTER

I thought at least he would have said 'the King'.
Or did he make the jest against his will?   30

WARWICK

Is not a dukedom, sir, a goodly gift?

RICHARD OF GLOUCESTER

Ay, by my faith, for a poor earl to give.
I'll do thee service for so good a gift.

WARWICK

'Twas I that gave the kingdom to thy brother.

KING EDWARD

Why then, 'tis mine, if but by Warwick's gift.   35

19–20 In Hall, Warwick is incensed not
with *our scouts* but with Montague, his
own brother, 'for lettyng kyng Edward
passe' (293).
20 **repair** return (*OED sb.*[1] 4 *Obs.*)
21–4 Hall says Edward's attempt to win
over Warwick happened before the
capture of Henry and after Clarence
had rejoined his brothers: 'Then was it
concluded emongest the. iii. bretherne
to attempte therle of Warwycke, if by
any fayre meanes he might be reconciled or by any promise allured to their
parte' (293). According to Hall,

Clarence made the first overture.
25 **draw . . . hence** remove
26 **who . . . down** See 2.3.37n.
32 **for . . . give** Richard may be alluding
to Warwick's offer to create Edward
Duke of York (see 4.3.34n.). Ard[1] suggests that Richard's offer to do
Warwick service (33) is a mocking use
of feudal deference, since Richard out-
ranks Warwick.
34 Warwick appears to be thinking of the
power he has wielded on Edward's
behalf and his initiative in insisting
that Edward be crowned (2.1.191–3).

WARWICK

   Thou art no Atlas for so great a weight;

   And, weakling, Warwick takes his gift again,

   And Henry is my King, Warwick his subject.

KING EDWARD

   But Warwick's King is Edward's prisoner.

   And, gallant Warwick, do but answer this: 40

   What is the body when the head is off?

RICHARD OF GLOUCESTER

   Alas, that Warwick had no more forecast,

   But whiles he thought to steal the single ten,

   The King was slyly fingered from the deck.

   You left poor Henry at the bishop's palace   45

   And ten to one you'll meet him in the Tower.

KING EDWARD

   'Tis even so, yet you are Warwick still.

RICHARD OF GLOUCESTER

   Come, Warwick, take the time, kneel down, kneel down.

   Nay, when? Strike now, or else the iron cools.

---

36 **Atlas** 'the poets feigned, that he susteigned the firmament with his shoulders' (Cooper). Cf. *AC* 1.5.24.

37 **takes . . . again** retracts, takes back his gift

41 alluding to the commonplace that the monarch governs the kingdom as reason (in the head) governs passions (in the body), and perhaps to the proverb 'If the head is off no beast can live' (Dent, H257.1)

42–9 Hitherto Warwick has replied to each speech from the Yorkists since Edward entered. This sequence of unanswered speeches by Edward and Richard may indicate Warwick's dismay and momentary confusion on hearing of Henry's capture for the first time.

42 **forecast** foresight. Shakespeare's only

use of this word, perhaps influenced by Hall's phrase, 'pollitique fore-castynges' (304; not in Holinshed).

43 **ten** 'The nearest card to a court or royal card' (Ard¹)

45 **bishop's palace**. See 4.8.33n.

47 **you . . . still** After Richard's gloating in 42–6, Edward tries to win Warwick over with a respectful acknowledgement of his status and influence.

48 **take the time** seize the opportunity. Proverbial: 'Take time when time comes' (Dent, T312).

49 **when?** i.e. when are you going to act? Cf. *R2* 1.1.162.

Strike . . . cools. Strike the iron when it is hot from the forge, i.e. seize the opportunity when you have a chance. Proverbial (Tilley, I94).

48] *Pope; F lines Warwicke, / downe: /*

WARWICK

    I had rather chop this hand off at a blow   50

    And with the other fling it at thy face

    Than bear so low a sail to strike to thee.

KING EDWARD

    Sail how thou canst, have wind and tide thy friend,

    This hand, fast wound about thy coal-black hair,

    Shall, whiles thy head is warm and new cut off,   55

    Write in the dust this sentence with thy blood,

    'Wind-changing Warwick now can change no more.'

       Enter OXFORD *with Drum and Colours.*

WARWICK

    O cheerful colours, see where Oxford comes!

OXFORD

    Oxford, Oxford for Lancaster!

    [*Oxford and his forces enter the city.*]

---

52 **bear . . . thee** When Warwick at last responds, he uses *strike* to mean 'lower your sail in token of surrender' (see 3.3.5n.).

53 **have . . . friend** i.e. even if you have the wind and tide with you. Edward seems to imply that Warwick is taking his chances by continuing to resist, but Cam[1] compares 57 and notes that Warwick is frequently associated with wind and tide (see 3.3.48, 4.3.59), 'because he seems (*a*) able to command the elements, and (*b*) as changeable as both'.

57.1 Oxford marches onto the main stage, presumably from the opposite direction to that from which Edward came. He is accompanied by a drummer and a bearer of his heraldic banner on a staff ('*Colours*').

59 O specifies that with this line, Oxford exits, presumably through one of the doors at the rear of the stage that acts as the city gate; he would then re-enter in the tiring-house façade when Warwick welcomes him at 66. O specifies similar exits for Montague and Somerset, in order to clear the stage for Clarence's arrival and reconciliation with his brothers. Montague and Somerset may also join Warwick in the tiring-house façade, but he does not welcome them, as he does Oxford, perhaps because of limited space in the upper acting area or limited men in the company: they could be imagined simply as in the *city*, and the same actors could march through twice, picking up new identifying tabards and banners backstage before entering the second time. See Appendix 2.

50 I had] *F; I'd Pope*   53] *Pope; F lines* canst, / friend, /   59 SD] *Capell*

RICHARD OF GLOUCESTER

The gates are open; let us enter, too. 60

KING EDWARD

So other foes may set upon our backs.
Stand we in good array, for they no doubt
Will issue out again and bid us battle.
If not, the city being but of small defence,
We'll quickly rouse the traitors in the same. 65

[*Enter Oxford on the walls.*]

WARWICK

O welcome, Oxford, for we want thy help.

Enter MONTAGUE *with Drum and Colours.*

MONTAGUE

Montague, Montague, for Lancaster!

[*Montague and his forces enter the city.*]

RICHARD OF GLOUCESTER

Thou and thy brother both shall buy this treason

60–3 Richard's comment and Edward's reply explain a necessary bit of stage action: the door at the rear of the main stage must be open so that Oxford, Montague and Somerset can pass through and proceed to the upper level of the tiring-house façade, where they join Warwick. But if the *gate* of the *city* is open, why shouldn't the enemy enter as well? Edward's concern about an attack from the besiegers' rear (61) would be valid whether the Yorkists allowed enemy cohorts into Coventry or not, and Richard passes over another obvious question: why not attack each party of reinforcements before it enters the city to increase Warwick's strength? A necessary dramatic action is thus covered with a dubious military explanation that

nonetheless suffices in the theatre.

61 **backs** rear of an armed force (*OED sb.*[1] 11). Cf. *2H4* 1.3.79.

62 **Stand . . . array** Let's keep good battle order.

64 **but . . . defence** not well fortified. Warwick later refers again to the unsuitability of Coventry as a defensive site (109). Cam[1] notes: 'Nothing in the chron. to justify these hints as to the condition of the walls, which prob. reflect their appearance in Sh.'s time'. On the economic decline of Coventry in the sixteenth century, see Phythian-Adams.

65 **rouse** move with violence, rush (*OED v.*[2] 11)

66 **want** need

68 **buy** suffer the consequences of (*OED v.* 3a)

65 SD] Cam[2] *subst.*   67 SD] Capell *subst.*

339

Even with the dearest blood your bodies bear.

KING EDWARD

    The harder matched, the greater victory.   70

    My mind presageth happy gain and conquest.

Enter SOMERSET *with Drum and Colours.*

SOMERSET

    Somerset, Somerset, for Lancaster!

    [Somerset and his forces enter the city.]

RICHARD OF GLOUCESTER

    Two of thy name, both Dukes of Somerset,

    Have sold their lives unto the House of York,

    And thou shalt be the third, if this sword hold.   75

Enter [GEORGE OF] CLARENCE *with Drum and Colours.*

WARWICK

    And lo, where George of Clarence sweeps along,

    Of force enough to bid his brother battle;

    With whom an upright zeal to right prevails

    More than the nature of a brother's love.

    Come, Clarence, come. Thou wilt, if Warwick call.   80

GEORGE OF CLARENCE

    Father of Warwick, know you what this means?

---

69 **dearest** most precious

70 proverbial: 'the more danger the more honour' (Tilley, D35)

71.1 SOMERSET Edmund Beaufort, fourth Duke. See List of Roles, 32n. Though Warwick had anticipated the arrival of Oxford, Montague and Clarence earlier in the scene, he had not looked for Somerset.

73 **Dukes of Somerset** For the various Dukes of Somerset, see List of Roles, 31n. and 32n.

75 **hold** holds out, lasts, i.e. to kill you

76 **sweeps along** as a peacock sweeps its tail behind it. Cf. *1H6* 3.3.6.

78–9 'whose love to do the right thing is greater than his love for his brother'. The dramatic irony of these lines emphasizes the moral morass in which everyone is caught: both Warwick and Clarence are motivated by personal pique, not by 'upright zeal to right', and Clarence is about to perjure himself in switching his allegiance back to his brother.

81–2 In F Clarence has already made up

72 SD] *Capell subst.*   78 whom an] *F2 subst.*; whom, in *F1*

[Takes the red rose out of his hat.]
Look here, I throw my infamy at thee!
[Throws it at Warwick.]
I will not ruinate my father's house,
Who gave his blood to lime the stones together,
And set up Lancaster. Why, trowest thou, Warwick,   85
That Clarence is so harsh, so blunt, unnatural,
To bend the fatal instruments of war
Against his brother and his lawful King?
Perhaps thou wilt object my holy oath.
To keep that oath were more impiety   90
Than Jephthah, when he sacrificed his daughter.

---

his mind to rejoin Edward when he enters, but O has a different version: Clarence enters with a shout for Lancaster, and Edward exclaims in dismay at Clarence's treachery: 'Et tu Brute, wilt thou stab *Cesar* too? / A parlie sirra to *George* of Clarence'. (The phrase 'Et tu Brute' occurs in no source but recurs famously in *JC* 3.1.77.) O then has this SD: 'Sound a Parlie, and *Richard* and *Clarence* whispers togither, and then Clarence takes his red Rose out of his hat, and throwes it at *Warwike*.' O's reference to a hat indicates Elizabethan military costuming for officers (see 1.1.0.2–3n.). O's portrayal of Richard's rhetoric affecting a reconciliation follows Hall and is arguably more dramatic than F's version of Clarence with his mind already made up: 'When eche host was in sight of other, Rychard duke of Glocester, brother to them both, as though he had bene made arbitrer betwene them, fyrst rode to the duke, and with hym commoned very secretly: from him he came to kyng Edward, and with the lyke secretnes so vsed hym, that in conclusion no vnnaturall warre, but a fraternall amitie was concluded and proclaymed' (293).

81 **Father of Warwick** i.e. 'Father Warwick'. Warwick was Clarence's father-in-law.
83–8 These lines echo a passage in Hall describing how Clarence's wife sent an anonymous 'damosell' to Clarence at Calais in 1470, to persuade him 'that it was neither naturall, nor honorable to hym, either to condiscende or take parte, against the house of Yorke (of which he was lineally discended) and to set vp again the house of Lancastre' (281).
83 **ruinate** destroy
84 **lime** cement
85 **trowest** do you believe
86 **blunt** unfeeling (*OED adj.* 4b)
87 **bend** turn. Cf. *AC* 1.1.4.
89 **my holy oath** In 1469, Clarence visited Warwick in Calais, where, 'after that the duke had sworne on the Sacrament to kepe his promise and pacte inuiolate made and concluded with the erle of Warwicke [to oppose Edward], he maried the Lady Isabell, eldest daughter to thesaid erle' (Hall, 272).
91 **Than Jephthah** than Jephthah showed. A biblical reference to 'Jephthah who made a vow to God that if God gave him victory over the Ammonites, he would sacrifice "for a burnt offring" whatever came first out

81, 82 SDs] *O subst.*   91 Jephthah] *(Iephah)*; Jepthah *F3*; Jephtah's *Rowe³*

I am so sorry for my trespass made
That, to deserve well at my brother's hands,
I here proclaim myself thy mortal foe.
With resolution, wheresoe'er I meet thee –   95
As I will meet thee, if thou stir abroad –
To plague thee, for thy foul misleading me.
And so, proud-hearted Warwick, I defy thee
And to my brothers turn my blushing cheeks.
Pardon me, Edward, I will make amends.   100
And Richard, do not frown upon my faults,
For I will henceforth be no more unconstant.

KING EDWARD
Now, welcome, more, and ten times more, beloved
Than if thou never hadst deserved our hate.

RICHARD OF GLOUCESTER
Welcome, good Clarence, this is brother-like.   105

WARWICK
O passing traitor, perjured and unjust.

KING EDWARD
What, Warwick, wilt thou leave the town and fight?
Or shall we beat the stones about thine ears?

WARWICK
Alas, I am not cooped here for defence.
I will away towards Barnet presently   110

of his house to greet him. His only
daughter was first to greet him, and he
"did with her according to his vowe".
Judges 11:30–39' (Shaheen, 70).
Shakespeare's only other reference to
Jephthah is in *Ham* 2.2.403–12.
96 **stir abroad** leave the city
106 Hall says that after Clarence's messengers told Warwick of the Duke's
defection, Warwick said 'he had leuer
be always lyke hym selfe, then lyke a
false & a periured duke' (293).
passing surpassing, extreme (*OED*

ppl. a. 3)
108 **shall** must
109 **cooped** confined, shut up. It is hard
to know why Warwick is cooped in
Coventry, if not for defence, or why he
would point out the city's poor
defences to those who are besieging
him, or why Edward would let him
leave the city so easily. See 110–12n.
110–12 Warwick's challenge to Edward to
fight him at Barnet is again militarily
dubious: why would Warwick select a
site near London, some eighty miles

99 brothers] *O;* Brother *F*   107] *Pope; F lines* Warwicke, / fight? /

And bid thee battle, Edward, if thou dar'st.

KING EDWARD

Yes, Warwick, Edward dares, and leads the way.

Lords, to the field. Saint George, and victory!

Exeunt. March. Warwick and his company follows.

[**5.2**]   *Alarum and excursions. Enter* [KING] EDWARD
                bringing forth WARWICK *wounded.*

KING EDWARD

So lie thou there. Die thou and die our fear,

For Warwick was a bug that feared us all.

Now, Montague, sit fast: I seek for thee,

away, and why would Edward let Warwick choose the battle venue? Again, however, once Shakespeare had decided to postpone Clarence's reconciliation with Edward at Coventry until after Henry's capture, it was necessary to provide a reason for the battle happening at Barnet, rather than Coventry. In Hall, Edward is reconciled with Clarence on 'a playne by the citie', confronts Warwick in Coventry (29 March), and proceeds to London, where he captures Henry (11 April). Warwick, trying too late to prevent Edward from reaching London, meets him at Barnet as he is leaving London, so Barnet is the place where at last they join battle (14 April).

110 **presently** immediately

113 SD Edward and his company exit below, while Warwick and his company presumably leave the upper area, re-enter below through one of the rear stage doors, as if leaving the city, and exit to meet Edward at Barnet.

5.2 The battle of Barnet was fought on Easter Sunday, 14 April 1471. It lasted most of the day, with neither side able to gain a decisive advantage, until

Warwick, attempting to rally his men, 'rushed into the middest of his enemies, where as he (aventured so farre from his awne compaignie, to kill and sley his aduersaries, that he could not be rescued) was in the middes of his enemies, strike doune and slaine' (Hall, 296). His brother Montague was killed trying to rescue him. The indecisiveness of the battle may be suggested in the first SD, but the scene goes straight to the climax: Warwick's death.

0.1–2 O has 'Alarmes, and then enter *Warwike* wounded', with no mention of Edward. F's version gives the impression that Edward killed Warwick and gives Edward a brief speech that emphasizes how much the momentum of events has shifted in York's favour.

0.2 *bringing forth* Edward may drag the wounded Warwick, leaving him to lie on the stage (1).

2 **bug** object of terror. Proverbial: 'bug[bear]s to scare babes' (Dent, B703).
feared frightened

3 **sit fast** hold on, watch out

That Warwick's bones may keep thine company.   *Exit.*

WARWICK

Ah, who is nigh? Come to me, friend or foe,   5

And tell me who is victor, York or Warwick?

Why ask I that? My mangled body shows –

My blood, my want of strength, my sick heart shows –

That I must yield my body to the earth

And, by my fall, the conquest to my foe.   10

Thus yields the cedar to the axe's edge

Whose arms gave shelter to the princely eagle,

Under whose shade the ramping lion slept,

Whose top branch overpeered Jove's spreading tree

And kept low shrubs from winter's powerful wind.   15

These eyes, that now are dimmed with death's black

     veil,

Have been as piercing as the midday sun

To search the secret treasons of the world.

The wrinkles in my brows, now filled with blood,

Were likened oft to kingly sepulchres,   20

For who lived king but I could dig his grave?

And who durst smile when Warwick bent his brow?

Lo, now my glory smeared in dust and blood.

My parks, my walks, my manors that I had

Even now forsake me, and of all my lands   25

7–8 **My . . . blood** an implicit SD. Cf. 37.

11–13 **cedar . . . eagle . . . lion** Warwick still views himself very much as the kingmaker, even as he lies dying, comparing himself to the noblest of trees, sheltering the noblest of birds and mammals, respectively.

12 **arms** branches. Cf. Sonnet 73.3, where 'boughs' are metaphoric arms.
   eagle suggesting Warwick's support for York. See 2.1.91.

13 **ramping** rearing. A ramping lion appears on the royal arms of England,

and Warwick may therefore suggest his support for both Edward IV and Henry VI.

14 **Jove's spreading tree** the oak, from Virgil, *Georgics*, 3.332–3, 'magna Iouis . . . quercus'

21–2 This is the play's final allusion to Warwick the kingmaker.

22 **bent his brow** frowned, scowled (*OED* bend *v.* 6b)

24 **walks** supervised tracts of forest land (*OED sb.*[1] 10a)

14 top branch] (top-branch)

Is nothing left me but my body's length.
Why, what is pomp, rule, reign but earth and dust?
And live we how we can, yet die we must.

Enter OXFORD *and* SOMERSET.

SOMERSET
　　Ah, Warwick, Warwick, wert thou as we are
　　We might recover all our loss again.   30
　　The Queen from France hath brought a puissant power;
　　Even now we heard the news. Ah, couldst thou fly.
WARWICK
　　Why, then, I would not fly. Ah, Montague,
　　If thou be there, sweet brother, take my hand
　　And with thy lips keep in my soul awhile.   35
　　Thou lov'st me not, for, brother, if thou didst,
　　Thy tears would wash this cold congealed blood
　　That glues my lips and will not let me speak.
　　Come quickly, Montague, or I am dead.
SOMERSET
　　Ah, Warwick, Montague hath breathed his last;   40
　　And to the latest gasp cried out for Warwick
　　And said, 'Commend me to my valiant brother.'
　　And more he would have said, and more he spoke,
　　Which sounded like a cannon in a vault,
　　That mought not be distinguished, but at last   45

26–7 proverbial: 'Six feet of earth make all men equal' (Dent, F582)
28 **die we must** proverbial: 'All men must die' (Dent, M505)
31 Hall says that Margaret 'gathered together no small compaignie, of hardy and valiaunt souldiours' when she heard that Edward had returned to England (297). Bad weather hindered her passage, however, and she arrived at Weymouth, on the Dorset coast, on the same day Warwick was defeated at Barnet (Boswell-Stone, 337).
37 **congealed** congealèd
45 **mought** could, i.e. could hardly be heard. This is the only instance of *mought* in Shakespeare, though it is frequent in *FQ*, whose first three books were published in 1590. The comparison to a cannon presumably describes the explosive force of Montague's character, but he is not portrayed that way in this play.

I well might hear, delivered with a groan,
'O, farewell, Warwick.'

WARWICK

Sweet rest his soul. Fly, lords, and save yourselves,
For Warwick bids you all farewell to meet in heaven!   [*Dies.*]

OXFORD

Away, away, to meet the Queen's great power!   50
              Here they bear away his body. Exeunt.

[5.3]   *Flourish. Enter* KING EDWARD *in triumph, with*
        RICHARD [OF GLOUCESTER], [GEORGE OF]
           CLARENCE *and the rest.*

KING EDWARD

Thus far our fortune keeps an upward course
And we are graced with wreaths of victory.
But in the midst of this bright-shining day,
I spy a black, suspicious, threat'ning cloud
That will encounter with our glorious sun   5
Ere he attain his easeful western bed.

50 O includes six lines here that are not in
F.

50 SD *Here . . . body.* On an uncurtained
stage, 'dead' bodies had to be carried
off in order to clear the stage for the
next scene.

5.3 Edward has just won the battle of
Barnet, as he mentions (20), fought on
14 April 1471. The scene echoes a
speech by Somerset to Margaret that
Hall records before the battle of
Tewkesbury. He urges her not to give
up and return to France but to stay and
fight, lest their own force be diminished 'and kyng Edwardes power
encreased and *augmented*' after his
narrow victory at Barnet. Though '*fortune shone* on him' then, it may turn in
her favour now (Hall, 298; not in

Holinshed).

0.1 *in triumph* The phrase may indicate
that Edward wears a crown of laurel
leaves, in the fashion of a triumphant
Roman general, as he suggests at 2.
Hall says Edward entered London 'in
moste triumphant maner' (297);
Holinshed, 'like a triumphant conqueror' (314).

2 The line appears verbatim in Marlowe's
Massacre at Paris (*c.* 1593), 794.

5 **sun** See 2.1.39–40.

6 **his . . . bed** literally the sunset, but
Edward's infamous lasciviousness and
identification of himself with the sun
may make this another of his sexual
Freudian slips. If so, even Richard, for
once, does not take him up on it.

48] *Steevens; F lines* Soule: / sclues, /   49 SD] *O*   5.3] *Capell*

I mean, my lords, those powers that the Queen
Hath raised in Gallia have arrived our coast
And, as we hear, march on to fight with us.

GEORGE OF CLARENCE

A little gale will soon disperse that cloud   10
And blow it to the source from whence it came.
Thy very beams will dry those vapours up,
For every cloud engenders not a storm.

RICHARD OF GLOUCESTER

The Queen is valued thirty thousand strong,
And Somerset with Oxford fled to her: 15
If she have time to breathe, be well assured
Her faction will be full as strong as ours.

KING EDWARD

We are advertised by our loving friends
That they do hold their course toward Tewkesbury.
We, having now the best at Barnet Field,   20
Will thither straight, for willingness rids way,
And as we march our strength will be augmented
In every county as we go along.
Strike up the drum. Cry 'Courage!' and away!   *Exeunt.*

7–9 See 5.2.31n.
8 **Gallia** France
   arrived arrived on, reached
12 **beams** Clarence continues Edward's
   solar allusions.
13 proverbial: 'All clouds bring not rain'
   (Tilley, C443)
14 **thirty thousand** Hall and Holinshed
   do not indicate the size of Margaret's
   force. Ard[1] notes Commines's figure of
   40,000.
15 **fled** is (i.e. has) fled
18 **advertised** informed (accented on
   second syllable, as at 2.1.115)
19 **they** the Queen and her forces. Time
   is collapsed here for dramatic conve-
   nience. Edward did not learn of

Margaret's landing until 16 April, two
days after Barnet field. He did not
leave Windsor in pursuit until 24
April, and he finally compelled her to
fight at Tewkesbury on 4 May
(Boswell-Stone, 338).
Tewkesbury an abbey town in
Gloucestershire, about ten miles north
of Gloucester, where Margaret had
hoped to escape westwards across the
Severn
21 **straight** immediately
   rids way moves ahead, makes progress
   (*OED* rid *v.* 8b)
24 **Strike . . . drum.** an implicit SD for a
   march

[5.4] *Flourish. March. Enter* QUEEN [MARGARET], *young*
[PRINCE] EDWARD, SOMERSET, OXFORD *and Soldiers.*

QUEEN MARGARET

Great lords, wise men ne'er sit and wail their loss
But cheerly seek how to redress their harms.
What though the mast be now blown overboard,
The cable broke, the holding-anchor lost
And half our sailors swallowed in the flood?   5
Yet lives our pilot still. Is't meet that he

5.4 The battle of Tewkesbury, 'the last ciuile battayl that was fought in kynge Edwardes dayes' (Hall, 301), took place on 4 May 1471. Edward's speed again gave him the advantage, as the Earl of Oxford notes (62–3), for Margaret hoped to escape to Wales, in order to increase her force, but Gloucester stood in the way of her crossing the Severn, and the city refused to yield, so Edward brought her to bay before she was ready. Taking Warwick's place as Lancaster's principal commander, Somerset planned the battle, entrenching his men on high ground, where Richard attacked them. When he saw he could not dislodge them, he pretended a retreat in order to draw them out of their position. The ruse was successful, and when he turned, 'the Quenes part went almost all to wrecke, for the most parte were slayne' (Hall, 300; Holinshed, 319). *R3* contains a reminiscence of the battle that is neither in the chronicles nor in the dramatic texts, when Edward recalls Clarence's rescue of him (2.1.112–14).

0.1 *Flourish* the last of the play's ambiguous royal fanfares, playing both for Edward as he departs to find Margaret, and for Margaret as she enters to rally her army (J. Long, 30)

0.2 OXFORD Oxford fought at Barnet, not at Tewkesbury, and he held out against

Edward at St Michael's Mount until 1474, when he was forced to surrender and was sent to Hammes Castle in Picardy (Hall, 304; Holinshed, 329).

1–38 Margaret's elaborate conceit may be suggested by Somerset's encouragement for Margaret to 'turne her saile on the otherside' (Hall, 298), but it directly imitates Arthur Brooke's *Romeus and Juliet* (1562) (1359–77; reprinted in Ard², 176–7). Margaret's first reaction to the defeat at Barnet was devastation and despair, and she decided to stay and fight only after much persuasion by Somerset and others (Hall, 298–9). She therefore comes across as more consistently strong and determined in the play than in the chronicles.

1–2 echoed in *R2* 3.2.178–9. Proverbial: 'One must not wail mischief but find a remedy for it' (Tilley, M999a).

2 cheerly cheerfully (as in *AYL* 2.6.13)

4 holding-anchor anchor that holds; not in *OED* but may indicate a 'sheet-anchor', or 'largest of a ship's anchors, used only in emergency' (*OED*), as Cam² suggests

6 pilot Henry VI. Though Henry's kingdom has effectively been reduced to little more than the army Margaret leads, her metaphor has an influential precedent in Plato's elaborate description of the state as a ship, with its leader as the pilot (*Republic*, 488a–3).

5.4] *Capell*

Should leave the helm and, like a fearful lad,
With tearful eyes add water to the sea
And give more strength to that which hath too much,
Whiles in his moan the ship splits on the rock,   10
Which industry and courage might have saved?
Ah, what a shame; ah, what a fault were this.
Say Warwick was our anchor, what of that?
And Montague our topmast, what of him?
Our slaughtered friends the tackles, what of these?   15
Why, is not Oxford here another anchor?
And Somerset another goodly mast?
The friends of France our shrouds and tacklings?
And, though unskilful, why not Ned and I
For once allowed the skilful pilot's charge?   20
We will not from the helm to sit and weep,
But keep our course, though the rough wind say no,
From shelves and rocks that threaten us with wrack.
As good to chide the waves as speak them fair.
And what is Edward but a ruthless sea?   25
What Clarence but a quicksand of deceit?
And Richard but a ragged fatal rock?
All these the enemies to our poor bark.
Say you can swim: alas, 'tis but awhile;
Tread on the sand: why, there you quickly sink;   30
Bestride the rock: the tide will wash you off
Or else you famish; that's a threefold death.
This speak I, lords, to let you understand,

---

meet appropriate
7   **fearful** full of fear
8–9 **add . . . much** proverbial: 'to cast
    water into the sea' (Tilley, W106)
10 **in** at. See Abbott, 161, for the use of *in*
    for 'at' or 'during'.
11 **industry** diligent effort
15 **tackles** ship's rigging, ropes

18 **of France** from France, French
    shrouds ropes securing a ship's mast
    tacklings rigging
21 **from** go away from, leave
23 **shelves** shallow areas, shoals
24 **them fair** to them courteously
27 **ragged** broken, jagged (*OED a.*[1] 2b)
28 **bark** sailing vessel

27 ragged] *(raged)*

If case some one of you would fly from us,
That there's no hoped-for mercy with the brothers   35
More than with ruthless waves, with sands and rocks.
Why, courage, then! What cannot be avoided
'Twere childish weakness to lament or fear.

PRINCE EDWARD

Methinks a woman of this valiant spirit
Should, if a coward heard her speak these words,   40
Infuse his breast with magnanimity
And make him, naked, foil a man at arms.
I speak not this as doubting any here,
For did I but suspect a fearful man,
He should have leave to go away betimes,   45
Lest in our need he might infect another
And make him of like spirit to himself.
If any such be here, as God forbid,
Let him depart before we need his help.

OXFORD

Women and children of so high a courage,   50
And warriors faint? Why, 'twere perpetual shame!
O brave young Prince, thy famous grandfather
Doth live again in thee. Long mayst thou live
To bear his image and renew his glories.

---

34 **If case** if it were the case, in case
37–8 **What . . . fear.** proverbial: 'What cannot be cured must be endured' (Dent, C922)
41 **magnanimity** lofty courage, fortitude
42 **naked** unarmed
   foil defeat
43–7 Henry V says something very similar in *H5* 4.3.33–7. Oxford's allusion to Henry V at 52–3 suggestively connects this passage to the later one, as if Shakespeare wrote it to confirm what Oxford says here.
44 **did . . . man** 'if I so much as suspected that any man was afraid'. Cf. *fearful* at 7.

45 **betimes** at once, forthwith
50 **children** Prince Edward. Shakespeare consistently understates the Prince's maturity, perhaps to make his death more pitiable. He was born in 1453 and was therefore eighteen by this time – the same age Edward Plantagenet was when he inherited the dukedom of York and became the Yorkists' leader.
51 **faint** fainthearted
52 **grandfather** Henry V. See 43–7n.
53–4 **Long . . . glories.** Given the Prince's death in the next scene, the dramatic irony of Oxford's words is so strong that they amount almost to an omen.
54 **bear his image** look like him

SOMERSET

> And he that will not fight for such a hope,   55
> Go home to bed and, like the owl by day,
> If he arise, be mocked and wondered at.

QUEEN MARGARET

> Thanks, gentle Somerset; sweet Oxford, thanks.

PRINCE EDWARD

> And take his thanks that yet hath nothing else.

Enter a Messenger.

MESSENGER

> Prepare you, lords, for Edward is at hand,   60
> Ready to fight; therefore be resolute.   [*Exit.*]

OXFORD

> I thought no less; it is his policy
> To haste thus fast to find us unprovided.

SOMERSET

> But he's deceived; we are in readiness.

QUEEN MARGARET

> This cheers my heart, to see your forwardness.   65

OXFORD

> Here pitch our battle; hence we will not budge.

Flourish and march. Enter [KING] EDWARD, RICHARD
[OF GLOUCESTER], [GEORGE OF] CLARENCE *and Soldiers.*

KING EDWARD

> Brave followers, yonder stands the thorny wood
> Which by the heaven's assistance and your strength

---

56 **owl by day** proverbial: 'To be like an owl to wonder at' (Dent, O94.1)
62 **policy** tactics; expedient, advantageous procedure (*OED* 4)
63 **unprovided** unprepared, not having provided adequately for what happens

65 **forwardness** readiness, eagerness
66 **pitch our battle** set our troops in fighting formation
67–9 Cf. Richard's image of a *thorny wood* at 3.2.174–5.

61 SD] *this edn*

Must by the roots be hewn up yet ere night.
I need not add more fuel to your fire,   70
For well I wot ye blaze to burn them out.
Give signal to the fight, and to it, lords!

QUEEN MARGARET

Lords, knights, and gentlemen, what I should say
My tears gainsay, for every word I speak
Ye see I drink the water of my eye.   75
Therefore, no more but this: Henry, your sovereign,
Is prisoner to the foe, his state usurped,
His realm a slaughterhouse, his subjects slain,
His statutes cancelled and his treasure spent,
And yonder is the wolf that makes this spoil.   80
You fight in justice. Then in God's name, lords,
Be valiant and give signal to the fight!

Alarum, retreat, excursions. Exeunt.

[5.5]   *Flourish. Enter* [KING] EDWARD, RICHARD
        [OF GLOUCESTER *and* GEORGE OF] CLARENCE,[*with*]
        QUEEN [MARGARET], OXFORD [*and*] SOMERSET[, *prisoners*].

---

70 **add . . . fire** proverbial: 'add fuel to
  the fire' (Tilley, F745)
71 **wot** know
74 **gainsay** hinder
82 SD O's SD offers a good deal more (see
  t.n.). The flight and return that O specifies for Edward may reflect an understanding and recollection of the tactics
  Hall describes (see 5.4n.), and the scene
  could be staged to show them.
5.5 Of five references to the battle of
  Tewkesbury in *R3*, all but one refer to
  the most infamous incident associated
  with the battle: the murder of Prince
  Edward. Yet Edward was not a child at

the time; he was eighteen, and the earliest records indicate that he died
fighting. His murder appears only in
later chronicles, and Shakespeare's
staging of it is the principal reason for
its infamy. It balances the murder of
Rutland (who was about the same age
as Edward when he died; see 1.3.8n.)
and leaves a dark stain on the Yorkist
triumph.
0.3 O's long SD for the battle of
  Tewkesbury (5.4.82 SD) specifies the
  capture of Margaret, Oxford and
  Somerset, who presumably enter as
  prisoners under guard.

---

82 SD] *F; Alarmes to the battell, Yorke flies, then the chambers be discharged. Then enter the king.
Cla & Glo. & the rest, & make a great shout, and crie, for Yorke, for Yorke, and then the Queene is
taken, & the prince, & Oxf. & Sum. and then sound and enter all againe.* O 5.5] Capell
0.2–3 CLARENCE *with . . . prisoners*] Capell; *Queene, Clarence, Oxford, Somerset. F*

KING EDWARD

Now here a period of tumultuous broils.
Away with Oxford to Hammes Castle straight;
For Somerset, off with his guilty head.
Go bear them hence; I will not hear them speak.

OXFORD

For my part, I'll not trouble thee with words.   5

[*Exit Oxford, under guard.*]

SOMERSET

Nor I, but stoop with patience to my fortune.

[*Exit Somerset, under guard.*]

QUEEN MARGARET

So part we sadly in this troublous world
To meet with joy in sweet Jerusalem.

KING EDWARD

Is proclamation made that who finds Edward
Shall have a high reward, and he his life?   10

RICHARD OF GLOUCESTER

It is, and lo where youthful Edward comes.

Enter the PRINCE [*under guard*].

1 **Now . . . period** now we have come to the end
   period conclusion, end
   broils quarrels
2 **Oxford . . . Castle** See 5.4.0.2n.
   straight straight away, at once
3 **For** as for
   Somerset . . . head 'And on the Monday next ensuing was Edmond duke of Somerset . . . behedded in the market place at Tewkesbury' (Hall, 301). See List of Roles, 32n.
5–6 O specifies an exit for Oxford and Somerset as each says his line. They would probably be accompanied by those guarding them when they first enter (5.5.0.3n.).

8 **sweet Jerusalem** biblical: heaven, the eschatalogical 'new Jerusalem' of Revelation, 21.2, 10 (Shaheen, 72)
9–10 **proclamation** 'After the felde ended, kyng Edward made Proclamation, that who so euer could bring prince Edward to him alyue or dead, shoulde haue an annuities of an .C.l. during his lyfe, and the Princes life to be saued' (Hall, 301; not in Holinshed). Edward's assurance for the Prince's life is the play's final public promise, broken by Edward himself almost as soon as he makes it (38 SD).
9 **who** he who, whoever. See Abbott, 251, for the use of *who* as a full pronoun.

5 SD] *O subst.*   6 SD] *O subst.; Exeunt. F*   11.1 *under guard*] *Capell subst.*

KING EDWARD

    Bring forth the gallant; let us hear him speak.

    What? Can so young a thorn begin to prick?

    Edward, what satisfaction canst thou make

    For bearing arms, for stirring up my subjects   15

    And all the trouble thou hast turned me to?

PRINCE EDWARD

    Speak like a subject, proud ambitious York.

    Suppose that I am now my father's mouth:

    Resign thy chair, and where I stand, kneel thou,

    Whilst I propose the selfsame words to thee   20

    Which, traitor, thou wouldst have me answer to.

QUEEN MARGARET

    Ah, that thy father had been so resolved!

RICHARD OF GLOUCESTER

    That you might still have worn the petticoat

    And ne'er have stol'n the breech from Lancaster.

PRINCE EDWARD

    Let Aesop fable in a winter's night;   25

    His currish riddles sorts not with this place.

---

12 **Bring forth** Edward's command indicates that the Prince is guarded and echoes Hall, who says that Prince Edward was captured by Sir Richard Crofts, who 'brought furth his prisoner' when he heard of the offered reward (Hall, 301).

13 **thorn** Cf. 5.4.67. Proverbial: 'It early pricks that will be a thorn' (Tilley, T232).

14 **what ... make** 'how can you make up' **satisfaction** atonement

17 **York** The Prince acknowledges Edward only as Duke of York, not as king. Cf. 4.3.29–34.

18 **I ... mouth** I speak for my father

19 **chair** royal seat, throne

22 **resolved** resolute. Cf. *E3* 2.2.168–9: 'Resolute to be dissolved' (RP).

24 **stol'n the breech** assumed the authority or rule. Proverbial, as noted by Prince Edward (25–6): 'She wears the breeches' (Tilley, B645). Also applied to Margaret in *2H6* 1.3.147. **breech** breeches

25 **Aesop** ascribed author of the famous book of fables

26 **currish riddles** alluding to Richard's mordant and proverbial style. Richard has more proverbs than anyone else in the play.
currish about beasts; quarrelsome, mean-spirited, cynical (the etymology of 'cynic' is 'dog' in Greek, as noted by Ard²). Cf. 5.6.77.
riddles sorts For third-person plural *-s* inflection see Abbott, 333.
riddles enigmatic sayings

RICHARD OF GLOUCESTER

By heaven, brat, I'll plague ye for that word!

QUEEN MARGARET

Ay, thou wast born to be a plague to men.

RICHARD OF GLOUCESTER

For God's sake, take away this captive scold!

PRINCE EDWARD

Nay, take away this scolding crookback, rather!   30

KING EDWARD

Peace, wilful boy, or I will charm your tongue.

GEORGE OF CLARENCE

Untutored lad, thou art too malapert.

PRINCE EDWARD

I know my duty: you are all undutiful.

Lascivious Edward, and thou perjured George,

And thou misshapen Dick, I tell ye all   35

I am your better, traitors as ye are,

And thou usurp'st my father's right and mine.

KING EDWARD

Take that, the likeness of this railer here!   *Stabs him.*

RICHARD OF GLOUCESTER

Sprawl'st thou? Take that to end thy agony!

Richard stabs him.

---

sorts answers or corresponds to, befits or suits (*OED v.*[1] 8 *trans.*)

27 **plague** torment, trouble

that word those words

31 **charm your tongue** silence you

32 **Untutored** a verbal detail that may trigger reminiscence of Rutland's murder (RP)

malapert presumptuous, saucy

35 **misshapen** See 1.4.75n.

37 This is Prince Edward's last line, and he would appear to die shortly thereafter, perhaps with Clarence's blow (40), as Margaret seems to imply at 41.

38 **likeness . . . here** alluding to

Margaret. Hall says Prince Edward was 'a goodly femenine & a well feautered yonge gentleman' (301).

38 SD Edward is not the first to stab the Prince in Hall, 'but with his hand thrust hym from hym (or as some say, stroke [struck] him with his gauntlet)' (301).

39 **Sprawl'st thou?** Do you convulse and shudder? (*OED* sprawl *v.* 1). Used also with this meaning in *Tit* 5.1.51 (the only other occurrence in Shakespeare). Richard's cruel mockery may contain an implicit SD to the actor playing Prince Edward.

GEORGE OF CLARENCE

  And there's for twitting me with perjury!   40

  Clarence stabs him.

QUEEN MARGARET

  O, kill me too!

RICHARD OF GLOUCESTER

  Marry, and shall.   *Offers to kill her.*

KING EDWARD

  Hold, Richard, hold, for we have done too much.

RICHARD OF GLOUCESTER

  Why should she live to fill the world with words?

KING EDWARD

  What, doth she swoon? Use means for her recovery.   45

RICHARD OF GLOUCESTER

  Clarence, excuse me to the King my brother;

  I'll hence to London on a serious matter.

  Ere ye come there, be sure to hear some news.

GEORGE OF CLARENCE

  What? What?   49

RICHARD OF GLOUCESTER

  The Tower. The Tower!   *Exit.*

40 **twitting** blaming, reproaching, taunting

42 **Marry** 'Why, to be sure' (*OED int.* a). *Marry, and shall* is proverbial (Dent, M699.1). Richard's near murder of Margaret is not in the chronicles, but it suits his character in this play and in *R3*.

45 **What . . . swoon?** an implicit SD for the actor playing Margaret

46–50   This exchange is presumably not overheard by others, who are distracted by Margaret's swoon (45). See 83. The chronicles offer no explanation for how Richard got from Tewkesbury to the Tower of London.

50 O has 'The Tower man, the Tower'

and adds 'Ile root them out', creating a full regular verse line, in contrast to F, and perhaps reflecting Hall: 'now is there no heire male of kynge Edwarde the thirde, but wee of the house of Yorke' (343). Clarence's repeated question at 49 (where O has 'About what prethe tell me?') indicates that Richard has whispered or mouthed something to his brother, now repeated more audibly but still elliptically. Richard's dropping of the customary *the* before *Tower* in F may suggest that he has been mouthing or whispering the single word in an effort to make Clarence understand and finally adds *the* to clarify his intent.

50 The Tower. The Tower!] O (The Tower man, the Tower,); Tower, the Tower F

QUEEN MARGARET

O Ned, sweet Ned, speak to thy mother, boy.
Canst thou not speak? O traitors, murderers!
They that stabbed Caesar shed no blood at all,
Did not offend, nor were not worthy blame,
If this foul deed were by to equal it. 55
He was a man; this, in respect, a child,
And men ne'er spend their fury on a child.
What's worse than murderer, that I may name it?
No, no, my heart will burst an if I speak –
And I will speak, that so my heart may burst. 60
Butchers and villains! Bloody cannibals!
How sweet a plant have you untimely cropped!
You have no children, butchers; if you had,
The thought of them would have stirred up remorse.
But if you ever chance to have a child, 65
Look in his youth to have him so cut off
As, deathsmen, you have rid this sweet young Prince!

KING EDWARD

Away with her. Go, bear her hence perforce.

---

51 Margaret addresses her dead son, perhaps holding him in her arms. She is more pitiable in this and the following lines than at any earlier point in the *H6* plays. Hall says that after Prince Edward's death, Margaret's life 'was more lyke a death then a lyfe, languishing and mornyng in continuall sorowe . . . for the losse of prince Edward her sonne' (301).

53 **They . . . Caesar** the senators who assassinated Julius Caesar. Cf. 5.1.81–2n.

54 **worthy blame** worthy of blame, blameworthy

55 'compared to this foul deed'
   equal it compare with it

56 **He . . . this** Caesar . . . Prince Edward

respect comparison

57 Margaret forgets or overlooks Clifford's murder of Rutland (1.3).

59 **an if** if

62 **untimely** prematurely, out of season
   cropped harvested, cut down

63 **You . . . butchers** proverbial: 'He that has no children knows not what love is' (Tilley, C341). Cf. *Mac* 4.3.217: 'He has no children'.

65–7, 82 Margaret anticipates her role in *R3*.

67 **deathsmen** death's men, executioners (as in *2H6* 3.2.217, *KL* 4.6.253)
   rid destroyed, done away with

68 **perforce** by force, forcibly. This is an implicit SD to those guarding Margaret.

QUEEN MARGARET

Nay, never bear me hence; dispatch me here.
Here sheath thy sword; I'll pardon thee my death.   70
What, wilt thou not? Then, Clarence, do it thou.

GEORGE OF CLARENCE

By heaven, I will not do thee so much ease.

QUEEN MARGARET

Good Clarence, do; sweet Clarence, do thou do it.

GEORGE OF CLARENCE

Didst thou not hear me swear I would not do it?

QUEEN MARGARET

Ay, but thou usest to forswear thyself.   75
'Twas sin before, but now 'tis charity.
What, wilt thou not? Where is that devil's butcher,
    Richard?
Hard-favoured Richard? Richard, where art thou?
Thou art not here. Murder is thy alms-deed;
Petitioners for blood thou ne'er put'st back.   80

KING EDWARD

Away, I say! I charge ye bear her hence.

QUEEN MARGARET

So come to you and yours as to this Prince!
                    Exit Queen [guarded, with one bearing her son].

69–70 **here. / Here** in this place; in my
  body
69–71 **Nay . . . not?** Margaret addresses
  Edward, before turning to Clarence
  (71, 73) and Richard (77).
74 **hear me swear** *By heaven* (72)
75 Margaret alludes to Clarence's perjury
  in abandoning Warwick. See 5.1.89n.
  usest . . . thyself are accustomed to
  perjuring yourself
77 **Richard** The line is hypermetric, and
  Richard may be a printer's error, but
  the rough verse may also reflect
  Margaret's state of mind, as Cam² sug-

gests. Alternatively *Where is* may elide
  to 'Where's'.
78–9 Richard's ominous threat at 46–50
  lends dramatic irony to Margaret's
  panicky question about where Richard
  is as she calls him a murderer.
78 **Hard-favoured** ill-favoured, ugly
79 **alms-deed** charity bestowed as one of
  the seven acts of mercy
80 **Petitioners** suppliants, seekers
  put'st back put off, rejected
82 **So come** so may it happen
82 SD Margaret presumably holds Prince
  Edward in her arms while sitting on

82 SD *guarded . . . son*] *Cam² subst.*

KING EDWARD

> Where's Richard gone?

GEORGE OF CLARENCE

> To London all in post and, as I guess,
> To make a bloody supper in the Tower.   85

KING EDWARD

> He's sudden if a thing comes in his head.
> Now march we hence. Discharge the common sort
> With pay and thanks, and let's away to London
> And see our gentle Queen how well she fares.   89
> By this I hope she hath a son for me.   *Exeunt.*

[5.6]   *Enter* [KING] HENRY *the Sixth and* RICHARD
        [OF GLOUCESTER], *with the* Lieutenant *on the* [*Tower*] *walls.*

---

the stage in 51–67. Edward's order to
bear her hence (81) indicates she exits
guarded. If she and Prince Edward
were both played by boys, it is difficult
to see how the Queen could have carried out the Prince. Presumably the
Prince's body leaves the stage in someone else's arms.

84 **post** haste

85 **bloody supper** Clarence is either
repelled by what he suspects Richard
is up to or makes a mordant joke about
it.

86 Edward's inability to comprehend
Richard anticipates their relationship
in *R3*.

87 **common sort** common soldiers

90 **By this** by this time

5.6 Richard's sudden decision to murder
King Henry (5.5.46–50) is not in the
chronicles, which provide no transi-
tion from Tewkesbury field to the
Tower. The battle was fought on 4
May 1471, and Henry was murdered
on 21 or 22 May (Boswell-Stone, 340).
Both Hall and Holinshed fill the inter-
im with the Jack Cade-like uprising of
Thomas Falconbridge, which Shake-

speare ignores. Yet as early as 3.2.130,
Richard mentions 'Henry and his son,
young Edward' as two of those who
stand in his way to the throne, so the
climactic murder of the Lancastrian
King is arguably the culmination of
long and careful thought on Richard's
part, and the only surprise is how close
it is to the forefront of his consciousness, prompting him to act immediately when the opportunity presents
itself. The particular circumstances of
Henry's murder are also invented. Hall
writes simply that 'Poore kyng Henry
the sixte, a litle before depriued of his
realme, and Imperiall Croune, was
now in the Tower of London, spoyled
of his life, and all worldly felicitie, by
Richard duke of Gloucester (as the
constant fame ranne) which, to thin-
tent that king Edward his brother,
should be clere out of all secret suspicion of sodain inuasion, murthered the
said kyng with a dagger' (303;
Holinshed, 324).

0.1–2 O has 'Enter *Gloster* to king *Henry*
in the Tower.' F's Lieutenant is not in
O; he has no lines and is dismissed

90 SD] *O; Exit. F*   **5.6]** *Capell*   0.2 *Tower*] *O subst.*

RICHARD OF GLOUCESTER

Good day, my lord. What, at your book so hard?

KING HENRY

Ay, my good lord. 'My lord' I should say, rather.

'Tis sin to flatter; 'good' was little better.

'Good Gloucester' and 'good devil' were alike,

And both preposterous. Therefore, not 'good lord'.   5

RICHARD OF GLOUCESTER

Sirrah, leave us to ourselves. We must confer.

                              [*Exit Lieutenant.*]

KING HENRY

So flies the reckless shepherd from the wolf;

So first the harmless sheep doth yield his fleece

And next his throat unto the butcher's knife.

What scene of death hath Roscius now to act?   10

RICHARD OF GLOUCESTER

Suspicion always haunts the guilty mind;

The thief doth fear each bush an officer.

KING HENRY

The bird that hath been limed in a bush

---

almost at once by Richard. His purpose may be to signal the imagined location with a distinctive costume. F's '*on the walls*' may suggest that only the Lieutenant is in the upper acting area, overlooking Richard and Henry on the main stage, since it is unlikely that such a climactic and dramatic action would be performed '*on the walls*' with nothing else happening below (GWW).

1 **at your book** an implicit SD: Henry is reading, and it may be a prayer book, as at 3.1.12 SD. See *OED book sb.* 5b and Fig. 13.

3 **little better** little better than flattery

5 **preposterous** in the literal Latin sense of 'front to back', hence inverted, perverse. On the devil and preposterous-

ness, in this sense, see Clark, 43–93.

6 **Sirrah** form of address used to a social inferior. Emphasis on first syllable.
  leave us an implicit SD, dismissing the Lieutenant

7 **reckless** careless, heedless

10 **Roscius** Roman actor, identified by Elizabethan dramatists with tragedy (as in *Ham* 2.2.390–1), though Cooper knew better: 'a player in comedies, whom for his excellencie in pronunciation and gesture, the noble Cicero called his iewell'

11 proverbial: 'Who is guilty suspects everybody' (Tilley, F117)

12 proverbial (Tilley, T112)
  doth ... bush is afraid that each bush is

13–17 'Henry seems to be saying that, being innocent, he does not fear as the

6 SD] *Rowe*

360

With trembling wings misdoubteth every bush.
And I, the hapless male to one sweet bird,   15
Have now the fatal object in my eye
Where my poor young was limed, was caught and
        killed.

RICHARD OF GLOUCESTER

Why, what a peevish fool was that of Crete
That taught his son the office of a fowl!
And yet for all his wings the fool was drowned.   20

KING HENRY

I, Daedalus; my poor boy, Icarus;
Thy father, Minos, that denied our course;
The sun that seared the wings of my sweet boy,
Thy brother Edward; and thyself, the sea,
Whose envious gulf did swallow up his life.   25
Ah, kill me with thy weapon, not with words!
My breast can better brook thy dagger's point
Than can my ears that tragic history.
But wherefore dost thou come? Is't for my life?

thief does; nor does he fear every bush, since he has "the fatal object" before him' (Ard²).

13 **limed** limèd, i.e. caught with birdlime (sticky substance for catching small birds) (*OED sb.*¹ 1a). Proverbial: 'Birds once limed fear all bushes' (Tilley, B394). Cf. *2H6* 1.3.89, 2.4.54, 3.3.16.

14 **misdoubteth** fears, suspects

15 **hapless** unfortunate, unlucky
male to begetter of (as opposed to breeder; cf. 2.1.42)
one sweet bird Prince Edward. Henry has either heard of his son's murder in less time than Richard has taken to reach him, or he somehow guesses it from Richard's demeanour. In any case, Richard's telling Henry of Prince Edward's death (34) parallels Margaret's boasting of Rutland's mur-

der as she torments York before killing him in 1.4.

18–20 The *peevish fool* is Daedalus, who taught his son Icarus to fly, so he could escape the Cretan labyrinth. Icarus flew too near the sun and melted the wax that attached the feathers to his body. Henry explicates the allusion in 21–5.
fool . . . fowl . . . fool pronounced similarly in Elizabethan English (Cercignani, 198)

18 **peevish** silly, foolish (*OED a.*1)

19 **office** function (*OED sb.* 3b)

23 **sun** Edward's heraldic symbol. See 2.1.39–40.

25 **envious** malicious, spiteful (*OED a.* 2), possibly echoing Hall (see 49–56n.)
gulf whirlpool (*OED* 3). Cf. *H5* 2.4.10.

RICHARD OF GLOUCESTER

    Think'st thou I am an executioner?   30

KING HENRY

    A persecutor I am sure thou art;

    If murdering innocents be executing,

    Why then, thou art an executioner.

RICHARD OF GLOUCESTER

    Thy son I killed for his presumption.

KING HENRY

    Hadst thou been killed when first thou didst presume   35

    Thou hadst not lived to kill a son of mine.

    And thus I prophesy – that many a thousand

    Which now mistrust no parcel of my fear,

    And many an old man's sigh, and many a widow's,

    And many an orphan's water-standing eye,   40

    Men for their sons, wives for their husbands,

    Orphans for their parents' timeless death,

    Shall rue the hour that ever thou wast born.

    The owl shrieked at thy birth, an evil sign;

    The night-crow cried, aboding luckless time;   45

    Dogs howled; and hideous tempests shook down trees;

    The raven rooked her on the chimney's top;

    And chatt'ring pies in dismal discords sung.

    Thy mother felt more than a mother's pain,

    And yet brought forth less than a mother's hope: 50

---

34 **presumption** four syllables
38 'which now have no inkling of what I fear'
    mistrust suspect (*OED v.* 3a)
    parcel small part
40 **water-standing eye** eye with water standing in it, i.e. tearful
42 **timeless** untimely, premature
43 **rue** regret
44 **owl shrieked** See 2.6.56.
45 **aboding** foreboding, ominous

47 **rooked** rucked, i.e. crouched, huddled (*OED* ruck *v.*[1])
    her herself
48 **pies** magpies
49–56 Henry's description of Richard is taken from Hall, who in turn borrowed directly from Thomas More's *History of King Richard the Third* (1513–18): 'he was litle of stature, eiuill featured of limnes, croke backed, the left shulder muche higher than the righte,

46 tempests] *O;* Tempest *F*

To wit, an undigested and deformed lump,
Not like the fruit of such a goodly tree.
Teeth hadst thou in thy head when thou wast born
To signify thou cam'st to bite the world.
And if the rest be true, which I have heard,   55
Thou cam'st –

RICHARD OF GLOUCESTER
I'll hear no more! Die, prophet, in thy speech,
   Stabs him.
For this amongst the rest was I ordained.

KING HENRY
Ay, and for much more slaughter after this.
O God, forgive my sins and pardon thee.   *Dies.*   60

RICHARD OF GLOUCESTER
What? Will the aspiring blood of Lancaster
Sink in the ground? I thought it would have mounted.
See how my sword weeps for the poor King's death.
O may such purple tears be alway shed
From those that wish the downfall of our house.   65
If any spark of life be yet remaining,
Down, down to hell, and say I sent thee thither!
   Stabs him again.

harde fauoured of visage . . . . He was
malicious, wrothfull and enuious, and
as it is reported, his mother the duches had muche a dooe in her trauaill,
that she could not be deliuered of hym
vncut, and that he came into the
worlde the fete forwarde, as menne bee
borne outwarde, and as the fame
ranne, not vntothed' (342–3).
51 **To wit** namely
undigested . . . lump Ard² suggests
an echo of Ovid's description of chaos
as *rudis indigestaque moles* (*Meta-morphoses*, 1.7). Cf. Richard's comparison of himself to 'a chaos or an
unlicked bear whelp' at 3.2.161–2.
deformed deformèd

56 Richard stabs Henry just as he seems
about to say the line that Richard concludes at 71. O has 'Thou camst into
the world'.
57 **prophet** alluding to the idea that
dying men speak the truth; cf. *R2*
2.1.31 (RP).
58 **was I ordained** by Providence.
Richard may allude sardonically to
Henry's prophecy (37–43), or he may
frankly acknowledge the part he plays,
like that of the devil, in the divine
scheme. Cf. 78.
63 **my sword weeps** Blood may be dripping from his sword. Cf. 1.1.13–14.
64 **purple tears** The same phrase
describes drops of blood in *VA* 1054.

51 undigested] *(indigested)*   57] *Pope; F lines* more: / speech, /

I that have neither pity, love nor fear.
Indeed, 'tis true that Henry told me of,
For I have often heard my mother say   70
I came into the world with my legs forward.
Had I not reason, think ye, to make haste,
And seek their ruin that usurped our right?
The midwife wondered and the women cried,
'O, Jesus bless us, he is born with teeth!'   75
And so I was, which plainly signified
That I should snarl, and bite and play the dog.
Then, since the heavens have shaped my body so,
Let hell make crook'd my mind to answer it.
I have no brother; I am like no brother.   80
And this word 'love', which greybeards call divine,
Be resident in men like one another
And not in me: I am myself alone.
Clarence, beware: thou keep'st me from the light,
But I will sort a pitchy day for thee;   85
For I will buzz abroad such prophecies
That Edward shall be fearful of his life;
And then to purge his fear, I'll be thy death.
King Henry and the Prince his son are gone;
Clarence, thy turn is next, and then the rest,   90
Counting myself but bad till I be best.
I'll throw thy body in another room,
And triumph, Henry, in thy day of doom!

Exit [with the body].

---

83 **I . . . alone** See p. 79.
84–8 Richard has already threatened his
  brother at 3.2.130. He now outlines the
  plot that he puts into effect in *R3*
  1.1–4.
85 **sort** choose, select (*OED v.*[1] 14a). Cf.
  1H6 2.3.26.
  pitchy dark, black (like pitch)

87 **of** for. See Abbott, 174, for *of* meaning
  'regards' or 'concerning'.
91 **bad . . . best** proverbial: 'Bad is the
  best' (Dent, B316)
92 **throw . . . room** On removal of a body
  to another room, cf. *R3* 1.4.157–8 and
  Ham 3.4.219.

84 keep'st] (keept'st) 93 SD *with the body*] *Capell subst.*

[5.7]   *Flourish. Enter* KING [EDWARD],
QUEEN [ELIZABETH], [GEORGE OF] CLARENCE,
RICHARD [OF GLOUCESTER], HASTINGS,
Nurse [with infant Prince Edward,] and Attendants.

KING EDWARD

Once more we sit in England's royal throne,
Repurchased with the blood of enemies.
What valiant foemen like to autumn's corn
Have we mowed down in tops of all their pride!
Three Dukes of Somerset, threefold renowned   5
For hardy and undoubted champions;
Two Cliffords, as the father and the son;
And two Northumberlands, two braver men
Ne'er spurred their coursers at the trumpet's sound.
With them the two brave bears, Warwick and Montague,   10
That in their chains fettered the kingly lion

5.7 The scene is invented to show Richard as a sinister threat to his own family, now that he has just dispatched the last hopes of the Lancastrians in the previous two scenes. In 4.4 Queen Elizabeth is pregnant when she takes sanctuary, following Warwick's recent capture of Edward. Her newborn son is now presented as the hope of the Yorkists, even as his future murderer pretends to adore him. The hollow triumph of the Yorkists is complemented by a bitter reference to arrangements for Margaret's exile (37–41) that did not actually take place for another four years. Despite this apparent tying up of loose ends where Margaret is concerned, Shakespeare decided to bring her back again unhistorically and posthumously as a Senecan chorus of revenge at Edward's court in *R3* 1.3 and 4.4.

0.2 QUEEN This is the only time in F when this character is given the appropriate title in SDs or SPs.

0.4 O specifies 'with the young prince' following 'Nurse'.

4 **in tops** at the top or height

5 **Three . . . Somerset** See List of Roles, 31n. and 32n.

7 **Two Cliffords** Only the younger Clifford appears in *3H6*. His father is killed at the first battle of St Albans in *2H6* 5.1–5.2.
as introducing instances in exemplification or illustration of a general designation, 'namely', 'for example' (*OED adv.* 26). Cf. *TN* 1.5.242.

8 **two Northumberlands** See List of Roles, 35n.

9 **coursers** war horses

10 **bears** Warwick's heraldic symbol was 'The rampant bear chained to the ragged staff' (*2H6* 5.1.203).

11 **fettered** tied with fetters, chained
kingly lion The lion is the royal

5.7] *Capell*   0.2 ELIZABETH] *O*   0.4 SD *with . . . Edward*] *O* (with the young prince)   5 renowned]
Q3; renowmd *O*; Renowne *F*

And made the forest tremble when they roared.
Thus have we swept suspicion from our seat
And made our footstool of security.
Come hither, Bess, and let me kiss my boy.   15
Young Ned, for thee, thine uncles and myself
Have in our armours watched the winter's night,
Went all afoot in summer's scalding heat,
That thou mightst repossess the crown in peace,
And of our labours thou shalt reap the gain.   20

RICHARD OF GLOUCESTER [*aside*]

I'll blast his harvest, if your head were laid;
For yet I am not looked on in the world.
This shoulder was ordained so thick to heave,
And heave it shall some weight or break my back.
Work thou the way and that shalt execute.   25

KING EDWARD

Clarence and Gloucester, love my lovely queen,
And kiss your princely nephew, brothers both.

---

symbol (cf. 5.2.13). Edward may refer
to Warwick's imprisonment of both
Henry and himself, or more broadly to
Warwick's reputation as kingmaker.

14 **made . . . security** 'made security our
footstool'
security Edward clearly means 'the
condition of being protected from or
not exposed to danger' (*OED* 1), but
Richard's presence and ominous aside
(21–5) gives the word an ironic double
sense, 'culpable absence of anxiety,
carelessness' (*OED* 3). Cf. *Mac*
3.5.32–3.

15 **my boy** the future Edward V, who
lived from 1471 to 1483

16–20 Edward omits to mention
Clarence's defection to Lancaster, and,
of course, he does not know of the
treachery Richard has expressed earlier and reiterates immediately after this
speech.

21 **blast** blight
your . . . laid (1) the head on your
shoulders were cut off; (2) the top of a
stalk containing mature grain were
harvested (continuing the harvesting
metaphor in 20), i.e. 'if you were
mown down'

25 From describing his shoulder in the
third person (23–4), Richard now
switches to familiar direct address, as if
his shoulder were an intimate companion in crime: addressing it as *thou*,
Richard tells it to determine his course
and 'heave . . . some weight' (*that*), i.e.
remove those who stand in his way to
the throne, with 'thou' understood as
the subject of *shalt execute*.
that i.e. heaving some weight off his
back (24)
shalt i.e. thou shalt (still addressing
his shoulder)
execute carry out, effect

16 Young] *F1c* (Yong); Kong *F1u*   21 SD] *Rowe*   25 and] *F1c*; add *F1u*   27 kiss] *F1c* (kis); 'tis *F1u*

GEORGE OF CLARENCE

The duty that I owe unto your majesty
I seal upon the lips of this sweet babe.

QUEEN ELIZABETH

Thanks, noble Clarence; worthy brother, thanks.   30

RICHARD OF GLOUCESTER

And that I love the tree from whence thou sprang'st,
Witness the loving kiss I give the fruit. –
[*aside*] To say the truth, so Judas kissed his master
And cried, 'All hail!', when as he meant all harm.

KING EDWARD

Now am I seated as my soul delights,   35
Having my country's peace and brothers' loves.

GEORGE OF CLARENCE

What will your grace have done with Margaret?
Reynard, her father, to the King of France
Hath pawned the Sicils and Jerusalem,
And hither have they sent it for her ransom.   40

KING EDWARD

Away with her and waft her hence to France.

---

30 SP F assigns the line to Clarence; O, to Elizabeth, as her only line in the scene. Without O's suggestion, the line could equally well be assigned to Edward.

33–4 Hall describes Richard as 'not let-tynge to kisse whom he thought to kill' (343), but Richard himself calls atten-tion to Matthew, 26.49, 'When he came to Iesus, he said, Haile master: and kissed him' (Shaheen, 73).

34 **when as** when. See Abbott, 116.

38–41 taken from Hall, who comments on the fatuity of Margaret's life: 'King Reiner her father raunsomed her with money, which summe (as the French writers afferme) he borowed of kyng Lewes ye xi. and, because he was not of power nor abilitie to repaye so great a

dutie, he solde to the French kyng & his heyres, the kingdomes of Naples and both the Sciciles, wyth the countie of Prouynce . . . After the raunsom payed, she was conueyed in to Fraunce with small honor, which with so great triumphe and honorable enterteyn-ment was with pompe aboue al pryde, receyued in this Realme xxviii. yeres before' (Hall, 301). What Henry VI lost in the form of an unpaid dowry (*2H6* 1.1), Edward IV thus gains in the form of Margaret's ransom: her com-ing to England involved financial loss for the crown, while her departure brought it gain.

38 **Reynard** See List of Roles, 28n.

39 **the Sicils** See 1.4.122n.

30 SP QUEEN ELIZABETH] *O (subst.); Cla. F*   Thanks] *O;* Thanke *F*   33 SD] *Rowe*

367

And now what rests but that we spend the time
With stately triumphs, mirthful comic shows,
Such as befits the pleasure of the court.
Sound drums and trumpets! Farewell, sour annoy,   45
For here I hope begins our lasting joy.

> *[Drums and trumpets.] Exeunt omnes.*

42 **rests** remains
45 **Sound . . . trumpets!** The line indi-
    cates that drums and a flourish would
    accompany the final clearing of the
    stage.

42 rests] *F1c;* tests *F1u*   46 SD *Drums and trumpets*] *this edn; Flourish / Capell*

APPENDIX 1

THE OCTAVO (1595)

Reproduced in reduced photographic facsimile from Malone[a] 876 by courtesy of the Bodleian Library, Oxford.

The top-of-page references indicate the corresponding act, scene and line reference in the present edition, and the corresponding through line numbers (TLN) in *The First Folio of Shakespeare: The Norton Facsimile*, prepared by Charlton Hinman (New York, London, 2nd edn, 1996)

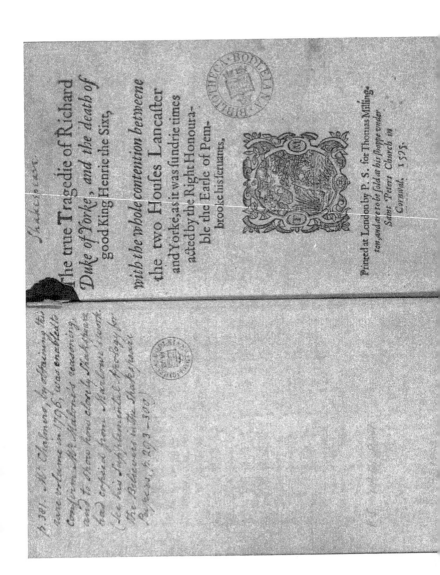

Shakespeare

The true Tragedie of Richard Duke of Yorke, and the death of good King Henrie the Sixt,

with the whole contention betweene the two Houses Lancaster and Yorke, as it was sundrie times acted by the Right Honoura- ble the Earle of Pem- brooke his seruants.

Printed at London by P. S. for Thomas Milling- ton, and are to be solde at his shoppe vnder Saint Peters Church in Cornwal. 1595.

p. 301. Mr Chalmers, by straining this same volume in 1796, was enabled to confirm Mr Malone's reasoning, and to shew how closely Shakspeare had copied from Marlowe's work. (See his Supplemental Apology for the Believers in the Shakspeare Papers, p. 293-300)

The true Tragedie of Richard Duke
of *Yorke*, and the good King
Henry the Sixt.

Enter *Richard Duke* of *Yorke*, The Earle of *Warwicke*,
The *Duke* of *Norffolke*, *Marquis Montague*, *Edward*
Earle of *March*, *Crookeback Richard*, and the yong *Earle*
of *Rutland* with Drumme and Souldiers, with white Roses in their hats.

Warwke.

Wonder how the king escapt our hands,
Yorke. Whilst we pursuede the horssemen
of the North,
He slilie stole awaie and left his men:
Whereat the great Lord of Northum-
land,
Whose warlike eares could neuer brooke retrait,
Chargde our maine battels front, and there with him
Lord *Stafford* and Lord *Clifford* all abrest (slaine,
Brake in and were by the hands o common Souldiers
Edw. Lord *Staffords* father Duke of *Buckingham,*
Is either slaine or wounded dangerouslie,

A 2   I clest

The Tragedie of Richard D. of

I cleft his Beuer with a downe right blow:
Father that this is true behold his bloud.
Mont. And brother heeres the Earle of *Wiltshires*
Bloud, whom I encountred as the battailes ioind.
Rich. Speake thou for me and tell them what I did.
York. What is your grace dead my L. of *Sommerfet?*
Norf. Such hope haue all the line of *Iohn* of *Gaunt.*
Rich. Thus doe I hope to shape king *Henries* head.
War. And so do I victorious prince of *Yorke;*
Before I see thee seated in that throne
Which now the house of *Lancaster* vsurpes,
I vow by heauens these eies shal neuer close.
This is the pallace of that fearefull king,
And that the regall chaire? Possessie it *Yorke:*
For this is thine and nocking *Henries* heires.
Tork. Assist me then sweet *Warwike,* and I will
For hither are we broken in by force.
Norf. Weele all assist thee, and he that flies shall die.
Tork. I thanks gentle *Norffolke,* Staie by me my Lords,
and souldiers staie you heere and lodge this night;
War. And when the king comes offer him no
Violence, vnlesse he seeke to put vs out by force.
Rich. Arm'de as we be, lets staie within this house?
War. The bloudie parliment shall this be calde,
Vnlesse *Plantaginet* Duke of *Yorke* be king
And bashfull *Henrie* be depolde, whose cowardise
Hath made vs by-words to our enemies.
Tork. Then leaue me not my Lords : for now I meane
To take possession of my right.

War.

Yorkes, and Henrie the sixt.

War. Neither the king, nor him that loues him best,
The proudest he that holds vp *Lancaster*
Dares stirre a wing, if *Warwike* shake his bels.
Ile plant *Plantagenet* : and root him out who dares?
Resolue thee *Richard:* Claime the English crowne.

Enter king Henrie the sixt, with the Duke of Exceter,
The Earle of Northumberland, the Earle of Westmerland
and Clifford, the Earle of Cumberland, with red Roses in
their hats.

King. Looke Lordings where the sturdy rebel sits,
Euen in the chaire of state : belike he meanes
Backt by the power of *Warwike* that false peere,
To aspire vnto the crowne, and raigne as king.
Earle of *Northumberland,* he slew thy father,
And thine *Clifford* : and you both haue vow'd reuenge,
On him, his sonnes, his fauorites, and his friends.
Northu. And if I be not, heauens be reuengd on me.
Clif. The hope thereof, makes *Clifford* mourn in steel.
West. What? shall we suffer this, lets pull him downe.
My hart for anger breakes, I cannot speake.
King. Be patient gentle Earle of *Westmerland.*
Clif. Patience is for pultroons such as he
He durst not sit there, had your father liu'd?
My gratious Lord : here in the Parlement,
Let vs assaile the familie of *Yorke.*
North. Well hast thou spoken cosen, be it fo.
King. O know you not the Cittie fauours them,

A 3. And

The Tragedie of Richard D. of

And they haue troopes of souldiers at their becke?
Exet. But when the D. is slaine, theile quicklie slie.
King. Far be it from the thoughts of *Henries* hart,
To make a shambles of the parlement house,
Cosen of *Exeter*, words, frownes, and threats,
Shall be the warres that *Henrie* meanes to vse.
Thou factious duke of *Yorke*, descend my throne,
I am thy soueraigne.
  Yorke. Thou art deceiu'd: I am thine.   (Yorke.
  Exet. For shame come downe, he made the D. of
  Yorke. T'was mine inheritance as the kingdome is.
  Exet. Thy father was a traytor to the crowne.
  War. Exeter thou art a traitor to the crowne,
In following this vsurping *Henry*.
  Clif. Whom should he follow but his naturall king.
  War. True *Clif.* and that is *Richard* Duke of *Yorke.*
  King. And shall I stande while thou sittest in my
    throne?
  Yorke. Content thy selfe it must and shall be so.
  Wa. Be Duke of *Lancaster*, let him be King.
  West. Why? he is both king & Duke of *Lancaster,*
And that the Earle of *Westmerland* shall maintaine.
  War. And *warwike* shall disproue it. You forget
That we are those that chaste you from the field
And slew your father, and with colours spred,
Marcht through the Citie to the pallas gates.
  Nor. No *Warwike* I remember it to my griefe,
And by his soule thou and thy house shall rewit.
  West. *Plantagenet* of office and of thy sonnes,
    Thy

Yorke, and Henrie the sixt.

Thy kinsmen and thy friendes, Ile haue more liues,
Then drops of bloud were in my fathers vaines.
  Clif. Vrge it no more, least in reuenge thereof,
I send thee *Warwike* such a messenger,
As shall reuenge his death before I stirre.
  War. Poore *Clifford*, how I skorn thy worthles threats
  Yorke. Wil ye we shew our title to the crowne,
Or else our words shall pleadit in the field?
  King. What title hast thou traitor to the Crowne?
Thy father was as thou art Duke of *Yorke,*
Thy grandfather *Roger Mortimer* earle of *March,*
I am the sonne of *Henrie* the fift who tamde the *French*,
And made the Dolphin stoope, and seaz'd vpon their
Townes and prouinces.
  War. Talke not of *France* since thou hadst lost it all
  King. The Lord protector lost it and not I,
When I was crownd I was but nine months old.
  Rich. You are olde enough now and yet me thinks
    you lose,
Father teare the Crowne from the Vsurpers head.
  Edw. Do so sweet father, set it on your head.
  Mont. Good brother as thou louest & honorst armes,
Lets fight it out and not stand cauilling thus.
  Rich. Sound drums and trumpets & the king will fly.
  York. Peace sonnes:
  Northum. Peace thou and giue king *Henry* leaue to
    speake.   (met
  King. Ah *Plantagenet*, why seekest thou to depose
Are we not both both *Plantagenets* by birth,
    And

A 4

The Tragedie of Richard D. of Yorke

And from two brothers lineallie difcent?
Suppofe by right and equitie thou be king,
Thinkft thou that I will leaue my kinglie feate
Wherein my father and my grandfire fat?
No, firft fhall warre vnpeople this my realme,
I and our colours often borne in *France*,
And now in *England* to our harts great forrow
Shall be my winding fheete, why faint you Lords?
My titles better farre than his,

War. Proue it *Henrie* and thou fhalt be king?

King. Why *Henrie* the fourth by conqueft got the
   Crowne.

York. T'was by rebellion gainft his foueraigne,

King. I know not what to faie my titles weake,
Tell me maie not a king adopt an heire?

War. What then?

King. Then am I lawfull king. For *Richard*
The fecond in the view of manie Lords
Refignde the Crowne to *Henrie* the fourth,
Whofe heire my Father was, and I am his.

York. I tell thee he rofe againft him being his
Soueraigne, & made him to refigne the crowne perforce,

War. Suppofe my Lord he did it vnconftrainde,
Thinke you that were preiudiciall to the Crowne?

Exet. No for he could not fo refigne the Crowne,
But that the next heire muft fucceed and raigne,

King. Art thou againft vs, Duke of *Exeter*?

Exet. His is the right, and therefore pardon me.

King. All will reuolt from me and turne to him.
   Nor-

Yorke, and Henrie the fixt.

Northum. *Plantagenet* for all the claime thou laift,
Thinke not king *Henry* fhall be thus depofde?

War. Depofde he fhall be in defpight of thee.

North. Tufh *Warwike*, Thou art deceiued ? 'tis not thy
Southerne powers of *Effex*, *Suffolke*, *Norffolke*, and of
Kent that makes thee thus prefumpuous and proud,
Can fet the Duke vp in defpight of me.

Cliff. King *Henrie* be thy title right or wrong
Lord *Clifford* vowes to fight in thy defence.
Maie that ground gape and fwallow me aliue,
Where I do kneele to him that flew my father.

King. O *Clifford* how thy words reuiue my foule,

York. *Henry* of *Lancafter* refigne thy crowne,
What mutter you? or what confpire you Lords?

War. Doe right vnto this princelie Duke of *Yorke*,
Or I will fill the houfe with armed men,

   Enter Souldiers.

And ouer the chaire of state where now he fits,
Wright vp his title with thy vfurping blood.

King. O *Warwike*, heare me fpeake.
Let me but raigne in quiet whileft I liue.

York. Confirme the crowne to me and to mine heires,
And thou fhalt raigne in quiet whilft thou liuft.

King. Conuey the fouldiers hence, and then I will,

War. Captaine conduct them into *Tuthill* fieldes,

Clif. What wrong is this vnto the Prince your fone?

War. What good is this for *England* and himfelfe?

Northam. Bafe, fearefull, and defpairing *Henry*.

Clif. How haft thou wrong'd both thy felfe and vs?
   Weft.

The Tragedie of Richard D. of

Warw. I cannot staie to heare these Articles. *Exit.*

Clif. Nor I. Come cosen lets go tell the Queene.

Northum. Be thou a praie vnto the houfe of *Yorke*,
And die in bands for this vnkingly deed.

Clif. In dreadfull warre maist thou be overcome, *Exit.*
Or liue in peace abandon'd and despifde. *Exit.*

Exet. They seeke reuenge, and therefore will not
yeeld my Lord.

King. Ah *Exeter*?

War. Why shoulld you sigh my Lord?

King. Not for my felfe Lord *Warwike*, but my fonne,
Whom I vnnaturallie shall disinherit.
But be it as it maie: I heere intaile the Crowne
To thee and to thine heires, conditionallie,
That heere thou take thine oath to ceafe these ciuill
Broiles, and whilft I liue to honour me as thy king and
Soueraigne.

York. That oath I willinglie take and will performe.

War. Long liue king *Henry*, *Plantagenet* embrace
him?

King. And long liue thou and all thy forward fonnes.

Yorke. Now *Yorke* and *Lancaster* are reconcilde. *Exit.*

Exet. Accurft be he that feekes to make them foes.

Sound Trumpets.

Tork. My Lord Ile take my leaue, for Ile to *Wakefield*
To my castell. *Exit Yorke and his sonnes.*

War. And Ile keepe *London* with my fouldiers. *Exit.*

Norf. And Ile to *Norffolke* with my followers. *Exit.*

Mont. And I to the fea from whence I came. *Exit*

Enter

Yorke, and Henrie the fixt.

Enter the *Queene* and the *Prince.*

Exet. My Lord here comes the Queen, Ile fteale away.

King. And fo will I.

Queene. Naie ftaie, or elfe Ile follow thee.

King. Be patient gentle *Queene*, and then Ile ftaie.

Que. What patience can there? ah timerous man,
Thou haft vndoone thy felfe, thy fonne, and me,
And giuen our rights vnto the houfe of *Yorke*.
Art thou a king and wilt be forft to yeeld?
Had I beene there, the fouldiers fhould haue roft
Me on their launces poins before I would haue
Granted to their wils. The Duke is made
Protector of the land : Sterne *Fawconbridge*
Commands the narrow feas. And thinkft thou then
To fleepe fecure? I heere diuorce me *Henry*
From thy bed, vntill that Act of Parlement
Be recalde, wherein thou yeeldest to the houfe of *Yorke*,
The Northen Lords that haue forfworne thy colours,
Will follow mine if once they fee them fpred,
And fpread they fhall vnto thy deepe difgrace.
Come fonne, lets awaie and leaue him heere alone.

King. Staie gentle *Margaret*, and heere me fpeake.

Queene. Thou haft fpoke too much already, therefore be ftill.

King. Gentle fonne *Edwarde*, wilt thou ftaie with me?

Que. I, to be murdred by his enimies. *Exit.*

Prin. When I returne with victorie from the field,
Ile fee your Grace, till then Ile follow her. *Exit.*

King. Poore *Queene*, her loue to me and to the prince

Her

The Tragedie of Richard D. of

Her fonne,
Makes hir in fine thus forget hir felfe.
Reuenged maie fhe be on that a curfed Duke,
Come cofen of *Exeter*, ftaie thou here,
For *Clifford* and thofe Northern Lords be gone
I feare towards *Wakefield* to diffurbe the Duke.

Enter *Edward* and *Richard*, and *Montague*.
Edw. Brother, and cofen *Montague*, giue mee leaue to
      fpeake,
Rich. Nay, I can better plaie the Orator.
Mont. But I haue reafons ftrong and forceable.

            Enter the Duke of *Yorke*.
York. Howe nowe fonnes what a iarre among'ft you
felues?
Rich. No father, but a fweete contention , about that
which concernes your felfe and vs, The crowne of Eng-
land father.
York. The crowne boy, why *Henrie* yet aliue,
And I haue fworne that he fhall raigne in quiet till
His death.
Edw. But I would breake an hundred othes to raigne
one yeare.
Rich. And fir pleafe your grace to giue me leaue,
Ile fhew your grace the waie to faue your oath,
And difpoffeffe King *Henrie* from the crowne.
Yorke. I pray the *Dicke* let me heare thy deuife.
Rich. Then thus my Lord. An oath is of no moment
                                                    Being

Yorke, and Henrie the fixt.

Being not I wone before a lawfull magiftrate.
Henry is none but doth vfurpe your right,
And yet your grace ftands bound to him by oath,
Then noble father refolue your felfe,
And once more claime the crowne,
Yorke. I faift thou fo boie, why then it fhall be fo.
I am refolude to winne the crowne, or die.
Edward, thou fhalt to *Edmund Brooke* Lord *Cobham*,
With whom the *Kentifhmen* will willingly rife:
Thou cofen *Montague*, fhalt to *Norffolke* ftraight,
And bid the Duke to mufter vp his fouldiers,
And come to me to *Wakefield* prefentlie.
And *Richard* thou to *London* ftrait fhalt poft,
And bid *Richard Neuill* Earle of *Warwie*
To leaue the cittie, and with his men of warre,
To meete me at Saint *Albons* ten daies hence.
My felfe heere in *Sandall* caftell will prouide
Both men and monie to furder our attempts.
Now, what newes?   Enter a Meffenger.
Mef. My Lord, the *Queene* with thirtie thoufand men,
Accompanied with the Earles of *Cumberland*,
Northumberland and *Weftmerland* , and others of the
Houfe of *Lancafter*, are marching towards *Wakefield*,
To befiedge you in your caftell heere.
      Enter fir *Iohn* and fir *Hugh Mortimer*.
Yorke. A Gods name, let them come. Cofen *Montine*
gue poft you hence: and bois ftaie you with me.
Sir *Iohn* and fir *Hugh Mortimers* mine vncles,
                                                    You

Your welcome to Sandall in as happie houre,
The armie of the Queene meanes to beleger vs.
Sir *Iohn.* Shee shall not neede my Lorde, wee le meete
      herin the field.
Yorke. What? with fiue thousand souldiers vnckle?
Rich. I Father, with fiue hundred for a need,
A womans generall, what should you feare?
Yorke. Indeed, manie braue battells haue I woon
In *Normandie,* when as the enimie
Hath bin ten to one and why should I now doubt
Of the like successe? I am resolu'd Come lets goe.
Edw. Lets march awaie, I heare their drums.   *Exit.*

Alarms, and then Enter the yong Earle of
Rutland and his Tutor.

Tutor. Oh flie my Lord, lets leaue the Castell,
And flie to *Wakefield* straight.
                                   Enter Clifford.

Rut. O Tutor, looke where bloudie *Clifford* comes,
Clif. Chaplin awaie, thy Preisthood saues thy life,
As for the brat of that accursed Duke
Whose father slew my father, he shall die,
Tutor. Oh *Clifford* spare this tender Lord, least
Heauen reuenge it on thy head: Oh saue his life.
Clif. Soldiers awaie and drag him hence perforce:
Awaie with the villaine,   *Exit the Chaplein.*
How now, what dead alreadie? or is it feare that
Makes him close his eies? Ile open them.
Rut. So lookes the peut vp Lion on the lambe,
                                              And

And so he walkes insulting ouer his praie,
And so he turnes againe to rend his limmes in sunder,
Oh *Clifford,* kill me with thy sword, and
Not with such a cruell threatning looke,
I am too meane a subiect for thy wrath,
Be thou reuengde on men, and let me liue.
Clif. In vaine thou speakest poore boy: my fathers
Bloud hath stopt the passage where thy wordes shoulde
enter.
Rut. Then let my fathers blood ope it againe? he is a
Man, and *Clifford* cope with him.
Clif. Had I thy brethren here, their liues and thine
Were not reuenge sufficient for me.
Or should I dig vp thy forefathers graues,
And hang their rotten coffins vp in chaines,
It could not slake mine ire, nor ease my hart,
The sight of anie of the house of *Yorke,*
Is as a furie to torment my soule,
Therefore till I root out that cursed line
And leaue not one on earth, Ile liue in hell therefore,
Rut. Oh let me praie, before I take my death,
To thee I praie: Sweet *Clifford* pittie me.
Clif. I such pittie as my rapiers point affords.
Rut. I neuer did thee hurt, wherefore wilt thou kill
mee?
Clif. Thy father hath.
Rut. But twas ere I was borne:
Thou hast one sonne, for his sake pittie me,
Least in reuenge thereof, sith God is iust,

He s

The Tragedie of Richard D. of Yorke

He be as miserable slaine as I.
Oh, let me liue in prison all my daies,
And when I giue occasion of offence,
Then let me die, for now thou hast no cause.
Clif. No cause? Thy Father slew my father, therefore
Die.
Plantagenet I come *Plantagenet,*
And this thy sonnes bloud cleauing to my blade,
Shall rust vpon my weapon, till thy bloud
Congeald with his, doe make me wipe off both.   *Exit.*
Alarmes. Enter the Duke of Yorke solus.
Yor. Ah *Yorke,* post to thy castell, saue thy life,
The goale is lost thou house of *Lancaster,*
Thrise happie chance is for thee and thine,
That the rauen abridge my daies and eals me hence,
But God knowes what chance hath beside my sonnes?
But this I know they haue demean'd themselues,
Like men borne to renowne by life or death:
Three times this daie came *Richard* to my sight,
And cried courage Father: Victorie or death.
And twise so oft came *Edward* to my view,
With purple Faulchen painted to the hilts,
In bloud of those whom he had slaughtered.
Oh harke, I heare the drums: No waie to flie:
No waie to saue my life: And heere I staie:
And heere my life must end.

Enter the Queene, Clifford, Northumberland,
and souldiers.
Come

Yorke, and Henrie the sixt.

Come bloudie *Clifford,* rough *Northumberland,*
I dare your quenchlesse furie to more bloud:
This is the But, and this abides your shot.
Northum. Yeeld to our mercies proud *Plantagenet,*
Clif. I, to such mercie as his ruthfull arme
With downe right painem lent vnto my father,
Now *Phaeton* hath tumbled from his carre,
And made an euening at the noone tide pricke,
Yor. My ashes like the *Phoenix* maie bring forth
A bird that will reuenge it on you all,
And in that hope I cast mine eies to heauen,
Skorning what ere you can afflict me with:
Why stale you Lords? what, multitudes and feares?
Clif. So cowards fight when they can flie no longer:
So Doues doe pecke the Rauens piercing tallents:
So desperate theeues all hopelesse of their liues,
Breath out inuectiues gainst the officers.
Yor. Oh *Clifford,* yet bethinke thee once againe,
And in thy minde oreruu my former time:
And bite thy toung that slaunderst him with cowardise,
Whose verie looke hath made thee quake ere this,
Clif. I will not bandie with thee word for word,
But buckle with thee blowes twise two for one.
Queene. Hold valiant *Clifford,* for a thousand causes,
I would prolong the traitors life a while.
Wrath makes him death, speake thou *Northumberland.*
Nor. Hold *Clifford,* doe not honour him so much,
To pricke thy finger though no wound his haire:
What valure were it when a curre doth grin,
For one to thrust his hand betweene his teeth,
When he might spurne him with his foote awaie?
B

The Tragedie of Richard D. of

'Tis warres prise to take all aduantages,
And ten to one, is no impeach in warres,
   Fight and take him.
Cliff. I, I, so thriues the Woodcocke with the gin.
North. So doth the cunnie struggle with the net.
Yorke. So triumphs theeues vpon their conquered
Bootie: So true men yeeld by robbers ouermatcht:
North. What will your grace haue done with him?
Queen. Braue warriors *Clifford* & *Northumberland*
Come make him stand vpon this molehill here,
That aimde at mountaines with outstretched arme,
And parted but the shaddow with his hand,
Was it your that reuelde in our Parlement,
And made a prechment of your high descent?
Where are your messe of sonnes to backe you now?
The wanton *Edward*, and the lustie *George*?
Or where is that valiant *Crookbacke* prodegie?
Dickey your boy, that with his grumbling voice,
Was wont to cheare his Dad in mutinies?
Or among'st the rest, where is your darling *Rutland*?
Looke *Yorke*, I dipt this napkin in the bloud,
That valiant *Clifford* with his rapiers point,
Made issue from the bosome of thy boy,
And if thine eies can water for his death,
I giue thee this to drie thy cheeks withall,
Alas poore *Yorke*? But that I hate thee much,
I should lament thy miserable state?
I prethee greeue to make me merrie *Yorke*?
Stamp, raue and fret, that I maie sing and dance.
What, hath thy fierie hart so parcht thine entrails,
That not a teare can fall for *Rutlands* death?

                  Thou

Yorke, and Henrie the sixt.

Thou would'st be fee'de I see to make me sport,
Yorke cannot speake, vnlesse he weare a crowne.
A crowne for *Yorke*? and Lords bow low to him.
So: hold you his hands, whilst I doe set it on:
I, now lookes he like a king?
This is he that tooke king *Henries* chaire,
And this is he was his adopted aire.
But how is it that great *Plantagenet*,
Is crown'd so soone, and broke his holie oath,
As I bethinke me you should not be king,
Till our *Henry* had shooke hands with death,
And will you inpale your head with *Henries* glorie,
And rob his temples of the Diadem
Now in his life againſt your holie oath?
Oh, tis a fault too too vnpardonable.
Off with the crowne, and with the crowne his head,
And whilst we breath, tak'e time to doe him dead.
  Clif. That is my office for my fathers death.
  Queen. Yet stay: & lets here the Orisons he makes,
  Yorke. She wolfe of *Fraunce*, but worse than Wolues of
      France.
Whose tongue more poison'd than the Adders tooth:
How ill beseeming is it in thy sexe,
To triumph like an *Amazonian* trull
Vpon his woes, whom Fortune captiuates?
But that thy face is visard like, vnchanging,
Made impudent by vse of euill deeds:
I would assaie, proud Queene to make thee blush;
To tell thee of whence thou art, from whom deriu'de,
I were shame enough to shame thee, wert thou not
    shamelesse.

        B 2,   Thy

The Tragedie of Richard D. of

Thy father beares the type of king of *Naples*,
Of both the *Sicils* and *Ierusalem*,
Yet not so wealthie as an English Yeoman.
Hath that poore Monarch taught thee to insult?
It needes not, or it bootes thee not proud Queene,
Vnlesse the Adage must be verifide:
That beggers mounted, run thou horse to death.
Tis beautie, that oft makes women proud,
But God he wots thy share thereof is small.
Tis gouernment, that makes them most admirde,
The contrarie doth make thee wondred at.
Tis vertue that makes them seeme deuine,
The want thereof makes thee abhominable.
Thou art as opposite to euerie good,
As the *Antipodes* are vnto vs,
Or as the South to the Septentrion.
Oh Tygers hart wrapt in a womans hide?
How couldst thou draine the life bloud of the childe,
To bid the father wipe his eies withall,
And yet be seene to beare a womans face?
Women are milde, pitifull, and flexible,
Thou indurate, sterne, rough, remorceleſſe.
Bids thou me rage? why now thou hast thy will,
Wouldst haue me weepe? why so thou hast thy wish,
For raging windes blowes vp a storme of teares,
And when the rage alaies the raine begins.
These teares are my sweet *Rutlands* obsequies,
And euerie drop begs vengeance as it fals,
On thee fell *Clifford*, and the falce French woman.
North. Beshrew me but his pitions moue me so,
As hardlie can I checke mine eies from teares.

Yorke.

Yorke, and Henrie the sixt.

York. That face of his the hungrie Cannibals
Could not haue tucht, would not haue staind with bloud
But you are more inhumaine, more inexorable,
O ten times more then Tygers of *Arcadia*.
See ruthleſſe *Queene* a haplesse fathers teares.
This cloth thou dipst in bloud of my sweet boy,
And loe with teares I wash the bloud awaie.
Keepe thou the napkin and go boast of that,
And if thou tell the heauie storie well,
Vpon my soule the hearers will shheed teares,
Ieuen my foes will shheed saft falling teares,
And saie, alas it was a pitteous deed.
Here take the crowne, and with the crowne my curse,
And in thy need such comfort come to thee,
As now I reape at thy two cruell hands.
Hard-harted *Clifford*, take me from the world,
My soule to heauen, my bloud vpon your heads.
North. Had he bin slaughterman of all my kin,
I could not chuse but weepe with him to see,
How inlie anger gripes his hart.
Quee. What weeping ripe, my Lorde *Northumberland?*
Thinke but vpon the wrong he did vs all,
And that will quickle drie your melting tears.
Clif. I heare for my oath, that cares for my faubers death,
Queene. And bears to right our gentle-harted kind.
Yorke. Open thy gates of mercie gratious God,
My soule flies foorth to meet with thee.
Queene. Off with his head and set it on *Yorke* Gates,
So *Yorke* maie ouerlooke the towne of *Yorke*,

Exeunt omnes.

B 3.   Enter

The Tragedie of Richard D. of

Enter *Edward* and *Richard*, with drum
and Souldiers.

Edw. After this dangerous fight and haplesse warre,
How doth my noble Brother *Richard* fare?
Rich. I cannot ioy vntil I be resolu'te,
Where our right valiant father is become,
How often did I see him beare himselfe,
As doth a lion midst a heard of neat,
So fled his enemies our valiant father,
Me thinkes its pride enough to be his sonne.
   Three sunnes appeare in the aire.
Edw. Loe how the morning opes her golden gates,
And takes her faire well of the glorious sun,
Dast I mine eies or do I see three suns?
Rich. Three glorious suns, each one seperated by a racking
Cloud, but seuered in a pale cleere shining skie,
See, see, they ioine, embrace, and seeme to kisse,
As if they vowde some league inuiolate:
Now are they but one lampe, one light, one sun,
In this the heauens doth figure some euent.
Edw. I thinke it cites vs brother to the field,
That we the sonnes of braue *Plantagenet*,
Alreadie each one shining by his meed,
May ioine in one and outpeere the world,
As this the earth, and therefore henceforward,
Ile beare vpon my Targ three faire shining suns.
But what art thou that lookest so heauilie?

Mes. Oh one that was a wofull looker on,
When as the noble Duke of *Yorke* was slaine.

Edw. O speake no more, for I can heare no more.
Rich. Tell on thy tale, for I will heare it all.

                                                    Mes.

Yorke, and Henrie the sixt.

Mes. When as the noble Duke was put to flight,
And then pursude by *Clifford* and the *Queen*,
And manie souldiers moe, who all at once
Let driue at him and forst the Duke to yeeld:
And then they set him on a molehill there,
And crowned the gratious Duke in high despite,
Who then with teares began to waile his fall.
The ruthlesse *Queene* perceiuing he did weepe,
Gaue him a handkercher to wipe his eies,
Dipt in the bloud of sweete yong *Rutland*
By rough *Clifford* slaine: who weeping tooke it vp.
Then during his breft they thrust their bloudy swordes,
Who like a lambe fell at the butchers feete.
Then on the gates of *Yorke* they set his head,
And there it doth remaine the pitteous spectacle
That ere mine eies beheld.

Edw. Sweet Duke of *Yorke* our prop to leane vpon,
Now thou art gone there is no hope for vs:
Now my foules pallace is become a prison,
Oh would she breake from compasse of my breast,
For neuer shall I haue more ioie.

Rich. I cannot weepe, for all my breasts moisture
Scarse serues to quench my furnace burning hart.
I cannot ioie till this white rose be dide,
Euen in the hart bloud of the house of *Lancaster.*
Richard, I bare thy name, and Ile reuenge thy death,
Or die my selfe in seeking of reuenge.

Edw. His name that valiant Duke hath left with thee,
His chaire and Dukedome that remaines for me.
Rich. Nay, if thou be that princely Eagles bird,
Shew thy descent by gazing gainst the sunne.

                                                       B 4

                                                        Fos

The Tragedie of Richard D. of

For chaire, and dukedome, Throne and kingdome faie:
For either that is thine, or else thou wert not his?

Enter the Earle of Warwike, Montague, with
dium, ancient, and souldiers.

War. How now faire Lords: what fare? what
newes abroad?

Rich. Ah *Warwike?* should we report the balefull
Newes, and at each words deliuerance stab poiniardes
In our flesh till all were told, the words would adde
More anguish then the wounds.
Ah valiant Lord the Duke of *Yorke* is slaine.

Edw. Ah *Warwike, Warwike,* that *Plantagenet,*
Which held thee deere: Euen as his soules redemption,
Is by the sterne L. *Clifford* done to death.

War. Ten daies a go I drownd these newes in teares,
And now to adde more measure to your woes,
I come to tell you things since then befalne.
After the bloudie fraie at *Wakefield* fought,
Where your braue father breath'd his latest gaspe,
Tidings as swift as the post could runne,
Was brought me of your losse, and his departure.
I then in London keeper of the *King,*
Mustred my souldiers, gathered flockes of friends,
And verie well appointed as I thought,
Marcht to faint *Albons* to entercept the *Queene,*
Bearing the *King* in my behalfe along,
For by my scoutes I was aduertised,
That she was coming, with a full intent
To dash your late decree in parliament,
Touching king *Henries* heires and your succession.
Short tale to make, we at Saint *Albons* met,

Our

Yorke, and Henrie the sixt.

Our battels ioynd, and both sides fiercelie fought,
But whether twas the coldnesse of the king,
He looktfull gentle on his warlike *Queene,*
That robd my souldiers of their heated spleene,
Or whether twas report of his successe,
Or more then common feare of *Cliffords* rigor,
Who thunders to his captaines bloud and death,
I cannot tell: But to conclude with truth,
Their weapons like to lightnings went and came,
Our souldiers like the night Owles lasie flight,
Or like an idle thresher with a flaile,
Fel gentle downe as if they fauoure their friends.
I cheerd them vp with iustice of the cause,
With promise of hie paie: and great rewardes,
But all in vaine, they had no harts to fight,
Nor we in them no hope to winne the daie,
So that we fled: The king vnto the *Queene,*
Lord *George* your brother, *Norffolke,* and my selfe,
In halt, post halt are come to ioyne with you,
For in the marches here we heard you were,
Making another head to fight againe.

Edw. Thankes gentle *Warwike.*
How farre hence is the Duke with his power?
And when came *George* from *Burgundie* to *Englande?*
War. Some fiue miles off the Duke is with his power,
But as for your brother he was latelie sent
From your kind Aunt, Duches of *Burgundie,*
With aide of souldiers gainst this needfull warre.

Rich. Twas odd belike, when valiant *Warwike* fled,
Oft haue I heard thy praises in pursute,
But ne're till now thy scandall of retire.

War.

The Tragedie of Richard D. of

War. Nor now my selfe and I Richard dost thou heare,
For thou that know that this right hand of mine,
Can plucke the Diadem from faint Henries head,
And wring the awefull scepter from his fift,
Were he as famous and as bold in warre,
As he is fam'de for mildnesse, peace and praier.
Rich. I know it well Lord Warwike blame me not,
T was loue I bare thy glories made me speake.
But in this troublous time, whats to be done?
Shall we go throw a way our coates of steele,
And clad our bodies in blacke mourning gownes,
Numbring our Auemaries with our beades?
Or shall we on the helmets of our foes,
Tell our deuotion with reuengefull armes?
Ffor the last, saie I, and so I Lords.
War. Why therefore Warwike came to find you out,
And therefore comes my brother Montague.
Attend me Lords, the proud insulting Queene,
With Clifford and the haught Northumberland,
And of their feather manie mo proud birdes,
Haue wrought the easie melting king like waxe,
He sware consent to your succession,
His oath inrolled in the Parliament.
But now to London all the crew are gone,
To suffrate his oath or what besides
May make against the house of Lancaster.
Their power I gesse them fifty thousand strong,
Now if the helpe of Norfolke and my selfe,
Can but amount to 48. thousand,
With all the friends that thou braue earle of March,
Among the louing Welshmen canst procure,
  Why

Yorke, and Henrie the sixt.

Why vs, To London will we march amaine,
And once againe bestride our foming steedes,
And once againe crie charge vpon the foe,
But neuer once againe turne backe and flie.
Rich. I, now me thinkes I heare great Warwike speake,
Nere maie the lue to see a sunshine daie,
That cries retire, when Warwike bids him stay.
Edw. Lord Warwike, on thy shoulder will I leane,
And when thou faints, must Edward fall:
Which perill heauen forefend.
War. No longer Earle of March, but Duke of Yorke,
The next degree is Englands royall king:
And king of England shalt thou be proclaimde,
In euery burrough as we passe along,
And he that casts not vp his cap for ioie,
Shall for the offence make forfeit of his head,
King Edward, valiant Richard Montague,
Say we no longer dreaming of renowne,
But forward to effect these resolutions.
          Enter a Messenger.
Mes. The Duke of Norffolke sends you word by me,
The Queene is comming with a puissant power,
And craues your companie for speedie councell.
War. Why then it forts braue Lordes. Lets march a-
way.   Exeunt Omnes.
Enter the King and Queene, Prince Edward, and
        the Northerne Earles, with drum
              and Souldiers.
Quee. Welcome my Lord to this braue town of Yorke,
Yonder is the head of that ambitious enemie,
That sought to be impaled with your crowne.
                    Doth

The Tragedie of Richard D. of

Doth not the obiect please your eie my Lord?
King. Euen as the rockes please them that feare their
   wracke.
Withhold reuenge deare God, tis not my fault,
Nor wittinglie haue I infringde my vow.
Cliff. My gracious Lord, this too much lenitie,
And harmefull pittie must be laid aside,
To whom do I yees cast their gentle lookes?
Nor to the beast that would vsurpe his den.
Whose hand is that the sauge Beare doth licke?
Not his that spoiles his young before his face.
Whose scapes the lurking serpentes mortall sting?
Not he that sets his foote vpon her backe.
The smallest worme will turne being troden on,
And Doues will pecke in seure of their broode,
Ambicious *Yorke* did leuell at thy Crowne,
Thou smiling, while he knit his angrie browes.
He but a Duke, would haue his sonne a king,
And raise his issue like a louing fire.
Thou being a king blest with a goodlie sonne,
Didst giue consent to disinherit him,
Which argude thee a most vnnaturall father.
Vnreasonable creatures feed their yong,
And though mans Face be fearefull to their eies,
Yet in protection of their tender ones,
Who hath not seene them euen with those same wings
Which they haue sometime wide in fearefull flight,
Make warre with him, that climes vnto their nest,
Offing their owne liues in their yongs defence?
For shame my Lord, make them your presidents,
Were it not pittie that this goodlie boy,
                                        Should

Yorke, and Henrie the sixt.

should lofe his birthright through his fathers fault?
And long hereafter saie vnto his child,
What my great grandsire and grandsire got,
My carelesse father fondlie gaue awaie?
Looke on the boy and let his manlie face,
Which promiseth successefull fortune to vs all,
Steele thy melting thoughts,
To keepe thine owne, and leaue thine owne with him.
King. Full wel hath *Clifford* plaid the Orator,
Inferring arguments of mightie force.
But tell me, didst thou neuer yet heare tell,
That things well got had euer bad successe,
And happie euer was it for that sonne,
Whose father for his hoording went to hell?
I leaue my sonne my vertuous deedes behind,
And would my father had left me no more,
For all the rest is held at such a rate,
As askes a thousand times more care to keepe,
Then maie the present profit counteruaile.
Ah cosen *Yorke*, would thy best friendes did know,
How it doth greeue me that thy head stands there.
Quee. My Lord, this harmefull pittie makes your fol-
   lowers faint.
You promisde knighthood to your princelie sonne,
Vnsheath your sword, and straight doe dub him knight,
Kneele downe *Edward.*
   King. Edward Plantagenet, arise a knight,
And learne this lesson boy, draw thy sword in right.
   Prince. My gratious father, by your kinglie leaue,
Ile draw it as apparant to the crowne,
And in that quarrell vse it to the death.

                                        Northum.

The Tragedie of Richard D. of

Northumb. Why this is spoken like a toward prince.

Enter a Messenger.

Mes. Royall commaunders be in readinesse,
For with a band of fiftie thousand men,
Comes *Warwike* backing of the Duke of *Yorke*.
And in the townes whereas they passe along,
Proclaimes him king, and manie flies to him,
Prepare your battels, for they be at hand
Clif. I would your highnesse would depart the field,
The *Queene* hath best successe when you are absent.
Quee. Do good my Lord, and leaue vs to our fortunes
King. Why thats my fortune, therefore Ile stay still.
Clif. Be it with resolution then to fight.
Prince. Good father cheere these noble Lords,
Vnsheath your sword, sweet father crie Saint *George*.
Clif. Pitch we our battell heere, for hence wee will not
moue.

Enter the house of *Yorke*.

Edward. Now periurie *Henrie* wilt thou yeelde thy
crowne,
And kneele for mercie at thy soueraignes feete?
Quee. Go rate thy minions proud insulting boy,
Becomes it thee to be thus male pert,
Before thy king and lawfull soueraigne?
Edw. I am his king, and he should bend his knee,
I was adopted heire by his consent,
George. Since when he hath broke his oath,
For as we heare you that are king
Though he doe weare the Crowne,
Haue caus'de him by new act of Parlement
To blot our brother out, and put his owne sonne in.

Clif.

Yorke, and Henrie the sixt.

Clif. And reason *George.* Who should succeede the fa-
ther but the sonne?
Rich. Are you their butcher?
Clif. I *Crookebacke*, here I stand to answere thee, or any
of your sort.
Rich. Twas you that kild yong *Rutland*, was it not?
Clif. Yes, and old *Yorke* too, and yet not satisfide.
Rich. For Gods sake Lords giue signall to the fight.
War. What faiest thou *Henry*? wilt thou yeelde thy
crowne?
Quee. What, long tongde *War*, dare you speake?
When you and *I* met at saint *Albones* last,
Your legs did better seruice than your hands;
War. I, then twas my turne to flee, but now tis thine.
Clif. You said so much before, and yet you fled.
War. Twas not your valour *Clifford*, that droue mee
thence.
Northum. No, nor your manhood *Warwike*, that could
make you staie.
Rich. *Northumberland*, *Northumberland*, wee holde
Thee reuerentlie: Breake off the parlie, for I scarse
I can refraine the execution of my big swolne
Hart, against that *Clifford* there, that
Cruell child-killer.
Clif. Why I kild thy father, call'st thou him a child?
Rich. I like a villaine, and a trecherous coward,
As thou didst kill our tender brother *Rutland*,
But ere sunne set Ile make thee curse the deed.
King. Haue doone with words great Lordes, and
Heare me speake.
Quee. Defie them then, or else hold close thy lips.

King.

The Tragedie of Richard D. of

King. I prethe giue no limits to my tongue,
I am a king and priuiledge to speake.
Clif. My Lord the wound that bred this meeting here
Cannot be cur'd with words, therefore be still,
Rich. Then executioner vnsheathe thy sword,
By him that made vs all I am resolu'de,
That Clifford manhood hangs vpon his tongue.
Eaw. What saist thou Henry, shall I haue my right
         or no?
A thousand men haue broke their fast to daie,
That nere shall dine, vnlesse thou yeeld the crowne.
War. If thou denie their blouds be on thy head,
For Yorke in iustice puts his armour on.
Prin. If all be right that Warwike saies is right,
There is no wrong but all things must be right.
Rich. Whosoeuer got thee, there thy mother stands,
For well I wot thou hast thy mothers tongue.
Queen. But thou art neither like thy sire nor dam,
But like a foule misshapen stigmaticke
Markt by the destinies to be auoided,
As venome Todes or Lizards fainting lookes.
Rich. Iron of Naples, hid with English gilt,
Thy father beares the title of a king,
As if a channell should be calde the Sea;
Shame sthou not, knowing from whence thou art de-
Riu'de, to parlie thus with Englands lawfull heires?
Edw. A wispe of straw were worth a thousand crownes,
To make that shamelesse callet know her selfe,
Thy husbands father reueld in the hart of France,
And tam'de the French, and made the Dolphin stoope:
And had he match according to his state,
                                                            He

Yorke, and Henrie the sixt.

He might haue kept that gorie till this daie,
But when he tooke a begger to his bed,
And graeft thy fun-shine fire with his bridall daie,
Then that fun-shine bred a showre for him
Which washt his fathers fortunes out of France,
And heapt seditions on his crowne at home,
For what hath mou'd these tumults but thy pride?
Hadst thou bene meeke, our title yet had slept,
And we in pitie of the gentle king,
Had slipt our claime vntill an other age.
George. But when we saw our summer brought the
         gaine,
And that the haruest brought vs no increase,
We set the axe to thy vsurping root,
And though the edge haue something hir our selues,
Yet know thou we wil neuer cease to strike,
Till we haue hewne thee clowne,
Or bath'd thy growing with our heated blouds,
Edw. And in this resolution, I defie thee,
Not willing anie longer conference,
Since thou denest the gentle king to speake.
Sound trumpets, let our bloudie colours waue,
And either victorie or else a graue.
Quee. Staie Edward staie.
Edw. Hence wrangling woman, Ile no longer staie,
Thy words will cost ten thousand liues to daie.
         Exeunt Omnes.   Alarmes.
                 Enter Warwike.
War. Sore spent with toile as runners with the race,
I laie me downe a litle while to breath,
For strokes receude, and manie blowes repaide,   Hath

C

The Tragedie of Richard D. of

Hath robd my strong knit sinews of their strength,
And spent the force to force needs must I rest my selfe.

Enter Edward.

Edw. Smile gentle heauens or strike vngentle death,
That we may die, vnlesse we gaine the daie:
What fatall starre malignant frownes from heauen,
Vpon the hart melesse line of *Yorke* true house?

Enter George.

George. Come brother, come, lets to the field againe,
For yet theres hope inough to win the daie:
Then let vs back to cheere our fainting Troupes,
Lest they retire now we haue left the field.

War. How now my Lords, what hap, what hope of good?

Enter Richard running.

Rich. Ah *Warwike* why hast thou withdrawne thy selfe?
Thy noble father in the thickest throngs,
Cride still for *Warwike* his thrife valiant son,
Vntill with thousand swords he was beset,
And manie wounds made in his aged brest,
And as he tottering sate vpon his steede,
He waft his hand to me and cride aloud:
Richard, commend me to my valiant sonne,
And still he cride *Warwike* reuenge my death,
And with those words he tumbled off his horse,
And so the noble *Salsbury* gaue vp the ghost.

War. Then let the earth be drunken with his blood,
Ile kill my horse because I will not flie:
And here to God of heauen I make a vow,
Neuer to passe from forth this bloudy field
Till I am full reuenge for his death.

Edw. Lord *Warwike*, I doe bend my knees with thine,
And

Yorke, and Henrie the sixt.

And in that vow now ioine my soule to thee,
Thou setter vp and puller downe of kings,
vouchsafe a gentle victorie to vs,
Or let vs die before we loose the daie:

George. Then let vs shaft to cheere the souldiers harts,
And call them pillers that will stand to vs,
And hiely promise to remuncrate
Their trustie seruice, in these dangerous warres.

Rich. Come, come awaie, and stand not to debate,
For yet is hope of fortune good enough.
Brothers, giue me your hands, and let vs part,
And take our leaues vntill we meet againe,
Where ere it be in heauen or in earth.
Now I that neuer wept, now melt in wo,
To see these dire mishaps continue so.
Warwike farewel.

War. A waie, awaie, once more sweet Lords farewell.

Exeunt Omnes.

*Alarmes, and then enter Richard at one dore,
and Clifford at the other.*

Rich. A *Clifford* a *Clifford.*

Clif. A *Richard* a *Richard.*

Rich. Now *Clifford*, for *Yorke* & young *Rutlands* death,
This thirstie sword that longs to drinke thy blood,
Shall lop thy limmes, and slise thy curssed hart,
For to reuenge the murders thou hast made.

Clif. Now *Richard*, I am with thee here alone,
This is the hand that stabd thy father *Yorke*,
And this the hand that slew thy brother *Rutland*,
And heeres the heart that triumphes in their deaths,
And cheeres these hands that slew thy sire and brother,

To

C. 2.

The Tragedie of Richard D. of Yorke

To execute the like vpon thy selfe,
And so haue at thee.

   Alarmes. They Fight, and then enters Warwike,
   and rescues Richard, & then exeunt omnes.
   Alarmes still, and then enter Henry solus.

Hen. Oh gratious God of heauen looke downe on vs,
And let some ende to these miserting griefes,
How like a mastlesse ship vpon the seas,
This wofull battaile doth continue still.
Now leauing this way, now to that side driue,
And none doth know to whom the daie will fall:
O would my death might staie these ciuilians!
Would I had neuer raind, nor nere bin king,
Margret and *Clifford*, chide me from the fielde,
Swearing they had best successe when I was thence,
Would God that I were dead, so all were well,
Or would my crowne suffice, I were content
To yeeld it them and liue a priuate life.

   Enter a souldier with a dead man in his armes.

Sould. Ill blowes the winde that profits no bodie,
This man that I haue slaine in fight to daie,
Maie be possesed of some store of crownes,
And I will search to find them if I can,
But stay, Methinkes it is my fathers face,
Oh I tis he whom I haue slaine in fight,
From London was I prest out by the king,
My father he came on the part of *Yorke*,
And in this conflict I haue slaine my father:
Oh pardon God, I knew not what I did,
And pardon father, for I knew thee not,

   Enter an other souldier with a dead man.

          2. Sould.

Yorke, and Henrie the sixt.

2. Sould. Lie there thou that fought'st with me so stoutly,
Now let me see what store of gold thou hast,
But stay, me thinkes this is no famous face:
Oh no it is my sonne that I haue slaine in fight,
O monstrous times begetting such euents,
How cruell bloudy, and ironious,
This deadlie quarrell daile doth beget,
Poore boy thy father gaue thee life too late,
And hath bereau'de thee of thy life too soone.

King. Wo aboue wo, griefe more then common griefe,
Whilst Lyons warre and battaile for their dens,
Poore lambs do feele the riger of their wraths:
The red rose and the white are on his face,
The fatall colours of our striuing houses,
Wither one rose, and let the other flourish,
For if you thriue, ten thousand liues must perish.

1. Sould. How will my mother for my fathers death,
Take on with me and nere be satisfide?
2. Sol. How will my wife for slaughter of my son,
Take on with me and nere be satisfide?

King. How will the people now misdeeme their king,
Oh would my death their minds could satisfie.

1. Sould. Was euer son so rude his fathers bloud to spill?
2. Sould. Was euer father so vnnaturall his son to kill?
King. Was euer king thus grieued and vexed still?
1. Sould. Ile beare thee hence from this accursed place,
For wo is me to see my fathers face.
            Exit with his father.
2. Sould. Ile beare thee hence & let them fight that wil,
For I haue murdered where I should not kill.
            Exit with his sonne.

                 King.

C 3

The Tragedie of Richard D. of

K.Hen. Weepe wretched man, Ile lay thee teare for teare,
Here is a kings woe begone as thee.
   Alarues and enter the Queene.
Queen. Away my Lord to *Barwike*, preſende,
The dale is loft, our friends are murdered,
No hope is left for vs, therefore awaie.
   Enter prince Edward,
Prince. Oh father flie our men haue left the field,
Take houſe ſweet father, lets ſaue our ſelues,
   Enter Exeter,
Exet. Awaie my Lord for vengeance comes along with (him.
Nay ſtand not to expoſtulate make haſt,
Or elſe come after, Ile awaie before,
K.Hen. Nae flaie good *Exeter*, for Ile along with thee.
   Enter Clifford wounded, with an
   arrow in his necke.
Clif. Heere burnes my candell out,
That whilſt it laſted gaue king *Henry* light.
Ah *Lancaster*, I feare thine ouerthrow,
More then my bodies parting from my ſoule,
My loue and feare glude manie friendes to thee,
And now I die, that tough commixture melts,
Impairing *Henry* ſtrength breeding proud *Yorke*,
The common people ſwarme like ſummer flies,
And whither flies the Gnats but to the ſun?
And who ſhines now but *Henries* enemie?
Oh *Phoebus* hadſt thou neuer giuen conſent,
That *Phaeton* ſhould checke thy fierie fleedes,
Thy burning carre had neuer ſcurcht the earth,
And *Henry* hadſt thou liud as kings ſhould doe,
And as thy father and his father did,

    Gi-

Yorke, and Henrie the ſixt.

Giuing no foot vnto the houſe of *Yorke*,
I and ten thouſand in this wofull land,
Hadſt left no mourning Widdowes for our deathes,
And thou this daie hadſt kept thy throne in peace.
For what doth cheriſh weedes but gentle aire?
And what makes robbers bolds but lenitie?
Bootleſſe are plaints, and cureleſſe are my wounds,
No waie to flie, no ſtrength to hold our flight,
The foe is mercileſſe and will not pitie me,
And at their hands I haue deſerude no pitie.
The aire is got into my bleeding wounds,
And much effuſe of blond doth make me faint,
Come *Yorke* and *Richard*, *Warwike* and the reſt,
If ſtabd your fathers, now come ſplit my breſt.
   Enter Edward, Richard and Warwike,
   and Souldiers.

Edw. Thus farre our fortunes keepes an vpward
Courſe, and we are graft with wreaches of victorie.
Some troopes purſue the bloudie minded Queene,
That now towards *Barwike* doth poſte amaine,
But thinke you that *Clifford* is fled awaie with them?
Wm. No, tis impoſſible he ſhould eſcape,
For though before his face I ſpeake the words,
Your brother *Richard* marke him for the graue,
And where ſo ere he be I warrant him dead.

   Clifford groanes and then dies.

Edm. Harke, what ſoule is this that takes his heauy leaue?
Rich. A deadlie grone, like lhe and deaths departure.
Edw. See who it is: and now the battailes ended,
Friend or foe, let him be friendlie vſed.
Rich. Reuerſe that doome of mercie, for tis *Clifford*,
       Who

     C 4

The Tragedie of Richard D. of

Who kild our tender brother *Rutland*,
And ftabd our princelie father Duke of *Yorke*.
War. From off the gates of *Yorke* fetch downe the
Head, Your fathers head, which *Clifford* placed there,
Inftead of that, let his fupplie the roome.
Meafure for meafure muft be anfwered.
Edw. Being forth that fatall skinch owle to
ourhoufe,
That nothing fling to vs but bloud and death,
Now his euill boding tongue no more fhall fpeake.
War. I thinke his vnderftanding is bereft.
Say *Clifford*, do-ft thou know who fpeakes to thee?
Darke cloudie death ore fhades his beames of life,
And he no fees nor heares vs what we faie.
Rich. Oh would he did, and fo perhaps he doth,
And tis his policie that in the time of death,
He might auoid fuch bitter ftormes as he
In his houre of death did giue vnto our father.
George. Richard did thou thinkeft fo, vex him with ea-
ger words.
Rich. Clifford, aske mercie and obtaine no grace.
Edw. Clifford, repent in booteleffe penitence.
War. Clifford deuife excufes for thy fault.
George. Whilft we deuife fell tortures for thy fault.
Rich. Thou pitiedft *Yorke*, and I am fonne to *Yorke*.
Edw. Thou pitiedft *Rutland*, and I will pitie thee.
George. Wheres captaine *Margaret* to fence you
now?
War. They mocke thee *Clifford*, fweare as thou waft
wont.
Rich. What not an oath? Nay then I know hees dead,
Tis

Yorke, and Henrie the fixt.

Tis hard, when *Clifford* cannot foord his friend an oath,
By this I know hees dead, and by my foule,
Would this right hand buy but an howres life,
That I in all contempt might raile at him.
Ile cut it off and with the iffuing bloud,
Stifle the villaine whose infamed thirft,
Yorke and young *Rutland* could not fatisfie.
War. I, but he is dead off with the traitors head,
And reare it in the place your fathers ftands.
And now to London with triumphant march,
There to be crowned *Englands* lawfull king,
From thence fhall *Warwike* croffe the feas to *France*,
And aske the ladie *Bona* for thy *Queene*,
So fhalt thou finew both thefe landes together,
And hauing *France* thy friend thou needft not dread,
The fcattered foe that hopes to rife againe.
And though they cannot greatly fling to hurt,
Yet looke to haue them bufie to offend thine eares.
Firft Ile fee the coronation done,
And afterward Ile croffe the feas to *France*,
To effect this marriage if it pleafe my Lord.
Edw. Euen as thou wilt good *Warwike* let it be,
But firft before we goe, *George* kneele downe.
We here create thee Duke of *Clarence*, and girt thee with
the fword
Our yoonger brother *Richard* Duke of *Gloecefter*.
Warwike as my felic fhal do & vndo as him pleafeth beft.
Rob. Let me be Duke of *Clarence*, *George* of *Glofter*,
For *Glofters* Dukedome is too ominous.
War. Tufh thats a childifh obferuation.
Richard be Duke of *Glofter*, Now to London.
To

390

The Tragedie of Richard D. of

To see thee here in possession.   *Exeunt Omnes.*
Entertwo keepers with bow and arrowes.
Keeper. Come, lets take our stands vpon this hill,
And by and by well come this waie.
But staie, here comes a man, leu s teal him a while.

Enter king Henrie disguisde.
Hen. From *Scotland* am I stolne euen of pure loue,
And this disguise to greet my natiue land.
No, *Harrie* no, It is no land of thine,
No bending knee will call thee *Cæsar* now,
No humble sutes, no letters to thee for right,
For how canst thou helpe them and not thy selfe.
Keeper. I marrie sir, here is a deere, his skin is a
Keepers fee. Sirra stand close, for as I thinke.
This is the king king *Edward* hath deposde,
Hen. My *Queene* and sonne poore soules are gone to
France, and as I heare the great commanding *Warwike,*
To intreat a marriage with the ladie *Bona,*
If this be true, poore *Queene* and sonne,
Your labour is but spent in vaine,
For *Lewis* is a prince soone wonn with words,
And *Warwike* is a subtill Orator.
He laughes and saies, his *Edwards* misfalde.
She weepes and saies, her *Henry* is depposde,
He on his right hand asking a wife for *Edward,*
She on his left side crauing aide for *Henry,*
Hen. More then I seeme, for lesse I should not be,
A man at least, and more I cannot be,
And men maie talke of kings, and why not I?
  Keeper

Yorke, and Henrie the sixt.

Keeper. I but thou talkest as if thou wert a king thy selfe.
Hen. Why so I am in mind though not in shew.
Keeper. And if thou be a king where is thy crowne?
Hen. My crowne is in my hart, not on my head
My crowne is calde content, a crowne that
Kings doe seldome times enjoy.
Keeper. And if thou be a king crownd with content,
Your crowne content and you must be content
To go with vs vnto the officer, for as we thinke
You are our quondam king, *K. Edward* hath depo_
de,
And therefore we charge you in Gods name & the kings
To go along with vs vnto the officers.
Hen. Gods name be fulfild, your kings name be
Obaide, and be you king, command, and I le obay.
  Exeunt Omnes.

Enter King Edward, Clarence, and Gloster, Montague,
Hastings, and the Lady Gray.
K. Edw Brothers of *Clarence* and of *Gloster,*
This ladies husband heere Sir *Richard Gray,*
At the battaile of faint *Albones* did lose his life,
His lands then were seazed on by the conqueror.
Her sute is now to repossesse those lands,
And sith in quarrell of the house of *Yorke,*
The noble gentleman did lose his life,
In honor we cannot denie her sute.
Glo. Your highnesse shall doe well to grant it then.
K. Edw I, so I will, but yet lle make a pause.
Gla. I, is the wind in that doore?
Clarence. I see the Lady hath some thing to grant,
Before the king will graunt her humble sute.
Gla. He knowes the game, how well he keepes the winde
  K. Edw.

The Tragedie of Richard D. of

K. Ed. Widow we come some other time to know our mind.
La. May it please your grace I cannot brooke delaies,
I beseech your highnesse to dispatch me now.
K. Ed. Lords giue vs leaue, wee meane to trie this wi-
                    dowes wit.
Cla. I good leaue haue you.
Glo. For you will haue leaue till youth take leaue,
And leaue you to your crouch.
K. Ed. Come hither widow, how, how many children haste
                    thou?
Cla. I thinke he meanes to begge a child on her.
Glo. Nay whip me then, heele rather giue hir two.
La. Three my most gratious Lord.
Glo. You shall haue foure and you will be rulde by him.
K. Ed. Were it not pittie they should loose their fathers
                    lands?
La. Be pitifull then dread L. and grant it them.
K. Edw. Ile tell thee how these lands are to be got.
La. So shall you bind me to your highnesse seruice.
K. Ed. What seruice wilt thou doe me if I grant it them?
La. Euen what your highnesse shall command.
Glo. Naie then widow Ile warrant you all your
Husbands lands, if you grant to do what he
Commands, Fight close or in good faith
You catch a clap.
Cla. Naie I feare her not vnlesse she fall.
Glo. Marie gods forbot man, for heele take vantige
                    then.
La. Why stops my Lord, shall I not know my taske?
K. Ed. An easie taske, tis but to loue a king.
La. That is soone performde, because I am a subiect.
                                                    K. Edw.

Torke, and Henrie the fixt.

K. Ed. Why then thy husbands landes, I freelie giue
                    thee.
La. I take my leaue with manie thousand thankes.
Cla. The match is made, shee seales it with a cursie.
K. Ed. Staie widdow staie, what loue dost thou thinke
I sue so much to get?
La. My humble seruice, such as subiects owes and
                    the lawes commands.
K. Ed. No by my troth, I meane no such loue,
But to tell thee, the the troth, I aime to lie with thee.
La. To tell you plaine my Lord, I had rather lie
                    in prison.
K. Edw. Why then thou canst not get thy husbands
                    lands.
La. Then mine honestie shall be my dower,
For by that losse I will not purchase them.
K. Ed. Herein thou wrongst thy children mightilie.
La. Herein your highnesse wrongs both them and
Me, but my thie Lord, this merrie inclination
Agrees not with the sadnesse of my sute.
Please it your highnes to dismisse me either with I or no.
K. Ed. I, if thou saie I, to my request,
No, if thou saie no, to my demand.
La. Then no my Lord, my suite is at an end.
Glo. The widdow likes him not, shee bends the brow.
Cla. Why he is the bluntest wooer in christendome,
K. Ed. Her lookes are all repleat with maiestie,
One waie or other shee is for a king,
And shee shall be my loue or else my *Queene*,
Saie that king *Edward* tooke thee for his *Queene*.
La. Tis better said then done, my gratious Lord,

I

The Tragedie of Richard D. of

I am a ſubiect fit to ieſt withall,
But farre vnfit to be a Soueraigne.
K.Edw. Sweet widdow, by my ſtate I ſweare, I ſpeake
No more then what my hart intends,
And that is to enioy thee for my loue.
La. And that is more then I will yeeld vnto,
I know I am too bad to be your *Queene,*
And yet too good to be your Concubine.
K.Edw. You caull widdow, I did meane my *Queene.*
La. Your grace would be loath my ſonnes ſhould call
    you father.
K.Edw. No more then when my daughters call thee
Mother. Thou art a widow and thou haſt ſome children,
And by Gods mother I being but a bachelor
Haue other ſome. Why tis a happy thing
To be the father of manie children.
Argue no more, for thou ſhalt be my Queene.
Glo. The ghoſtlie father now hath done his ſhrift.
Cla. When he was made a ſhrifter twas for ſhift.
K.Edw. Brothers, you muſe what all the widdow
And I haue had you would thinke it ſtrange
If I ſhould marrie her.
Cla. Marrie her my Lord, to whom?
K.Edw. Why *Clarence* to my ſelfe.
Glo. That would be ten daies wonder at the leaſt.
Cla. Why thars a daie longer then a wonder laſtes.
Glo. And ſo much more are the wonders in extreames.
K.Edw. Well, ieaſt on brothers, I can tell you, hir
Sute is graunted for her husbands lands.
    Enter a Messenger.
Meſ. And it pleaſe your grace, *Henry* your foe is
                                                Taken,

Yorke, and Henrie the ſixt.

Taken, and brought as priſoner to your pallace gates.
K.Edw. A waie with him and ſend him to the Tower,
And let vs go queſtion with the man about
His apprehenſion. Lords along, and vietnis
Ladie honorable.   *Exeunt Omnes.*
    Manet Gloſter and ſpeakes.
Glo. I, *Edward* will vſe women honourable,
Would he were waſted marrow, bones and all,
That from his loines no iſſue might ſucceed
To hinder me from the golden time I looke for,
For I am not yet looke on in the world.
Firſt is there *Edward, Clarence,* and *Henry*
And his ſonne, and all their looke for iſſue.
Of their loines ere I can plant my ſelfe,
A cold premeditation for my purpoſe,
What other pleaſure is there in the world beſides?
I will go clad my bodie in gaie ornaments,
And huſſe my ſelfe within a ladies lap,
And witch ſweet Ladies with my words and lookes,
O monſtrous man, to harbour ſuch a thought,
Why loue did I come me in my mothers wombe,
And for I ſhould not deale in hir affaires,
Shee did corrupt fraile nature in the fleſh,
And plaſie an enuious mountaine on my backe,
Where ſits deformity to mocke my bodie,
To drie mine armes vp like a withered ſhrimpe,
To make my legges of an vnequall ſize,
And am I then a man to be belou'd?
Eaſier for me to compaſſe twentie crownes,
Tut I can ſmile, and murder when I ſmile,
I crie content to that that grieues me moſt,

The Tragedie of Richard D. of

I can adde colours to the Camelion,
And for a neede change shapes with *Proteus*,
And set the aspiring *Catalin* to schoole.
Can *I* doe this and cannot get the crowne?
Tush, were it ten times higher, Ile pullit downe.   *Exit*

Enter king Lewis and the ladie Bona, and Queene
Margaret, Prince Edward, and Oxford
and others.

Lewes. Welcome *Queene Margaret* to the Court of
France,
It fits not *Lewis* to sit while thou dost stand,
Sit by my side, and heere *I* vow to thee,
Thou shalt haue aide to repossesse thy right,
And beare proud *Edward* from his vsurped seats,
And place king *Henry* in his former rule.

Queen. I humble thanke your royall maiestie,
And pray the God of heauen to blesse thy state,
Great king of *France,* that thus regards our wrongs.
Enter Warwike.

Lew. How now, who is this?
Queen. Our Earle of *Warwike Edwardes* chiefest friend.
Lew. Welcome braue *Warwike,* what brings thee to
France?

War. From worthy *Edward* king of *England,*
My Lord and Soueraigne and thy vowed friend,
I come in kindnes and vnfained loue,
First to do greetings to thy royall person,
And then to craue a league of amitie,
And lastlie to confirme that amitie
With nuptiall knot, if thou vouchsafe to grant
That vertuous ladie *Bona* thy faire sister,

To.

Yorke, and Henrie the sixt.

To Englands king in lawfull marriage.
Queen. And if this go forward all our hope is done.
War. And gracious Madam in our kings behalfe,
I am commanded with your loue and fauour,
Humble to kisse your hand and with my tongue,
To tell the passions of my soueraines hart,
Where fame late entring at his heedfull eares,
Hath plast thy glorious image and thy vertues,
Queen. King *Lewes* and Lady *Bona* heare me speake,
Before you answere *Warwike* or his words,
For hee it is hath done vs all these wrongs.

War. Iniurious *Margaret.*
Prince Ed. And why not Queene?
War. Because thy father *Henry* did vsurpe,
And thou no more art Prince then shee is Queene.

Ox. Then *Warwike,* disanuls great *Iohn* of *Gaunt,*
That did subdue the greatest part of *Spaine,*
And after *Iohn* of *Gaunt,* wise *Henry* the fourth,
Whose wisedome was a mirrour to the world,
And after this wise prince *Henry* the fift,
Who with his prowesse conquered all *France,*
From these our *Henries* linealie discent.

War. Oxford, how haps that in this smooth discourse
You told not how *Henry* the sixt had lost
All that *Henry* the fift had gotten.
Me thinkes these peeres of *France* should smile at that,
But for the rest youre like a pettigree
Of threescore and two yeares a slice time,
To make prescription for a kingdomes worth.

Oxf. Why *Warwike,* canst thou deny thy king,
Whom thou obeydst thirtie and eight yeares,

And

D.

The Tragedie of Richard D of

And bewray thy treasons with a blush?
War. Can *Oxford* that did euer fence the right,
Now buckler falshood with a pettigree?
For I haue leaue *Henry* and call *Edward* king.
Oxf. Call him my king, by whom mine elder
Brother the Lord *Awbrey Vere* was done to death?
And more than so, my father euen in the
Downefall of his mellowed yeares,
When age did call him to the dore of death?
No *Warwike* no, whilst life vpholds this arme,
This arme vpholds the house of *Lancaster*.
War. And I the house of *Yorke*.
K *Lew.* Queene *Margaret*, prince *Edward* and
Oxford vouchsafe to forbeare a while,
Till I doe talke a word with *Warwike*.
Now *Warwike* euen vpon thy honor tell me true,
Is *Edward* lawfull king or no?
For I were loath to linke with him, that is not lawful heir.
War. Thereon I pawne mine honour and my credit.
Lew. What is he gratious in the peoples eies?
War. The more, that *Henry* is vnfortunate.
Lew. What's his loue to our sister *Bona*?
War. Such it seemes
As maie beseeme a monarke like himselfe.
My selfe haue often heard him saie and sweare,
That this his loue was an eternall plant,
Thereof was fixt in vertues ground,
The leaues and fruite maintainde with beauties sun,
Exempt from enuie, but not from disdaine,
Vnlesse the ladie *Bona* quite his paine.
Lew. Then sister let vs heare your firme resolue.

Yorke, and Henrie the first.

Bona. Your grant or your deniall shall be mine,
But ere this daie, I must confesse, when I
Haue heard your kings defects recounted,
Mine cares haue tempted iudgement to desire.
Lew. Then draw neere Queene *Margaret*: and be a
Witnesse, that *Bona* shall be wife to the English king.
Prince Edw. To *Edward*, but not the English king.
War. Henry now liues in *Scotland* at his ease,
Where hauing nothing, nothing can he lose.
And as for you your selfe our *quondam* Queene,
You haue a father able to maintaine your state,
And better twere to trouble him then *France*.
    Sound for a post within.
Lew. Here comes some post *Warwike* to thee or vs,
Post. My Lord ambassador this letter is for you,
Sent from your brother Marquis *Mountague.*
This from our king vnto your Maiestie,
And these to you Madam, from whom I know not.
Oxf. I like it well that our faire Queene and mistresse,
Smiles at her newes when *Lewes* stamps as his.
P. Ed. And marke how *Lewes* stamps as his.
Lew. Now *Margaret* & *Warwike*, what are your news?
Queen. Mine such as fils my hart full of ioie.
War. Mine full of sorrow and hars discontent.
Lew. What hath your king married the Ladie *Grey,*
And now to excuse himselfe sends vs a post of papers?
How dares he presume to vse vs thus?
Quee. This proueth *Edwards* loue, & *Warwike,* honestly.
War. King *Lewis*, I here protest in sight of heauen,
And by the hope I haue of heauenlie blisse,
That I am cleare from this misldeed of *Edwards.*
        No

D 2.   *Bona*

The Tragedie of Richard D. of

No more my king, for he dissembles,
And most himselfe, if he could see his shame.
Did I forget that by the house of Yorke,
My father came vntimelie to his death?
Did I let passe the abuse done to my neece?
Did I impale him with the regall Crowne,
And chruit king *Henry* from his natiue home,
And most vngratefull doth he vie me thus?
My gratious *Queene* pardon what is past,
And henceforth I am thy true seruitour,
I will reuenge the wrongs done to ladie *Bona*,
And replant *Henry* in his former state.

Queen. Yes *Warwike* I doe quite forgetfly former
Faultes, if now thou wilt become king *Henries* friend.

War. So much his freind, This vnfained friend,
That if king *Lewes* vouchsafe to furnish vs
With some few bands of chosen souldiers,
Ile vndertake to land them on our coast,
And force the Tyrant from his seate by warre,
Tis not his new made bride shall succour him,

Lew. Then at the last I sinelie am resolud,
You shall haue aide: and English messenger returne
In post, and tell false *Edward* thy supposed king,
That *Lewes* of France is sending ouer Maskers
To reuell it with him and his new bride,

Bona. Tell him in hope heele be a Widower shortlie,
Ile weare the willow garland for his sake.

Queen. Tell him my mourning weedes be laide aside,
And I am readie to put armour on.

War. Tell him from me, that he hath done me wrong,
And therefore Ile vncrowne him ere't be long.

Thean

Yorke, and Henrie the sixt.

Then thy reward, begone.

Lew. But now tell me *Warwike*, what assurance
I shall haue of thy true loyaltie?

War. This shall affirme my constant loyaltie,
If that our Queene and this young prince agree,
Ile ioine mine eldest daughter and my ioie
To him forthwith in holie wedlockes bandes.

Quee. Withall my hart, that match / like full wel,
Loue her sonne *Edward*, shee is faire and yong,
And giue thy hand to *Warwike* and thy loue.

Lew. It is enough, and now we will prepare,
To leuie foldiers for to go with you.
And you Lord *Bowbon*, our high Admirall,
Shall wafttie ouer safelie to the English coast,
And chase proud *Edward* from his slumbring traunce,
For mocking marriage with the name of *France*.

War. I came from *Edward* as his ballador,
But Ireturne his fworne and mortall foe:
Matter of marriage was the charge he gaueme,
But dreadfull warre shall answere his demand.
Had he none else to make it but me?
Then none but I shall turne his iest to sorrow.
I was the chiefe that raisde him to the crowne,
And Ile be chiefe to bring him downe againe,
Not that I pittie *Henries* miserie,
But seeke reuenge on *Edwards* mockerie.   *Exit.*

Enter king *Edward*, the Queene and *Clarence*, and
Gloster, and *Montague* and *Hastings*, and
Penbrooke, with souldiers.

Edw. Brothers of *Clarence*, and of *Gloester*,
What thinke you of our marriage with the ladie *Gray*?
                                              Cla-

D 3.

The Tragedie of Richard D. of

Cla. My Lord, we thinke as *Warwike* and *Leeues*
That are so slacke in iudgement that their take
No offence at this suddaine marriage,
Edw. Suppose they doe, they are but *Leeues* and
Warwike, and I am your king and *Warwike*,
    And will be obaid.
Glo. And finally, because our king doe yet such
Sudden marriages seldome prooueth well.
Edw. Yea brother *Richard*, are you againſt vs too?
Glo. Not I my Lord, no God forefend that I should
Once giue fate your highneſſe pleaſure, (ther.
I Kit were a pittie to funder them that yoake ſo well togi-
Edw. Setting your skornes and your diflikes aſide,
Shew me some reaſons why the Ladie *Gray*,
Maie not be my loue and Englands *Queene*?
Speake freelie *Clarence*, *Gloſter*,
Montague and *Haſting*.
Cla. My Lord then this is my opinion,
That *Warwike* being diſhonored in his embaſſage,
Doth ſeeke reuenge to quite his iniuries,
Glo. And *Leeues* in regard of his ſiſters wrongs,
Doth ioine with *Warwike* to implant your ſtate.
Edw. Suppoſe that *Lewes* and *Warwike* be appeaſd,
By ſuch meanes as I can beſt deuiſe.
Clan. But yet to haue more haue ſ ſtrengthened this our
Alliance, would more haue ſtrengthened this our
Common wealth, gainſt forraine formes,
Then all theſe bred marriage.
Haſt. Let England be true within it ſelfe,
We need not France nor any alliance with them.
Cla. For this ſome ſpeech the Lord *Haſtings* well deſerues,
    To

Yorke, and Henrie the ſixt.

To haue the daughter and heire of the Lord *Hungerford*.
Edw. And what then? It was our will it ſhould be ſo?
Cla. I, and for ſuch a thing too the Lord *Scales*
Did well deſerue at your hands, to haue the
Daughter of the Lord *Bonfield*, and left your
Brother to go ſeeke elſewhere, but in
Your madnes, you burie brotherhood.
Edw. Alaſſe poore *Clarence*, is it for a wife,
That thou art mal-content,
Why man be of good cheere, I will prouide thee one.
Cla. Naie you miſtake the broker ſo ill for your ſelfe,
That you ſhall giue me leaue to make my
Choiſe as I thinke good, and ſo I take my leaue.
I ſhortlie meane to leaue you.
Edw. Leaue me or tarrie I am full reſolued,
Edward will not be tried to his brothers will.
Queen. My Lords doe me: but right and you muſt
Confeſſe, before it pleaſd his highneſſe to aduance
My ſtate to title of a Queene,
That I was not ignoble of my birth.
Edw. Forbeare my loue to honor vpon their frownes,
For thee they muſt obey, nay ſhall ſo, (France,
And if they looke for fauour at my hands,
Maſt. My Lord heere is the meſſenger returnd from

    Enter a Meſſenger.

Edw. Now ſirra, What letters or what newes?
Meſſ. No letters my Lord, and ſuch newes as without
your highneſſe ſpeciall pardon I dare not relate.
Edw. We pardon thee, and as neere as thou canſt
Tell me, What ſaid *Lewes* to our letters?
Meſſ. At my departure theſe were his verie words,
       D 4   Go

Yorke, and Henrie the fixt.

Goe tell falfe *Edward* thy fuppofed king,
That *Lewes* of France is (fending ouer Maskers,)
To reuill it with him and his new bride.
Edw. Is *Lewis* fo braue, belike he thinkes me *Henry* .
But what faid Lady *Bona* to thefe wrongs?
Mef. Tell him thus quoth fhe, in hope he'le proue a widdow-
er fhortly, Ile weare the willow garland for his fake.
Edw. She had the wrong, indeed fhe could faie
Little lefle. But what faide *Henrie* Queene, for as
I heare, fhe was then in place?
Mef. Tell him, quoth fhe my mourning weeds be
Doone, and I am readie to put armour on.
Edw. Then belike fhe meanes to plaie the *Amazon*.
But what faid *Warwike* to thefe iniuries?
Mef. He more incemfed then the reft my Lord,
Tell him, quoth he, that he hath done me wrong,
And therefore Ile vnarme him ere't be long.
Ed. Ha? Durft the traytor breath out fuch proude words?
But I will arme me to preuent the worft.
But what is *Warwike* friends with *Clarence* are?
Mef. I my good Lord, he are fo linkt in friendfhip,
That young Prince *Edward* maries *Warwikes* daughter.
Cla. The eldeft belike *Clarence* fhall haue the
yonger. All you that loue me and *Warwike*
Follow me.   *Exit Clarence and Summerfet.*
Edw. *Clarence* and *Summerfet* both fled to *Warwike.*
What faies your brother *Richard*, will you ftand to vs?
Glo. I my Lord, in defpight of all that fhall
With ftand you. For why hath Nature
Made me halfe downe right, but that I
Should be a valiant villaine and ftand it, for if

The Tragedie of Richard D. of

I would, I cannot runne awaie.
Edw. Penbrooke, go raife an armie prefentlie,
Pitch vp my tent, for in the field this night
I meane to reft, and on the morrow morne,
Ile march to meet proud *Warwike* ere he land
Thofe ftraging troups which he hath got in France,
But ere I goe *Montague* and *Haftings*,
You of all the reft are neereft allied
In bloud to *Warwike*, therefore tell me, if
You fauour him more then me or not:
Speake truelie, for I had rather haue you open
Enemies, then hollow friends.
Mont. So God helpe *Montague* as he proues true.
Haft. And *Haftings* as hee fauours *Edwards* caufe.
Edw. It fhall fuffice, come then lets march awaie.
                                Exeunt Omnes.
    Enter Warwike and Oxford, with fouldiers.
War. Truft me my Lords all hitherto goes well,
The common people by numbers fwarme to vs.
But fee where *Sommerfet* and *Clarence* comes,
Speake fuddenlie my Lords, are we allfriends?
Cla. Feare not that my Lord.
War. Then gentle *Clarence* welcome vnto *Warwike*,
And welcome *Summerfet*, I holdit cowardife,
To reft miftruftfull where a noble hart,
Hath pawnde an open hand in figne of loue;
Elfe might I thinke that *Clarence, Edwards* brother,
We're but a fained friend to our proceedings,
But welcome fweet *Clarence* my daughter fhal be thine.
And now what refts but in nights couerture,
Thy brother being carelefle encampt,

His

The Tragedie of Richard D. of

His souldiers lurking in the towne about,
And but attended by a simple guarde,
We maie surprise and take him at our pleasure,
Our skouts haue found the aduenture very easie,
Then crie king *Henry* with resolued mindes,
And breake we presentlie into his tent.

Cla. Why then lets on our waie in silent sort,
For *Warwike* and his friends God and saint *George.*

War. This is his tent, and see where his guard doth
Stand, Courage my souldiers, now or neuer,
But follow me now, and *Edward* shall be ours.

All. A *Warwike,* a *Warwike,*

Alarmes, and Glofter and Haftings flies.

Oxf. Who goes there?   (*Duke.*
War. Richard and *Hafting* let them go, heere is the
Edw. The Duke, why *Warwike* when we parted
Laft, thou caldft me king?
War. I, but the cafe is altred now,
When you difgraft me in my embaffage,
Then I difgrade you from being king,
And now am come to create you Duke of *Yorke,*
Alaffe how fhould you goucrne anie kingdome,
That knowes not how to vfe embaffadors,
Nor how to vfe your brothers brotherlie,
Nor how to fhrowd your felfe from enimies,
Edw. Well *Warwike,* let fortune dou: her worft,
Edward in mind will beare himfelfe a king,
War. Then for his minde be *Edward* Englands king,
But *Henry* now fhall weare the Englifh crowne:
Go conuaic him to our brother archbifhop of *Yorke,*
And when I haue fought with *Pembrooke* & his followers,

Ie

Yorke, and Henrie the fixt.

He come and tell thee what the ladie *Bona* faies,
And fo for a while farewell good Duke of *Yorke,*

Exeunt fome with Edward

Cla. What followes now, all hitherto goes well,
But we muft difpatch fome letters to *Fraunce,*
To tell the Qweene of our happy fortune,
And bid hir come with fpeed to ioine with vs,
War. Thats the firft thing that we haue to doe,
And free king *Henry* from imprifonment,
And feeling him feated in his regall throne,
Come let vs hafte awaie, and hauing paft thefe cares,
Ile poft to *Yorke,* and fee how *Edward* fares.

Exeunt Omnes.

Enter Glofter, Haftings, and fir William Stanly.

Glo. Lord *Haftings,* and fir *William Stanly,*
Know that the caufe I fent for you is this:
I looke my brother with a flender trayne,
Should come a hunting in this forreft heere,
The Bifhop of *Yorke* befriends him much,
And lets him vfe his pleafure in the chafe,
Now I haue priuilie fent him word,
How *I* am come with you to refcue him,
And fee where the huntfman and he doth come.

Enter Edward and a Huntfman.

Hunt. This waie my Lord, the deere is gone,
Edw. No this vait huntfman, fee where the
Keepers ftand: Now brother and thereft,
What are you prouided to depart?
Glo. I, the horfe ftands at the parke corner,
Come, to *Lynne,* and fo take fhipping into *Flanders,*
Edw. Come then, *Haftings,* and *Stanlie,* I will

Re

The Tragedie of Richard D. of

Require your loues. Bishop farewell,
Sheelth the from Warwicke soone,
And praie that I maie repossesse the crowne.
Now huntsman what will you doe?
Hunt. Marrie my Lord, I thinke I had as good
Goe with you, as tarrie heere to be hangde.
Edw. Come then lets awaie with speed.
                              Exeunt Omnes.

Enter the Queene and the Lord Riuers.
Riuers. Tel me good madam, why is your grace
So passionate of late?
Queen. Why brother Riuers, heare you not the newes,
Of that succeslie king Edward had of late?
Riu. What? loste of some pitcht battaile against Warwike,
Tush, feare not faire Queene but cast those cares aside.
King Edwards noble minde his honours doth display:
And Warwike maie loose, though then he got the day.
Queen. If that were all my griefes were at an end:
But greater troubles will I feare befall.
Riu. What, is he taken prisoner, by the foe,
To the danger of his royall person then?
Queen. I, theare my griefe, king Edward is surprisde,
And led awaie, as prisoner vnto Yorke.
Riu. The newes is passing strange I must confesse,
Yet comfort your selfe, for Edward hath more friends,
Then Lancaster at this time must perceiue,
That some will set him in his throne againe.
Queen. God grant they maie, but gentle brother come,
And let me leane vpon thine arme a while,
Vntill I come vnto the sanctuarie.
There to preserue the fruit within my wombe,

K.

Yorke, and Henrie the sixt.

K. Edwards fled true heire to Englands crowne. Exit.
Enter Edward and Richard, and Hastings, with a
troope of Hollanders.
Edw. Thus far from Belgia haue we past the feas,
And marcht from Ravenspur hauen vnto Yorke:
But soft the gates are shut, / like not this.
Rich. Sound vp the drum and call them to the wals.
Enter the Lord Maire of Yorke vpon the wals.
Mair. My Lords we had notice of your comming,
And thats the cause we stand vpon our garde,
An I shut the gates for to preserue the towne.
Henry now is king, and we are sworne to him.
Edw. Why my Lord Maire, if Henry be your king,
Edward I am sure at least, is Duke of Yorke.
Mair. Truth my Lord, we know you for no lesse.
Edw. I craue nothing but my Dukedome,
Rich. But when the Fox hath gotten his head,
Heele quicklie make the bodie follow after.
Hast. Why my Lord Maire, what stand you vpon points
Open the gates, we are king Henries friends.
Mair. Saie you so, then Ile open them presentlie.
                              Exit Maire.
Ri. By my faith, a wise stout captain & soone perswaded,
The Maire opens the dore, and bringes the
keies in his hand.
Edw. So my Lord Maire, these gates must not be shut,
But in the time of warre giue me the keies:
What feare not man for Edward will defend
the towne and you, despight of all your foes.
Enter sir John Mountgommery with
drumme and souldiers.

How

Torke, and Henrie the sixt.

For this night weele harbour here in *Yorke*,
And then as earlie as the morning sunne,
Lifts vp his beames aboue this horizon,
Weele march to London, to meete with *VVarwike*:
And pull false *Henry* from the Regall throne,

             Exeunt Omnes.

Enter *VVarwike* and *Clarence*, with the Crowne, and
then king *Henry*, and *Oxford*, and *Summerset*,
and the yong Earle of *Richmond*.

King. Thus from the prison to this princelie feat,
By Gods great mercies am I brought
Againe, *Clarence* and *VVarwike* doe you
Keepe the crowne, and gouerne and protect
My realme in peace, and I will spend the
Remnant of my daies, to finnes rebuke
And my Creators praise.
VVar. What answeres *Clarence* to his soueraignes will?
Cla. *Clarence* agrees to what king *Henry* likes.
King. My Lord of *Summerset*, what prettie
Boie is that you seeme to be lo carefull of?
Sum. And it pleafe your grace, it is yong *Henry*,
Earle of *Richmond*.
King. *Henry* of *Richmond*, Come hither prettie Ladde,
If heauenlie powers doe ettime aright,
To my diuining thoughts, thou pretie boy,
Shalt proue this Countries bliffe,
Thy head is made to weare a princelie crowne,
Thy lookes are all repleat with Maieftie,
Make much of him my Lords,

                    For

The Tragedie of Richard D. of

How now *Richard*, who is this?
Rich. Brother, this is fir *Iohn Mungummery*,
A trustie friend vnleffe I be deceiude.
Edw. Welcome fir *Iohn*. Wherefore come you in armes?
Sir Iohn. To helpe king *Edward* in this time of stormes,
As euerie loyall fubiect ought to doe.
Edw. Thankes braue *Mountgummery*,
But I onlie claime my Dukedom,
Vntill it pleafe God to fend the rest.
Sir Iohn. Then fare you wele Drum ftrike vp and let vs
March away, I came to serue a king and not a Duke,
Edw. Nay ftaie fir *Iohn*, and let vs fift debate,
With what fecuritie we maie doe this thing.
Sir Iohn. What ftand you on debating to be briefe,
Except you prefently proclaime your felfe our king,
Ile hence a gaine, and keepe them backe that come to
Succour you, why fhould we fight when
you pretend no title?
Rich. fie brother, fie, ftand you vpon tearmes?
Refolue your felfe, and let vs claime the crowne.
Edw. I am refolude once more to claime the crowne,
And win it too or else to loofe my life.
Sir Iohn. I now my foueraigne fpeaketh like himfelfe,
And now will I be *Edwards* Champion,
Sound Trumpets, for *Edward* fhall be proclaimd.
Edward the fourth by the grace of God, king of England
and France, and Lord of Ireland, and who foeuer gain-
faies king *Edwards* right, by this I challenge him to
fingle fight, long liue *Edward* the fourth.
All. Long liue *Edward* the fourth.
Edw. We thanke you all, Lord Maire leade on the ware.

                    For

The Tragedie of Richard D. of

For this is he shall helpe you more,
Then you are hurt by me.
 Enter one with a letter to Warwike.
War. What Councell Lords, *Edward* from *Belgia*,
With hastie Germaines and blunt *Hollanders*,
Is past in safetie through the narrow seas, (*London*,
And with his troopes doe march amaine towardes
And manie giddie people follow him.
Oxf. Tis best to looke to this betimes,
For if this fire doe kindle any further,
Yt wilbe hard for vs to quench it out.
War. In *Warwike* shire I haue true harted friends,
Not mutinous in peace, yet bold in warre,
Them will I muster vp, and thou soone *Clarence* shalt
In *Essex, Suffolke, Norfolke*, and in *Kent*,
Stirre vp the knights and gentlemen to come with thee.
And thou brother *Montague*, in *Leister* shire,
Buckingham and *Northampton* shire shalt finde,
Men well inclinde to doe what thou commands,
And thou braue *Oxford* wondrous well beloud,
Shalt in thy countries muster vp thy friends.
My soueraigne with his louing Citizens,
Shall rest in London till we come to him.
Faire Lords take leaue and stand not to replie,
Farewell my soueraigne.
King. Farewell my *Hector*, my *Troyes* true hope.
War. Farewell sweet Lords, lets meet at *Couentrie*.
All. Agreed.   *Exeunt Omnes.*
 Enter Edward and his traine.
Edw. Seaze on the shamefast *Henry*,
And once againe conuaie him to the Tower, Awaite

Yorke, and Henrie the sixt.

Awaie with him, I will not heare him speake.
And now towards *Couentrie* let vs bend our course
To meet with *Warwike* and his confederates.
  Exeunt Omnes.
 Enter Warwike on the walles.
War. Where is the post that came from valiant *Oxford?*
How farre hence is thy Lord my honest fellow?
Oxf post. By this at *Dauntree* marching hitherward.
War. Where is our brother *Montague?*
Where is the post that came from *Montague?*
Poss. I left him at *Dansmore* with his troopes.
War. Say *Summerfield*, where is my louing son?
And by thy gesse, how farre is *Clarence* hence?
Sommer. At *Southam* my Lord I left him with
His force, and doe expect him two houres hence.
War. Then *Oxford* is at hand, I heare his drum.
 Enter Edward and his power.
Glo. See brother, where the sunlie *Warwike* mans the wal,
War. O vnbid spight, is sportfull *Edward* come?
Where slept our scoutes or how are they seducde,
That we could haue no newes of their repaire?
Edw. Now *Warwike* wilt thou be sorrie for thy faults,
And call *Edward* king, and he will pardon thee.
War. Nae rather wilt thou draw thy forces backe?
Conselfe who set thee vp and pluld thee downe?
Call *Warwike* patron and be penitent,
And thou shalt still remaine the Duke of *Yorke.*
Glo. I had thought at least he would haue said the king,
Or did he make the iest against his will.
War. I was *Warwike* gaue the kingdome to thy brother.
Edw. Why then tis mine, if but by *Warwikes* gift. *War.*

E

The Tragedie of Richard D. of

War. I but thou art no Atlas for fo great a waight,
And weaking *Warwike* takes his gift againe,
Henry is my king, *Warwike* tell me this?
Edw. I prethe gallant *Warwike* tell me this,
What is the bodie when the head is off?

Glo. Alafte that *Warwike* had no more foresight,
But whilft he fought to fticale the fingleton,
The king was finelie fingerd from the decke?
You left poore *Henry* in the Bifhops pallace,
And ten to one you'le meet him in the Tower,
Edw. Tis euen fo, and yet you are olde *Warwike* ftill
War. O cheerefull colours, fee where Oxford comes.

Enter Oxford with drum and fouldiers & a cffie.   *Exit.*

Oxf. Oxford, Oxford, for Lancafter.   *Exit.*
Edw. The Gates are open, fee they enter in,
Lets follow them and bid them battaile in the ftreetes,
Glo. No, fo fome other might flee vpon our backes,
Wee'le ftaie till all be entered, and then follow them.

Enter Summerfet with drum and fouldiers.

Sum. Summerfet, Summerfet, for Lancafter.   *Exit.*
Glo. Two of thy name both Dukes of Summerfet,
Haue folde their liues vnto the houfe of *Yorke*,
And thou fhalt be the thud and my fword hold.

Enter Montague with drum and fouldiers.

Mont. Montague, Montague, for Lancafter.   *Exit.*
Edw. Traitorous *Montague*, thou and thy brother
Shall deerelie abie this rebellious act.

Enter Clarence with drum and fouldiers.

War. And loe where *George* of *Clarence* fweepes
Along, of powre enough to bid his brother batell.
Cla. Clarence, Clarence, for Lancafter.

        Edw.

Yorke, and Henrie the fixt:

War. Et tu Brute, wilt thou ftab Cæfar too?
parlie firft to *George* of *Clarence*.

Sounds a Parlie, and Richard and Clarence whispers to-
gither, and then Clarence takes his red Rofe out of his
hat, and throwes it at Warwike.

War. Com *Clarence* come, thou wilt if *Warwike* call.
Cla. Father of *Warwike*, know you what this means?
throw mine infamie at thee,
will not ruinate my fathers houfe,
Who gaue his bloud to lime the ftones togither,
And fet vp *Lancaſter.* Thinkeft thou
that *Clarence* is fo harfh vnnaturall,
To lift his fword againft his brothers life,
And fo proud harted *Warwike* I defie thee,
And to my brothers curne my blufhing cheekes?
Pardon me *Edward*, for I haue done amiſſe,
And *Richard* doe not frowne vpon me,
For henceforth I will proue no more vnconftant.

Edw. Welcome *Clarence*, and ten times more welcome,
Then if thou neuer hadft deferud our hate.
Glo. Welcome good *Clarence*, this is brotherlie.
War. Oh paffing traytor, periurd and vniuft.
Edw. Now *Warwike*, wilt thou leaue
the towne and fight? or fhall we beate the
ftones about thine eares?

War. Why I am not coopt vppe heere for defence,
will awaie to Barnet prefently,
And bid thee battaile *Edward* : if thou dareft.
Edw. Yes *Warwike* he dares, and leades the waie,
Lods to the field, faint *George* and victorie.

    Exeunt Omnes.   *Alarmes,*

        E 2.

The Tragedie of Richard D. of

Alarmes, and then enter Warwike wounded,

War. Ah, who's neere? Come to me friend or foe?
And tell me who is victor Yorke or Warwike?
Why aske I that? my mangled bodie shewes,
That I must yeeld my bodie to the earth,
And by my fall the conquest to my foes.
Thus yeelds the Cedar to the axes edge,
Whose armes gaue shelter to the princelie Eagle,
Vnder whose shade the ramping Lion slept,
Whose top branch ouerpeerd Ioues spreading tree,
And kept low shrubs from winters powerfull winde.
These eyes that now are dimd with deaths blacke vaile,
Haue beene as piercing as the mid-day Sunne,
To search the secret treasons of the world:
The wrinkles in my browes now fild with bloud,
Were likened oft to kinglie sepulchers.
For who liud king, but I could dig his graue?
And who durst smile, when Warwike bent his brow?
Lo now my glorie smeerd in dust and bloud,
My parkes, my walkes, my mannors that I had,
Euen now forsake me, and of all my lands,
Is nothing left me but my bodies length.

Enter Oxford and Summerset.

Oxf. Ah Warwike, Warwike, cheere vp thy selfe and liue,
For yet theres hope enough to win the daie,
Our warlike Queene with troopes is come from *France,*
And at *South-hampton* landed all hir traine,
And mightst thou liue then would we neuer flie.
War. Why then I would not flie, nor haue I now,
But *Hercules* himselfe must yeeld to ods,
For manie wounds receiu'd, and manie moe repaid,
Hath robd my strong knit sinews of their strength,
And spite of spites needs must I yeeld to death.
Som. Thy brother *Mountague* to the earth his last,
And at the pangs of death I heard him crie

Yorke, and Henrie the sixt.

And fate commend me to thy valiant brother.
And more he would haue spoke, and more he said,
Which sounded like a clamor in a vault,
That could not be distinguisht for the sound,
And so the valiant *Mountague* gaue vp the ghost.
War. What is pompe, rule, raigne, but earth and dust?
And liue we how we can, yet die we must.

Sweet rest his soule, flie Lords and saue your selues,
For *Warwike* bids you all farewell to meet in Heauen.

He dies.

Oxf. Come noble *Summerset,* lets take our horse,
And cause retrait be founded through the campe,
That all our friends that yet remaine aliue,
Maie be warn'd and haue themselues by flight.
That done, with them weele post vnto the Queene,
And once more trie our fortune in the field *Ex. ambo.*

Enter Edward, Clarence, Gloster, with souldiers.

Edw. Thus still our fortune giues vs victorie,
And girts our temples with triumphant ioies,
The big boond traytor *Warwike* hath breathde his last,
An, heauen this daie hath smilde vpon vs all,
But in this cleere and brightsome daie,
I see a blacke suspitious cloud appeare,
That will encounter with our glorious sunne,
Before he gaine his eastfull welkeme beames,
I meane those powers which the *Queene* hath gotten in *France*
Are landed and meant once more to menace vs.
Glo. Oxford and Summerset are fled to hir,
And tis like if the haue time to breath,
Hir faction will be full as strong as ours,
Edw. We are aduertisde by our louing friends,

That

E 3

Yorke, and Henrie the sixt.

And Warriors faint, why were perpetuall
Shame? Oh braue yong Prince, thy
Noble grandfather doth liue againe in thee,
Long maiest thou liue to beare his image,
And to renew his glories.

        Enter a Messenger.

Mes. My Lords, Duke *Edward* with a mighty power,
Is marching hitherwards to fight with you.
Oxf. I thought it was his pollicie to take vs vnprouided,
But here we will we stand and fight it to the death.

   Enter king *Edward, Cla. Glo. Hast.* and Souldiers.

Edw. See brothers, yonder stands the thornie wood,
Which by Gods assistance and your prowesse,
Shall with our swords yer night be cleane cut downe.
Queen. Lords, Knights & gentlemen, what I should say,
My teares gainesaie, for as you see, I drinke
The water of mine eies. Then no more
But this, *Henry* your king is prisoner
In the tower, his land and all our friends
Are quite distrest, and yonder stands
The Wolfe that makes all this,
Then on Gods name Lords together cry saint *George*.
All. Saint *George* for *Lancaster*.

Alarms to the battell, *Yorke* flies, then the chamber be
discharged. Then enter the king, *Cla.* & *Glo.* & the rest,
& make a great shout, and crie for *Yorke*, for *Yorke*, and
then the *Queene* is taken, & the prince, & *Oxf.* & *Som.*
and then found and enter all againe.
                               Exit.

            E 4.

The Tragedie of Richard D. of

That they do hold their course towards *Tewkesburie.*
Thither will we, for willingnes ride wate,
And in euerie countie as we passe along,
Our strengthus shall be augmented.
Come lets goe, for if we flacke this faire
Bright Summers daie, sharpe winters
Showers will marre our hope for haie.   *Ex. Omnes.*

   Enter the *Queene, Prince Edward, Oxford* and *Som-*
merset, with drum and souldiers.

Que. Welcome to *England* my louing friends of *Frãce,*
And welcome *Summerset,* and *Oxford* too.
Once more haue we spread our sailes abroad,
And though our tackling be almost consumde,
And *Warwicke* as our maine mast ouerthrowne,
Yet warlike Lords raise you that sturdie post,
That beares the sailes to bring you vnto rest,
And *Ned* and I as willing Pilots should
For once with carefull mindes guide on the sterne,
To beare vs through that dangerous gulfe,
That heretofore hath swallowed vp our friends.

Prince. And if there be, as God forbid there should,
Amongst vs a timorous or fearefull man,
Let him depart before the battels ioine,
Leaft he in time of need intise another,
And so withdraw the souldiers harts from vs,
I will not stand aloofe and bid you fight,
But with my sword presse in the thickest thronges,
And single *Edward* from his thronged guard,
And hand to hand enforce him for to yeeld,
Or leaue my bodie as witnesse of my thoughts.
Oxf. Women and children of so high resolue,

                                   And

The Tragedie of Richard D. of

Edw. Lo there a period of tumultuous broiles,
Awaie with Oxford to *Hames* castell straight,
For *Summerset* of with his guiltie head.
Awaie I will not heare them speake.
Oxf. For my part Ile not trouble thee with words.
             Exet Oxford.
Som. Not I, but stoope with patience to my death.
             Exet Som.

Edw. Now *Edward* what satisfaction canst thou make,
For stirring vp my subiects to rebellion?
Prin. Speake like a subiect proud ambitious *Yorke,*
Suppose that I am now my fathers mouth,
Resigne thy chaire, and where I stand kneele thou,
Whilst I propose the selfe same words to thee,
Which traytor thou wouldst haue me answere to.
Queen. Oh that thy father had bin so resolu'd:
Glo. That you might still haue kept your
Persone, and nere haue stolne the
Breech from *Lancaster.*
Prin. Let *Æsop* fable in a winters night,
His currish Riddles sorts not with this place.
Glo. By heauen brat Ile plague you for that word.
Queen. I, thou wast borne to be a plague to men.
Glo. For Gods sake take away this captiue scold.
Prin. Naie take away this scolding Crookebacke rather.
Edw. Peace wilfull boy, or I will tame your tongue.
Cla. Vntutor'd lad thou art too malepert,
Prin. I know my dutie, you are all vndutifull,
Lasciuious *Edward,* and thou periurd *George,*
And thou misshapen *Dicke,* I tell you all,
I am your better traytors as you be.
             Edw.

Yorke, and Henrie the sixt.

Edw. Take that, the likenes of this railer heere.
Queen. Oh, kill me too.
Glo. Marrie and shall.   (much alredie.
Edw. Hold *Richard* hold, for we haue doone too
Glo. Why should she liue to fill the world with words?
Edw. What doth she swound: make meanes for
             Her recouerie?
Glo. Clarence excuse me to the king my brother,
I must to London on a serious matter,
Ere you come there, you shall heare more newes.
Cla. About what, prethee tell me?
Glo. The Tower man, the Tower, Ile root them out
             Exit Gloster.
Queen. Ah *Ned* speake to thy mother boy? ah
Thou canst not speake.
Traytors, Tyrants, bloudie Homicides,
They that stabd *Cæsar* shed no bloud at all,
For he was a man, this in respect a childe,
And men nere spend their furie on a child,
Whats worse then tyrant that I maie name,
You haue no children Deuils if you had,
The thought of them would then haue stopt your rage,
But if you euer hope to haue a sonne,
Looke in his youth to haue him so cut off,
As Traitors you haue doone this sweet young prince.
Edw. Awaie, and beare her hence.
Queen. Naie nere beare me hence, dispatch
Me heere, heere sheath thy sword,
Ile pardon thee my death. Wilt thou not?
Then *Clarence,* doe thou doe it?
Cla. By Heauen I would not doe thee so much ease.
             Queen.

The Tragedie of Richard D. of

Queen. Good Clarence doe, ſweet Clarence kill me too.
Cla. Didſt thou not heare me ſweare I would not do it?
Queen. I, but thou wilt to ſortweare thy ſelſe,
T'was ſinne before, but now tis charitie.
Whe as the Duels butcher, hard fauored Richard,
Richard where art thou? He is not heere,
Murder is his almes deed, petitioners
For bloud he nere put backe.
Edw. Awaie I ſaie, and take her hence perforce.
Queen. So come to you and yours, as to this prince. Ex.
Eliz. Clarence, whithers Glaſter gone?
Cla. Marrie my Lord to London, and as I gueſſe, to
Make a bloude ſupper in the Tower.
Edw. He is ſudden if a thing come in his head.
Well, diſcharge the common ſouldiers with paie
And thankes, and now let vs towards London,
To ſee our gentle Queene how ſhee doth fare,
For by this I hope ſhee hath a ſonne for vs.
Exeunt Omnes.

Enter Glaſter to king Henry in the Tower.
Glo. Good day my Lord: What at your booke ſo hard?
Hen. I my good Lord, Lord I ſhould ſaie rather,
Tis ſinne to flatter, good was little better,
Good Glaſter, and good Diuell, were all alike,
What ſcene of Death leath Roſſue now to act?
Glo. Suſpition alwaies haunts a guiltie mind,
Hen. The birde once limde, doth feare the ſatall buſh,
And I the hapleſſe male to one poore birde,
Haue now the ſatall obiect in mine eie,
Where my poore young was limde, was caught & kild.
Glo. Why, what a foole was that of Creete?
That

Yorke, and Henrie the fixt.

That taught his ſonne the office
Of a birde, and yet for all that the poore
Foule was drownde.
Hen. I Dedalus, my poore ſonne Icarus,
Thy father Minos that denide our courſe,
Thy brother Edward, the ſunne that ſearde his wings,
And thou the enuious gulfe that ſwallowed him.
Oh, better can my breſt abide thy daggers point,
Then can mine eares that tragicke hiſtorie.
Glo. Why doſt thou thinke I am an executioner?
Hen. A perſecutor I am ſure thou art,
And if murdering innocents be executions,
Then I know thou art an executioner.
Glo. Thy ſonne I kild for his preſumption.
Hen. Hadſt thou bin kild when firſt thou didſt preſume,
Thou hadſt not liude to kill a ſonne of mine,
And thus I propheſie of thee.
That manie a Widdow for her husbands death,
And many an infants water ſtanding eie,
Widdowes for their husbands, children for their fathers,
Shall curſe the time that euer thou wert borne.
The owle ſhriekt at thy birth, an euill ſigne,
The night Crow cride, aboding luckleſſe rune,
Dogs howld and hideous tempeſſe ſhooke down trees,
The Rauen rookt her on the Chimnies top,
And chattering Pies in diſmall diſcord ſung,
Thy mother felt more then a mothers paine;
And yet brought forth leſſe then a mothers hope,
To wit an vndigeſt created lumpe,
Not like the fruit of ſuch a goodly tree,
Teeth hadſt thou in thy head when thou waſt borne,
To

The Tragedie of Richard D. of

To ſignifie thou cam'ſt to bite the world,
And if the reſt be true that I haue heard,
Thou cam'ſt into the world   *He ſtabs him.*
Glo. Die propheta in thy ſpeech, Ile beare
No more, for this among ſt the reſt, was I ordainde.
How, I and for much more ſlaughter after this.
O God forgiue my ſinnes, and pardon thee. *He dies.*
Glo. What? will the aſpiring bloud of *Lancaſter*
Sinke into the ground, I had thought it would haue
       mounted.

See how my ſword weepes for the poore kings death.
Now maie ſuch purple teares be alwaies ſhed,
For ſuch as ſeeke the downefall of our houſe,
If anie ſparke of life remaine in thee,
       Stab him againe.
Downe, downe to hell, and ſaie I ſent thee thither.
I that haue neither pitie, loue nor feare,
Indeed t'was true that *Henry* told me of,
For I haue often heard my mother ſaie,
That I came into the world with my legs forward,
And had I not reaſon thinke you to make haſt,
And ſeeke their ruines that vſurpt our right?
The women wept and the midwiſe cride,
O Jeſus bleſſe vs, he is borne with teeth.
And ſo I was in deed, which plainelie ſignifie,
That I ſhould ſnarle and bite and plaie the dogge.
Then ſince Heauen hath made my bodie ſo,
Let hell make crook'd my mind to anſwere it.
I had no father, I am like no father,
I haue no brothers, I am like no brothers,
And this word *Loue* which gray beards call deuine,

B2

Yorke, and Henrie the ſixt.

Bereſident in men like one another,
And not in me, I am my ſelfe alone.
Clarence beware, thou keptſt me from the light,
But I will ſort a pitchie daie for thee:
For I will buz abroad ſuch propheſies,
As *Edward* ſhall be fearefull of his life,
And then to purge his feare, Ile be thy death.
Henry and his ſonne are gone, thou *Clarence* next,
And by one and one I will diſpatch the reſt,
Counting my ſelfe but bad, till I be beſt.
Ile drag thy bodie in another roome,
And triumph *Henry* in thy daie of doome.
           Exit.

Entering Edward, Queene Elizabeth, and a Nurſe
   with the young prince, and Clarence,
   and Haſtings, and others.

Edw. Once more we ſit in Englands royall throne,
Repurchaſte with the bloud of enemies.
What valiant foemen like to *Autumnes* corne,
Haue we mow'd downe in tops of all their pride?
Three Dukes of *Sommerſet* threefold renownd
For hardie and vndoubted champions.
Two *Cliffords,* as the father and the ſonne,
And two *Northumberlands,* two braver men
Nere ſpurd their courſers at the trumpets ſound.
With them the two rough Beares, *Warwicke* and
    Mountagu,
That in their chaines fettered the kinglie Lion,
And made the Foreſt tremble when they roard,

This

The Tragedie of Richard D. of

Thus haue we swept suspition from our seat,
And made our footstoole of securitie.
Come hither *Besse*, and let me kisse my boie,
Young *Ned*, for thee, thine Vncles and my selfe,
Haue in our armors watcht the Winters night,
Marcht all a foote in summers skalding heat,
That thou mightst repossesse the crowne in peace.
And of our labours thou shalt reape the gaine.
Glo. I le blast his haruest: and your head were laid,
For yet I am not lookt on in the world.
This shoulder was ordaind so thicke to heaue,
And heaue it shall some waight or breake my backe,
Worke thou the waie, and thou shalt execute.
Edward. Clarence and *Gloster*, loue my louelie
    Queene,
And kisse your princely nephew brothers both.
Cla. The dutie that I owe vnto you, Maiestie,
I seale vpon the rosiate lips of this sweet babe.
Queen. Thankes noble *Clarence* worthie brother
    thankes.
Gloster. And that I loue the fruit from whence thou
    Sprangst,
witnesse the louing kisse I giue the child,
To saie the truth so *Indas* kist his maister,
And so he cride all haile, and meant all harme.
Edward Now, am I seated as my soule
    delights,
Hauing my countries peace, and brothers loues.
Cla. What will your grace haue done with *Margaret*,
Reuerd her father to the king of *France*,
Hath pawnd the *Cysels* and *Ierusalem*,
And hither haue they sent it for her ransome.
    Edward

Yorke, and Henrie the sixt.

Edw. Awaie with her, and wafte hir hence to *France*,
And now what rests but that we spend the time,
With stately Triumphs and mirthhull comicke shewes,
Such as befits the pleafures of the Court,
Sound drums and Trumpets, farewell to sower annoy,
For heere I hope begins our lasting ioie.
    Exeunt Omnes,

F I N I S.

APPENDIX 2

CASTING

The casting requirements for *3 Henry VI* are unusually burdensome and complex. By our reckoning, sixty-seven roles require twenty-one adult actors, all of whom are on stage at once in tense confrontation between York and Lancaster in 1.1, while four other scenes require fifteen or more actors to be on stage at the same time. Many of these actors would have been extras who were hired to play roles with no lines, but even hired men would have had to know their entrances and exits, how to handle a guarded prisoner, and how to move on stage and manage themselves convincingly in fight scenes.

No less notable than sheer numbers is the burden placed on the principal adult actors, who not only have several hundred lines apiece but are also required to be on stage for an unusually large number of scenes. Whereas large Shakespearean roles typically require actors to appear in seven to nine scenes, the actors playing Richard and Edward are on stage in nineteen and eighteen scenes respectively, while George is on for fourteen scenes, Warwick for thirteen, and Henry and Margaret for seven each. A benchmark is Hamlet, one of Shakespeare's longest roles, who is on stage for twelve scenes in the Folio (T. King).

The following chart lists actors in order of their relative contribution to the play, reckoned in numbers of lines. It assumes that eight actors each took parts of more than 100 lines (for a total of 2,313 lines), while the remaining 163 lines for adult actors were parcelled out among five of the hirees. To achieve this result, the chart assumes that actor number 8 performed twelve separate roles in seventeen scenes, though the roles are all short, and some, like the body of the dead son, are silent and require little imagination to perform.

The chart assumes that four boys were required to play the parts of four women and three boys in *3 Henry VI*. A senior boy actor was required for Margaret's role, which is unusually demanding. Though Lady Grey/Queen Elizabeth and Prince Edward of Lancaster do not appear in the same scene, their roles nonetheless require a boy each, because the transition between Prince Edward's exit at 3.3.255 and Queen Elizabeth's entrance at 4.1.7.1 is too brief (a mere sixteen lines) to allow for the costume change that the actor playing Queen Elizabeth would have had to undertake. Covering the prince's costume with a wig and a simple dress might be accomplished in such a short time, but Queen Elizabeth appears in 4.1 for the first time as Queen and may be assumed to be elaborately dressed and coiffed – certainly more so than when she appeared as a widow. Prince Edward and Queen Margaret appear on stage with Lady Bona in 3.3, necessitating three boy actors for those roles. Since Lady Bona has a very small speaking role (nine lines in 3.3), it seems reasonable to assign the boy playing her part to Rutland as well (twenty-four lines in 1.3). The Nurse in 5.7 has no lines and could have been played by anyone without a beard, but since a boy had been assigned to play Lady Bona anyway, he may well have been assigned to both the Nurse and Richmond, another silent role, as well.

T.J. King has much to teach anyone who compiles a doubling chart, since he has compiled one for each of Shakespeare's plays and some twenty-three others. Our line count for the roles in *3 Henry VI* frequently differs from his, however; he occasionally omits roles in some scenes; and we have combined roles differently, assuming less spoken acting was required of hirees than he does. (His eighth 'major part' requires eighty-one lines, while one of his 'minor' parts involves sixty-one lines and another fifty-five.)

We also differ from King in assigning only one pair of '*Drum and Colours*' to 5.1, because we assume that a rapid costume change for the drummer and standard bearer accompanying

Oxford could enable the same pair of actors to accompany Montague and Somerset as well. Entering the main stage, these retainers immediately exit with their respective lords. If the retainers slipped off one tabard and immediately donned another, while the standard bearer ('Colours') exchanged one heraldic banner for another at the same time, they could re-enter within seconds as retainers of the next lord, thus reducing the number of actors required for the scene. (F does not indicate that they enter 'above'; that area could hardly have held so many actors in any case.) This rapid costume change for the drummer assumes that the drum was attached only to his belt, as in the famous illustration of Richard Tarlton, thus enabling a rapid change of his tabard.

DOUBLING CHART

Actor	Role	1.1	1.2	1.3	1.4	2.1	2.2	2.3	2.4	2.5	2.6	3.1	3.2	3.3	4.1	4.2
1	Edward	5	9			40	38	15			22		57		68	
2	Warwick	44				79	7	13	0		31			90		26
3	Richard	6	20			65	18	18	6		24		93		21	
4	King Henry	76			99		23			78		68				
5	York	35	37													
6	George						7	11			3		8		24	1
	Clifford	18		26	13		46		7		30					
	Oxford													19		0
7	Northumberland	13			15		2									
	Father									27						
	King Lewis													65		
	Montgomery															
8	Exeter	12								3						
	Tutor			3												
	Messenger [York]		4			24										
	Messenger [Lanc.]						6									

413

Actor	Role	1.1	1.2	1.3	1.4	2.1	2.2	2.3	2.4	2.5	2.6	3.1	3.2	3.3	4.1	4.2
	Dead Son									0						
	Soldier										0					
	Nobleman												2		18	
	Post													6		
	1Watchman															
	Rivers															
	Mayor of York															
	Somerville															
9	Westmorland	11														
	Son									22		14				
	2 Keeper					0	0									0
	Soldier															
	Somerset															
	Third Duke														2	
10	Montague	5	3			0	0				0				5	
	1 Keeper											17				
	Hastings														8	
11	Norfolk	3					0									
	John Mortimer		1													
	Soldier				0											
	Dead Father									0						0

Actor	Role	1.1	1.2	1.3	1.4	2.1	2.2	2.3	2.4	2.5	2.6	3.1	3.2	3.3	4.1	4.2
	Bourbon													0		
	2 Watchman															
	Stanley															
	Lieutenant															
	Alderman															
	Mayor of Coventry				0											
12	Soldier	0									0					0
	Hugh Mortimer		0												0	
	Pembroke															
	3 Watchman															
	Huntsman															
	Alderman															
	Messenger					3										
	Attendant															
13	Soldier	0				0					0					0
	Stafford														0	
	2 Messenger															
	Attendant															
14	Soldier	0				0					0					0
	Drum						0									

415

Actor	Role	1.1	1.2	1.3	1.4	2.1	2.2	2.3	2.4	2.5	2.6	3.1	3.2	3.3	4.1	4.2
15	Soldier	0									0					0
	Trumpet															
16	Soldier	0				0	0				0					
	Trumpet															
17	Soldier	0				0	0				0					
	Colours										0					
18	Soldier	0				0					0					
19	Soldier	0				0					0					
20	Soldier	0				0										
21	Soldier	0					0									
22†	Queen Margaret	40			53		22			6			35	72		
23†	L. Grey /Q. Elizabeth														8	
24†	Prince Edward	4			0		8			3				6		
25†	Rutland			24												
	Lady Bona													9		
	Richmond															
	Nurse															

† boy actor

416

Actor	Role	4.3	4.4	4.5	4.6	4.7	4.8	5.1	5.2	5.3	5.4	5.5	5.6	5.7	Lines per role	Lines per actor
1	Edward	11		8		43	10	27	4	16	6	23		30		432
2	Warwick	27			22		22	34	33							428
3	Richard	0		18		12	3	19		4	0	12	43	9		391
4	King Henry				47		22						49			363
5	York														171	
6	George	0			9		3	22		4	0	7		6	105	276
	Clifford														140	
7	Oxford	2			2		1	1	1		8	1			35	175
	Northumberland														30	
	Father														27	
	King Lewis														65	
8	Montgomery					14									14	136
	Exeter						2								17	
	Tutor														3	
	Messenger [York]														28	
	Messenger [Lanc.]														6	
	Dead Son														0	
	Soldier										0	0			0	
	Nobleman														2	

Actor	Role	4.3	4.4	4.5	4.6	4.7	4.8	5.1	5.2	5.3	5.4	5.5	5.6	5.7	Lines per role	Lines per actor
	Post				7										31	
	1Watchman	8													8	
	Rivers		7												7	
	Mayor of York					5									5	112
	Somerville							5							5	
9	Westmorland														11	
	Son														22	
	2 Keeper														14	
	Soldier											1			0	
	Somerset	1			13			1	12		4				32	81
	Third Duke						1	1							2	
10	Montague				0										5	
	1 Keeper														17	
	Hastings			2		10								0	20	52
11	Norfolk	0													3	
	John Mortimer									0	0	0			1	
	Soldier														0	
	Dead Father														0	

Actor	Role	4.3	4.4	4.5	4.6	4.7	4.8	5.1	5.2	5.3	5.4	5.5	5.6	5.7	Lines per role	Lines per actor
	Bourbon														0	
	2 Watchman	7													7	
	Stanley			0											0	
	Lieutenant				3								0		3	
	Alderman					0									0	
	Mayor of Coventry						0	0							0	
12	Soldier						0			0					0	14
	Hugh Mortimer											0			0	
	Pembroke														0	
	3 Watchman	9													9	
	Huntsman			2											2	
	Alderman					0									0	
	Messenger							1			2				3	
	Attendant													0	0	
13	Soldier			0		1	0			0		0			1	14
	Stafford														0	
	2 Messenger							1							1	
	Attendant													0	0	
14	Soldier						0			0					0	2
	Soldier		0												0	0

Actor	Role	4.3	4.4	4.5	4.6	4.7	4.8	5.1	5.2	5.3	5.4	5.5	5.6	5.7	Lines per role	Lines per actor
	Drum					0		0							0	0
15	Soldier			0			0	0			0				0	0
	Trumpet														0	0
16	Soldier			0		0		0			0				0	0
	Trumpet														0	0
17	Soldier			0		0					0				0	0
	Colours														0	0
18	Soldier	0		0		0		0			0				0	0
19	Soldier	0						0			0				0	0
20	Soldier	0									0				0	0
21	Soldier	0									0				0	0
22†	Queen Margaret										50	31			274	274
23†	L. Grey / Q. Elizabeth		28											1	72	72
24†	Prince Edward										12	13			46	46
25†	Rutland														24	
	Lady Bona														9	
	Richmond				0										0	
	Nurse													0	0	33

† boy actor

APPENDIX 3

THE BATTLES IN
3 HENRY VI

3 Henry VI has sometimes been dismissed as a battle play, and it is true that most of the battles in the Wars of the Roses are staged, summarized or mentioned in the third play about Henry VI's reign. (Presumably in recognition of this fact, Malone included notes about the battles in *3 Henry VI* immediately following the play in his edition (6.393–5).) But in fact the Wars of the Roses involved few major battles, they were spread out over sixteen years, and *3 Henry VI* actually stages just five of them, omitting four of those listed below and alluding to one that concludes the action in *2 Henry VI*. (Ferrybridge was a brief skirmish on the day before the battle of Towton, remembered chiefly in *3 Henry VI* as the occasion of Clifford's death.) Shakespeare makes *3 Henry VI* a battle play by compressing time, rearranging the course of events and suggesting a late surge of momentum in York's favour, whereas the two decisive Yorkist victories at Barnet and Tewkesbury were won two years after the previous battle had been fought.

Battle location	Date	Won by	Scripted in
St Albans (1)	22 May 1455	York	*2H6* 5.1–5.2
Northampton	10 July 1460	York	omitted (conflated with St Albans (1) in *3H6* 1.1)
Wakefield	30 December 1460	Lancaster	1.3 and 1.4
Mortimer's Cross	2 February 1461	York	omitted (see 2.1n.)
St Albans (2)	17 February 1461	Lancaster	described in 2.1.111–40
Ferrybridge	28 March 1461	Lancaster	2.3
Towton	29 March 1461	York	2.3–2.6
Hexham	15 May 1464	York	omitted (see 3.1n.)
Edgcote	26 July 1469	Warwick (not yet declared an ally of Lancaster)	omitted (see 4.2n.)
Barnet	14 April 1471	York	5.2
Tewkesbury	4 May 1471	York	5.4

APPENDIX 4
GENEALOGICAL TABLES

1 The House of Lancaster

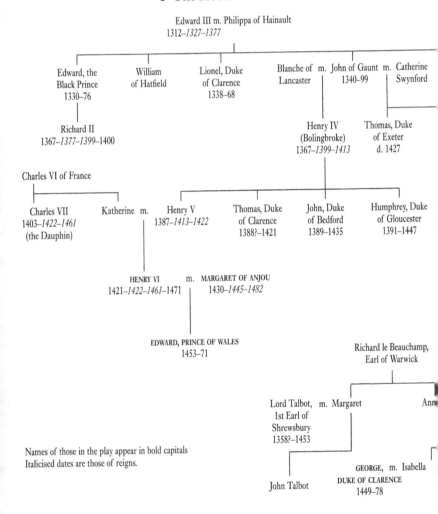

Edward III m. Philippa of Hainault
1312–*1327–1377*

Edward, the Black Prince 1330–76

William of Hatfield

Lionel, Duke of Clarence 1338–68

Blanche of Lancaster m. John of Gaunt 1340–99 m. Catherine Swynford

Richard II 1367–*1377–1399*–1400

Henry IV (Bolingbroke) 1367–*1399–1413*

Thomas, Duke of Exeter d. 1427

Charles VI of France

Charles VII 1403–*1422–1461* (the Dauphin)

Katherine m. Henry V 1387–*1413–1422*

Thomas, Duke of Clarence 1388?–1421

John, Duke of Bedford 1389–1435

Humphrey, Duke of Gloucester 1391–1447

HENRY VI 1421–*1422–1461*–1471 m. MARGARET OF ANJOU 1430–*1445–1482*

EDWARD, PRINCE OF WALES 1453–71

Richard le Beauchamp, Earl of Warwick

Lord Talbot, 1st Earl of Shrewsbury 1358?–1453 m. Margaret

Ann

John Talbot

GEORGE, DUKE OF CLARENCE 1449–78 m. Isabella

Names of those in the play appear in bold capitals
Italicised dates are those of reigns.

424

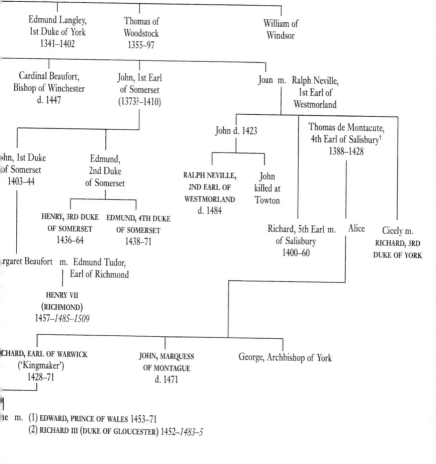

Edmund Langley,
1st Duke of York
1341–1402

Thomas of
Woodstock
1355–97

William of
Windsor

Cardinal Beaufort,
Bishop of Winchester
d. 1447

John, 1st Earl
of Somerset
(1373?–1410)

Joan m. Ralph Neville,
1st Earl of
Westmorland

John d. 1423

Thomas de Montacute,
4th Earl of Salisbury[†]
1388–1428

hn, 1st Duke
of Somerset
1403–44

Edmund,
2nd Duke
of Somerset

**RALPH NEVILLE,
2ND EARL OF
WESTMORLAND**
d. 1484

John
killed at
Towton

**HENRY, 3RD DUKE
OF SOMERSET**
1436–64

**EDMUND, 4TH DUKE
OF SOMERSET**
1438–71

Richard, 5th Earl m.
of Salisbury
1400–60

Alice

Cicely m.
**RICHARD, 3RD
DUKE OF YORK**

rgaret Beaufort m. Edmund Tudor,
Earl of Richmond

**HENRY VII
(RICHMOND)**
1457–*1485–1509*

CHARD, EARL OF WARWICK
('Kingmaker')
1428–71

**JOHN, MARQUESS
OF MONTAGUE**
d. 1471

George, Archbishop of York

ne m. (1) **EDWARD, PRINCE OF WALES** 1453–71
(2) **RICHARD III (DUKE OF GLOUCESTER)** 1452–*1483–5*

2 The Houses of York and Mortimer

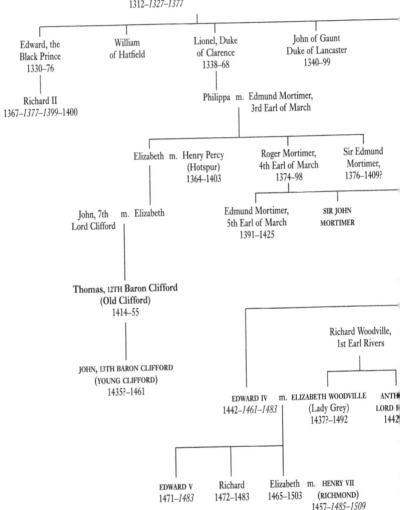

Names of those in the play appear in bold capitals
Italicised dates are those of reigns.

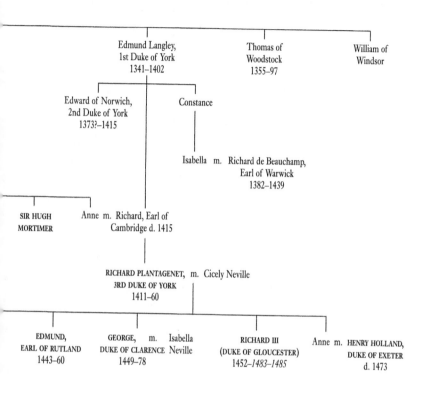

ABBREVIATIONS AND REFERENCES

References to Shakespeare's works other than *3H6* are to the Arden 3 editions published at the time of writing, namely *AC*, *H5*, *1H6*, *2H6*, *JC*, *KL*, *LLL*, *MW*, *Oth*, *Son*, *TC*, *Tem*, *Tit*, *TNK*; otherwise to *The Complete Works of Shakespeare*, ed. David M. Bevington, 4th edn (New York and London, 1997). References to *E3* are to *The Reign of King Edward the Third*, ed. G. Melchiori (Cambridge, 1998). Biblical references are taken from the Geneva Bible (1560; Madison, Wisconsin, 1969). In all references, place of publication is London unless otherwise stated.

ABBREVIATIONS

ABBREVIATIONS USED IN NOTES

*	precedes commentary notes involving readings altered from the text on which this edition is based
n.	(in cross-references) commentary note
n.p.	no place
n.d.	no date
SD	stage direction
SP	speech prefix.
subst.	substantially
this edn	a reading adopted for the first time in this edition
TLN	through line numbering in *The Norton Facsimile: The First Folio of Shakespeare*, prepared by Charlton Hinman (New York, 1968)
t.n.	textual note

SHAKESPEARE'S WORKS AND WORKS PARTLY BY SHAKESPEARE

AC	*Antony and Cleopatra*
AW	*All's Well That Ends Well*
AYL	*As You Like It*
CE	*The Comedy of Errors*
Cor	*Coriolanus*
Cym	*Cymbeline*
E3	*King Edward III*
Ham	*Hamlet*
1H4	*King Henry IV, Part 1*
2H4	*King Henry IV, Part 2*
H5	*King Henry V*
1H6	*King Henry VI, Part 1*
2H6	*King Henry VI, Part 2*
3H6	*King Henry VI, Part 3*
H8	*King Henry VIII*
JC	*Julius Caesar*
KJ	*King John*
KL	*King Lear*
LC	*A Lover's Complaint*
LLL	*Love's Labour's Lost*
Luc	*The Rape of Lucrece*
MA	*Much Ado About Nothing*
Mac	*Macbeth*
MM	*Measure for Measure*
MND	*A Midsummer Night's Dream*
MV	*The Merchant of Venice*
MW	*The Merry Wives of Windsor*
Oth	*Othello*
Per	*Pericles*
PP	*The Passionate Pilgrim*
R2	*King Richard II*
R3	*King Richard III*
RJ	*Romeo and Juliet*
Son	*Sonnets*
STM	*Sir Thomas More*
TC	*Troilus and Cressida*
Tem	*The Tempest*
TGV	*The Two Gentlemen of Verona*
Tim	*Timon of Athens*
Tit	*Titus Andronicus*
TN	*Twelfth Night*
TNK	*The Two Noble Kinsmen*

TS	*The Taming of the Shrew*
VA	*Venus and Adonis*
WT	*The Winter's Tale*

REFERENCES

EDITIONS OF SHAKESPEARE COLLATED

Alexander	*The Complete Works*, ed. Peter Alexander, 4 vols (London and Glasgow, 1951)
Ard¹	*The Third Part of King Henry the Sixth*, ed. H.C. Hart, The Arden Shakespeare (Indianapolis, 1910)
Ard²	*The Third Part of King Henry VI*, ed. Andrew S. Cairncross, The Arden Shakespeare (1964)
Bevington	*The Complete Works of Shakespeare*, ed. David M. Bevington, 4th edn (New York and London, 1997)
Cam¹	*The Third Part of King Henry VI*, ed. John Dover Wilson (Cambridge, 1952)
Cam²	*The Third Part of King Henry VI*, ed. Michael Hattaway (Cambridge, 1993)
Capell	*Mr. William Shakespeare His Comedies, Histories and Tragedies*, ed. Edward Capell, 10 vols (1767–8)
Collier MS	MS annotations in the Perkins' Second Folio, 1632 (Huntington Library)
Delius	*Shakesperes Werke*, ed. Nicolaus Delius, 7 vols (Elberfeld, Germany, 1844–53)
Dyce	*The Works of William Shakespeare*, ed. Alexander Dyce, 6 vols (1857)
Dyce²	*The Works of William Shakespeare*, ed. Alexander Dyce, 2nd edn, 9 vols (1864–7)
F, F1	*Mr William Shakespeares Comedies, Histories and Tragedies*, The First Folio (1623)
F1c	F1 corrected state
F1u	F1 uncorrected state
F2	*Mr William Shakespeares Comedies, Histories and Tragedies*, The Second Folio (1632)
F3	*Mr William Shakespeares Comedies, Histories and Tragedies*, The Third Folio (1663)
F4	*Mr William Shakespeares Comedies, Histories and Tragedies*, The Fourth Folio (1685)
Hanmer	*The Works of Shakespeare*, ed. Thomas Hanmer, 6 vols (Oxford, 1743–4)
Hudson	*The Complete Works of William Shakespeare*, ed. Henry N. Hudson, 11 vols (1851–6)

Hulme	Hilda M. Hulme, *Explorations in Shakespeare's Language* (1962)
Johnson	*The Plays of William Shakespeare*, ed. Samuel Johnson, 8 vols (1765)
Malone	*The Plays and Poems of William Shakespeare*, ed. Edmond Malone, 10 vols (1790)
O	*The True Tragedy of Richard Duke of York* (1595)
Oxf	William Shakespeare, *The Complete Works*, ed. Stanley Wells and Gary Taylor with John Jowett and William Montgomery (Oxford, 1986)
Pope	*The Works of Shakespear*, ed. Alexander Pope, 6 vols (1723–5)
Q2	*The True Tragedy of Richard Duke of York*, the Second Quarto (1600)
Q3	*The Whole Contention between the Two Famous Houses, Lancaster and York*, the Third Quarto (n.d. [1619])
Rowe	*The Works of Mr William Shakespeare*, ed. Nicholas Rowe, 6 vols (1709)
Rowe[2]	*The Works of Mr William Shakespeare*, ed. Nicholas Rowe, 2nd edn, 6 vols (1709)
Rowe[3]	*The Works of Mr William Shakespeare*, ed. Nicholas Rowe, 3rd edn, 8 vols (1714)
Singer	*The Dramatic Works of William Shakespeare*, ed. Samuel Weller Singer, 10 vols (1826)
Steevens	*The Plays of William Shakespeare*, ed. Samuel Johnson and George Steevens, 10 vols (1773)
Steevens[2]	*The Plays of William Shakespeare*, ed. Samuel Johnson and George Steevens, 10 vols (1778)
Theobald	*The Works of Shakespeare*, ed. Lewis Theobald, 7 vols (1733)
Warburton	*The Works of Shakespeare*, ed. William Warburton, 8 vols (1747)

OTHER WORKS

Abbott	Edwin A. Abbott, *A Shakespearian Grammar*, 2nd edn (New York, 1897). Numbers refer to numbered paragraphs, not pages.
Abel	Lionel Abel, *Metatheatre: A New View of Dramatic Form* (New York, 1963)
Addenbrooke	David Addenbrooke, *The Royal Shakespeare Company* (1971)
Adelman	Janet Adelman, *Suffocating Mothers: Fantasies of Maternal Origin in Shakespeare's Plays: Hamlet and The Tempest* (New York and London, 1992)

AEB	*Analytical and Enumerative Bibliography*
Aeneid	Virgil, *Aeneid*, trans. H.R. Fairclough, 2 vols (Cambridge, Massachusetts, and London, 1935)
Albright	E.M. Albright, *Elizabethan Dramatic Publication 1580–1640* (New York, 1927)
Alexander, *Shakespeare's*	Peter Alexander, *Shakespeare's Henry VI and Richard III* (Cambridge, 1929)
Alexander, *TLS*	Peter Alexander, '*3 Henry VI and Richard, Duke of York*', *TLS*, 13 November 1924, 730
Arber	Edward Arber (ed.), *A Transcript of the Registers of the Company of Stationers of London*, 5 vols (1875)
Ard² *1H6*	*The First Part of King Henry VI*, ed. Andrew S. Cairncross, The Arden Shakespeare (1962)
Ard² *2H6*	*The Second Part of King Henry VI*, ed. Andrew S. Cairncross, The Arden Shakespeare (1957)
Ard³	The Arden Shakespeare, 3rd series. General editors: Richard Proudfoot, Ann Thompson and David Scott Kastan
Aristotle	Aristotle, *Poetics*, trans. Gerald F. Else (Ann Arbor, Michigan, 1973)
Ashcroft	Peggy Ashcroft, 'Margaret of Anjou', *Shakespeare Jahrbuch West*, 1973, 7–9
Astington	John Astington, '"Fault" in Shakespeare', *SQ*, 36 (1985), 330–4
Aycock	Roy Aycock, 'Dual progression in "Richard III"', *SAB*, 38 (1973), 70–8
Baldwin	T.W. Baldwin, *William Shakspere's Small Latine & Lesse Greeke*, 2 vols (Urbana, Illinois, 1944)
Barroll	J. Leeds Barroll, *Artificial Persons: The Formation of Character in the Tragedies of Shakespeare* (Columbia, South Carolina, 1974)
Barthes	Roland Barthes, 'The death of the author', in *Image Music Text*, trans. Stephen Heath (New York, 1977)
Barton and Hall	John Barton and Peter Hall, *The Wars of the Roses* (1970)
Bawcutt	N.W. Bawcutt, '"Policy", Machiavellianism, and the Earlier Tudor Drama', *ELR*, 1 (1971), 195–209
BCP	*The Book of Common Prayer, 1559: The Elizabethan Prayer Book*, ed. John E. Booty (Charlottesville, Virginia, 1976)
Beauman	Sally Beauman, *The Royal Shakespeare Company* (Oxford, 1982)
Beckerman	Bernard Beckerman, *Shakespeare at the Globe* (New York, 1962)
Bergeron	David Bergeron, 'The play-within-the-play in *3 Henry VI*', *TSL*, 22 (1977), 37–45

Berman — Ronald S. Berman, 'Fathers and sons in the *Henry VI* plays', *SQ*, 13 (1962), 487–97

Berry, E. — Edward Berry, *Patterns of Decay* (Charlottesville, Virginia, 1975)

Berry, F. — Francis Berry, *The Shakespearean Inset* (1965)

Bevington, 'Domineering' — David M. Bevington, 'The domineering female in *1 Henry VI*', *SSt*, 2 (1966), 51–8

Bevington, *Mankind* — David M. Bevington, *From* Mankind *to Marlowe: Growth of Structure in the Popular Drama of Tudor England* (Cambridge, Massachusetts, 1962)

Bevington, *Tudor* — David M. Bevington, *Tudor Drama and Politics: A Critical Approach to Topical Meaning* (Cambridge, Massachusetts, 1968)

Billings — Wayne L. Billings, 'Ironic lapses: plotting in *Henry VI*', *SLI*, 5 (1972), 27–49

Birney — Alice Birney, *Satiric Catharsis in Shakespeare* (Berkeley and Los Angeles, California, 1973)

Blanpied — John W. Blanpied, *Time and the Artist in Shakespeare's English Histories* (Newark, Delaware, 1983)

Blayney, 'Compositor B' — Peter W.M. Blayney, '"Compositor B" and the Pavier Quartos: problems of identification and their implication', *Library*, 5th series, 27 (1972), 179–206.

Blayney, 'Publication' — Peter W.M. Blayney, 'The publication of playbooks', in Cox and Kastan, 383–422

Bloom — Harold Bloom, *Shakespeare: The Invention of the Human* (New York, 1998)

Boas — F.S. Boas, 'Aspects of classical legend and history in Shakespeare', *PBA*, 29 (1943), 107–32

Boris — Edna Zwick Boris, *Shakespeare's English Kings, the People, and the Law* (Rutherford, New Jersey and London, 1978)

Boswell-Stone — W.G. Boswell-Stone, *Shakespeare's Holinshed: The Chronicle and the Plays Compared* (1907; New York, 1968)

Bowers — Fredson Bowers, 'Establishing Shakespeare's text: notes on short lines and the problem of verse division', *Studies in Bibliography*, 33 (1980), 74–130

Boyd — Michael Boyd, conversation with John D. Cox, Ann Arbor, Michigan, 10 March 2001

Bradbrook — M.C. Bradbrook, *Shakespeare and Elizabethan Poetry* (1951)

Bradley, A. — A.C. Bradley, *Shakespearean Tragedy*, 2nd edn (1905)

Bradley, D. — David Bradley, *From Text to Performance in the Elizabethan Theatre* (Cambridge, 1992)

Brecht — Bertolt Brecht, *The Messingkauf Dialogues*, trans. John Willett (1965)

Bristol   Michael Bristol, 'How good does evidence have to be?', in
                           *Textual and Theatrical Shakespeare: Questions of
                           Evidence*, ed. Edward Pechter (Iowa City, 1996), 22–43

Brockbank, 'Frame'   J.P. Brockbank, 'The frame of disorder – Henry VI', in
                           Early Shakespeare, ed. John Russell Brown and Bernard
                           Harris (1961), 72–99

Brockbank,   John Philip Brockbank, 'Shakespeare's historical myth: a
  'Shakespeare's'   study of Shakespeare's adaptation of his sources in mak-
                           ing the plays of *Henry VI* and *Richard III*', Ph.D.
                           dissertation, University of Cambridge, 1953

Bromley   John C. Bromley, *The Shakespearean Kings* (Boulder,
                           Colorado, 1971)

Brooke   Nicholas Brooke, 'Marlowe as provocative agent in
                           Shakespeare's plays', *SS 14* (1961), 34–44

Brooks   Cleanth Brooks, *The Well Wrought Urn* (New York, 1947)

Brown   James Bucham Brown, *Bible Truths with Shakespearian
                           Parallels* (1872)

Brownlow   F.W. Brownlow, *Two Shakespearean Sequences* (Pittsburgh,
                           Pennsylvania, 1977)

Bucknill   Charles Bucknill, *The Psychology of Shakespeare* (1859)

Bullough   Geoffrey Bullough, *Narrative and Dramatic Sources of
                           Shakespeare*, 8 vols (London and New York, 1957–75)

BWVACET   *Bulletin of the West Virginia Association of College English
                           Teachers*

Cadoux   Arthur Temple Cadoux, *Shakespearean Selves: An Essay
                           in Ethics* (1938)

Cairncross   Andrew S. Cairncross, 'Shakespeare and the history play',
                           Explorations in Renaissance Culture, 1 (1973), 65–78

Calderwood   James L. Calderwood, *Shakespearean Metadrama*
                           (Minneapolis, 1971)

Campbell, *Heroes*   Lily B. Campbell, *Shakespeare's Tragic Heroes: Slaves of
                           Passion* (Cambridge, 1930)

Campbell, *Histories*   Lily B. Campbell, *Shakespeare's 'Histories': Mirrors of
                           Elizabethan Policy* (San Marino, California, 1947)

Candido   Joseph Candido, 'Getting loose in the *Henry VI* plays',
                           SQ, 35 (1984), 392–406

CD   *Comparative Drama*

CE   *College English*

Cercignani   Fausto Cercignani, *Shakespeare's Works and Elizabethan
                           Pronunciation* (Oxford, 1981)

Chambers,   E.K. Chambers, *The Mediaeval Stage*, 2 vols (Oxford,
  Mediaeval   1903)

Chambers, *WS*   E.K. Chambers, *William Shakespeare: A Study of Facts
                           and Problems*, 2 vols (Oxford, 1930)

Champion	Larry S. Champion, *Perspective in Shakespeare's English Histories* (Athens, Georgia, 1980)
Chillington	Carol Chillington, 'Theatre in review', *ETJ*, 29 (1977), 566–9
CHum	*Computers and the Humanities*
Clark	Stuart Clark, *Thinking with Demons: The Idea of Witchcraft in Early Modern Europe* (Oxford, 1997)
Clarke, C.	Charles Cowden Clarke, *Shakespeare-Characters; Chiefly Those Subordinate* (1863)
Clarke, M., *Girlhood*	Mary Cowden Clarke, *The Girlhood of Shakespeare's Heroines*, 3 vols (1850–1)
Clarke, M., *Proverbs*	Mary Cowden Clarke, *Shakespeare Proverbs; or, The Wise Saws of Our Wisest Poet Collected into a Modern Instance* (1848)
Clemen, *Development*	Wolfgang Clemen, *The Development of Shakespeare's Imagery* (Cambridge, Massachusetts, 1951)
Clemen, 'Past'	Wolfgang Clemen, 'Past and future in Shakespeare's drama', *PBA*, 52 (1966), 231–52
Clemen, 'Style'	Wolfgang Clemen, 'Some aspects of style in the *Henry VI* plays', in *Shakespeare's Styles: Essays in Honour of Kenneth Muir*, ed. Philip Edwards, Inga-Stina Ewbank and G.K. Hunter (Cambridge, 1980), 9–24
Cochrane	Claire Cochrane, *Shakespeare and the Birmingham Repertory Theatre 1913–1929* (1993)
Cohen	Hennig Cohen, 'Shakespeare in Charleston on the eve of the revolution', *SQ*, 4 (1953), 327–30
Coleridge	S.T. Coleridge, *Coleridge's Shakespearean Criticism*, ed. T.M. Raysor, 2 vols (1930)
Cooper	Thomas Cooper, *Thesaurus Linguae Romanae et Britannicae* (1565; Menston, England, 1969)
Coursen, 'Bard'	H.R. Coursen, 'The Bard and the tube', in James C. Bulman and H.R. Coursen (eds), *Shakespeare on Television* (Hanover, New Hampshire and London, 1988)
Coursen, *Shakespeare*	Herbert R. Coursen, *Shakespeare in Production: Whose History?* (Athens, Ohio, 1996)
Courtenay	Thomas Peregrine Courtenay, *Commentaries on the Historical Plays of Shakespeare*, 2 vols (London, 1840)
Cox, '3 Henry VI'	John D. Cox, '*3 Henry VI* and the Shakespearean history play', *CD*, 12 (1978–9), 42–60
Cox, *Devil*	John D. Cox, *The Devil and the Sacred in English Drama 1350–1642* (Cambridge, 2000)
Cox, *Shakespeare*	John D. Cox, *Shakespeare and the Dramaturgy of Power* (Princeton, New Jersey, 1989)
Cox and Kastan	John D. Cox and David Scott Kastan (eds), *A New History of Early English Drama* (New York, 1997)

435

Craig	Hardin Craig, 'Shakespeare and the history play', in *Joseph Quincy Adams Memorial Studies*, ed. James G. McManaway, Giles E. Dawson and Edwin E. Willoughby (Washington, D.C., 1948), 55–64
Crane	Milton Crane, 'Shakespeare on television', *SQ*, 12 (1961), 323–7
Crosse	Gordon Crosse, *Shakespearian Playgoing 1890–1952* (1941)
Cunliffe	J.W. Cunliffe, *The Influence of Seneca on Elizabethan Tragedy* (1893)
Danby	John F. Danby, *Shakespeare's Doctrine of Nature: A Study of King Lear* (1949)
Daniell, 'Opening'	David Daniell, 'Opening up the text: Shakespeare's *Henry VI* in performance', in *Drama and Society*, ed. James Redmond (Cambridge, 1979), 247–77
Daniell, 'Reading'	David Daniell, 'Reading the Bible', in Kastan, *Companion*, 158–71
Davidson	Clifford Davidson, 'Saint plays and pageants of medieval Britain', *EDAM*, 22 (1999), 11–37
Dayton	Paige Dayton, 'The making of a misogynist', *Journal of Evolutionary Psychology*, 9 (1988), 346–51
Dean	Paul Dean, 'Shakespeare's *Henry VI* trilogy and Elizabethan "Romance" histories: the origins of a genre', *SQ*, 33 (1982), 34–48
De Grazia	Margreta De Grazia, *Shakespeare Verbatim* (Oxford, 1991)
Dent	R.W. Dent, *Shakespeare's Proverbial Language: An Index* (Berkeley, California and London, 1981)
Déprats	Jean-Michel Déprats, 'Shakespeare in France', *SQ*, 32 (1981), 390
Dessen	Alan Dessen, 'Oregon Shakespearean Festival', *SQ*, 29 (1978), 278–85
Dickins	Richard Dickins, *Forty Years of Shakespeare on the English Stage. August, 1867 to August, 1907* (n.p., n.d.)
Dobson	Michael Dobson, *The Making of the National Poet: Shakespeare, Adaptation and Authorship, 1660–1709* (Oxford, 1992)
Dollimore, 'Introduction'	Jonathan Dollimore, 'Introduction: Shakespeare, cultural materialism and the new historicism', in Dollimore and Sinfield, 2–17
Dollimore, *Radical*	Jonathan Dollimore, *Radical Tragedy: Religion, Ideology and Power in the Drama of Shakespeare and His Contemporaries* (Chicago, 1984)
Dollimore and Sinfield	John Dollimore and Alan Sinfield (eds), *Political Shakespeare* (Ithaca, New York and London, 1985)

Doran	Madeleine Doran, *Henry VI, Parts II and III: Their Relation to* The Contention *and* The True Tragedy, *University of Iowa Studies*, 4 (1928)
Dowden	Edward Dowden, *Shakespere: A Critical Study of His Mind and Art*, 12th edn (1901)
Driver	Tom F. Driver, *The Sense of History in Greek and Shakespearean Drama* (New York, 1960)
Dutton	Richard Dutton, 'Shakespeare and Lancaster', *SQ*, 49 (1998), 1–21
Eaton	T.R. Eaton, *Shakespeare and the Bible* (1858)
Eccles	Christine Eccles, *The Rose Theatre* (London and New York, 1990)
EDAM	*Early Drama, Art, and Music Review*
Elliott and Valenza	Ward Elliott and Robert Valenza, *Matching Shakespeare, 1994: Computer Testing of Elizabethan Texts for Common Authorship with Shakespea*re (Claremont, California, 1994)
Ellis-Fermor	Una Ellis-Fermor, *The Frontiers of Drama* (1945)
ELR	*English Literary Renaissance*
ES	*English Studies*
ETJ	*Educational Theatre Journal*
Evans	Gareth Lloyd Evans, 'Shakespeare, Seneca, and the kingdom of violence', in *Roman Drama*, ed. T.A. Dorey and Donald R. Dudley (New York, 1965), 123–59
Ewbank	Inga-Stina Ewbank, 'The fiend-like Queen: a note on "Macbeth" and Seneca's "Medea"', *SS 19* (1966), 82–94
Farmer	Richard Farmer, *An Essay on the Learning of Shakespeare*, 3rd edn (1821)
Fiedler	Leslie Fiedler, *The Stranger in Shakespeare* (New York, 1972)
Fleay	F.G. Fleay, 'Who wrote *Henry VI?*' *Macmillan's Magazine*, 33 (1875), 50–62
Fly	Richard Fly, 'The evolution of Shakespearean metadrama: Abel, Burckhardt, and Calderwood', *CD*, 20 (1986), 124–39
Foster, 'Claremont'	Donald W. Foster, 'The Claremont Shakespeare Authorship Clinic: how severe are the problems?' *CHum*, 32 (1998), 491–510
Foster, 'Response'	Donald W. Foster, 'Response to Elliott and Valenza, "And then there were none"', *CHum*, 30 (1996), 147–55
FQ	Edmund Spenser, *Faerie Queene*, ed. J.C.Smith, 2 vols (Oxford, 1909)
French, A., 'Henry VI'	A.L. French, '*Henry VI* and the ghost of Richard II', *ES*, 50 (1969), Anglo-American Supplement, xxxvii–xliii
French, A., 'Mills'	A.L. French, 'The Mills of God and Shakespeare's early history plays' *ES*, 55 (1974), 313–24

French, G.	George Russell French, *Shakespeareana Genealogica* (1869)
French, M.	Marilyn French, *Shakespeare's Division of Experience* (New York, 1981)
Freud	Sigmund Freud, 'Some character-types met with in psycho-analytic work', trans. E. Colburn Mayne, *Collected Papers*, ed. Ernest Jones, 10 vols (1925), 4.318–44
Frey	David L. Frey, *The First Tetralogy: Shakespeare's Scrutiny of the Tudor Myth* (The Hague and Paris, 1976)
Fulwell	Ulpian Fulwell, *Like Will to Like*, ed. J.A.B. Somerset, in *Four Tudor Interludes* (1974)
Furness	Horace Howard Furness, ed. *Much Ado About Nothing: A New Variorum Edition* (Philadelphia, 1899)
Garber	Marjorie Garber, 'Descanting on deformity: Richard III and the shape of history', in *The Historical Renaissance*, ed. Heather Dubrow and Richard Strier (Chicago and London, 1988), 79–103
Gaw, 'Actors' names'	Allison Gaw, 'Actors' names in basic Shakespearean texts, with special reference to *Romeo and Juliet* and *Much Ado*', *PMLA*, 40 (1925), 530–57
Gaw, *Origin*	Allison Gaw, *The Origin and Development of 1 Henry VI* (Los Angeles, 1926)
Gaw, 'Sincklo'	Allison Gaw, 'John Sincklo as one of Shakespeare's actors', *Anglica*, 49 (1925), 289–303.
Geertz	Clifford Geertz, *The Interpretation of Cultures* (New York, 1973)
Geneva Bible	*The Bible and Holy Scriptures* (1560; Madison, Wisconsin, 1969)
George	Louise Wright George, 'Shakespeare in La Ceiba', *SQ*, 3 (1952), 359–65
Gerould	Daniel C. Gerould, 'Principles of dramatic structure in *Henry VI*', *ETJ*, 20 (1968), 376–88
Goddard	Harold Goddard, *The Meaning of Shakespeare* (Chicago, 1951)
Gouhier	Henri Gouhier, 'Shakespeare, Lee Falk, André Roussin, Pirandello', *La Table Ronde*, 229 (1967), 107–11
Greenblatt 'Exorcists'	Stephen Greenblatt, 'Shakespeare and the Exorcists', in Patricia Parker and Geoffrey Hartman (eds), *Shakespeare and the Question of Theory* (London and New York, 1985), 163–87
Greenblatt, 'Invisible'	Stephen Greenblatt, 'Invisible bullets: Renaissance authority and its subversion: *Henry IV* and *Henry V*', in Dollimore and Sinfield, 18–47
Greene	*Greene's Groatsworth of Wit*, ed. D. Allen Carroll (Binghamton, New York, 1994)

Greg, *BEPDR* W.W. Greg (ed.), *A Bibliography of English Printed Drama to the Restoration*, 4 vols (1939)

Greg, *Dramatic Documents* W.W. Greg, *Dramatic Documents from the Elizabethan Playhouses: Stage Plots; Actors' Parts; Prompt Books*, 2 vols (Oxford, 1931)

Greg, *Editorial Problem* W.W. Greg, *The Editorial Problem in Shakespeare* (Oxford, 1942)

Greg, *First Folio* W.W. Greg, *The Shakespeare First Folio: Its Bibliographical and Textual History* (Oxford, 1955)

Greg, *Henslowe* W.W. Greg, *Henslowe's Diary*, 2 vols (1904)

Greg, *MWW* W.W. Greg (ed.), *Shakespeare's Merry Wives of Windsor 1602* (Oxford, 1910)

Greg, *Parallel Texts* W.W. Greg (ed.), *Marlowe's 'Doctor Faustus' 1604–1616: Parallel Texts* (Oxford, 1950)

Grivelet and Monsarrat Michel Grivelet and Gilles Monsarrat (eds), *Shakespeare's Œuvres Complètes*, bilingual edition (Paris, 1997)

Gurr Andrew Gurr, *The Shakespearian Playing Companies* (Oxford, 1996)

GWW George Walton Williams, private communication

Hall Edward Hall, *Hall's Chronicle* (1809; New York, 1965)

Harbage Alfred Harbage, *As They Liked It: An Essay on Shakespeare and Morality* (New York, 1947)

Hardison O.B. Hardison, *Christian Rite and Christian Drama in the Middle Ages* (Baltimore, Maryland, 1965)

Hart, *Homilies* Alfred Hart, *Shakespeare and the Homilies* (Melbourne, 1934)

Hart, *Stolne* Alfred Hart, *Stolne and Surreptitious Copies: A Comparative Study of Shakespeare's Bad Quartos* (Melbourne, 1942)

Hattaway Michael Hattaway, *Elizabethan Popular Theatre* (1982)

Hawkins Richard Henry Hawkins, 'Some effects of techniques developed in the native English drama on the structure of Shakespeare's plays', Ph.D. dissertation, Washington State University, 1970

Hawley William M. Hawley, *Critical Hermeneutics and Shakespeare's Plays* (New York, 1992)

Hazlitt William Hazlitt, *Characters of Shakespeare's Plays* (1817)

Henslowe *Henslowe's Diary*, ed. R.A. Foakes and R.T. Rickert (Cambridge, 1961)

Herald *Stratford-upon-Avon Herald*

Heywood Thomas Heywood, *An Apology for Actors* (1612), ed. Richard H. Perkinson (New York, 1941)

Hinman Charlton Hinman, *The Printing and Proof-Reading of the First Folio of Shakespeare*, 2 vols (Oxford, 1963)

Hirsch	Foster Hirsch, 'The New York Shakespeare Festival – 1970' '*SQ*', 21 (1970), 477–80
Hodgdon, *End*	*The End Crowns All: Closure and Contradiction in Shakespeare's History* (Princeton, New Jersey, 1991)
Hodgdon, 'Two *Lears*'	Barbara Hodgdon, 'The two *King Lears*: discovering the film text', *Literature/Film Quarterly*, 11 (1983), 143–51
Hodgdon, '*Wars*'	Barbara Hodgdon, '*The Wars of the Roses*: scholarship speaks on the stage', *Shakespeare Jahrbuch West* (1972), 170–84
Holderness, 'Boxing'	Graham Holderness, 'Boxing the Bard: Shakespeare and television', in *The Shakespeare Myth* (Manchester, 1988), 173–89
Holderness, 'Radical'	Graham Holderness, 'Radical potentiality and institutional closure: Shakespeare in film and television', in Dollimore and Sinfield, 182–201
Holderness, *Shakespeare*	Graham Holderness, *Shakespeare: The Histories* (New York, 2000)
Holderness, *Shakespeare's*	Graham Holderness, *Shakespeare's History* (Dublin and New York, 1985)
Holinshed	Raphael Holinshed, *Holinshed's Chronicles* (1808; New York, 1965)
Hornstein	Lillian Herlands Hornstein, 'Analysis of imagery: a critique of literary method', *PMLA*, 57 (1942), 638–53
Hortmann	Wilhelm Hortmann, *Shakespeare on the German Stage* (Cambridge, 1998)
Hosley	Richard Hosley, 'The gallery over the stage in the public playhouse of Shakespeare's time', *SQ*, 8 (1957), 15–31
Howard-Hill	T.H. Howard-Hill, 'Crane's 1619 "promptbook" of *Barnavelt* and theatrical processes', *Modern Philology*, 86 (1988), 146–70
Howse	Ernest Marshall Howse, *Spiritual Values in Shakespeare* (New York, 1955)
Humphreys	A.R. Humphreys, 'Shakespeare's histories and "the emotion of multitude"', *PBA*, 54 (1968), 265–87
Hunt	Maurice Hunt, 'Unnaturalness in Shakespeare's *3 Henry VI*', *ES*, 80 (1999), 146–67
Hunter, 'Afterword'	G.K. Hunter, 'Afterword: notes on the genre of the history play', in Velz, 229–40
Hunter, 'Royal'	G.K. Hunter, 'The Royal Shakespeare Company plays *Henry VI*', *RenDr*, 9 (1978), 91–108
Hunter, 'Seneca'	G.K. Hunter, 'Seneca and the Elizabethans: a case-study in influence', *Dramatic Identities and Cultural Tradition* (Liverpool, 1978), 159–73
Irace	Kathleen Irace, *Reforming the 'Bad' Quartos: Performance and Provenance of Six Shakespearean First Editions* (Newark, Delaware, 1994)

Jackson, B.	Sir Barry Jackson, 'On producing *Henry VI*', *SS* 6 (1953), 49–52
Jackson, G.	Gabriele Bernhard Jackson, 'Topical ideology: witches, Amazons, and Shakespeare's Joan of Arc', *ELR*, 18 (1988), 40–65.
Jackson, M., 'Langbaine'	MacD.P. Jackson, 'Langbaine and the memorial versions of *Henry VI, Parts II* and *III*', *Notes and Queries*, 209 (1964), 134
Jackson, M., *Wars*	MacD.P. Jackson, '*The Wars of the Roses*: the English Shakespeare Company on tour', *SQ*, 40 (1989), 208–12
Jackson, R.	Russell Jackson, 'Shakespeare at Stratford-upon-Avon 1994–95', *SQ*, 46 (1995), 340–57
Jackson, W.A.	William A. Jackson (ed.), *Records of the Court of the Stationers' Company, 1602 to 1640* (1957)
Jackson and Smallwood	Russell Jackson and Robert Smallwood (eds), *Players of Shakespeare 3* (Cambridge, 1993)
Jenkins	*Hamlet*, ed. Harold Jenkins, The Arden Shakespeare, 2nd series (1982)
JH	Jonathan Hope, private communication
Johnson, F.	Francis R. Johnson, 'Notes on English retail book-prices, 1550–1640', *Library*, 5th series, 5 (1950–1), 83–112
Johnson, G.	Gerald Johnson, 'Thomas Pavier, publisher, 1600–25', *Library*, 6th series, 14 (1992), 12–50
Johnson, S.	Samuel Johnson, *Johnson on Shakespeare*, ed. Arthur Sherbo (1968), vols 7 and 8 of *The Yale Edition of the Works of Samuel Johnson*, 16 vols (New Haven, Connecticut, 1958–90)
Jones, E.	Emrys Jones, *The Origins of Shakespeare* (Oxford, 1977)
Jones, R.	Robert C. Jones, *These Valiant Dead: Renewing the Past in Shakespeare's Histories* (Iowa City, 1991)
Jonson	*Ben Jonson*, ed. C.H. Herford and Percy and Evelyn Simpson, 11 vols (Oxford, 1925–52)
Jordan	John E. Jordan, 'The reporter of *Henry VI, Part 2*', *PMLA*, 64 (1949), 1089–113
Jump	John Jump, 'Shakespeare and history', *Critical Quarterly*, 17 (1975), 33–44
Kahn	Coppélia Kahn, *Man's Estate: Masculine Identity in Shakespeare* (Berkeley and Los Angeles, California, 1981)
Kantorowicz	Ernst Kantorowicz, *The King's Two Bodies: A Study in Medieval Political Theology* (Princeton, New Jersey, 1957)
Kastan, *Companion*	David Scott Kastan (ed.), *A Companion to Shakespeare* (Oxford and Malden, Massachusetts, 1999)
Kastan, *Shakespeare*	David Scott Kastan, *Shakespeare and the Shapes of Time* (Hanover, New Hampshire, 1982)
Kastan, 'Shape'	David Scott Kastan, 'The shape of time: form and value in the Shakespearean history play', *CD*, 7 (1972–3), 259–77

Kay	Carol McGinnis Kay, 'Traps, slaughter, and chaos: a study of Shakespeare's *Henry VI* plays', *SLI*, 5 (1972), 1–26
Kelly, F.	Faye L. Kelly, 'Oaths in Shakespeare's *Henry VI* plays', *SQ*, 24 (1973), 357–71
Kelly, H.	Henry Asgard Kelly, *Divine Providence in the England of Shakespeare's Histories* (Cambridge, Massachusetts, 1970)
Kemp	T.W. Kemp, 'Acting Shakespeare: modern tendencies in playing and production', *SS 7* (1954), 121–7
Kennedy, D.	Dennis Kennedy, *Granville Barker and the Dream of Theatre* (Cambridge, 1985)
Kennedy, R.	Richard F. Kennedy, 'Speech prefixes in some Shakespearean quartos', *Papers of the Bibliographical Society of America*, 92 (1998), 177–209
Kenny	Thomas Kenny, *The Life and Genius of Shakespeare* (1864)
Kermode	Frank Kermode, *Shakespeare's Language* (New York, 2000)
Kernan	Alvin B. Kernan, 'A comparison of the imagery in *3 Henry VI* and *The True Tragedie of Richard Duke of York*', *SP*, 51 (1954), 431–42
King, L., '*2 and 3*'	Lucille King, '*2 and 3 Henry VI* – which Holinshed?' *PMLA*, 50 (1935), 745–52
King, L., 'Hall'	Lucille King, 'The use of Hall's *Chronicles* in the Folio and Quarto texts of *Henry VI*', *PQ*, 13 (1934), 321–32
King, L., 'Text'	Lucille King, 'Text sources of the Folio and Quarto *Henry VI*', *PMLA*, 51 (1936), 702–18
King, T.	T.J. King, *Casting Shakespeare's Plays* (Cambridge, 1992)
Kingsford, *English*	Charles Lethbridge Kingsford, *English Historical Literature in the Fifteenth Century* (Oxford, 1913)
Kingsford, *Prejudice*	Charles Lethbridge Kingsford, *Prejudice and Promise in XVth Century England* (Oxford, 1925)
Kirsch, *Jacobean*	Arthur C. Kirsch, *Jacobean Dramatic Perspectives* (Charlottesville, Virginia, 1972)
Kirsch, *Passions*	Arthur C. Kirsch, *The Passions of Shakespeare's Tragic Heroes* (Charlottesville, Virginia, 1990)
Kirsch, *Shakespeare*	Arthur C. Kirsch, *Shakespeare and the Experience of Love* (Cambridge, 1981)
Kitchin	Laurence Kitchin, 'Shakespeare on screen', *SS 18* (1965), 70–4
Knight	Charles Knight, 'An essay on the three Parts of *King Henry VI* and *Richard III*', *The Pictorial Edition of the Comedies, Histories, Tragedies and Poems of William Shakespeare*, 10 vols (London, 1838), 5.ix–xcii
Knights	L.C. Knights, *How Many Children Had Lady Macbeth? An Essay in the Theory and Practice of Shakespeare Criticism* (Cambridge, 1933)

Knox and Leslie	Father Ronald Knox and Shane Leslie, *The Miracles of King Henry VI* (Cambridge, 1923)
Kolve	V.A. Kolve, *The Play Called Corpus Christi* (Stanford, California, 1966)
Langbaine	Gerard Langbaine, *An Account of the English Dramatic Poets* (Oxford, 1691)
Law, 'Chronicles'	Robert Adger Law, 'The Chronicles and the three Parts of *Henry VI*', *University of Texas Studies in English*, 33 (1955), 13–32
Law, 'Links'	Robert Adger Law, 'Links between Shakespeare's history plays', *SP*, 50 (1953), 168–87
Law, 'Rejoinder'	Robert Adger Law, 'Shakespeare's historical cycle: rejoinder', *SP*, 51 (1954), 40–1
Lee, J.	Jane Lee, 'On the authorship of the second and third Parts of *Henry VI* and their originals', *New Shakespeare Society's Transactions*, 3–4 (1875–6), 219–313
Lee, P.	Patricia-Ann Lee, 'Reflections of power: Margaret of Anjou and the dark side of queenship', *RQ*, 39 (1986), 183–217
Leech	Clifford Leech, 'The two-part play: Marlowe and the early Shakespeare', *Shakespeare Jahrbuch*, 94 (1958), 90–106
Leggatt	Alexander Leggatt, 'The death of John Talbot', in Velz, 12–30
Leiter	Samuel L. Leiter, *Shakespeare around the Globe: A Guide to Notable Postwar Revivals* (New York, 1986)
Lennox	Charlotte Lennox, *Shakespear Illustrated: or the Novels and Histories on Which the Plays of Shakespeare Are Founded*, 3 vols (1773–4)
Levin, *New*	Richard Levin, *New Readings vs. Old Plays* (Chicago, 1979)
Levine	Nina S. Levine, *Women's Matters: Politics, Gender, and Nation in Shakespeare's Early History Plays* (Newark, Delaware and London, 1998)
Liebler	Naomi Conn Liebler, 'King of the hill: ritual and play in the shaping of *3 Henry VI*', in Velz, 31–54
Liebler and Shea	Naomi C. Liebler and Lisa Scancella Shea, 'Shakespeare's Queen Margaret: unruly or unruled?', in Pendleton, 79–96.
Long, J.	John H. Long, *Shakespeare's Use of Music: The Histories and Tragedies* (Gainesville, Florida, 1971)
Long, W. 'Perspective'	William B. Long, 'Perspective on provenance: the context of varying speech-heads', in G. Williams, 21–44
Long, W., 'Precious'	William B. Long, '"Precious few": English manuscript playbooks', in Kastan, *Companion*, 414–33

Lower	Charles B. Lower, 'Separated stage groupings: instances with editorial gain', *Renaissance Papers 1970*, 55–72
Lucas	F.L. Lucas, *Seneca and Elizabethan Tragedy* (Cambridge, 1922)
Lynch	Stephen Lynch, *Shakespearean Intertextuality: Studies in Selected Sources and Plays* (Westport, Connecticut and London, 1998)
McDonald	Russ McDonald, *Shakespeare Reread: The Texts in New Contexts* (Ithaca, New York, 1994)
McElroy	Bernard McElroy, 'The Plantagenets in Chicago', *SQ*, 39 (1988), 495–500
McKernan and Terris	Luke McKernan and Oliver Terris, *Walking Shadows: Shakespeare in the National Film and Television Archive* (1994)
McKerrow, 'Bad Quartos'	R.B. McKerrow, 'A note on the "Bad Quartos" of *2* and *3 Henry VI* and the Folio text', *RES*, 13 (1937), 64–72
McKerrow, '*Henry VI*'	R.B. McKerrow, 'A note on *Henry VI, Part II*, and *The Contention of York and Lancaster*', *RES*, 9 (1933), 157–69
McKerrow, 'Suggestion'	R.B. McKerrow, 'A suggestion regarding Shakespeare's manuscripts', *RES*, 9 (1935), 459–65
McMillin	Scott McMillin, 'Casting for Pembroke's men: the *Henry VI* Quartos and *The Taming of a Shrew*', *SQ*, 23 (1972), 141–59
McNeal	Thomas H. McNeal, 'Margaret of Anjou: romantic princess and troubled queen', *SQ*, 9 (1958), 1–10
Maguire	Laurie Maguire, *Shakespearean Suspect Texts: The 'Bad' Quartos and Their Contexts* (Cambridge, 1996)
Maguire and Berger	Laurie Maguire and Thomas Berger (eds), *Textual Formations and Reformations* (1998)
Malone, *Historical*	Edmond Malone, *An Historical Account of the Rise and Progress of the English Stage* (1790)
Manheim, 'English'	Michael Manheim, 'The English history play on screen', in Anthony Davies and Stanley Wells (eds), *Shakespeare and the Moving Image* (Cambridge, 1994), 121–45
Manheim, *Weak King*	Michael Manheim, *The Weak King Dilemma in the Shakespearean History Play* (Syracuse, New York, 1973)
Marcus	Leah Marcus, *Puzzling Shakespeare: Local Reading and Its Discontents* (Berkeley, California, 1988)
Marder	Louis Marder, 'History cycle at Antioch College', *SQ*, 4 (1953), 57–8
Martin and Cox	Randall Martin and John D. Cox, 'Who is "Somerville" in *3 Henry VI?*', *SQ*, 51 (2000), 332–52
Marx	Steven Marx, *Shakespeare and the Bible* (Oxford, 2000)
Masefield	John Masefield, *William Shakespeare* (New York and London, 1911)

Masten	Jeffrey Masten, 'Playwrighting: authorship and collaboration' in Cox and Kastan, 357–82
Matthews	Honor Matthews, *Character and Symbol in Shakespeare's Plays* (Cambridge, 1962)
Merriam	Thomas Merriam, 'Tamburlaine stalks in *Henry VI*', *CHum*, 30 (1996), 267–80
Merrix	Robert P. Merrix, 'Shakespeare's histories and the new Bardolators', *SEL*, 19 (1979), 179–96
Metamorphoses	Ovid, *Metamorphoses*, trans. Frank Justus Miller, 2 vols (Cambridge, Massachusetts and London, 1916)
Mirror	*The Mirror for Magistrates*, ed. Lily B. Campbell (Cambridge, 1938)
Moore	J.K. Moore, *Primary Materials Relating to Copy and Print in English Books of the Sixteenth and Seventeenth Centuries* (Oxford, 1992)
More	Thomas More, *Utopia*, ed. Edward Surtz and J.H. Hexter, *Complete Works of St. Thomas More*, 12 vols (New Haven, Connecticut, 1961–), vol. 4.
Moxon	Joseph Moxon, *Mechanic Exercises on the Whole Art of Printing* (1683)
Mroz	Sister Mary Bonaventure Mroz, *Divine Vengeance: A Study in the Philosophical Backgrounds of the Revenge Motif As It Appears in Shakespeare's Chronicle History Plays* (Washington, D.C., 1941)
MSR	Malone Society Reprints
Muir	Kenneth Muir, *The Sources of Shakespeare's Plays* (London, 1977)
Nashe	*The Works of Thomas Nashe*, ed. R.B. McKerrow, 6 vols (Oxford, 1958)
Neill	Michael Neill, 'Shakespeare's Halle of Mirrors: play, politics, and psychology in *Richard III*' *SSt*, 8 (1975), 99–129
Noble	Richmond Noble, *Shakespeare's Biblical Knowledge and Use of the Book of Common Prayer, As Exemplified in the Plays of the First Folio* (London, 1935)
Norvell	Betty G. Norvell, 'The dramatic portrait of Margaret in Shakespeare's *Henry VI* plays', *BWVACET*, 8 (1983), 38–44
Odell	George C.D. Odell, *Shakespeare from Betterton to Irving*, 2 vols (New York, 1920)
OED	*Oxford English Dictionary*, 2nd edn, prepared by J.A. Simpson and E.S.C. Weiner (Oxford, 1989)
Onions	C.T. Onions, *A Shakespeare Glossary*, rev. edn (Oxford, 1953)
Ornstein	Robert Ornstein, *A Kingdom for a Stage* (Cambridge, Massachusetts, 1972)

Palmer	John Palmer, *Political Characters of Shakespeare* (London, 1945)
Paris, *Character*	Bernard J. Paris, *Character as a Subversive Force in Shakespeare: The History and Roman Plays* (London and Toronto, 1991)
Paris, 'Richard III'	Bernard J. Paris, 'Richard III: Shakespeare's first great mimetic character', *Aligarh Journal of English Studies*, 8 (1983), 40–67
Partridge	Eric Partridge, *Shakespeare's Bawdy* (New York, 1969)
Payne-Gallwey	Ralph Payne-Gallwey, *The Crossbow* (London, 1903)
PBA	*Proceedings of the British Academy*
Pendleton	Thomas A. Pendleton, *Henry VI: Critical Essays* (New York, 2001).
Phythian-Adams	Charles Phythian-Adams, *Desolation of a City: Coventry and the Urban Crisis of the Late Middle Ages* (Cambridge, 1979)
Pierce	Robert B. Pierce, *Shakespeare's History Plays: The Family and the State* (Columbus, Ohio, 1971)
Pilkington	Ace G. Pilkington, *Screening Shakespeare from Richard II to Henry V* (Newark, Delaware and London, 1991)
Pitt	Angela Pitt, *Shakespeare's Women* (London and Totowa, New Jersey, 1981)
Plantagenets	*The Plantagenets: Adapted by the Royal Shakespeare Company from William Shakespeare's Henry VI parts I, II, III and Richard III as Henry VI, the rise of Edward IV, Richard III, his death.* Introduction by Adrian Noble (London, 1989)
PMLA	*Publications of the Modern Language Association*
Pollard, *Fight*	A.W. Pollard, *Shakespeare's Fight with the Pirates* (1917)
Pollard, *Folios*	A.W. Pollard, *Shakespeare Folios and Quartos: A Study in the Bibliography of Shakespeare's Plays 1594–1685* (1909)
Pope, *Shakespear*	*The Works of Shakespear*, ed. Alexander Pope, William Warburton and William Dodd, 8 vols (Edinburgh, 1753)
Potter	Lois Potter, 'Recycling the early histories: "The Wars of the Roses" and "The Plantagenets"', *SS 43* (1990), 171–81
PQ	*Philological Quarterly*
Price, 'Construction'	Hereward T. Price, 'Construction in Shakespeare', *University of Michigan Contributions in Modern Philology*, 17 (1951), 1–42
Price, 'Shakespeare'	Hereward T. Price, 'Shakespeare as a critic', *PQ*, 20 (1941), 390–9
Prior, *Drama*	Moody Prior, *The Drama of Power* (Evanston, Illinois, 1973)
Prior, 'Imagery'	Moody Prior, 'Imagery as a test of authorship', *SQ*, 6 (1955), 381–6

Quinn   Michael Quinn, 'Providence in Shakespeare's Yorkist
                         plays', *SQ*, 10 (1959), 45–52
Quinones, 'Lineal'   Ricardo P. Quinones, '"Lineal honour" and augmentative
                         time in Shakespeare's treatment of the Bolingbroke line',
                         Topic, 4 (1964), 12–32
Quinones, 'Views'   Ricardo P. Quinones, 'Views of time in Shakespeare',
                         Journal of the History of Ideas, 26 (1965), 327–52
Rabkin   Norman Rabkin, *Shakespeare and the Common
                         Understanding* (New York and London, 1967)
Rasmussen,   Eric Rasmussen, 'Rehabilitating the A-text of Marlowe's
  'Rehabilitating'   *Doctor Faustus*', *Studies in Bibliography*, 46 (1993), 221–38
Rasmussen,   Eric Rasmussen, 'The year's contributions to Shakespeare
  'Textual studies'   studies: editions and textual studies', *SS 52* (1999),
                         302–26
Ravich   Robert A. Ravich, 'A psychoanalytic study of Shake-
                         speare's early plays', *Psychoanalytic Quarterly*, 33 (1964),
                         388–410
REED   *Records of Early English Drama*
Rees   James Rees, *Shakespeare and the Bible* (Philadelphia, 1876)
Reese   M.M. Reese, *The Cease of Majesty* (London, 1961)
RenDr   *Renaissance Drama*
RES   *Review of English Studies*
Rhodes, E.L.   Ernest L. Rhodes, *Henslowe's Rose: The Stage and
                         Staging* (Lexington, Kentucky, 1976)
Rhodes, R.C.   Raymond Crompton Rhodes, *Shakespeare's First Folio*
                         (Oxford, 1923)
Ribner   Irving Ribner, *The English History Play in the Age of
                         Shakespeare* (Princeton, New Jersey, 1957)
Richmond   H.M. Richmond, *Shakespeare's Political Plays* (New
                         York, 1967)
Ricks   Don M. Ricks, *Shakespeare's Emergent Form: A Study of
                         the Structures of the Henry VI Plays* (Logan, Utah, 1968)
Riggs   David Riggs, *Shakespeare's Heroical Histories*: Henry VI
                         and Its Literary Tradition (Cambridge, Massachusetts,
                         1971)
Righter   Anne Righter, *Shakespeare and the Idea of the Play* (1962)
Robinson   Horace Robinson, 'Shakespeare, Ashland, Oregon', *SQ*, 6
                         (1955), 447–51
Rolfe   W.J. Rolfe (ed.), *'Shakespeare's Proverbs' by Mary
                         Cowden Clark* (New York, 1908)
Root   R.K. Root, *Classical Mythology in Shakespeare* (New
                         York, 1903)
Rose   Mark Rose, *Shakespearean Design* (Cambridge,
                         Massachusetts, 1972)

Rossiter, 'Prognosis' A.P. Rossiter, 'Prognosis on a Shakespeare problem', *Durham University Journal*, 33 (1940–1), 126–39

Rossiter, *Woodstock* A.P. Rossiter (ed.), *Woodstock A Moral History* (1946)

Rothwell and Melzer Kenneth S. Rothwell and Annabelle Henkin Melzer, *Shakespeare on Screen: An International Filmography and Videography* (New York and London, 1990)

Rowell George Rowell, *The Old Vic Theatre: A History* (Cambridge, 1993)

RP Richard Proudfoot, private communication

RQ *Renaissance Quarterly*

Rubinstein Frankie Rubinstein, *A Dictionary of Shakespeare's Sexual Puns and Their Significance* (1984)

SAB *South Atlantic Bulletin*

Saccio, 'Images' Peter Saccio, 'Images of history in *3 Henry VI*', *SB*, 2 (1984), no. 8, 13–20

Saccio, *Shakespeare's* Peter Saccio, *Shakespeare's English Kings*, 2nd edn (Oxford, 2000)

Salgādo Gamini Salgādo, *Eyewitnesses of Shakespeare* (1975)

Sandoe James Sandoe, 'The Oregon Shakespeare Festival', *SQ*, 1 (1950), 6–11

Sarlos Robert K. Sarlos, 'Dingelstedt's celebration of the tercentenary: Shakespeare's histories as a cycle', *Theatre Studies*, 5 (1964), 117–31

Sasayama Takashi Sasayama, J.R. Mulryne and Margaret Shewring (eds), *Shakespeare and the Japanese Stage* (Cambridge, 1998)

SB *Shakespeare Bulletin*

Schelling F.E. Schelling, *The English Chronicle Play* (New York, 1902)

Scott-Giles C.W. Scott-Giles, *Shakespeare's Heraldry* (1950)

SEL *Studies in English Literature 1500–1900*

Shaheen Naseeb Shaheen, *Biblical References in Shakespeare's History Plays* (Newark, Delaware, 1989)

Shaughnessy Robert Shaughnessy, *Representing Shakespeare: England, History and the RSC* (Hemel Hempstead, England, 1994)

Siegel Paul N. Siegel, 'Tillyard lives: historicism and Shakespeare's history plays', *Clio*, 9 (1979), 5–23

Simpson, P. Percy Simpson, *Studies in Elizabethan Drama* (Oxford, 1955)

Simpson, R. Richard Simpson, 'The politics of Shakespere's historical plays', *New Shakspere Society Transactions*, 2nd series (1874), 396–441

Sims James H. Sims, *Dramatic Uses of Biblical Allusions in Marlowe and Shakespeare* (Gainesville, Florida, 1966)

Sinfield Alan Sinfield, 'Royal Shakespeare: theatre and the making of ideology', in Dollimore and Sinfield, 158–81

SLI *Studies in the Literary Imagination*

Smart	J.S. Smart, *Shakespeare: Truth and Tradition* (1928)
Smith, B.	Bruce R. Smith, *Ancient Scripts and Modern Experience on the English Stage, 1500–1700* (Princeton, New Jersey, 1988)
Smith, C.	Charles G. Smith, *Shakespeare's Proverb Lore: His Use of the* Sententiae *of Leonard Culman and Pubilius Syrus* (Cambridge, Massachusetts, 1963)
Smith, G.	G. Gregory Smith (ed.), *Elizabethan Critical Essays*, 2 vols (1904)
Somerset, *REED*	J.A.B. Somerset (ed.), *REED Warwickshire* (forthcoming)
Somerset, *Stratford*	J.A.B. Somerset, *The Stratford Festival Story* (New York, 1991)
SP	*Studies in Philology*
Spencer, C.	Christopher Spencer, *Five Restoration Adaptations of Shakespeare* (Urbana, Illinois, 1965)
Spencer, H.	Hazleton Spencer, *Shakespeare Improved* (Cambridge, Massachusetts, 1987)
Spencer, T.	Theodore Spencer, *Shakespeare and the Nature of Man*, 2nd edn (New York, 1961)
Spivack	Bernard Spivack, *Shakespeare and the Allegory of Evil* (New York, 1958)
Sprague	Arthur Colby Sprague, *Shakespeare's Histories: Plays for the Stage* (1964)
Spurgeon	Caroline F. Spurgeon, *Shakespeare's Imagery and What It Tells Us* (Cambridge, 1935)
SQ	*Shakespeare Quarterly*
SS	*Shakespeare Survey*
SSt	*Shakespeare Studies*
Starnes and Talbert	D.T. Starnes and E.W. Talbert, *Classical Myth and Legend in Renaissance Dictionaries* (Chapel Hill, North Carolina, 1955)
Stone, *Crisis*	Lawrence Stone, *The Crisis of the Aristocracy 1558–1641* (Oxford, 1965)
Stone, *Family*	Lawrence Stone, *The Family, Sex, and Marriage in England 1500–1800* (New York, 1977)
Sugden	Edward H. Sugden, *A Topographical Dictionary to the Works of Shakespeare and His Fellow Dramatists* (Manchester, 1925)
Swander	Homer Swander, 'The Rediscovery of *Henry VI*', *SQ*, 29 (1978), 146–63
Swayne	Mattie Swayne, 'Shakespeare's King Henry VI as a pacifist', *CE*, 3 (1941), 143–9
Talbert	E.W. Talbert, *Elizabethan Drama and Shakespeare's Early Plays* (Chapel Hill, North Carolina, 1963)
Taylor and Warren	Gary Taylor and Michael Warren (eds), *The Division of the Kingdoms* (Oxford, 1983)

Thomas, K., 'Anthropology'	Keith Thomas, 'An anthropology of religion and magic', *Journal of Interdisciplinary History*, 6 (1975), 91–109
Thomas, K., *Religion*	Keith Thomas, *Religion and the Decline of Magic* (1971)
Thomas, S.	Sidney Thomas, 'McKerrow's thesis re-examined', in G. Williams, 17–20
Thompson	Marvin and Ruth Thompson, *Shakespeare and the Sense of Performance* (Newark, Delaware, 1989)
Thomson, J.	J.A.K. Thomson, *Shakespeare and the Classics* (1952)
Thomson, W.	W.H. Thomson, *Shakespeare's Characters: A Historical Dictionary*, 2nd edn (1951; New York, 1966)
Tilley	Morris P. Tilley, *A Dictionary of the Proverbs in England in the Sixteenth and Seventeenth Centuries* (Ann Arbor, Michigan, 1950)
Tillyard, 'Cycle'	E.M.W. Tillyard, 'Shakespeare's historical cycle: organism or compilation?', *SP*, 51 (1954), 34–9
Tillyard, *Elizabethan*	E.M.W. Tillyard, *The Elizabethan World Picture* (1943)
Tillyard, *History Plays*	E.M.W. Tillyard, *Shakespeare's History Plays* (1944)
TLS	*The Times Literary Supplement*
Torrey	Michael Torrey, '"The plain devil and dissembling looks": ambivalent physiognomy and Shakespeare's *Richard III*', *ELR*, 30 (2000), 123–53
Towneley	*The Towneley Plays*, ed. Martin Stevens and A.C. Cawley, 2 vols (Oxford, 1994)
TSL	*Tennessee Studies in Literature*
Tucker Brooke	C.F. Tucker Brooke, *The Authorship of the Second and Third Parts of 'King Henry VI'* (New Haven, Connecticut, 1912)
Turner, 'Characterization'	Robert Y. Turner, 'Characterization in Shakespeare's early history plays', *ELH*, 31 (1964), 241–58
Turner, *Shakespeare's*	Robert Y. Turner, *Shakespeare's Apprenticeship* (Chicago and London, 1974)
TxC	Stanley Wells and Gary Taylor, with John Jowett and William Montgomery, *William Shakespeare: A Textual Companion* (Oxford, 1987)
Tynan	Kenneth Tynan, *Curtains* (New York, 1961)
Urkowitz, 'If'	Steven Urkowitz, '"If I mistake in those foundations which I build upon": Peter Alexander's textual analysis of *Henry VI Parts 2* and *3*', *ELR*, 18 (1988), 230–56
Urkowitz, *Revision*	Steven Urkowitz, *Shakespeare's Revision of 'King Lear'* (Princeton, New Jersey, 1980)
Utterback	Raymond V. Utterback, 'Public men, private wills, and kingship in *Henry VI, Part III*', *Renaissance Papers 1978*, 47–54

Van Laan	Thomas F. Van Laan, *Role-Playing in Shakespeare* (Toronto, 1978)
Vaughan	Henry H. Vaughan, *New Readings and Renderings of Shakespeare's Tragedies*, 3 vols (1886)
Velz	John W. Velz (ed.), *Shakespeare's English Histories: A Quest for Form and Genre* (Binghamton, New York, 1996)
Vickers	Brian Vickers, *Shakespeare: The Critical Heritage*, 6 vols (London and Boston, 1974–80)
Walbran	C.J. Walbran, *Dictionary of Shakespere Quotations* (1849)
Warren, M.	Michael Warren, 'Quarto and Folio *King Lear* and the interpretation of Albany and Edgar', in David Bevington and Jay Halio (eds), *Shakespeare, Pattern of Excelling Nature* (Newark, Delaware and London, 1978), 95–107
Warren, R.	Roger Warren, 'Comedies and histories at two Stratfords, 1977', *SS 31* (1978), 141–53
Watson, D.	Donald G. Watson, *Shakespeare's Early History Plays: Politics at Play on the English Stage* (1990)
Watson, R.	Robert N. Watson, *Shakespeare and the Hazards of Ambition* (Cambridge, Massachusetts, 1984)
Weinberg	Bernard Weinberg, *A History of Literary Criticism in the Italian Renaissance*, 2 vols (Chicago, 1961)
Wentersdorf, 'Authenticity'	Karl P. Wentersdorf, 'The authenticity of *The Taming of the Shrew*', *SQ*, 5 (1954), 11–32
Wentersdorf, 'Imagery'	Karl P. Wentersdorf, 'Imagery as a criterion of authenticity: a reconsideration of the problem', *SQ*, 23 (1972), 231–59
Werstine, 'Actors' names'	Paul Werstine, 'Actors' names in printed English Renaissance drama', paper presented at the Shakespeare Association of America meeting, 1989
Werstine, 'Editing'	Paul Werstine, 'Editing after the end of editing', *SSt*, 24 (1996), 47–54
Werstine, 'Line division'	Paul Werstine, 'Line division in Shakespeare's dramatic verse: an editorial problem', *AEB*, 8 (1984), 73–125
Werstine, 'Suggestion'	Paul Werstine, 'McKerrow's 'Suggestion' and twentieth-century Shakespeare textual criticism', *RenDr*, 19 (1989), 149–73
Werstine, 'Touring'	Paul Werstine, 'Touring and the construction of Shakespeare textual criticism', in Maguire and Berger, 45–66
Whateley	Thomas Whateley, *Remarks on Some of the Characters of Shakespere*, 3rd edn (1839)
White	Richard Grant White, *An Essay on the Authorship of the Three Parts of King Henry the Sixth* (Boston, 1859)
Wilders	John Wilders, *The Lost Garden: A View of Shakespeare's English and Roman History Plays* (Totowa, New Jersey, 1978)

Willcock   Gladys Willcock, 'Language and poetry in Shakespeare's
                      early plays', *PBA*, 40 (1954), 103–17
Williams, G.   George Walton Williams (ed.), *Shakespeare's Speech-
                      Headings: Speaking the Speech in Shakespeare's Plays*
                      (Newark, Delaware, and London, 1997)
Williams, S.   Simon Williams, *Shakespeare on the German Stage,
                      1586–1914* (Cambridge, 1990)
Williamson   Marilyn Williamson, '"When men are rul'd by women":
                      Shakespeare's first tetralogy', *SSt*, 19 (1987), 41–60
Willis, D.   Deborah Willis, *Malevolent Nurture: Witch-hunting and
                      Maternal Power in Early Modern England* (Ithaca, New
                      York, 1995)
Willis, E.   Eola Willis, *The Charleston Stage in the XVIII Century*
                      (Columbia, South Carolina, 1924)
Willis, S.   Susan Willis, *The BBC Shakespeare Plays: Making the
                      Televised Canon* (Chapel Hill and London, 1991)
Wilson, F., *Marlowe* F.P. Wilson, *Marlowe and the Early Shakespeare* (Oxford,
                      1953)
Wilson, F.,   F.P. Wilson, *Shakespearian and Other Studies*, ed. Helen
   Shakespearian   Gardner (Oxford, 1969)
Wilson, J.   John Dover Wilson, 'Malone and the upstart Crow', *SS 4*
                      (1951), 56–68
Wimsatt   W.K. Wimsatt and Monroe C. Beardsley, *The Verbal Icon*
                      (Lexington, Kentucky, 1954)
Winny   James Winny, *The Player King: A Theme of Shakespeare's
                      Histories* (New York, 1968)
Woolf   Rosemary Woolf, *The English Mystery Plays* (Berkeley
                      and Los Angeles, California, 1972)
Wordsworth   Charles Wordsworth, *Shakespeare's Knowledge and Use of
                      the Bible* (1864)
Worthen   W.B. Worthen, *Shakespeare and the Authority of
                      Performance* (Cambridge, 1997)
Wright   Celeste Turner Wright, 'The Elizabethan female wor-
                      thies', *SP*, 43 (1946), 628–43
Zeefeld   W. Gordon Zeefeld, 'The influence of Hall on
                      Shakespeare's English historical plays', *ELH*, 3 (1936),
                      317–53

INDEX

Abel, Lionel, 131
Adelman, Janet, 78, 116
Age of Kings, An, 35
alarum, stage direction (defined), 185n.
Albright, E.M., 169
Alciati, Andrea, 88
Alexander, Peter, 46, 161
Anderson, James, 16
Antioch College, 40
Appius and Virginia, 79
Aristotle, 103
Ashcroft, Peggy, actor, 53
Ashland Shakespeare Festival, 41–2
Atkins, Robert, director, 17

Baldwin, T. W., 87
Bale, John, 99, 104n.
Barroll, Leeds, 68
Barrymore, John, actor, 34
Barthes, Roland, 47
Barton, John, director, 18, 20–3, 27, 28,
   34, 36, 37, 41, 53, 140
   on adaptation, 22
Bawcutt, N. W., 207n.
BBC/Time-Life Shakespeare, 36–8
Beaumont, Francis and John Fletcher
   Philaster, 12
Beckerman, Bernard, 136–7
Believe as You List, 173
Benson, Frank, director, 16, 27, 33
   and political interpretation, 16–17
Berger, Thomas, 172n.
Bergeron, David, 132n.
Berman, Ronald S., 125n., 126
Berry, Edward
   on a good man possibly being a bad
      ruler, 72
   on Richard's psychological motivation, 81
   on thematic unity in *3 Henry VI*, 126
Berry, Francis, 108
Bevington, David M., 111n., 125n.
   on 'domineering female' in *1 Henry
      VI*, 141

   on Marlowe and Tudor morality
      plays, 106
   on topical interpretation, 111
Bible, The, 89–91
   Corinthians, 2nd 284n.
   Ecclesiastes, 249n.
   Ecclesiasticus, 91
   Exodus, 219n.
   Genesis, 249n.
   Job, 254n.
   Judges, 342n.
   Luke, 242n., 250n., 313n.
   Mark, 258n.
   Matthew, 89, 91, 263n., 367n.
   Revelation, 353n.
Billings, Wayne L., 105n.
Birmingham Repertory Theatre, 18
Birney, Alice, 142
Blanpied, John, 132
Blayney, Peter, 48, 151, 167
Bloom, Harold, 68, 78n.
Bogdanov, Michael, director, 27–8, 31,
   40, 140
   and political interpretation, 27
Book of Common Prayer, 89, 90, 91,
   263n., 284n.
Boris, Edna Zwick, 74, 111
Boswell-Stone, W. G., 83, 85
Bowmer, Angus, 40
Boyd, Michael, director, 31–3
   and 'magical realism', 31
   and political interpretation, 31, 32
Bradbrook, M.C.
   on garden imagery in *3 Henry VI*, 120
   and performance criticism, 135
   on the Tudor myth, 52
Bradford, William, 172n.
Bradley, A.C., 66, 114
Bradley, David, 163
Brecht, Bertolt, 22, 28, 28n., 37, 40, 43
   alienation effect, 28
Brighton, Pam, director, 31, 41
Bristol, Michael, 49

453